BUSINESS ISSUES, COMPETITION AND ENTREPRENEURSHIP

DISADVANTAGED SMALL BUSINESSES AND THE 8(A) PROGRAM

Business Issues, Competition and Entrepreneurship

Additional books in this series can be found on Nova's website under the Series tab.

Additional E-books in this series can be found on Nova's website under the E-books tab.

BUSINESS ISSUES, COMPETITION AND ENTREPRENEURSHIP

DISADVANTAGED SMALL BUSINESSES AND THE 8(A) PROGRAM

JAMES P. CARLSON
AND
ANDREA M. BERNARD
EDITORS

Nova Science Publishers, Inc.
New York

For permission to use material from this book please contact us:
Telephone 631-231-7269; Fax 631-231-8175
Web Site: http://www.novapublishers.com

LIBRARY OF CONGRESS CATALOGING-IN-PUBLICATION DATA

Disadvantaged small businesses and the 8(a) program / editors, James P. Carlson and Andrea M. Bernard.
p. cm.
Includes index.
ISBN 978-1-61209-309-3 (hbk.)
1. Minority business enterprises--Government policy--United States. 2. Federal aid to small business--United States. 3. Small business--United States--Finance. 4. Public contracts--United States--Evaluation. I. Carlson, James P. II. Bernard, Andrea M.
HD2358.5.U6D57 2011
354.2'7990973--dc22
2010051536

Published by Nova Science Publishers, Inc. † New York

CONTENTS

Preface

This new book discusses what constitutes a "disadvantaged" small business for purposes of federal and federally funded contracting programs and how firms are certified or otherwise designated as such. Disadvantaged groups include Indian tribes, Alaska Native Corporations, Native Hawaiian Organizations, and Community Development Corporations. In 2008, the federal government awarded $29.3 billion in contracts or subcontracts to SDBs, including $6.3 billion in contracts to 8(a) participants.

Chapter 1- This report discusses what constitutes a "disadvantaged" small business for purposes of federal and federally funded contracting programs and how firms are certified or otherwise designated as such. Three primary categories of disadvantaged small businesses are currently eligible for various contracting programs: (1) small businesses participating in the Small Business Administration's (SBA's) 8(a) Program (8(a) participants); (2) "small disadvantaged businesses" (SDBs) and (3) "disadvantaged business enterprises" (DBEs). These firms are characterized as "disadvantaged" because they are at least 51% unconditionally owned and controlled by socially and economically disadvantaged individuals or groups. Members of certain racial and ethnic groups are presumed to be disadvantaged, and other individuals can prove personal disadvantage by a preponderance of the evidence. Veterans and persons with disabilities are not presumed to be disadvantaged for purposes of these programs. However, there are separate contracting programs for them. Disadvantaged groups include Indian tribes, Alaska Native Corporations, Native Hawaiian Organizations, and Community Development Corporations. In FY2008, the federal government awarded $29.3 billion in contacts or subcontracts to SDBs, including $6.3 billion in contracts to 8(a) participants. Comparable data regarding contracting with DBEs are not readily available.

Chapter 2- This report provides an overview of the Small Business Administration's (SBA's) Minority Small Business and Capital Ownership Development Program. Based upon authorities given to the SBA by Sections 7(j) and 8(a) of the Small Business Act of 1958, as amended, this program is commonly known as the "8(a) Program." The 8(a) Program provides participating small businesses w ith training, technical assistance, and contracting opportunities in the form of set- asides and sole-source awards. A "set-aside" is an acquisition in which only certain contractors may compete, while a sole-source award is a contract awarded, or proposed for award, without competition. Eligibility for the 8(a) Program is generally limited to small businesses "unconditionally owned and controlled by one or more socially and economically disadvantaged individuals who are of good character and citizens of the United States" that demonstrate "potential for success." However, small businesses owned by Indian tribes, Alaska Native Corporations (ANCs), Native Hawaiian Organizations (NHOs), and Community Development Corporations (CDCs) are eligible for the 8(a) Program under somewhat different terms. In FY2008, 9,462 firms participated in the 8(a) Program, and the federal government spent $6.3 billion on contracts with 8(a) firms.

Chapter 3- The Small Business Administration's (SBA) 8(a) program helps eligible socially and economically disadvantaged small businesses compete in the economy by providing business development activities, such as counseling and technical assistance, and providing opportunities to obtain federal contracts on a set-aside basis. GAO was asked to review SBA's internal control procedures for determining 8(a) eligibility. Specifically, we (1) evaluated the procedures and processes that SBA has implemented to ensure that only eligible firms participate in the 8(a) program, and (2) assessed the extent to which SBA uses external mechanisms such as complaint information in helping to ensure that only eligible firms participate. To address these objectives, GAO reviewed SBA guidance and prior reports, interviewed SBA officials, and conducted site visits and file reviews of 123 randomly sampled 8(a) firms covering the most recent 2 years of annual reviews at five SBA locations.

Chapter 4- The Small Business Administration (SBA) helps socially and economically disadvantaged small businesses gain access to federal contracting opportunities through its 8(a) program. To participate, firms must be at least 51 percent owned and controlled by an individual who meets SBA's criteria of socially and economically disadvantaged. The firm must also qualify as a small business. Once certified, 8(a) firms are eligible to receive sole-source and set-aside contracts for up to 9 years.

GAO was asked to (1) determine whether ineligible firms are participating in the 8(a) program, (2) proactively test SBA's controls over the 8(a) application process, and (3) determine what vulnerabilities, if any, exist in SBA's fraud prevention system. To identify cases, GAO reviewed SBA data and complaints to GAO's fraud hotline. To perform its proactive testing, GAO created four bogus businesses and applied for 8(a) certification. GAO did not attempt to project the extent of fraud and abuse in the program.

Chapter 5- Alaska Native corporations (ANC) were created to settle land claims with Alaska Natives and foster economic development. In 1986, legislation passed that allowed ANCs to participate in the Small Business Administration's (SBA) 8(a) program. Since then, Congress has extended special procurement advantages to 8(a) ANC firms, such as the ability to receive sole-source contracts for any dollar amount and to own multiple subsidiaries in the 8(a) program. We were asked to testify on an earlier report where we identified (1) trends in the government's 8(a) contracting with ANC firms, (2) the reasons agencies have awarded 8(a) sole- source contracts to ANC firms and the facts and circumstances behind some of these contracts, and (3) how ANCs are using the 8(a) program. GAO also evaluated SBA's oversight of 8(a) ANC firms.

Chapter 6- According to some reports, federal contract dollars awarded to Alaska Native Corporations and their subsidiaries increased by 916% between FY2000 and FY2008, going from $508.4 million to $5.2 billion. The dollars awarded to ANC-owned firms through the Small Business Administration's (SBA's) 8(a) Program, in particular, reportedly tripled between FY2004 ($1.1 billion) and FY2008 ($3.9 billion). This widely reported increase has generated congressional and public interest in the legal authorities governing contracting with these entities. Of particular interest are the authorities creating the alleged "special procurement advantages" that ANC subsidiaries enjoy in contracting under the 8(a) Program.

Chapter 7- According to some reports, federal contract dollars awarded to Alaska Native Corporations and their subsidiaries increased by 916% between FY2000 and FY2008, going from $508.4 million to $5.2 billion. The dollars awarded to ANC-owned firms through the Small Business Administration's (SBA's) 8(a) Program, in particular, reportedly tripled between FY2004 ($1.1 billion) and FY2008 ($3.9 billion). This widely reported increase has generated congressional and public interest in the legal authorities governing contracting with these entities. Of particular interest are the authorities creating the alleged "special procurement advantages" that ANC subsidiaries enjoy in contracting under the 8(a) Program.

Chapter 8- This report discusses *Rothe Development Corporation v. Department of Defense*, a case involving a constitutional challenge to a minority contracting program authorized under Section 1207 of the Department of Defense (DOD) Authorization Act of 1987. This program allowed DOD to take 10% off the price of offers submitted by "small disadvantaged businesses" in determining which offer had the lowest price or represented the best value for the government. Section 1207 also incorporated a presumption that minorities are socially and economically disadvantaged.

In: Disadvantaged Small Businesses and the 8(a) Program ISBN: 978-1-61209-309-3
Editors: James P. Carlson and Andrea M. Bernard

Chapter 1

"DISADVANTAGED" SMALL BUSINESSES: DEFINITIONS AND DESIGNATIONS FOR PURPOSES OF FEDERAL AND FEDERALLY FUNDED CONTRACTING PROGRAMS

Kate M. Manuel

SUMMARY

This report discusses what constitutes a "disadvantaged" small business for purposes of federal and federally funded contracting programs and how firms are certified or otherwise designated as such. Three primary categories of disadvantaged small businesses are currently eligible for various contracting programs: (1) small businesses participating in the Small Business Administration's (SBA's) 8(a) Program (8(a) participants); (2) "small disadvantaged businesses" (SDBs) and (3) "disadvantaged business enterprises" (DBEs). These firms are characterized as "disadvantaged" because they are at least 51% unconditionally owned and controlled by socially and economically disadvantaged individuals or groups. Members of certain racial and ethnic groups are presumed to be disadvantaged, and other individuals can prove personal disadvantage by a preponderance of the evidence. Veterans and persons with disabilities are not presumed to be disadvantaged for purposes of these programs. However, there are separate contracting programs for them. Disadvantaged groups include Indian tribes, Alaska Native Corporations, Native Hawaiian Organizations, and Community Development Corporations. In FY2008, the federal government awarded $29.3 billion in contacts or subcontracts to SDBs, including $6.3 billion in contracts to 8(a) participants. Comparable data regarding contracting with DBEs are not readily available.

In part because of small businesses' widely reported role in job creation and concerns that the recent recession has disproportionately affected disadvantaged small businesses, the 111th Congress has enacted or proposed legislation that would assist disadvantaged small businesses in various ways (e.g., P.L. 111-5; P.L. 111-8; P.L. 111-88; H.R. 915; H.R. 2200; H.R. 2299; H.R. 3371; H.R. 3619; H.R. 4220; H.R. 4253; S. 1451; S. 2862).

INTRODUCTION

This report discusses what constitutes a "disadvantaged" small business for purposes of federal and federally funded contracting programs and how firms are certified or otherwise designated as such. Three primary categories of disadvantaged small businesses are currently eligible for various contracting programs: (1) small businesses participating in the Small Business Administration's (SBA's) 8(a) Program (8(a) participants); (2) "small disadvantaged businesses" (SDBs) and (3) "disadvantaged business enterprises" (DBEs).[1] These firms are characterized as "disadvantaged" because they are at least 51% unconditionally owned and controlled by socially and economically disadvantaged individuals or groups.[2] Members of certain racial and ethnic groups are presumed to be disadvantaged, and other individuals can prove personal disadvantage by a preponderance of the evidence. Veterans and persons with disabilities are not presumed to be disadvantaged for purposes of these programs. However, there are separate contracting programs for them.[3] Disadvantaged groups include Indian tribes, Alaska Native Corporations, Native Hawaiian Organizations, and Community Development Corporations.[4] In FY2008, the federal government awarded $29.3 billion in contacts or subcontracts to SDBs,[5] including $6.3 billion in contracts to 8(a) participants.[6] Comparable data regarding contracting with DBEs are not readily available.

In part because of small businesses' widely recognized role in job creation[7] and concerns that the recent recession has disproportionately affected disadvantaged small businesses,[8] the 111th Congress has enacted or proposed legislation that would assist disadvantaged small businesses in various ways (e.g., P.L. 111-5; P.L. 111-8; P.L. 111-88; H.R. 915; H.R. 2200; H.R. 2299; H.R. 3371; H.R. 3619; H.R. 4220; H.R. 4253; S. 1451; S. 2862).

CATEGORIES OF DISADVANTAGED SMALL BUSINESSES

8(a) Participants

Small businesses that are at least 51% unconditionally owned and controlled by "socially and economically disadvantaged individuals" or groups are eligible for the Minority Small Business and Capital Ownership Development Program.[9] Implemented by the SBA under the authority of Sections 7(j) and 8(a) of the Small Business Act, as amended,[10] this program is commonly known as the 8(a) Program, and participants in it are often called 8(a) participants or 8(a) firms.

Social Disadvantage

Owners of 8(a) firms must be "socially disadvantaged," or have experienced "racial or ethnic prejudice or cultural bias within American society because of their identities as members of groups and without regard to their individual qualities."[11] Members of the following racial and ethnic groups are presumed to be socially disadvantaged:

> Black Americans; Hispanic Americans; Native Americans (American Indians, Eskimos, Aleuts, or Native Hawaiians); Asian Pacific Americans (persons with origins from Burma, Thailand, Malaysia, Indonesia, Singapore, Brunei, Japan, China (including Hong Kong),

> Taiwan, Laos, Cambodia (Kampuchea), Vietnam, Korea, The Philippines, U.S. Trust Territory of the Pacific Islands (Republic of Palau), Republic of the Marshall Islands, Federated States of Micronesia, the Commonwealth of the Northern Mariana Islands, Guam, Samoa, Macao, Fiji, Tonga, Kiribati, Tuvalu, or Nauru); Subcontinent Asian Americans (persons with origins from India, Pakistan, Bangladesh, Sri Lanka, Bhutan, the Maldives Islands or Nepal); and members of other groups designated from time to time by SBA.[12]

Individuals who are not members of these groups must establish social disadvantage by a preponderance of the evidence, including (1) at least one objective distinguishing feature contributing to social disadvantage, such as race, ethnic origin, gender, or physical handicap; (2) personal experiences of substantial and chronic disadvantage in American society; and (3) negative impact on entry into or advancement in the business world because of the disadvantage.[13]

Economic Disadvantage

Owners of 8(a) firms must also be "economically disadvantaged" in that their "ability to compete in the free enterprise system has been impaired due to diminished credit and capital opportunities as compared to others in the same or similar line of business who are not socially disadvantaged."[14] Economic disadvantage is not presumed. Rather, all individuals upon whom an 8(a) firm's eligibility is based must describe their economic disadvantage in a narrative statement and submit personal financial information to the SBA.[15] This information must include, among other things, income for the past two years, personal net worth, and the fair market value of all assets.[16] Individuals' net worth, excluding ownership interests in 8(a) firms and equity in primary personal residences, must be less than $250,000 at the time of application to the 8(a) Program and less than $750,000 thereafter.[17] The value of retirement accounts is currently not excluded when the net worth of prospective 8(a) participants is calculated, although the SBA recently proposed changing its regulations to exclude it.[18] The SBA also compares the financial condition of firms applying to the 8(a) Program to the financial profiles of small businesses in the same primary industry classification[19] or similar line of business that are not owned by socially and economically disadvantaged individuals when determining economic disadvantage.[20]

Applications to the 8(a) Program

Firms must apply to participate in the 8(a) Program and may not receive contracting or other federal assistance based upon 8(a) status until the SBA approves their application.[21] The application form requires submission of various materials including, but not limited to, financial statements, federal personal and business tax returns, and personal history statements.[22]

Once accepted into the 8(a) Program, firms must inform the SBA in writing of any changes in circumstances that adversely affect their eligibility.[23] Each firm must also complete an annual review, which has its own form[24] and requires submission of (1) certifications that the firm meets the eligibility requirements and no changes in circumstances adversely affect its eligibility; (2) personal financial information for each disadvantaged owner; and (3) a financial statement for the firm, among other things.[25] Depending upon the firm's gross revenue, its financial statement may need to be audited by an independent public accountant,[26] as **Table 1** illustrates.

Table 1. Auditing Requirements Based on Firms' Gross Revenue

Amount of Revenue	Auditing Requirements
Over $5 million	Audited annual financial statement prepared by a licensed independent public accountant within 120 days of the close of the fiscal year
Between $1 million and $5 million	Reviewed financial statement prepared by a licensed independent public accountant within 90 days of the fiscal year close
Under $1 million	Annual financial statement prepared in-house, or a compilation statement prepared by a licensed independent public accountant, verified as to accuracy by an authorized officer, partner, limited liability member, or sole proprietor within 90 days of the fiscal year close

Source: Congressional Research Service, based on 13 C.F.R. § 1 24.602(a)-(c).

Maximum Nine-Year Term in the 8(a) Program

Firms may participate in the 8(a) Program one time, for a period of no more than nine years.[27] Once a firm has exited the program after participating in it for any period of time, it is generally ineligible for further participation.[28] Additionally, socially and economically disadvantaged individuals may confer eligibility for the 8(a) Program upon only one firm over their lives.[29] In contrast, disadvantaged groups (i.e., Indian tribes, Alaska Native Corporations, Native Hawaiian Organizations, and Community Development Corporations) may confer eligibility upon multiple 8(a) firms, which may participate in the 8(a) Program concurrently, subject to certain limitations on the primary industries in which they operate, or at different times.[30]

Contracting and Related Assistance for 8(a) Participants

Federal agencies "set aside" certain contracts for 8(a) firms by conducting procurements in which only 8(a) firms may compete.[31] They can also award contracts to 8(a) firms on a sole-source basis, sometimes in circumstances in which they could not otherwise make sole-source awards.[32] According to SBA data, federal agencies spent $6.3 billion on competitive and sole-source contracts with 8(a) participants in FY2008.[33] However, 8(a) participants are not guaranteed federal contracts, and only 44% percent of 8(a) firms not owned by Alaska Native Corporations received contracts in FY2008.[34]

8(a) firms are also eligible for (1) direct and guaranteed loans from the SBA; (2) transfer of technology and surplus property owned by the United States; and (3) management and technical assistance, including training in financing, management, accounting, bookkeeping, marketing, the operation of small businesses, and the identification and development of new business opportunities.[35] Additionally, the SBA sponsors a mentor-protégé program for eligible 8(a) participants.[36] Mentors are established firms that provide their 8(a) protégés with "technical and/or management assistance; financial assistance in the form of equity investments and/or loans; subcontracts; and/or assistance in performing prime contracts with the Government in the form of joint venture arrangements."[37] Mentors and protégés can also form joint ventures that may qualify as "small" for purposes of government procurements, including sole-source awards under Section 8(a).[38]

Small Disadvantaged Businesses

"Small disadvantaged businesses" (SDBs) include 8(a) participants and other small businesses that are at least 51% unconditionally owned and controlled by socially or economically disadvantaged individuals or groups.[39] SDBs that are not 8(a) firms need not demonstrate potential for success,[40] and individuals owning and controlling non-8(a) SDBs may have net worth of up to $750,000, excluding ownership interests in 8(a) firms and equity in primary personal residences, when their firms are first designated as SDBs.[41] Otherwise, however, SDBs must generally meet the same eligibility requirements as 8(a) firms, although they do not apply to the SBA to be designated SDBs in the same way that 8(a) firms do.

Certification of SDBs

At one time, SDBs had to be certified by the SBA, or a private certifying entity acting in compliance with SBA regulations, to qualify for certain federal programs as prime contractors.[42] However, most federal programs for SDB prime contractors have been discontinued, with only the government-wide and agency-specific goals for the percentage of federal contract dollars awarded to SDB contractors (and subcontractors) each year remaining.[43] Because of the discontinuance of these programs, the SBA ceased certifying SDBs in October 2008,[44] and no longer issues regulations for private certifiers.[45] In the few cases where SDB certification is currently required, 8(a) participants are deemed to be certified,[46] and other firms may be certified by the agency conducting the procurement, private certifying entities, or state and local governments.[47] Firms not relying on their 8(a) status that have submitted applications for SDB certification to a procuring agency are treated as if they are certified so long as the agency has not rejected their application.[48] Certification generally lasts for three years,[49] and the same firm may be certified as an SDB repeatedly, so long as it meets the requirements for certification.

Firms do not need to be certified SDBs to qualify for federal programs for subcontractors. Rather,

> A firm may represent that it qualifies as an SDB for any Federal subcontracting program if it believes in good faith that it is owned and controlled by one or more socially and economically disadvantaged individuals.[50]

Prime contractors "acting in good faith" may rely on subcontractors' written representation of their status as an SDB.[51] Although the Federal Acquisition Regulation (FAR) still contains contract clauses obligating prime contractors to verify firms' SDB status with the SBA,[52] agencies appear to be dropping this requirement in light of the SBA ceasing to certify SDBs.[53] However, the SBA still retains the authority to review the status of uncertified firms that represent themselves as SDBs for purposes of federal subcontracts when it receives "credible information" that they are not disadvantaged.[54]

Contracting Programs for SDBs

The government promotes contracting and subcontracting with SDBs by setting government-wide and agency-specific goals for the percentage of federal contract and subcontract dollars awarded to SDBs each fiscal year. The government-wide goal is that "not less than 5 percent of the total value of all prime contract and subcontract awards" be made to SDBs,[55] a goal that was met in FY2008, when $29.3 billion was awarded to SDBs.[56] Agency specific goals are generally also set at 5% of the total value of prime contracts and subcontracts awarded each fiscal year, although agency achievements range from 1.8% (Department of Energy) to 44.3% (SBA).[57] In the past, agencies also had authority to "us[e] less than full and open competitive procedures and partial set-asides," including a 10% price evaluation adjustment,[58] when evaluating bids or offers involving SDB contractors or subcontractors.[59] However, such authorities have either expired[60] or been subject to statutory conditions or judicial decisions precluding their use.[61]

Other federal programs focus specifically on promoting SDBs as subcontractors on federal prime contracts. Agencies must negotiate "subcontracting plans" with the apparently successful bidder or offeror on eligible prime contracts prior to awarding the contract.[62] Subcontracting plans set goals for the percentage of subcontract dollars to be awarded to SDBs, among others, and describe efforts that will be made to ensure that SDBs "have an equitable opportunity to compete for subcontracts."[63] Failure to make a good faith effort to comply with the subcontracting plan constitutes a material breach of the contract, potentially allowing the agency to terminate the contract for default[64] and subjecting the contractor to liquidated damages.[65] Federal agencies may also consider the extent of subcontracting with SDBs in determining to whom to award a contract,[66] or give contractors "monetary incentives" to subcontract with SDBs.[67] Such incentives reward prime contractors by paying them up to 10% of the amount by which their actual performance in subcontracting with SDBs exceeds their proposed performance.[68]

Disadvantaged Business Enterprises

Like 8(a) participants and SDBs, "disadvantaged business enterprises" (DBEs) are small businesses at least 51% unconditionally owned and controlled by socially and economically disadvantaged individuals.[69] However, DBEs differ from 8(a) participants and SDBs in that members of the following groups—which include women—are presumed to be both socially *and* economically disadvantaged:

> (i) "Black Americans," which includes persons having origins in any of the Black racial groups of Africa; (ii) "Hispanic Americans," which includes persons of Mexican, Puerto Rican, Cuban, Dominican, Central or South American, or other Spanish or Portuguese culture or origin, regardless of race; (iii) "Native Americans," which includes persons who are American Indians, Eskimos, Aleuts, or Native Hawaiians; (iv) "Asian-Pacific Americans," which includes persons whose origins are from Japan, China, Taiwan, Korea, Burma (Myanmar), Vietnam, Laos, Cambodia (Kampuchea), Thailand, Malaysia, Indonesia, the Philippines, Brunei, Samoa, Guam, the U.S. Trust Territories of the Pacific Islands (Republic of Palau), the Commonwealth of the Northern Marianas Islands, Macao, Fiji, Tonga, Kirbati, [T]uvalu, Nauru, Federated States of Micronesia, or Hong Kong; (v) "Subcontinent Asian Americans," which includes persons whose origins are from India, Pakistan, Bangladesh, Bhutan, the Maldives Islands, Nepal or Sri Lanka; (vi) Women; (vii) [a]ny additional groups whose members are designated as socially and economically disadvantaged by the SBA, at such time as the SBA designation becomes effective.[70]

Table 2. Comparison of the Various Types of Disadvantaged Small Businesses

	8(a) Participant	SDB	DBE
Social disadvantage	Presumed for designated racial and ethnic groups Not presumed for women	Presumed for designated racial and ethnic groups Not presumed for women	Presumed for designated racial and ethnic groups Presumed for women
Economic disadvantage	Not presumed Personal net worth of less than $250,000 at time of application ($750,000 thereafter) Retirement accounts not excluded from net worth	Not presumed Personal net worth of less than $750,000 Retirement accounts not excluded from net worth	Presumed for designated racial and ethnic groups and women Personal net worth of less than $750,000 Retirement accounts excluded from net worth
Application or certification process	Firms apply to the SBA Firms must be approved before participating Initial application form with supporting materials Mandatory disclosure of changes in circumstances Annual renewal form with supporting materials; may need audited financial statements	8(a) participants deemed to be SDBs; other firms certified by procuring agencies, private certifying entities, or state or local governments Firms can participate as prime contractors while certification is pending and as subcontractors with good faith belief in their eligibility	8(a) participants and SDBs not deemed to be DBEs, but their application can be denied only in certain circumstances; other firms must be certified by the Unified Certification Program for the state of the funding recipient Firms must be certified before participating in programs On-site reviews conducted Mandatory disclosure of changes in circumstances Sworn affidavit annually on anniversary of certification
Length of designation	One time eligibility for firms and disadvantaged individuals; no more than nine years in the 8(a) Program	Certification lasts three years; firms may seek and be certified multiple times	Certification lasts three years; firms may seek and be certified multiple times
Contracting and related programs	Set-asides and sole-source contracts Direct and guaranteed loans from the SBA Transfer of federal technology and surplus property Management and technical assistance Mentor-protégé program	5% government-wide goal for contracting and subcontracting Agency-specific goals for contracting and subcontracting Subcontracting plans Subcontracting an evaluation factor Monetary incentives for subcontracting	10% national goal for contracting and subcontracting Recipient-set goals, including on individual contracts Race-neutral means to meet goals, if possible Development programs Mentor-protégé programs

Source: Congressional Research Service, based on 13 C.F.R. §§ 124.1-12.1014 and 49 C.F.R. §§ 26.1-26.109.

Members of these groups must nonetheless submit a signed, notarized statement regarding their group membership,[71] as well as information concerning their economic disadvantage.[72] Additionally, their net worth cannot exceed $750,000,[73] excluding their ownership interest in the DBE firm, equity in their primary residence, and assets held in pension plans, IRAs, 401(k) accounts, or other retirement savings or investment programs which cannot be distributed prior to retirement age without "significant adverse tax or interest consequences."[74] Individuals who are not members of designated groups must demonstrate by a preponderance of the evidence that they are socially and economically disadvantaged.[75]

Certification of DBEs

8(a) firms and SDBs are not automatically deemed to be DBEs.[76] However, their application for 8(a) status or SDB certification generally suffices as their application for DBE certification,[77] and they must be granted DBE certification unless the certifying entity determines, based on an on- site visit to the firm and related information, that the firm does not meet eligibility requirements.[78] Firms that are not 8(a) participants or SDBs can only be certified as DBEs after they are found to be eligible based upon (1) an on-site visit with the firm, including interviews with its principal officers; (2) an on-site visit to any job sites operated by the firm; (3) an analysis of the ownership of stock in the firm, as well as its bonding and financial capacity; (4) the firm's work history, including the contracts it has received and the work it has completed; (5) a statement from the firm indicating its preferred type(s) of work and work locations; (6) a list of equipment owned by or available to the firm; and (7) a completed application form.[79] All certifications must be final before the due date for bids or offers for any contract on which a firm seeks to participate as a DBE.[80]

Once certified, DBEs must provide written notices of any changes in circumstances affecting their eligibility as these changes occur.[81] They must also produce a sworn affidavit affirming that there have been no changes in circumstances affecting the firm's eligibility each year on the anniversary of their date of certification.[82]

Certification generally lasts for three years, and the same firm may be certified as a DBE repeatedly, so long as it meets the requirements for certification.[83] Certifications are state-specific,[84] although states may recognize one another's certifications.[85]

Contracting Programs for DBEs

DBEs are eligible for various contracting programs, most of which are operated by state governments and other entities that receive certain federal highway or transit funds, or airport funds.[86] The federal government has as a goal that 10% of such funds be awarded to DBEs. However, this is "an aspirational goal at the national level" and "does not authorize or require [funding] recipients to set overall or contract goals at the 10 percent level, or any other particular level, or to take any special administrative steps if their goals are above or below 10 percent."[87]

Funding recipients also set goals for DBE participation overall and on individual contracts that have the possibility of subcontracting.[88] They are barred from using "quotas," or requiring that certain percentages of their contract dollars go to DBEs, and they can "set aside" contracts for DBEs only "in limited and extreme circumstances ... when no other method could be reasonably expected to redress egregious instances of discrimination."[89] Instead, they must use race-neutral means to meet "the maximum feasible portion" of these goals.[90] Such means include

- arranging solicitations, times for the presentation of bids, quantities, specifications, and delivery schedules so as to facilitate DBE participation (e.g., unbundling

contracts; encouraging prime contractors to subcontract work that they would otherwise perform in-house);
- limiting obstacles that DBEs may encounter in obtaining bonding or financing (e.g., simplifying bonding processes; eliminating surety costs from bids);
- providing technical assistance and other services;
- publicizing contract opportunities and providing information about contracting procedures (e.g., providing information in languages other than English);
- assisting DBEs in developing and improving their business management, record keeping, and financial and accounting capabilities;
- providing services to help DBEs develop, participate in various kinds of work, and achieve self-sufficiency;
- assisting new start-up firms, particularly in fields where DBE participation has historically been low;
- distributing DBE directories to potential prime contractors; and
- assisting DBEs to develop their capability to utilize emerging technology and conduct business through electronic media.[91]

Funding recipients cannot be penalized for failure to meet their goals unless they did not administer their DBE program in good faith. [92]

Recipients may also establish development and mentor-protégé programs for DBEs, although participants in any mentor-protégé programs do not enjoy the same "exemption" from the SBA size standards when they form joint ventures as 8(a) firms participating in the SBA mentor- protégé program do.[93]

Tabular Comparison of the Various Types of Disadvantaged Small Businesses

Table 2 provides a comparison of the various types of disadvantaged small businesses for purposes of federal and federally funded contracting programs.

CONSTITUTIONALITY OF FEDERAL PROGRAMS FOR DISADVANTAGED SMALL BUSINESSES

All federal programs for disadvantaged small businesses currently define "disadvantage," in part, based on the presumption that racial and ethnic minorities, or women, are disadvantaged.[94] Presumptions based on race have been found to constitute "explicit racial classifications,"[95] subjecting programs that incorporate them to "strict scrutiny" when such programs are challenged as violations of due process and equal protection under the U.S. Constitution.[96] For a challenged program to survive strict scrutiny, the government must show that the program is necessary to a compelling government interest.[97] The U.S. Court of Appeals for the Federal Circuit recently stuck down a Department of Defense program for SDBs because the government could not show a "strong basis in evidence" for concluding that the program was necessary to remedy discrimination in the defense industry.[98]

Presumptions based on sex may also be subjected to heightened scrutiny if challenged, because courts have required the government to show that other programs classifying individuals on the basis of sex are substantially related to important government objectives.[99] Something like a "strong basis in evidence" might thus be required for programs incorporating the presumption that women are disadvantaged.[100]

RECENTLY ENACTED OR PROPOSED LEGISLATION

In part because of small businesses' widely recognized role in job creation and concerns that the recent recession has disproportionately affected disadvantaged small businesses, the 111th Congress has enacted or proposed legislation that would assist disadvantaged small businesses in various ways. It has enacted legislation that (1) gives SDBs special consideration in the selection of grant recipients under the Broadband Technology Opportunities Program funded by the American Recovery and Reinvestment Act (ARRA);[101] (2) provides bonding assistance for DBEs performing transportation contracts funded under ARRA;[102] (3) allows the U.S. Agency for International Development to issue orders under certain multiple-award indefinite-delivery, indefinite quantity (ID/IQ) contracts funded by the Omnibus Appropriations Act, 2009 to SDBs, among others, without providing other firms a fair opportunity to be considered;[103] and (4) grants the Department of the Interior special authority to contract with SDBs, among others, for forest hazardous fuels reduction, watershed or water quality monitoring or restoration, wildlife or fish population monitoring, or habitat restoration or management.[104]

Legislation has also been proposed that would

- allow individuals with greater net worth to qualify as economically disadvantaged for purposes of the 8(a) and SDB programs;[105]
- exempt businesses that have not completed an 8(a) contract from time limits on participation in the 8(a) Program;[106]
- extend the maximum term of participation in the 8(a) Program for individuals called to "active duty" in the U.S. military for more than 30 days;[107]
- raise the government-wide goal for contracting with SDBs to 10%;[108]
- establish an SBA program to train 8(a) firms and SDBs for contracting opportunities in the construction industry;[109]
- establish a three-year pilot program (the State Trade and Export Promotion Grant Program) to make grants to states for use in carrying out programs that assist 8(a) firms, among others, in doing business abroad;[110]
- require that contractors holding Transportation Security Administration contracts in excess of $300 million implement[111] their plans for contracting with SBDs and report periodically on this implementation, including the percentages of contract dollars awarded to all tiers of SDB subcontractors;[112]
- encourage heads of certain federally funded laboratories at minority-serving institutions to establish partnerships with SDBs for the purpose of increasing R&D capacity, among other things;[113] and

- require that a "formal, structured certification training program" be established for DBE airport concessions and that the Secretary of Transportation issue regulations adjusting the net-worth threshold for inflation.[114]

End Notes

[1] There are other federal programs for SDBs and DBEs, in particular, that are agency-specific and smaller in scale, such as the Environmental Protection Agency's DBE program. *See* 33 C.F.R. §§ 33.101-33.503. Such programs are not addressed in this report. Also not addressed in this report are programs for "minority business enterprises" (MBEs), as defined by the Department of Commerce's Minority Business Development Agency (MDBA). MBEs need not be "small," and their owners can be either socially *or* economically disadvantaged. 15 C.F.R. § 1400.2(a). MBEs are not certified for purposes of federal programs, and there are no federal or federally funded contracting programs for MBEs that are not also 8(a) participants, SDBs, or DBEs.

[2] *See* 13 C.F.R. § 124.105 (8(a) participants); 13 C.F.R. § 124.1002(b)(2) (SDBs); 49 C.F.R. § 26.5 (DBEs).

[3] *See* 15 U.S.C. §§ 657b and 657c (programs for veteran-owned small businesses); 15 U.S.C. § 657f (programs for service-disabled veteran-owned small businesses); 41 U.S.C. §§ 46-47 (program to benefit "the blind and severely disabled"). The latter program is commonly known as the Javits-Wagner-O'Day Program (JWOD).

[4] For more on contracting with Alaska Native Corporations, see CRS Report R40855, *Contracting Programs for Alaska Native Corporations: Historical Development and Legal Authorities*, by John R. Luckey, Kate M. Manuel, and Roger Walke.

[5] Small Business Administration, Goals Achieved Government-Wide, *available at* http://www.sba.gov/idc/groups/public/documents/sba_homepage/goals_08_gov_wide.pdf.

[6] Small Business Administration, Goals Achieved Government-Wide, *available at* http://www.sba.gov/idc/groups/public/documents/sba_homepage/goals_08_gov_wide.pdf.

[7] *See, e.g.*, Mark Trumbull, Why Obama Job Creation Plan Focuses on Small Business, *The Christian Science Monitor*, Dec. 8, 2009, *available at* http://features.csmonitor.com/politics/ (noting that small businesses are reported to have created 65% of all new jobs in the United States over the past 15 years).

[8] *See, e.g.*, John Rosenthal, Tough Times Often Even Tougher on Minority Biz, *Chicago Business*, Nov. 30, 2009, *available at* http://www.chicagobusiness.com/cgi-bin/mag/article.pl?articleId=32738&seenIt=1.

[9] 13 C.F.R. § 124.101. Eligibility for the 8(a) Program is further limited to firms that demonstrate "potential for success" and whose owners are U.S. citizens and possess "good character." *Id.* Detailed regulations govern each of these requirements. *See* 13 C.F.R. § 124.105 (ownership); 13 C.F.R. § 124.106 (control); 13 C.F.R. § 124.107 (potential for success); 13 C.F.R. § 124.108(a) (good character).

[10] *See* 15 U.S.C. § 636(j); 15 U.S.C. § 637(a).

[11] 13 C.F.R. § 124.103(a). Such prejudice or bias must also be due to circumstances beyond the individuals' control. *Id.*

[12] 13 C.F.R. § 124. 103(b)(1). This presumption may be overcome by "credible evidence" to the contrary, and SBA may require individuals relying on the presumption to demonstrate that they held themselves out and are currently recognized by others as members of the group. 13 C.F.R. § 124. 103(b)(2)-(3). The SBA relies on a group petition process in recognizing additional groups. *See* 13 C.F.R. § 124. 103(d)(1)-(3).

[13] 13 C.F.R. § 124. 103(c)(2)(i)-(iii). In assessing the third factor, the SBA will consider all relevant evidence produced by the applicant, but must consider the applicant's education, employment, and business history to see if the totality of the circumstances shows disadvantage. 13 C.F.R. § 124. 103(c)(2)(iii).

[14] 13 C.F.R. § 124.104(a).

[15] 13 C.F.R. § 124.104(b)(1).

[16] 13 C.F.R. § 124.104(c).

[17] 13 C.F.R. § 124.104(c)(2).

[18] Small Business Administration, Small Business Size Regulations; 8(a) Business Development/Small Disadvantaged Business Status Determinations, 74 Fed. Reg. 55694, 55698 (Oct. 28, 2009).

[19] Businesses are classified by North American Industry Classification System (NAICS) codes. A firm's primary industry is that in which it earns the majority of its revenue.

[20] 13 C.F.R. § 124.104(c).

[21] 13 C.F.R. § 124.2.

[22] *See* 13 C.F.R. § 124.203; Small Business Administration, Application for 8(a) Business Development (8(a) BD) and Small Disadvantaged Business (SDB) Certification, *available at* http://www.sba.gov/idc/groups/public/documents/ sba_homepage/forms_trng1010banc.pdf. Despite the title of this form, SBA no longer certifies SDBs. *See infra* note 44 and accompanying text.

[23] 13 C.F.R. § 124.112(a).

[24] *See* Small Business Administration, 8(a) Annual Update, *available at* http://www.sba.gov/idc/groups/public/documents/sba_homepage/forms_1450.pdf.

[25] 13 C.F.R. § 124.112(b)(1)-(8); 13 C.F.R. § 124.603.

[26] 13 C.F.R. § 124.602(a)-(c).

[27] 13 C.F.R. § 124.2. Firms may be terminated or subjected to early graduation from the 8(a) Program before nine years have passed. 15 U.S.C. § 636(j)(10)(C)(i) (nine-year term); 15 U.S.C. § 637(a)(9) (termination and early graduation); 13 C.F.R. § 124.301 (exiting the 8(a) Program); 13 C.F.R. § 124.302 (early graduation); 13 C.F.R. § 124.303 (termination from the Program).

[28] 13 C.F.R. § 124.108(b). When at least 50% of the assets of one firm are the same as those of another firm, the firms are considered identical for purposes of eligibility for the 8(a) Program. 13 C.F.R. § 124.108(b)(4).

[29] 15 U.S.C. § 636(j)(11)(B)-(C); 13 C.F.R. § 124.108(b).

[30] 15 U.S.C. § 644(o); 13 C.F.R. § 125.6; 48 C.F.R. § 52.219-14.

[31] 13 C.F.R. §§ 124.501-124.519.

[32] *See, e.g.*, 48 C.F.R. 19.805-1(b)(2) (authorizing sole-source awards to 8(a) participants owned by Indian tribes or Alaska Native Corporations even when there is a reasonable expectation that at least two eligible and responsible 8(a) firms will submit offers at a fair market price).

[33] U.S. Small Business Administration, Fiscal Year 2008 Report to the U.S. Congress on Minority Small Business and Capital Ownership Development, at 7, *available at* http://www.sba.gov/idc/groups/public/documents/sba_program_office/8abd_408_fy2008report.pdf.

[34] Office of the Inspector General, U.S. Small Business Administration, Participation in the 8(a) Program by Firms Owned by Alaska Native Corporations, at 5 (July 10, 2009), *available at* http://www.sba.gov/idc/groups/public/ documents/sba_homepage/oig_reptbydatejuly9-15.pdf. In contrast, 63% of 8(a) firms owned by Alaska Native Corporations received contracts in FY2008.

[35] 13 C.F.R. § 124.404(a)-(c); 13 C.F.R. § 124.405; 13 C.F.R. §§ 124.701-704.

[36] Eligibility for the mentor-protégé program is generally limited to 8(a) firms that are in the developmental stage of the 8(a) Program; have never received an 8(a) contract; and have a size that is less than half the size standard corresponding to its primary NAICS code. 13 C.F.R. § 124.520(c)(1)(i)-(iii).

[37] 13 C.F.R. § 124.520(a).

[38] 13.C.F.R. § 124.520(d)(1). For the joint venture to qualify as "small," the 8(a) firm must qualify as "small" under the size standards for the procurement, and, in the case of sole-source contracts awarded under the authority of Section 8(a), must not have received a combined total of competitive and sole-source awards in excess of $100 million or other applicable threshold. *See* 13 C.F.R. § 519.

[39] 13 C.F.R. § 124.1002. The majority of the firm's earnings must also accrue to socially and economically disadvantaged individuals or groups for purposes of programs under 10 U.S.C. § 2323, discussed below. *Id.*

[40] 13 C.F.R. § 124.1002(e).

[41] 13 C.F.R. § 124.1002(c).

[42] *See, e.g.*, 13 C.F.R. § 124. 1004 and § 124.1008 (2007).

[43] *See infra* notes 55-6 1 and accompanying text.

[44] *See* Small Business Administration, Small Disadvantaged Business Program, 73 Fed. Reg. 57490 (Oct. 3, 2008 (announcing that SBA would not longer certify SDBs).

[45] *Id.*

[46] 13 C.F.R. § 124.1003(a).

[47] 13 C.F.R. § 124. 1003(b)-(c). It is the procuring agency's decision whether to accept certifications from private certifying entities or state or local governments.

[48] 13 C.F.R. § 124.1001(b)(4).

[49] 13 C.F.R. § 124.1005(a).

[50] 13 C.F.R. § 124.1001(c).

[51] 48 C.F.R. § 19.703(b).

[52] *See* 48 C.F.R. § 52.2 19-25.

[53] *See, e.g.*, Class Deviation to the Federal Acquisition Regulation: Small Disadvantaged Business Certification for Subcontractors, Nov. 19, 2009, at 3, *available at* http://www.acq.osd.mil/dpap/policy DPAP.pdf.

[54] 13 C.F.R. § 124.1006.

[55] 15 U.S.C. § 644(g)(1).

[56] Small Business Administration, Goals Achieved Government-Wide, *available at* http://www.sba.gov/idc/groups/public/documents/sba_homepage/goals_08_gov_wide.pdf. The goal for SBDs was the only government-wide goal for contracting and subcontracting with small businesses that was met in FY2008. *Id.* In FY2008, the government awarded 6.58% of its contract and subcontract dollars to SDBs. *Id.*

[57] *See* Small Business Administration, FY2008 Goals and Achievements, *available at* http://www.sba.gov/idc/group s/ public/documents/sba_homepage/fy2008goals_and_achievements.html.

[58] A price evaluation adjustment works as follows: when comparing a bid or offer from an SDB with one submitted by another business, the agency can subtract up to 10% of the price from the bid or offer submitted by the

SDB in determining which bid or offer has the lowest price or represents the best value. For example, if a business that is not an SDB bids $100,000 and an SDB bids $110,000, the SDB would win because it is the lower bidder after its price is reduced by 10% ($1 10,000-$1 1,000=$99,000).

[59] *See, e.g.*, Department of Defense Authorization Act for FY1987, P.L. 99-661, § 1207, 100 Stat. 3973-75 (Nov. 14, 1986) (codified at 10 U.S.C. § 2323) (procurements of defense agencies); Federal Acquisition Streamlining Act, P.L. 103-355, § 7102, 108 Stat. 3368-69 (Oct. 13, 1994) (procurements of civilian agencies).

[60] *See* P.L. 103-355, § 7102 (authority expiring at the end of FY2000).

[61] *See* Strom Thurmond National Defense Authorization Act for FY1999, P.L. 105-261, § 801, 112 Stat. 2080-8 1 (Oct. 17, 1998) (barring DOD from granting price evaluation adjustments in any fiscal year directly following a fiscal year in which DOD awarded at least 5% of its contract dollars to SDBs); Rothe Dev. Corp. v. Dep't of Defense, 545 F.3d 1023 (Fed. Cir. 2008) (finding 10 U.S.C. § 2323 unconstitutional on its face).

[62] 15 U.S.C. § 637(d)(4) & (5). Eligible contracts are those (1) exceeding $500,000 ($1 million, in the case of contracts to construct public facilities) and (2) offering subcontracting possibilities. *Id.* Agencies may not find a contractor affirmatively "responsible" for purposes of the award of a federal contract unless it agrees to any required subcontracting plan. For more on responsibility determinations, see CRS Report R40633, *Responsibility Determinations Under the Federal Acquisition Regulation: Legal Standards and Procedures*, by Kate M. Manuel.

[63] 15 U.S.C. § 637(d)(6).

[64] 15 U.S.C. § 637(d)(8).

[65] 48 C.F.R. § 19.705-7. Liquidated damages are damages whose amount was agreed upon, as compensation for specific breaches, by the parties during the contract's formation.

[66] 48 C.F.R. § 19.1202-3 ("In developing an SDB participation evaluation factor or subfactor for the solicitation, agencies may consider—(a) [t]he extent to which SDB concerns are specifically identified; (b) [t]he extent of commitment to use SDB concerns (for example, enforceable commitments are to be weighted more heavily than non- enforceable ones); (c) [t]he complexity and variety of the work SDB concerns are to perform; (d) [t]he realism of the proposal; (e) [p]ast performance of offerors in complying with subcontracting plan goals for SDB concerns and monetary targets for SDB participation; and (f) [t]he extent of participation of SDB concerns in terms of the value of the total acquisition.").

[67] 48 C.F.R. § 19.1203 ("The contracting officer may encourage increased subcontracting opportunities in the NAICS Industry Subsector as determined by the Department of Commerce for SDB concerns in negotiated acquisitions by providing monetary incentives.... Monetary incentives shall be based on actual achievement as compared to proposed monetary targets for SDB subcontracting.").

[68] 48 C.F.R. § 52.219-26(b) ("If the Contractor exceeds its total monetary target for subcontracting to small disadvantaged business concerns in the authorized, NAICS Industry Subsectors, it will receive [Contracting Officer to insert the appropriate number between 0 and 10] percent of the dollars in excess of the monetary target, unless the Contracting Officer determines that the excess was not due to the Contractor's efforts (e.g., a subcontractor cost overrun caused the actual subcontract amount to exceed that estimated in the offer, or the excess was caused by the award of subcontracts that had been planned but had not been disclosed in the offer during contract negotiations).").

[69] 49 C.F.R. § 26.5 (defining "disadvantaged business enterprise"). SBA size standards are used in determining whether DBE firms are "small." 49 C.F.R. § 26.65(a).

[70] 49 U.S.C. § 26.5. Members of these groups may be required to present evidence of their membership in the group, including showing that they held themselves out as a member of the group over a "long period of time prior to application for certification" and are regarded as a member of the group by the relevant community. 49 C.F.R. § 26.63(a)(1) & (b).

[71] 49 C.F.R. § 26.65(a).

[72] 49 C.F.R. § 26.6 1(c); 49 C.F.R. § 26.67(a)(2)(ii).

[73] 49 C.F.R. § 26.67(a)(2)(i).

[74] 49 C.F.R. § 26.67(a)(2)(iii)(D).

[75] 49 C.F.R. § 26.6 1(d).

[76] 49 C.F.R. § 26.84(c) (requiring the certifying entity to conduct an on-site review before certifying an 8(a) participant or SDB as a DBE).

[77] 49 C.F.R. § 26.84(a). However, the certifying entity may require 8(a) participants and SDBs to submit information not included in their applications for the 8(a) Program or SDB certification. 49 C.F.R. § 26. 84(b).

[78] 49 C.F.R. § 26.84(d).

[79] 49 C.F.R. § 26.83(c)(1)-(7). This application form can be found in Appendix F to Part 26 of Title 49 of the *Code of Federal Regulations*.

[80] 49 C.F.R. § 26.8 1(c).

[81] 49 C.F.R § 26.83(i).

[82] 49 C.F.R. § 26.83(j).

[83] 49 C.F.R. § 26.83(h).

[84] *See* 49 C.F.R. § 26.81(a) & (b)(1) (requiring all recipients of federal funding within a state to participate in a Unified Certification Program (UCP), whose DBE certifications are binding on recipients in that state).

[85] 49 C.F.R. § 26.8 1(e)-(f).

[86] 49 C.F.R. § 26.3(a).

[87] 49 C.F.R. § 26.4 1(b)-(c).

[88] 49 C.F.R. § 26.45(a)(1). These goals are to be based on demonstrable evidence of the availability of ready, willing and able DBEs relative to the availability of other firms ready, willing and able to participate on the contract. 49 C.F.R. § 26.45(b). *See also* 49 C.F.R. § 26.5 1(e)(1) (goals only on contracts with subcontracting possiblity); 49 C.F.R. § 26.4 1(f)(3) (requiring funding recipients to project the portions of the overall goal to be met through race-conscious and race-neutral means).

[89] 49 C.F.R. § 26.43.

[90] 49 C.F.R. § 26.51(b).

[91] 49 C.F.R. § 26.5 1(b)(1)-(9).

[92] 49 C.F.R. § 26.47(a).

[93] *See* Small Business Size Regulations; 8(a) Business Development/Small Disadvantaged Business Status Determinations, *supra* note 18, at 55694.

[94] *See* 13 C.F.R. § 124.103(b)(1) (8(a) participants); 13 C.F.R. § 124.1001(a) (SDBs); 49 C.F.R. § 26.5 (DBEs).

[95] Rothe Dev. Corp. v. Dep't of Defense, 545 F.3d 1023, 1035 (Fed. Cir. 2008).

[96] Due process under the Fifth Amendment includes equal protection, or the constitutional assurance that the government will apply the law equally to all people and not improperly prefer one class of people over another. *See* Bolling v. Sharpe, 347 U.S. 497 (1954).

[97] Adarand Constructors, Inc. v. Peña, 515 U.S. 200 (1995). See generally CRS Report RL33284, *Minority Contracting and Affirmative Action for Disadvantaged Small Businesses: Legal Issues*, by Jody Feder.

[98] Rothe Dev. Corp., 545 F.3d at 1049. In determining whether there was a "strong basis in evidence," the court examined the empirical studies upon which the government relied in concluding that there was discrimination in the defense industry, including their geographical scope, their currency, and whether they were "before" Congress. For more on the *Rothe* decision, see CRS Report R40440, *Rothe Development Corporation v. Department of Defense: The Constitutionality of Federal Contracting Programs for Minority-Owned and Other Small Businesses*, by Jody Feder and Kate M. Manuel.

[99] *See, e.g.*, Craig v. Boren, 429 U.S. 190, 197 (1976). In *United States v. Virginia*, the Court required the State of Virginia to provide an "exceedingly persuasive justification" for its policy of maintaining an all-male military academy. 518 U.S. 515 (1996). It is unclear whether this standard differs from the intermediate scrutiny standard of review.

[100] During the Bush Administration, the SBA extended the comment period on a proposed rule regarding set-asides for women-owned small businesses in order to "review" the evidence underlying its determinations regarding the industries in which women are underrepresented. *See* Small Business Administration, The Women-Owned Small Business Federal Contract Assistance Procedures: Eligible Industries, 74 Fed. Reg. 1153 (Jan. 12, 2009). Set-asides for women-owned firms are only possible in industries in which the SBA has determined that women-owned firms are underrepresented. *See* 15 U.S.C. § 637(m)(2)(A)-(F) & (m)(4). However, the Obama Administration recently issued a proposed rule that could lead to implementation of such set-asides. *See* Small Business Administration, Women-Owned Small Business Federal Contract Program: Proposed Rule, 75 Fed. Reg. 10029 (Mar. 4, 2010).

[101] P.L. 111-5, § 6001(h)(3), 123 Stat. 515 (Feb. 17, 2009).

[102] *Id.* at Title XII, 123 Stat. 207. Contractors are often required to post bid, performance, payment and/or patent infringement bonds, the proceeds of which are used to pay the government for any losses it sustains when the contractor fails to perform as required.

[103] P.L. 111-8, § 7034, 123 Stat. 877 (Mar. 11, 2009). The Federal Acquisition Streamlining Act of 1994 generally requires that all contractors holding a multiple-award ID/IQ contract be given a "fair opportunity to be considered" for the issuance of orders under that contract unless certain conditions are met. *See* 10 U.S.C. § 2304c(b)(1)-(4) (procurements of defense agencies) & 41 U.S.C. § 303j(b)(1) (procurements of civilian agencies). There is a similar provision in the Department of State, Foreign Operations, and Related Programs Appropriations Act, 2010, H.R. 3081, § 7034.

[104] Interior Department and Further Continuing Appropriations, Fiscal Year 2010, P.L. 111-88, § 413, 123 Stat. 2958- 59 (Oct. 30, 2009).

[105] Minority Small Business Enhancement Act of 2009, H.R. 2299, § 2 (proposing to increase the net-worth threshold to $1.5 million); An Act to Amend the Small Business Act to Change the Net Worth Amount Under the Small Business Program for Socially and Economically Disadvantaged Individuals from $750,000 to $978,722, and For Other Purposes, H.R. 4253, § 1

[106] H.R. 2299, at § 2.

[107] Promoting Jobs for Veterans Act of 2009, H.R. 4220, § 104. As used here, "active duty" has the same meaning it has under 10 U.S.C. § 101(d)(2).

[108] H.R. 2299, at § 5.

[109] An Act to Amend the Small Business Act to Establish Mentorship and Assistance Programs Designed to Help Minority, Veteran-Owned, and Women-Owned Small Businesses Operate in the Construction Industry, and For Other Purposes, H.R. 3773, § 2.

[110] Small Business Export Enhancement and International Trade Act of 2009, S. 2862.

[111] The focus upon implementation here potentially distinguishes this provision from existing law. Currently, contractors are required to make good faith efforts to comply with their subcontracting plans, but can be excused from implementing them in certain circumstances. *See* 15 U.S.C. § 637(d)(2)(F)(ii).

[112] Transportation Security Administration Authorization Act, H.R. 2200, § 103. H.R. 2200 would also require TSA to report annually to the House and Senate committees of jurisdiction on contractors' performance in subcontracting with SDBs.

[113] Coast Guard Authorization Act of 2010, H.R. 3619, § 221.

[114] FAA Air Transportation Modernization and Safety Improvement Act, S. 1451, § 703 and § 715. *See also* FAA Reauthorization Act of 2009, H.R. 915, §§ 115-116.

In: Disadvantaged Small Businesses and the 8(a) Program ISBN: 978-1-61209-309-3
Editors: James P. Carlson and Andrea M. Bernard

Chapter 2

THE "8(A) PROGRAM" FOR SMALL BUSINESSES OWNED AND CONTROLLED BY THE SOCIALLY AND ECONOMICALLY DISADVANTAGED: LEGAL REQUIREMENTS AND ISSUES

John R. Luckey and Kate M. Manuel

SUMMARY

This report provides an overview of the Small Business Administration's (SBA's) Minority Small Business and Capital Ownership Development Program. Based upon authorities given to the SBA by Sections 7(j) and 8(a) of the Small Business Act of 1958, as amended, this program is commonly known as the "8(a) Program." The 8(a) Program provides participating small businesses w ith training, technical assistance, and contracting opportunities in the form of set- asides and sole-source awards. A "set-aside" is an acquisition in which only certain contractors may compete, while a sole-source award is a contract awarded, or proposed for award, without competition. Eligibility for the 8(a) Program is generally limited to small businesses "unconditionally owned and controlled by one or more socially and economically disadvantaged individuals who are of good character and citizens of the United States" that demonstrate "potential for success." However, small businesses owned by Indian tribes, Alaska Native Corporations (ANCs), Native Hawaiian Organizations (NHOs), and Community Development Corporations (CDCs) are eligible for the 8(a) Program under somewhat different terms. In FY2008, 9,462 firms participated in the 8(a) Program, and the federal government spent $6.3 billion on contracts with 8(a) firms.

The report surveys the historical development of the 8(a) Program, as well as the legal requirements presently governing (1) eligibility for the 8(a) Program, (2) set-asides and sole-source awards under Section 8(a), and (3) related matters. It also discusses potential developments in the 8(a) Program in light of recently proposed legislation, changes in executive branch policies, and legal challenges and decisions. It includes the changes that SBA proposed to the regulations governing the 8(a) Program on October 28, 2009.

The 111th Congress has enacted legislation (P.L. 111-118) that would allow the Department of Defense to convert functions to performance by certain 8(a) firms without conducting the public- private competitions normally required under Office of Management and Budget Circular A-76. It is also considering bills that would modify various aspects of the 8(a) Program or otherwise promote contracting with 8(a) firms (e.g., H.R. 456, H.R. 2200, H.R. 2299, H.R. 2682, H.R. 3771, H.R. 4220, H.R. 4253, H.R. 4818, H.R. 4929, H.R. 5109, S. 1167, S. 2862).

INTRODUCTION

This report provides an overview of the Small Business Administration's (SBA's) Minority Small Business and Capital Ownership Development Program. Based upon authorities given to the SBA by Sections 7(j) and 8(a) of the Small Business Act of 1958, as amended, this program is commonly known as the "8(a) Program." The 8(a) Program provides participating small businesses with training, technical assistance, and contracting opportunities in the form of set- asides and sole-source awards. A "set-aside" is an acquisition in which only certain contractors may compete, while a sole-source award is a contract awarded, or proposed for award, without competition. Eligibility for the 8(a) Program is generally limited to small businesses "unconditionally owned and controlled by one or more socially and economically disadvantaged individuals who are of good character and citizens of the United States" that demonstrate "potential for success." However, small businesses owned by Indian tribes, Alaska Native Corporations (ANCs), Native Hawaiian Organizations (NHOs), and Community Development Corporations (CDCs) are eligible for the 8(a) Program under somewhat different terms. In FY2008, 9,462 firms participated in the 8(a) Program, and the federal government spent $6.3 billion on contracts with 8(a) firms.[1]

The report surveys the historical development of the 8(a) Program, as well as the legal requirements presently governing (1) eligibility for the 8(a) Program, (2) set-asides and sole-source awards under Section 8(a), and (3) related matters. It also discusses potential developments in the 8(a) Program in light of recently proposed legislation, changes in executive branch policies, and legal challenges and decisions. It includes the changes that SBA proposed to the regulations governing the 8(a) Program on October 28, 2009.

The 111th Congress has enacted legislation (P.L. 111-118) that would allow the Department of Defense to convert functions to performance by certain 8(a) firms without conducting the public- private competitions normally required under Office of Management and Budget Circular A-76. It is also considering bills that would modify various aspects of the 8(a) Program or otherwise promote contracting with 8(a) firms (e.g., H.R. 456, H.R. 2200, H.R. 2299, H.R. 2682, H.R. 3771, H.R. 4220, H.R. 4253, H.R. 4818, H.R. 4929, H.R. 5109, S. 1167, S. 2862).

HISTORY OF THE 8(A) PROGRAM

Origins of the 8(a) Program

The current 8(a) Program resulted from the merger of two distinct types of federal programs: those seeking to assist small businesses in general and those seeking to assist racial and ethnic minorities. This merger first occurred, as a matter of executive branch practice, in 1967 and was given a statutory basis in 1978.

Federal Programs for Small Businesses: The Origins of the SBA's Subcontracting Authority

Congress first authorized a federal agency to enter into prime contracts with other agencies and subcontract with small businesses for the performance of these contracts in 1942.[2] The agency was the Smaller War Plants Corporation (SWPC), which was created partly for this purpose, and Congress gave it these powers in order to ameliorate small businesses' financial difficulties while also "mobiliz[ing] the productive facilities of small business in the interest of successful prosecution of the war."[3] The SWPC's subcontracting authority expired along with the SWPC at the end of the World War II, but Congress created the Small Defense Plants Administration (SDPA), which was generally given the same powers that the SWPC had exercised, in 1951 at the start of the Korean War.[4] Two years later, in 1953, Congress transferred the SDPA's subcontracting authorities, among others, to the newly created Small Business Administration,[5] with the intent that the SBA would exercise these powers in peacetime, as well as in wartime.[6] When the Small Business Act of 1958 transformed the SBA into a permanent independent agency, this subcontracting authority was included in Section 8(a) of the act.[7] At its inception, the SBA's subcontracting authority was not limited to small businesses owned and controlled by the socially and economically disadvantaged. Under the original Section 8(a), the SBA could contract with any "small-business concerns or others,"[8] but the SBA seldom, if ever, employed this subcontracting authority, focusing instead upon its loan programs and other programs.[9]

Federal Programs for Minorities Merge with the SBA's Subcontracting Authority: Executive Branch Policy and Administrative Regulations

Federal programs for minorities began developing at approximately the same time as those for small businesses, although there was initially no explicit overlap between them. The earliest programs were created by executive orders, beginning with President Franklin Roosevelt's order on June 25, 1941, requiring that all federal agencies include a clause in defense-related contracts prohibiting contractors from discriminating on the basis of race, creed, color, or national origin.[10]

Subsequent Presidents followed Roosevelt's example, issuing a number of executive orders seeking to improve the employment opportunities of "Negroes, Spanish-Americans, Orientals, Indians, Jews, Puerto Ricans, etc."[11] These executive branch initiatives took on new importance after the Kerner Commission's report on the causes of the urban riots of 1966 concluded that African Americans would need "special encouragement" to enter the economic mainstream.[12]

Presidents Lyndon Johnson and Richard Nixon laid the foundations for the present 8(a) Program in the hope of providing such "encouragement." Johnson created the President's Test Cities Program (PTCP), which involved a small-scale use of the SBA's authority under Section 8(a) to award contracts to firms willing to locate in urban areas and hire unemployed individuals, largely African Americans, or sponsor minority-owned businesses by providing capital or management assistance. [13] Under the PTCP, small businesses did not have to be minority-owned to receive subcontracts under Section 8(a), though.[14] Nixon's program was larger and focused more specifically on minority-owned small businesses.[15] Under Nixon, the SBA promulgated its earliest regulations for the 8(a) Program. In 1970, the first of these regulations articulated the SBA's policy of using Section 8(a) to "assist small concerns owned by disadvantaged persons to become self-sufficient, viable businesses capable of competing effectively in the market place."[16] A later regulation, promulgated in 1973, defined "disadvantaged persons" as including, but not limited to, "black Americans, Spanish-Americans, oriental Americans, Eskimos, and Aleuts."[17] However, the SBA lacked explicit statutory authority for focusing its 8(a) Program on minority- owned businesses. [18]

The 1978 Amendments to the Small Business Act and Subsequent Regulatory Developments

In 1978, Congress amended the Small Business Act of 1958 to give the SBA statutory authority for its 8(a) Program for minority-owned businesses. [19] Under the 1978 amendments, SBA can only subcontract under Section 8(a) with "socially and economically disadvantaged small business concerns,"[20] or businesses which are least 51% owned by one or more socially and economically disadvantaged individuals and whose management and daily operations are controlled by such individual(s).[21]

Table 1. Groups Presumed to Be Socially Disadvantaged

Group	Countries of Origin Included Within Group
Black Americans	n/a
Hispanic Americans	n/a
Native Americans (including American Indians, Eskimos, Aleuts, Native Hawaiians)	n/a
Asian Pacific Americans	Burma, Thailand, Malaysia, Indonesia, Singapore, Brunei, Japan, China (including Hong Kong), Taiwan, Laos, Cambodia, Vietnam, Korea, The Philippines, U.S. Trust Territory of the Pacific Islands (Republic of Palau), Republic of the Marshall Islands, Federated States of Micronesia, Commonwealth of the Northern Mariana Islands, Guam, Samoa, Macao, Fiji, Tonga, Kiribati, Tuvalu, Nauru
Subcontinent Asian Americans	India, Pakistan, Bangladesh, Sri Lanka, Bhutan, the Maldives Islands, Nepal

Source: Congressional Research Service, based on 13 C.F.R. § 124.103(b) (2009).

The 1978 amendments established a basic definition of "socially disadvantaged individuals," which included those who have been "subjected to racial or ethnic prejudice or cultural bias because of their identity as a member of a group without regard to their individual qualities."[22] They also included congressional findings that "Black Americans, Hispanic Americans, Native Americans, and other minorities" are socially disadvantaged.[23] Thus, if an individual was a member of one of these groups, he or she was presumed to be socially disadvantaged. Otherwise, the amendments granted the SBA broad discretion to recognize additional groups or individuals as socially disadvantaged based upon criteria promulgated in regulations.[24] Under these regulations, which include a three-part test for determining whether minority groups not mentioned in the amendment's findings are disadvantaged,[25] the SBA recognized the racial or ethnic groups listed in **Table 1** as socially disadvantaged for purposes of the 8(a) Program.[26] The regulations also established standards of evidence to be met by individuals demonstrating personal disadvantage and procedures for rebutting the presumption of social disadvantage accorded to members of recognized minority groups.[27]

The 1978 amendments also defined "economically disadvantaged individuals," for purposes of the 8(a) Program, as "those socially disadvantaged individuals whose ability to compete in the free enterprise system has been impaired ... as compared to others in the same business area who are not socially disadvantaged."[28] Later, the SBA established by regulation that personal net worth of less than $250,000 at the time of entry into the 8(a) Program ($750,000 for continuing eligibility) constitutes economic disadvantage.[29]

Expansion of the 8(a) Program to Include Small Businesses Owned by "Disadvantaged" Groups

Originally the 8(a) Program was set up exclusively for the benefit of disadvantaged individuals. However, in the 1980's Congress expanded the program to include small businesses owned by four "disadvantaged" owner-groups.

The first owner-group included was Community Development Corporations (CDCs). A CDC is

> ... a nonprofit organization responsible to residents of the area it serves which is receiving financial assistance under part 1 [42 USCS § § 9805 et seq.] and any organization more than 50 percent of which is owned by such an organization, or otherwise controlled by such an organization, or designated by such an organization for the purpose of this subchapter [42 USCS §§ 9801 et seq.].[30]

Congress created CDCs with the Community Development Act of 1981[31] and instructed the SBA to issue regulations ensuring that CDCs could participate in the 8(a) Program.[32]

In 1986, two additional owner-groups, Indian tribes and Alaska Native Corporations, became eligible for the 8(a) Program when Congress passed legislation providing that firms owned by Indian tribes, which included Alaskan Native Corporations (ANCs),[33] were to be deemed "socially disadvantaged" for purposes of the 8(a) Program.[34] In 1992, ANCs were further deemed to be "economically disadvantaged."[35]

The last owner-group, that of Native Hawaiian Organizations (NHOs), was recognized in 1988.[36] An NHO was defined as

> ... any community service organization serving Native Hawaiians in the State of Hawaii which—(A) is a nonprofit corporation that has filed articles of incorporation with the director (or the designee thereof) of the Hawaii Department of Commerce and Consumer Affairs, or any successor agency, (B) is controlled by Native Hawaiians, and (C) whose business activities will principally benefit such Native Hawaiians.[37]

8(A) PROGRAM AT PRESENT: LEGAL REQUIREMENTS

Under the current 8(a) Program, participating firms are eligible for set-asides or sole-source awards of federal contracts, as well as training and technical assistance from SBA. Detailed statutory and regulatory requirements govern eligibility for the Program; set-asides and sole- source awards to 8(a) firms; and related issues. These requirements are generally the same for all participants in the 8(a) Program, although there are instances where there are "special rules" for 8(a) firms owned by groups.[38] The **Appendix** highlights commonalities and differences in the requirements for various types of 8(a) firms.

Requirements In General

Eligibility for the 8(a) Program

Key among the requirements is that eligibility for the 8(a) Program is limited to "small business[es] which [are] unconditionally owned and controlled by one or more socially and economically disadvantaged individuals who are of good character and citizens of the United States, and which demonstrate[] potential for success."[39] Each of these terms is further defined by the Small Business Act; regulations that the SBA has promulgated to implement Section 8(a); or judicial or administrative decisions.[40] The eligibility requirements are the same at the time of entry into the 8(a) Program and throughout the Program unless otherwise noted.[41]

"Small"

A business is "small" if it is independently owned and operated; is not dominant in its field of operations; and meets any definitions or standards established by the Administrator of the SBA.[42] These standards focus primarily upon the size of the business as measured by the number of employees or its gross income, but they also take into account the size of other businesses within the same industry.[43] For example, businesses in the field of "scheduled passenger air transportation" are "small" if they have fewer than 1,500 employees, while those in the data processing field are "small" if they have a gross income of less than $25 million.[44]

Affiliations between businesses, or relationships allowing one party control or the power of control over another,[45] generally count in size determinations, with the SBA considering "the receipts, employees, or other measure of size of the concern whose size is at issue and all of its domestic and foreign affiliates, regardless of whether the affiliates are organized for profit."[46] Businesses can thus be determined to be other than small because of their involvement in joint ventures,[47] subcontracting arrangements,[48] or franchise or license agreements,[49] among other things, provided that their personnel numbers or income, plus those of their affiliate(s), are over the pertinent size threshold.

"Business"

Except for small agricultural cooperatives, a "business" is a for-profit entity that has a place of business located in the United States and operates primarily within the United States or makes a significant contribution to the U.S. economy by paying taxes or using American products, materials, or labor.[50] For purposes of the 8(a) Program, businesses may take the form of individual proprietorships, partnerships, limited liability corporations, corporations, joint ventures, associations, trusts, or cooperatives.[51]

"Unconditionally owned and controlled"

Participants in the 8(a) Program must be "at least 51% unconditionally and directly owned by one or more disadvantaged individuals who are citizens of the United States" unless they are owned by an Indian tribe, ANC, NHO, or CDC.[52] Ownership is "unconditional" when it is not subject to any conditions precedent or subsequent, executory agreements, voting trusts, restrictions on voting rights, or other arrangements that could cause the benefits of ownership to go to another entity.[53] Ownership is "direct" when the disadvantaged individuals own the business in their own right and not through an intermediary (e.g., ownership by another business entity or by a trust that is owned and controlled by one or more disadvantaged individuals).[54] Non-disadvantaged individuals and non-participant businesses that own at least 10% of an 8(a) business may own no more than 10 to 20% of any other 8(a) firm.[55] Non-participant businesses that earn the majority of their revenue in the same or similar line of business are similarly barred from owning more than 10 to 20% of another 8(a) firm.[56]

Participants must also be controlled by one or more disadvantaged individuals.[57] "Control is not the same as ownership" and includes both strategic policy setting and day-to-day management and administration of business operations.[58] Management and daily business operations must also be conducted by one or more disadvantaged individuals unless the 8(a) business is owned by an Indian tribe, ANC, NHO, or CDC.[59] These individuals must have managerial experience "of the extent and complexity needed to run the concern" and generally must devote themselves full-time to the business "during the normal working hours of firms in the same or similar line of business."[60] A disadvantaged individual must hold the highest officer position within the business.[61] Non-disadvantaged individuals may otherwise be involved in the management of an 8(a) business, or may be stockholders, partners, limited liability members, officers, or directors of an 8(a) business.[62] However, they may not exercise actual control or have power to control, or receive compensation greater than that of highest officer without SBA approval.[63]

"Socially disadvantaged individual"

Socially disadvantaged individuals are "those who have been subjected to racial or ethnic prejudice or cultural bias within American society because of their identities as members of groups and without regard to their individual qualities."[64] Members of designated groups, listed in **Table 1**, are entitled to a rebuttable presumption of social disadvantage for purposes of the 8(a) Program,[65] although this presumption can be overcome with "credible evidence to the contrary."[66] Individuals who are not members of designated groups must prove they are socially disadvantaged by a preponderance of the evidence.[67] Such individuals must show (1) at least one objective distinguishing feature that has contributed to social disadvantage (e.g., race, ethnic origin, gender, physical handicap, long-term residence in an environment isolated from mainstream American society); (2) personal experiences of substantial and chronic social disadvantage in American society; and (3) negative impact on entry into or advancement in the business world.[68] In assessing the third factor, the SBA will consider all relevant evidence produced by the applicant, but must consider the applicant's education, employment, and business history to see if the totality of the circumstances shows disadvantage.[69] Other groups not included in **Table 1** may obtain listing by demonstrating disadvantage by a preponderance of the evidence. [70]

"Economically disadvantaged individual"

Economically disadvantaged individuals are "socially disadvantaged individuals whose ability to compete in the free enterprise system has been impaired due to diminished financial capital and credit opportunities as compared to others in the same or similar line of business who are not socially disadvantaged."[71] Individuals claiming economic disadvantage must describe it in a personal statement and submit financial documentation.[72] The SBA will examine their personal income for the past two years, their personal net worth, and the fair market value of the assets they own, as well as financial profiles of small businesses in the same primary industry or similar line of business.[73] However, principal ownership in a prospective or current 8(a) business is excluded when calculating net worth, as is equity in individuals' primary residence.[74] For initial eligibility, applicants to the 8(a) Program must have a net worth of less than $250,000.[75] For continued eligibility, net worth must be less than $750,000.[76]

"Good character"

In determining whether an applicant to or participant in the 8(a) Program possesses "good character," the SBA looks for criminal conduct, violations of SBA regulations, or current debarment or suspension from government contracting. [77]

"Demonstrated potential for success"

For a firm to have demonstrated potential for success, it generally must have been in business in the field of its primary industry classification for at least two full years immediately prior to the date of its application to the 8(a) Program.[78] However, the SBA may grant a waiver allowing firms that have been in business for less than two years to enter the 8(a) Program when (1) the disadvantaged individuals upon whom eligibility is based have substantial business management experience; (2) the business has demonstrated the technical experience necessary to carry out its business plan with a substantial likelihood of success; (3) the firm has adequate capital to sustain its operations and carry out its business plan; (4) the firm has a record of successful performance on contracts in its primary field of operations;

and (5) the firm presently has, or can demonstrate its ability to timely obtain, the personnel, facilities, equipment, and other resources necessary to perform contracts under Section 8(a).[79]

Set-Asides and Sole-Source Awards under Section 8(a)

Section 8(a) of the Small Business Act authorizes agencies to award contracts for goods or services, or to perform construction work, to the SBA for subcontracting to small businesses participating in the 8(a) Program.[80] A "set-aside" is an acquisition in which only certain contractors may compete, while a sole-source award is a contract awarded, or proposed for award, without competition.[81] Although the Competition in Contracting Act (CICA) generally requires "full and open competition" for government procurement contracts, set-asides and sole- source awards are both permissible under CICA. In fact, an 8(a) set-aside is a recognized competitive procedure.[82] Agencies are effectively encouraged to subcontract through the 8(a) Program because there are government-wide and agency-specific goals regarding the percentage of procurement dollars awarded to "small disadvantaged businesses," among others.[83] Awards made via set-asides or on a sole-source basis count toward these goals,[84] and businesses participating in the 8(a) Program are considered small disadvantaged businesses.[85]

Discretion to Subcontract Through the 8(a) Program

There are few limits on agency discretion to subcontract through the 8(a) Program.[86] By regulation, the SBA is prohibited from accepting procurements for award under Section 8(a) when

1. the procuring agency issued a solicitation for or otherwise expressed publicly a clear intent to reserve the procurement as a small business set-aside prior to offering the requirement to SBA for award as an 8(a) contract;[87]
2. the procuring agency competed the requirement among 8(a) firms prior to offering the requirement to SBA and receiving SBA's formal acceptance of it;
3. the SBA makes a written determination that "acceptance of the procurement for 8(a) award would have an adverse impact on an individual small business, a group of small businesses located in a specific geographical location, or other small business programs."[88]

Source: Congressional Research Service.

Figure 1. Acquisition Methods at Various Price Thresholds

SBA is also barred from awarding an 8(a) contract, either via a set-aside or on a sole-source basis, "if the price of the contract results in a cost to the contracting agency which exceeds a fair market price."[89] Otherwise, agency officials may offer contracts to the SBA "in [their] discretion," and the SBA may accept requirements for the 8(a) Program "whenever it determines such action is necessary or appropriate."[90] Moreover, the Government Accountability Office will generally not hear protests of agencies' determinations to procure, or not to procure, under the 8(a) Program absent a showing that the regulations may have been violated or that government officials acted in bad faith.[91]

Monetary Thresholds and Subcontracting Mechanism Under 8(a)

Once the SBA has accepted a contract for the 8(a) Program, the contract is awarded either through a set-aside or on a sole-source basis, with the amount of the contract generally determining the acquisition method used. When the anticipated total value of the contract, including any options, is less than \$3.5 million (\$5.5 million for manufacturing contracts), the contract is normally awarded without competition.[92] However, agencies can make competitive awards for contracts whose anticipated value is less than \$3.5 million (\$5.5 million for manufacturing contracts) provided that the SBA's Associate Administrator for 8(a) Business Development approves the agency's request to do so.[93] In contrast, when the anticipated value of the contract exceeds \$3.5 million (\$5.5 million for manufacturing contracts), the contract generally must be awarded via a set-aside with competition limited to 8(a) firms so long as there is a reasonable expectation that at least two eligible and responsible 8(a) firms will submit offers and the award can be made at fair market price.[94] Sole-source awards of contracts valued at \$3.5 million or more (\$5.5 million or more for manufacturing contracts) may only be made when (1) there is not a reasonable expectation that at least two eligible and responsible 8(a) firms will submit offers at a fair market price or (2) the SBA accepts the requirement on behalf of an 8(a) firm owned by an Indian tribe, an ANC or, in the case of Department of Defense contracts, an NHO.[95] Agencies may not divide acquisitions valued at more than \$3.5 million (\$5.5 million for manufacturing contracts) into several acquisitions at lesser amounts in order to make sole-source awards.[96]

Other Requirements

Other key requirements of the 8(a) Program include the following:

- ***Inability to protest an 8(a) firm's eligibility for an award***: When the SBA makes or proposes an award to an 8(a) firm, that firm's eligibility for the award cannot be challenged or protested as part of the solicitation or proposed contract award. Instead, information concerning a firm's eligibility for the 8(a) Program must be submitted to SBA in accordance with separate requirements contained in 13 C.F.R. § 124.517.[97]
- ***Maximum of nine years in the 8(a) Program***: Firms may participate in the 8(a) Program for no more than nine years from the date of their admission into the Program, although they may be terminated or graduate from the program before nine years have passed.[98]
- ***One-time eligibility for the 8(a) Program***: Once a firm or a disadvantaged individual upon whom a firm's eligibility was based has exited from the 8(a) Program after participating in it for any length of time, neither the firm nor the individual is eligible

to participate in the 8(a) Program again.[99] When at least 50% of the assets of one firm are the same as those of another firm, the firms are considered identical for purposes of eligibility for the 8(a) Program.[100]

- ***Limits on majority ownership in 8(a) firms***: Individuals who have been determined to be disadvantaged for purposes of one 8(a) firm, their immediate family members, and 8(a) firms themselves may generally not own more than 20% of any other 8(a) firm.[101]
- ***Limits on the amount of 8(a) contracts that a firm may receive***: 8(a) firms may generally not receive additional sole-source awards once they have received a combined total of competitive and sole-source awards in excess of $100 million, in the case of firms whose size is based on their number of employees, or in excess of an amount equivalent to the lesser of (1) $100 million or (2) five times the size standard for the industry, in the case of firms whose size is based on their revenues.[102] Additionally, 8(a) firms in either the "developmental stage," or the first four years of participation in the 8(a) Program, or the "transitional stage," or the last five years of participation, must achieve annual targets for the amount of revenues they receive from non-8(a) sources.[103] These targets increase over time, with firms required to attain 15% of their revenue from non-8(a) sources in the fifth year; 25% in the sixth year; 35% in the seventh year; 45% in the eight year; and 55% in the ninth year.[104] Firms that do not display the relevant percentages of revenue from non-8(a) sources are ineligible for sole-source 8(a) contracts "unless and until" they correct the situation.[105]
- ***Limitations on subcontracting***: Although not only under the authority of Section 8(a) of the Small Business Act or applicable only to 8(a) businesses, limitations on subcontracting require that small businesses receiving contracts under a set- aside perform minimum percentages of the contract work.[106] These percentages vary depending upon the type of the contract, with employees of the small business required to perform (1) at least 50% of the personnel costs of service contracts; (2) at least 50% of the costs of manufacturing (excluding materials) in supply contacts; (3) at least 15% of the costs of construction (excluding materials) in general construction contracts; and (4) at least 25% of the costs of construction (excluding materials) in "special trade" construction contracts.[107]

Requirements for Tribally, ANC-, NHO-, and CDC-Owned Firms

Tribes, ANCs, NHOs or CDCs themselves generally do not participate in the 8(a) Program. Rather, businesses that are at least 51% owned by such entities participate in the 8(a) Program,[108] although the rules governing their participation are, in places, somewhat different from those for the 8(a) Program generally.[109]

Eligibility for the 8(a) Program

"Small"

Firms owned by Indian tribes, ANCs, NHOs, and CDCs must be "small" under the SBA's size standards.[110] However, certain affiliations with the owning entity or other business enterprises of that entity are excluded in size determinations *unless* the Administrator of the SBA determines that, because of such exclusions, a small business owned by an Indian tribe, ANC, NHO, or CDC "[has] obtained, or [is] likely to obtain, a substantial unfair competitive advantage within an industry category."[111] Other affiliations of small businesses owned by Indian tribes, ANCs, NHOs, or CDCs can count in size determinations, and ANC-owned firms, in particular, have been subjected to early graduation from the 8(a) Program because they exceeded the size standards.[112]

"Business"

Firms owned by Indian tribes, ANCs, NHOs, and CDCs must be "businesses" under the SBA's definition.[113] Although ANCs themselves may be for-profit or non-profit, ANC-owned businesses must be for-profit to participate in the 8(a) Program.[114]

"Unconditionally owned and controlled"

Firms owned by Indian tribes, ANCs, NHOs, and CDCs must be unconditionally owned and substantially controlled by the tribe, ANC, NHO, or CDC, respectively.[115] However, under SBA regulations, tribally or ANC-owned firms may be managed by individuals who are not members of the tribe or Alaska Natives if the SBA determines

> ... that such management is required to assist the [firm's] development, that the tribe will retain control of all management decisions common to boards of directors, including strategic planning, budget approval, and the employment and compensation of officers, and that a written management plan exists which shows how disadvantaged tribal members will develop managerial skills sufficient to manage the concern or similar tribally-owned concerns in the future.[116]

The rules governing NHO-owned firms do not address this issue,[117] and although the general rules apply where no "special rules" exist,[118] it seems unlikely that NHO-owned firms are treated differently from tribally or ANC-owned firms in this regard. CDCs are to be managed and have their daily operations conducted by individuals with "managerial experience of an extent and complexity needed to run the [firm]."[119]

"Socially disadvantaged"

As owners of prospective or current 8(a) firms, Indian tribes, ANCs, NHOs, and CDCs are all presumed to be socially disadvantaged.[120]

"Economically disadvantaged"

By statute, ANCs are deemed to be economically disadvantaged,[121] and by regulation, CDCs are similarly presumed to be economically disadvantaged.[122] Indian tribes and NHOs, in contrast, must establish economic disadvantage at least once. Indian tribes must present data on, among other things, the number of tribe members; the tribal unemployment rate; the per capita income of tribe members; the percentage of the local Indian population above the poverty level; the tribe's assets as disclosed in current financial statements; and all businesses wholly or partially owned by tribal enterprises or affiliates, as well as their primary industry classification. [123] However, once a tribe has established that it is economically disadvantaged for purposes of one 8(a) business, it need not reestablish economic disadvantage in order to have other businesses certified for the 8(a) Program *unless* the Director of the Office of Business Development requires it to do so. [124] The rules governing NHO-owned firms do not address this issue,[125] and although the general rules apply where no "special rules" exist,[126] it seems unlikely that NHO-owned firms are treated differently from tribally owned firms in this regard.

"Good character"

When an organization owns an actual or prospective 8(a) firm, all members, officers, or employees of that organization are generally not required to show good character. The regulations governing tribally and ANC-owned firms explicitly address the issue, stating that the "good character" requirement applies only to officers or directors of the firm, or shareholders owning more than a 20% interest.[127] However, NHO-owned firms may be subject to the same requirements in practice.[128] With CDC-owned firms, the firm itself and "all of its principals" must have good character. [129]

"Demonstrated potential for success"

Firms owned by Indian tribes, ANCs, NHOs, and CDCs must either show demonstrated potential for success by having been in business in their primary industry for at least two full years immediately prior to the date of their application to the 8(a) Program or receive a waiver from the SBA.[130] Waivers are based on three criteria where firms owned by Indian tribes, ANCs, NHOs, and CDCs are involved: (1) the technical and managerial experience and competency of the individuals who will manage and control the firm's daily operations; (2) the firm's financial capacity; and (3) the firm's record of performance on prior federal or other contracts in its primary industry.[131] These criteria differ in their number and wording from the waiver criteria for other 8(a) firms.[132] However, these differences are unlikely to result in group-owned firms receiving waivers where other 8(a) firms would not because the criteria are analogous.

Set-Asides and Sole-Source Awards

Like other participants in the 8(a) Program, firms owned by Indian tribes, ANCs, NHOs, and CDCs are eligible for 8(a) set-asides and may receive sole-source awards valued at less than $3.5 million ($5.5 million for manufacturing contracts). However, firms owned by Indian tribes and ANCs can also receive sole-source awards in excess of $3.5 million ($5.5 million for manufacturing contracts) even when contracting officers reasonably expect that that at least two eligible and responsible 8(a) firms will submit offers and the award can be made at fair market price.[133] NHO-owned firms may receive sole-source awards from the Department of Defense under the same conditions.[134]

Table 2. Trends in 8(a) Participation FY2000-FY2008

Fiscal Year	Number of 8(a) Firms	Total Revenue Firms Received under 8(a)	Percentage of Firms' Revenue Received from 8(a)
FY2000	6383	3.78 billion	28.2%
FY2001	6942	4.66 billion	26.01%
FY2002	7585	4.4 billion	29.4%
FY2003	8431	5.4 billion	27.5%
FY2004	8900	5.6 billion	27.58%
FY2005	9470	7.0 billion	30.91%
FY2006	9667	7.1 billion	30.2%
FY2007	9423	6.7 billion	30.4%
FY2008	9462	6.3 billion	61.2%

Source: Congressional Research Service, based on data in Office of Business Development, Annual Report to Congress, 2000-2008.

Other Requirements

Firms owned by Indian tribes, ANCs, NHOs, and CDCs are governed by the same regulations as other 8(a) firms where certain of the "other requirements" are involved, including (1) inability to protest an 8(a) firm's eligibility for an award;[135] (2) maximum of nine years in the 8(a) Program (for individual firms);[136] and (3) limits on subcontracting.[137] However, the requirements for such firms differ somewhat from those for other 8(a) firms where one-time eligibility for the 8(a) Program; limits on majority ownership of 8(a) firms; and limits on the amount of 8(a) contracts that a firm may receive are involved. Firms owned by Indian tribes, ANCs, NHOs, and CDCs may participate in the 8(a) Program only one time.[138] However, unlike the disadvantaged individuals upon whom other firms' eligibility for the 8(a) Program is based, Indian tribes, ANCs, NHOs, and CDCs may confer eligibility for the 8(a) Program upon firms on multiple occasions and for an indefinite period.[139] Additionally, although Indian tribes, ANCs, NHOs, and CDCs may not own 51% or more of a firm obtaining the majority of its revenues from the same "primary" industry in which another firm they own or owned currently operates or has operated within the past two years, there are no limits on the number of firms they may own that operate in other primary industries.[140] Moreover, Indian tribes, ANCs, NHOs, and CDCs may own multiple firms that earn less than 50% of their revenue in the same "secondary" industries.[141] Finally, firms owned by Indian tribes or ANCs may continue to receive additional sole-source awards even after they have received awards valued at $100 million, or other applicable amount, although firms owned by NHOs and CDCs may not.[142] However, firms owned by any of these four types of entities are subject to the same requirements regarding the percentages of revenue received from non-8(a) sources at various stages of their participation in the 8(a) Program as other 8(a) firms are.[143]

FUTURE OF THE 8(A) PROGRAM?

Although the 8(a) Program has expanded fairly consistently since FY2000, as **Table 2** illustrates, and the SBA credited it with helping firms to make "significant contributions to the Federal, state and local tax base and contribute[ing] an estimated 191,973 jobs to the Nation's economy" in FY2008,[144] the Program is not static. Rather, it continues to evolve as the result of legislation, changes in executive branch policies, and legal challenges and decisions. This section provides an overview of emerging developments that may shape the future of the 8(a) Program.

Proposed Legislation

Recent Congresses have considered several bills that would modify the 8(a) Program. These proposed modifications often reflect concerns that Members or commentators have about the program, such as: (1) whether the Program's eligibility requirements exclude certain small businesses that could benefit from the Program;[145] (2) whether the Program adequately serves participating businesses;[146] (3) whether the federal government awards too few of its procurement dollars to small disadvantaged businesses;[147] (4) fraud by businesses participating in the Program;[148] and (5) whether SBA and/or contracting agencies adequately oversee 8(a) contracts.[149] Recently, sole-source awards to ANC-owned firms under the authority of Section 8(a) have been a particular concern.[150] Some worry that the increase in the percentage of federal contract dollars awarded to ANC-owned firms under Section 8(a), which reportedly went from $1.1 billion in FY2004 to $3.9 billion in FY2008, diminishes the percentage of contract dollars available for other small businesses or 8(a) firms.[151] They also fear that that agencies improperly use sole-source awards to ANC-owned firms,[152] sole-source awards to ANC-owned firms cost too much,[153] or SBA and/or other federal agencies do not properly administer sole-source contracts to ANC-owned firms.[154] However, others desire to preserve, if not expand, the contracting programs for ANCs because of the benefits they provide to Alaska Natives. [155] Bills introduced in the 110th and 111th Congress took various approaches to the 8(a) Program, as described below.

110th Congress

Several bills in the 110th Congress would have expanded eligibility for the 8(a) Program by allowing individuals with higher levels of net worth to qualify as economically disadvantaged for initial entry into, or continuing participation in, the Program, or by excluding certain properties from consideration when the SBA calculates net worth.[156] However, one bill would have narrowed eligibility in an attempt to combat fraud by requiring background checks of owners and officers of prospective 8(a) firms and creating a presumption that criminal convictions indicate a lack of business integrity.[157] Other bills would have made additional categories of small businesses (e.g., veteran-owned, women-owned) eligible for the 8(a) Program, or eligible for benefits like those provided under 8(a) or provided to 8(a) businesses under other federal programs.[158] Yet other bills would have restructured the 8(a) Program by (1) increasing the number of years that firms can participate in it;[159] (2) creating a pre-8(a) Program, which firms must generally complete prior to entering the 8(a) Program and eligibility for which cannot be based on several factors that SBA currently uses in determining eligibility for the 8(a) Program (e.g., potential for success, technical and managerial experience);[160] and (3) restricting set-asides to industries in which the Secretary of Commerce has determined that firms owned and controlled by socially and economically disadvantaged individuals are underrepresented.[161] Additional legislation would have increased the government-wide or agency-specific goals for contracting with small disadvantaged businesses, which include 8(a) firms;[162] allowed noncompetitive awards at higher values;[163] required agencies to develop plans to minimize the number of sole-source awards, including sole-source awards under Section 8(a);[164] and allowed protests of firms' eligibility for 8(a) awards.[165]

111th Congress

The 111th Congress is considering several bills that would make similar changes to the 8(a) Program, including

- allowing individuals with higher personal net worth to be eligible for the 8(a) Program;[166]
- requiring the SBA to periodically adjust the net-worth thresholds for inflation;[167]
- extending the length of the 8(a) Program and the developmental phase within the Program;[168]
- exempting businesses that have not completed an 8(a) contract from time limits on participation in the 8(a) Program;[169]
- extending the maximum term of participation in the 8(a) Program for individuals called to "active duty" in the U.S. military for more than 30 days;[170]
- increasing the government-wide goal for contracting with small businesses generally to 25% and that for contracting with small disadvantaged businesses to 10%; 171
- specifying that individual small businesses may count toward government contracting goals in no more than two of the following categories: small business, service-disabled veteran-owned small business, Historically Underutilized Business Zone (HUBZone) small business, woman-owned small business, and small disadvantaged business;[172] and
- making service-disabled veteran-owned small businesses eligible for contracts under Section 8(a) by, among other things, including service-disabled veterans within the definition of "disadvantaged owner" and including service-disabled veteran-owned small businesses within the definition of "disadvantaged business."[173]

Other proposals would promote contracting with 8(a) firms by establishing new programs to increase their involvement in foreign trade and the construction industry;[174] allowing the Department of Defense to convert functions to performance by certain 8(a) firms without conducting the public-private competitions normally required under Office of Management and Budget (OMB) Circular A-76 when outsourcing;[175] and requiring that contractors holding Transportation Security Administration contracts in excess of $300 million "implement"[176] their plans for contracting with small disadvantaged businesses (including 8(a) firms).[177]

None of the bills introduced in the 110th Congress was enacted, and only one bill introduced in the 111th Congress has been enacted to date, allowing the Department of

Defense to convert functions to performance by certain 8(a) firms without conducting the public-private competitions normally required under OMB Circular A-76.[178] However, the 8(a) Program will probably remain a topic of interest to Members, in part because of the changes in executive branch policies and legal developments affecting the program that are discussed in the following sections.

Changes in Executive Branch Policies

While proposed legislation in the 110th and 111th Congresses has focused upon the 8(a) Program generally, executive branch agencies have recently made or proposed changes to the Program focused upon contracting with ANC-owned firms specifically. First, in June, 2007, the Department of Homeland Security (DHS) issued "Guidance on the Use of 8(a) Firms Owned by Indian Tribes/Alaska Native Corporations," in which agency contracting officials were instructed to "be judicious" and rely on "appropriate safeguards" when entering sole-source contracts with tribally or ANC-owned firms. This guidance document called for DHS contracting officers to ensure that the firm has the technical ability to perform the work, the firm will perform the required percentage of the work, and the award is in the best interest of the government.[179] Later, in April 2008, the Air Force issued "Sole Source Actions Over $550K." This document notes that there is "scrutiny involved with using sole source contracts simply as a means to reach particular subcontractors" and requires that all sole-source awards over $550,000 be justified in writing and approved by the Command Competition Advocate.[180] The SBA also reports having recently trained its 8(a) Program specialists on handling ANC-owned firms and its field staff on compliance with the 8(a) regulations.[181]

Proposed Changes in SBA Regulations

On October 28, 2009, SBA issued a proposed rule that would change certain eligibility and other requirements pertaining to the 8(a) Program.[182] **Table 3** summarizes the key, program-wide changes that SBA proposes.

Several other proposed changes pertain only to group-owned 8(a) firms. One proposed rule specifies that

> ... a newly certified tribally-owned [or ANC-owned] Participant cannot receive an 8(a) contract in a secondary NAICS code that is the primary NAICS code of another Participant (or former participant that has left the program within two years of the date of application) owned by the tribe for a period of two years from the date of admission to the program.[183]

Other proposed rules would (1) remove the requirement that tribe members prove personal economic disadvantage in order to participate in the management of tribally owned firms;[184] (2) allow tribally and ANC-owned firms to be found to have potential for success if the tribe or ANC pledges to use its resources to support the firm and to not allow the firm to cease operations;[185] (3) require Indian tribes, ANCs, NHOs, and CDCs to submit information to the SBA annually showing how their participation in the 8(a) Program has benefited members of the group;[186] (4) change the location for SBA's initial review of ANC-owned firms' applications from the Anchorage District Office to the San Francisco Division of Program Certification and Eligibility;[187] (5) and prohibit non-8(a)firms that form joint ventures with 8(a) firms to perform sole-source contracts in excess of $3.5 million ($5.5 million for manufacturing contracts) from serving as subcontractors on the contract.[188]

Table 3. Key Changes to the 8(a) Regulations Proposed by the SBA in October 2009

Requirement	Proposed Changes
Economic disadvantage (13 C.F.R. § 124.104)	• Community property laws will not be taken into account when the SBA determines economic disadvantage, but the financial situation of individuals' spouses will be considered when determining individuals' access to credit and capital. (74 Fed. Reg. at 55698)
	• Funds in Individual Retirement Accounts (IRAs) and other official retirement accounts are exempted from the calculation of net worth provided that the funds cannot be withdrawn from the account prior to retirement age without a "significant penalty." (74 Fed. Reg. at 55698)
	• Income from S Corporations is exempted from the calculation of both income and net worth to the extent that such income is reinvested in the firm or used to pay taxes arising from the normal course of operations of an S corporation. (74 Fed. Reg. at 55698-99)
	• Individuals are presumed not to be economically disadvantaged if their adjusted gross income averaged over the past two years exceeds $200,000, but they can rebut this presumption by showing that their income does not indicate a lack of economic disadvantage. (74 Fed. Reg. at 55699)
	• Individuals are not economically disadvantaged if the fair market value of their assets exceeds $3 million at the time of application to the 8(a) Program or $4 million thereafter. (74 Fed. Reg. at 55699)
Ownership (13 C.F.R. § 124.105)	• Firms are not automatically disqualified from the 8(a) Program because the individual seeking to qualify the firm has an immediate family member already participating in the 8(a) Program. SBA will make determinations regarding eligibility on a case-by-case basis, potentially allowing such firms to qualify when (1) there are no or negligible connections between the two firms and (2) the individuals seeking to use their disadvantaged status to qualify the firm can demonstrate sufficient management and technical experience to operate the firm. (74 Fed. Reg. at 55700)
Control (13 C.F.R. § 124.106)	• Disadvantaged managers of 8(a) firms must reside in the United States and spend part of every month physically present at the firm's primary offices. (74 Fed. Reg. at 55700) • Reserve members who are called to active duty in the U.S. military may either (1) designate one or more individuals to control daily business operations of their 8(a) firm during the time that they are gone or (2) suspend their participation in the 8(a) program during their active duty call-up period. (74 Fed. Reg. at 55700-01)
Credit toward contracting goals (13 C.F.R. § 124.503)	• Agencies may receive 8(a) credit for orders placed with 8(a) firms under indefinite- quantity/indefinite-delivery (ID/IQ) contracts not set aside for 8(a) firms so long as the order is offered to and accepted for the 8(a) Program and competed exclusively among eligible 8(a) firms, and the limitations on subcontracting apply to the individual order. (74 Fed. Reg. at 55704)

Table 3. (Continued)

Requirement	Proposed Changes
Acceptance and release of requirements (13 C.F.R. § 124.504)	• SBA may not accept requirements for the 8(a) Program when the procuring agency has expressed a clear intent to make HUBZone or SDVOSB awards. (74 Fed. Reg. at 55705) • Follow-on or repetitive 8(a) procurements must remain in the 8(a) Program unless SBA consents to release them for non-8(a) competition. (74 Fed. Reg. at 55705)
Delegation of contract administration (13 C.F.R. § 124.512)	• Procuring agencies exercising authority delegated to them by the SBA must track firms’ compliance with the limitations on subcontracting. (74 Fed. Reg. at 55706-07) • When agencies’ contracting officers modify contracts or exercise options under them, they must submit copies thereof to the SBA within 10 business days. (74 Fed. Reg. at 55706-07) • SBA may conduct periodic on-site reviews of other agencies’ contract files to determine compliance with Program requirements. (74 Fed. Reg. at 55706-07)
Joint ventures involving 8(a) firms (13 C.F.R. § 124.513)	• 8(a) participants to 8(a) joint ventures must receive profits from the joint venture commensurate with the work they perform, and they must perform at least 40% of the work performed by the joint venture. (74 Fed. Reg. at 55707) • Each 8(a) firm that performs an 8(a) contract through a joint venture must report to the SBA on how these requirements regarding the performance of work were met. (74 Fed. Reg. at 55707) • SBA must approve any joint venture agreement prior to the award of an 8(a) contract to the joint venture. (74 Fed. Reg. at 55707)
Mentor/protégé program (13 C.F.R. § 124.520)	• Assistance provided through the mentor/protégé relationship must be tied to the protégé firm’s SBA-approved business plan. (74 Fed. Reg. at 55707-08) • One mentor may have no more than three protégés. SBA may approve a second mentor for an 8(a) firm in certain circumstances. (74 Fed. Reg. at 55707-09) • SBA may not approve mentor/protégé agreements when the protégé has less than 1 year left in the 8(a) Program. (74 Fed. Reg. at 55709) • Joint ventures between mentors and protégés qualify as “small” for purposes of federal subcontracts, as well as for federal prime contracts. (74 Fed. Reg. at 55709) • The mentor/protégé agreement must be approved by SBA prior to the submission of the bid or offer to take advantage of the exception to the size requirements. (74 Fed. Reg. at 55710) • Mentors that fail to provide the agreed upon assistance to their protégés are subject to sanctions, including stoppage of work on the contract, termination from the 8(a) Program and debarment from federal contracting. (74 Fed. Reg. at 55710)

Source: Congressional Research Service

SBA also seeks comments on, among other things, whether a “bright-line test” based on assets or net worth, or some other method, is best for determining whether an Indian tribe is economically disadvantaged; the implications of requiring Indian tribes to prove economic disadvantage only once to qualify firms for the 8(a) Program; and whether managers of tribally owned firms must be members of that tribe, or whether they need only be members of an Indian tribe.[189]

The comment period on SBA's proposed rule ended on December 28, 2009,[190] and SBA has yet to promulgate a final rule.

Legal Decisions and Challenges

The 8(a) Program has also been the subject of legal challenges or decisions that could influence its future development. A lawsuit is currently pending that challenges the constitutionality of the 8(a) Program because of its presumption that minorities are socially disadvantaged, while a March 2, 2010, decision by the U.S. Court of Federal Claims held that set-asides for Historically Underutilized Business zone (HUBZone) small businesses take precedence over set-asides for 8(a) small businesses.

Constitutionality of 8(a) Program

In *Dynalantic Corporation v. U.S. Department of Defense*, a lawsuit currently pending in U.S. District Court for the District of Columbia, the plaintiff corporation alleges, among other things, that the 8(a) Program unconstitutionally deprives it of equal protection because of the Program's presumption that racial minorities are socially disadvantaged. [191] This presumption would probably constitute a racial classification subject to "strict scrutiny" when reviewed by the courts,[192] and a Department of Defense (DOD) contracting program incorporating a similar presumption was recently found unconstitutional because Congress did not have a "strong basis in evidence" for determining that minorities had been discriminated against it enacted the program. [193] Under strict scrutiny, the government must show that challenged programs are necessary to further a compelling government interest.[194]

The 8(a) Program is potentially distinguishable from the DOD program in that the DOD program included both a goal for contracting with disadvantaged businesses and a mechanism for meeting that goal (i.e., a 10% price evaluation preference),[195] while there are no goals for the percentage of federal contract dollars awarded to 8(a) firms.[196] Alternatively, a court might find that Congress had a strong basis in evidence when it most recently reauthorized Section 8(a) of the Small Business Act, which allows SBA to subcontract only with "socially and economically disadvantaged small business concerns."[197] However, the plaintiff's case in *Dynalantic* survived DOD's initial motion for summary judgment in 2007,[198] and the parties have apparently not settled this litigation.

If the 8(a) Program as it presently exists, with its presumption that minorities are socially disadvantaged, were found unconstitutional, the 8(a) Program could potentially be reconstituted without the presumption. Such a program might require proof of actual social disadvantage from all applicants to the 8(a) Program, perhaps using the same three criteria currently used by individual applicants demonstrating personal social disadvantage. [199] This program could be similar to the HUBZone program, which currently provides set-asides for small businesses located in low-income areas that are often also socially disadvantaged. However, unlike with the HUBZone program, individuals who are socially and economically disadvantaged *and* in an area with average or above average employment and income could be eligible.[200] Alternatively, the 8(a) Program could continue as a program for small businesses owned by Indian tribes, ANCs, NHOs, or CDCs because tribes and other entities are not racial groups.[201] The presumption of social and/or economic disadvantage accorded to these groups would thus not implicate a racial classification and would probably be subject only to "rational basis" review. Rational basis review is characterized by deference to legislative judgment, and the party challenging a government program must show that it is not rationally related to a legitimate government interest.[202]

"Precedence" of HUBZone Set-Asides over 8(a) Set-Asides

In its March 2, 2010, decision in *Mission Critical Solutions v. United States*, the Court of Federal Claims held that set-asides for HUBZone small businesses take precedence over those for 8(a) small businesses.[203] *Mission Critical Solutions* was a bid protest filed with the court after the contracting agency, the U.S. Department of the Army, indicated that it would not comply with the recommendations that the GAO made in an earlier bid protest.[204] The GAO had recommended that the Army abandon its proposed sole-source award to an 8(a) firm in favor of a HUBZone set- aside because "mandatory" agency actions take precedence over "discretionary" ones, and it construed the HUBZone Act as *requiring* HUBZone set-asides whenever at least two HUBZone firms are expected to submit offers and Section 8(a) as *allowing* 8(a) set-asides whenever agency officials "determine[] such action is necessary or appropriate."[205] The Office of Legal Counsel (OLC) at the Department of Justice disagreed, finding that the provisions of the Small Business Act regarding the set-aside programs are ambiguous and the SBA regulations providing for parity among the set-aside programs constitute reasonable interpretations of the governing statute.[206] OLC instructed agencies that its decisions are "binding on all Executive Branch agencies, notwithstanding any GAO decisions to the contrary,"[207] and the Army proposed proceeding with the contested award.[208] Mission Critical Solutions then filed suit in the Court of Federal Claims to enjoin this award.[209]

Like the GAO, the Court of Federal Claims relied upon the text of the Small Business Act and principles of statutory interpretation to find that HUBZone set-asides have precedence over 8(a) set-asides. Three provisions of the Small Business Act—two in the HUBZone Act and one in Section 8(a)—were key to the court's decision. First, the court construed language in the HUBZone Act regarding set-asides "[n]otwithstanding any other provision of law" to mean that the "provisions of the 'notwithstanding' section override conflicting provisions of any other section," including those regarding 8(a) set-asides.[210] In so finding, the court rejected the government's argument that the phrase "notwithstanding any other provision of law" need not be construed literally.[211] It did so because it found that the cases the government relied upon in support of this argument involved statutes which clearly indicated that certain provisions were to be excluded from the application of the "notwithstanding" provisions and were thus distinguishable from the Small Business Act.[212] The court also found that language in 15 U.S.C. § 657a(b)(4) regarding the relationship between the HUBZone program and the Federal Prison Industries and Javits-Wagner-O 'Day programs indicated that "if Congress wished to establish the relationship of the HUBZone program to another contracting preference program, it knew how to do so."[213] Second, the court construed the use of "shall" in the HUBZone Act to indicate mandatory agency actions, and its absence in Section 8(a) to indicate discretionary agency actions.[214] It rejected the government's argument that HUBZone set-asides are only mandatory in comparison to HUBZone sole-source awards and that, notwithstanding the use of "shall" or "may" in a statute, the court may consider "indications of legislative intent to the contrary or obvious inferences from the structure or purpose of the statute."[215] Finally, the court construed the language in Section 8(a) about contracts "offered for award pursuant to this section" as further indicating that 8(a) awards are discretionary.[216] It found similar language—and discretion— lacking in the HUBZone Act.[217]

The court gave no weight to the alleged parity accorded to the various set-aside programs under 15 U.S.C. § 637(d) and 15 U.S.C. § 644(g), which, respectively, require certain prime contractors to agree to plans for subcontracting with small businesses and establish government-wide and agency-specific goals for the percentage of federal contract and subcontract dollars awarded to small businesses.[218] The court was not persuaded by the government's argument that the lack of mention of precedence among the set-aside programs in these sections indicated parity.[219] The court also gave no weight to those aspects of the legislative history that the government claimed indicated that Congress intended there to be parity among the set-aside programs.[220] It noted that examination of the legislative history is not necessary when the statutory language is clear because "[t]he language of the statute is the best indication of Congress's intent."[221] However, it also noted that key evidence in the government's resort to legislative history did not necessarily carry the significance that the government attributed to it.[222] Further, the court gave no deference to SBA regulations providing for parity among the set-aside programs because it found these regulations were not entitled to deference under *Chevron U.S.A., Inc. v. Natural Resources Defense Council, Inc.*[223] According to the court, because the statute's plain meaning is apparent and "Congress has directly spoken to the precise question at issue," the SBA's interpretation of the statute is given no deference, especially when it is at variance with the statutory language.[224]

The government has appealed the Court of Federal Claims decision,[225] and the Department of Justice sent a letter to SBA noting that the court, notwithstanding its finding that HUBZone set- asides have precedence over 8(a) set-asides under the Small Business Act, enjoined only the award of a particular contract, not the application of SBA's "parity rule" generally.[226] However, assuming the court's and GAO's interpretation of the Small Business Act ultimately prevails, it could lead to an increase in the percentage of federal contract dollars awarded to HUBZone small businesses and decreases in the percentages awarded to 8(a) firms and other small businesses.[227] Currently, the government-wide goal is that 3% of federal contract dollars go to HUBZone small businesses, while 5% of federal contract and subcontract dollars go to 8(a) small businesses.[228] Achieving the 8(a) goal, in particular, could be difficult if agencies *must* use a HUBZone set- aside whenever the contract officer reasonably expects that at least two qualified HUBZone small businesses will submit offers and the award can be made at a fair market price.

Members of the 111th Congress have introduced legislation that could make HUBZone set-asides discretionary (H.R. 3729, S. 1489, S. 3190) and remove the basis upon which the Court of Federal Claims and GAO found that HUBZone set-asides have precedence over 8(a) and SDVOSB set-asides.

APPENDIX. COMPARISON OF THE REQUIREMENTS PERTAINING TO 8(A) BUSINESSES GENERALLY, TRIBALLY OWNED BUSINESSES, ANC-OWNED BUSINESSES, AND OTHERS

Requirements	8(a) Businesses Generally	Tribally Owned 8(a) Businesses	ANC-Owned 8(a) Businesses	NHO-Owned 8(a) Businesses	CDC-Owned 8(a) Businesses
"Small"	Independently owned and operated; not dominant in field of operation; meets size standards (15 U.S.C. § 631(a)) All affiliations count (13 C.F.R. § 121.103)	Independently owned and operated; not dominant in field of operation; meets size standards (15 U.S.C. § 631(a)) Affiliations based on the tribe or tribal ownership, among others, do not count (15 U.S.C. § 636(j)(10)(J)(ii); 13 C.F.R. § 124.109(c)(2))	Independently owned and operated; not dominant in field of operation; meets size standards (15 U.S.C. § 631(a)) Affiliations based on the ANC or ownership by the ANC, among others, do not count (15 U.S.C. § 636(j)(10)(J)(ii); 13 C.F.R. § 124.109(c)(2))	Independently owned and operated; not dominant in field of operation; meets size standards (15 U.S.C. § 631(a)) Affiliations based on the NHO or ownership by the NHO, among others, do not count (15 U.S.C. § 636(j)(10)(J)(ii); 13 C.F.R. § 124.110(c))	Independently owned and operated; not dominant in field of operation; meets size standards (15 U.S.C. § 631(a)) Affiliations based on the CDC or ownership by the CDC, among others, do not count (15 U.S.C. § 636(j)(10)(J)(ii); 13 C.F.R. § 124.111(c))
"Business"	For-profit entity with its place of business in the United States; operates primarily within the United States or makes a significant contribution to the U.S. economy (13 C.F.R. § 121.105(a)(1))	For-profit entity with its place of business in the United States; operates primarily within the United States or makes a significant contribution to the U.S. economy (13 C.F.R. § 121.105(a)(1))	For-profit entity with its place of business in the United States; operates primarily within the United States or makes a significant contribution to the U.S. economy (13 C.F.R. § 121.105(a)(1)) Although ANC may be non-profit, ANC-owned firms must be for-profit to be eligible for 8(a) Program (13 C.F.R § 124.109(a)(3))	For-profit entity with its place of business in the United States; operates primarily within the United States or makes a significant contribution to the U.S. economy (13 C.F.R. § 121.105(a)(1))	For-profit entity with its place of business in the United States; operates primarily within the United States or makes a significant contribution to the U.S. economy (13 C.F.R. § 121.105(a)(1))

(Continued)

Requirements	8(a) Businesses Generally	Tribally Owned 8(a) Businesses	ANC-Owned 8(a) Businesses	NHO-Owned 8(a) Businesses	CDC-Owned 8(a) Businesses
"Unconditionally owned and controlled"	At least 51% unconditionally and directly owned by one or more disadvantaged individuals who are U.S. citizens (13 C.F.R. § 124.105) Management and daily business operations must be conducted by one or more disadvantaged individuals (13 C.F.R. § 124.106)	At least 51% tribally owned (13 C.F.R. § 124.109(b)) Management may be conducted by individuals who are not members of the tribe provided that the SBA determines that such management is necessary to assist the business's development, among other things (13 C.F.R. § 124.109(c)(4)(B))	At least 51% ANC-owned (13 C.F.R. § 124.109(a)(3)) Management may be conducted by individuals who are not Alaska Natives provided that the SBA determines that such management is necessary to assist the business's development, among other things (13 C.F.R. § 124.109(c)(4)(B))	At least 51% NHO-owned (13 C.F.R. § 124.110(a)) Not explicitly addressed in regulation[a]	At least 51% CDC-owned (13 C.F.R. § 124.111(a)) Management and daily business operations to be conducted by individuals having managerial experience of an extent and complexity needed to run the firm (13 C.F.R. § 124.111(b))
"Socially disadvantaged individual"	Members of designated groups presumed to be socially disadvantaged; other individuals may prove personal disadvantage by a preponderance of the evidence (13 C.F.R. § 124.103)	Indian tribes presumed to be socially disadvantaged (43 U.S.C. § 1626(e); 15 U.S.C. § 637(a)(4)(A)-(B); 13 C.F.R. § 124.109(b)(1))	ANCs presumed to be socially disadvantaged (43 U.S.C. § 1626(e); 15 U.S.C. § 637(a)(4)(A)-(B); 13 C.F.R. § 124.109(b)(1))	NHOs presumed to be socially disadvantaged (43 U.S.C. § 1626(e); 15 U.S.C. § 637(a)(4)(A)-(B); 13 C.F.R. § 124.109(b)(1))	CDCs presumed to be socially disadvantaged (42 U.S.C. § 9815(a)(2))
"Economically disadvantaged individual"	Financial information (e.g., personal income, personal net worth, fair market value of assets) must	Tribe must prove economic disadvantage the first time a tribally owned firm applies to the 8(a) Program;	Deemed to be economically disadvantaged (43 U.S.C. § 1626(e); 13 C.F.R. § 124.109(a)(2))	Not explicitly addressed in regulation[a]	CDCs presumed to be economically disadvantaged (42 U.S.C. § 9815(a)(2))

(Continued)

Requirements	8(a) Businesses Generally	Tribally Owned 8(a) Businesses	ANC-Owned 8(a) Businesses	NHO-Owned 8(a) Businesses	CDC-Owned 8(a) Businesses
	show diminished financial capital and credit opportunities (13 C.F.R. § 124.104)	thereafter, a tribe need only prove economic disadvantage at the request of the SBA (13 C.F.R. § 124.109(b)(2))			
"Good character"	No criminal conduct or violations of SBA regulations; cannot be debarred or suspended from government contracting (13 C.F.R. § 124.108(a))	No criminal conduct or violations of SBA regulations; cannot be debarred or suspended from government contracting (13 C.F.R. § 124.108(a)) Requirement applies only to officers, directors, and shareholders owning more than a 20% interest in the business, not to all members of the tribe (13 C.F.R. § 124.109(c)(7)(B)(ii))	No criminal conduct or violations of SBA regulations; cannot be debarred or suspended from government contracting (13 C.F.R. § 124.108(a)) Requirement applies only to officers, directors, and shareholders owning more than a 20% interest in the business, not to all ANC shareholders (13 C.F.R. § 124.109(c)(7)(B)(ii))	No criminal conduct or violations of SBA regulations; cannot be debarred or suspended from government contracting (13 C.F.R. § 124.108(a)) Regulations do not address to whom requirements applya	No criminal conduct or violations of SBA regulations; cannot be debarred or suspended from government contracting (13 C.F.R. § 124.108(a)) Requirements apply to the firm and "all its principals" (13 C.F.R. § 124.111(g))
"Demonstrated potential for success"	Firm must generally have been in business in primary industry for at least two full years prior to date of application to 8(a) Program unless SBA	Firm must generally have been in business in primary industry for at least two full years prior to date of application to 8(a) Program unless SBA	Firm must generally have been in business in primary industry for at least two full years prior to date of application to 8(a) Program unless SBA grants a waiver; waiver	Firm must generally have been in business in primary industry for at least two full years prior to date of application to 8(a) Program unless SBA	Firm must generally have been in business in primary industry for at least two full years prior to date of application to 8(a) Program unless SBA grants a waiver; waiver based on 3 conditions[c] (13 C.F.R. § 124.111(f)

(Continued)

Requirements	8(a) Businesses Generally	Tribally Owned 8(a) Businesses	ANC-Owned 8(a) Businesses	NHO-Owned 8(a) Businesses	CDC-Owned 8(a) Businesses
	grants a waiver; waiver based on 5 conditions[b] (13 C.F.R. § 124.107)	grants a waiver; waiver based on 3 conditionsc (13 C.F.R. § 124.109(c)(6))	based on 3 conditionsc (13 C.F.R. § 124.109(c)(6))	grants a waiver; waiver based on 3 conditionsc (13 C.F.R. § 124.110(e))	
Sole-source awards	With contracts valued at over $3.5 million ($5.5 million for manufacturing contracts), sole-source awards permissible only if there is not a reasonable expectation that at least two eligible 8(a) firms will submit offers and the award can be made at fair market price (48 C.F.R. § 19.805-1(b)(1)-(2))	Can be made with contracts valued at over $3.5 million ($5.5 million for manufacturing contracts) even if there is a reasonable expectation that at least two eligible 8(a) firms will submit offers and the award can be made at fair market price (15 U.S.C. § 637(a)(1)(D)(i)-(ii); 48 C.F.R. § 19.805-1(b)(1)-(2))	Can be made with contracts valued at over $3.5 million ($5.5 million for manufacturing contracts) even if there is a reasonable expectation that at least two eligible 8(a) firms will submit offers and the award can be made at fair market price (15 U.S.C. § 637(a)(1)(D)(i)- (ii); 48 C.F.R. § 19.805-1(b)(1)-(2))	Can be made with Department of Defense contracts valued at over $3.5 million ($5.5 million for manufacturing contracts) even if there is a reasonable expectation that at least two eligible 8(a) firms will submit offers and the award can be made at fair market price (48 C.F.R. § 219.805-1(b)(2)(A)-(B)). Otherwise cannot be made unless there is not a reasonable expectation that at least two eligible 8(a) firms will submit offers and the award can be made at fair market price (48 C.F.R. § 19.805-1(b)(1)-(2))	With contracts valued at over $3.5 million ($5.5 million for manufacturing)contracts, sole-source awards permissible only if there is not a reasonable expectation that at least two eligible 8(a) firms will submit offers and the award can be made at fair market price (48 C.F.R. § 19.805-1(b)(1)-(2))

(Continued)

Requirements	8(a) Businesses Generally	Tribally Owned 8(a) Businesses	ANC-Owned 8(a) Businesses	NHO-Owned 8(a) Businesses	CDC-Owned 8(a) Businesses
Inability to protest eligibility for award	Firm's eligibility for award cannot be challenged or protested as part of the solicitation or proposed contract award (48 C.F.R. § 19.805-2(d))	Firm's eligibility for award cannot be challenged or protested as part of the solicitation or proposed contract award (48 C.F.R. § 19.805-2(d))	Firm's eligibility for award cannot be challenged or protested as part of the solicitation or proposed contract award (48 C.F.R. § 19.805-2(d))	Firm's eligibility for award cannot be challenged or protested as part of the solicitation or proposed contract award (48 C.F.R. § 19.805-2(d))	Firm's eligibility for award cannot be challenged or protested as part of the solicitation or proposed contract award (48 C.F.R. § 19.805-2(d))
Maximum of nine years in the 8(a) Program	Firm receives "a program term of nine years" but could be terminated or graduated early (13 C.F.R. § 124.2)	Firm receives "a program term of nine years" but could be terminated or graduated early (13 C.F.R. § 124.2)	Firm receives "a program term of nine years" but could be terminated or graduated early (13 C.F.R. § 124.2)	Firm receives "a program term of nine years" but could be terminated or graduated early (13 C.F.R. § 124.2)	Firm receives "a program term of nine years" but could be terminated or graduated early (13 C.F.R. § 124.2)
One-time eligibility for 8(a) Program	Applies to both disadvantaged owners and firms (13 C.F.R. § 124.108(b))	Applies only to tribally owned firms, not tribes (15 U.S.C. § 636(j)(11)(B)-(C))	Applies only to ANC-owned firms, not ANCs (15 U.S.C. § 636(j)(11)(B)-(C))	Applies only to NHO-owned firms, not NHOs (15 U.S.C. § 636(j)(11)(B)-(C))	Applies only to CDC-owned firms, not CDCs (15 U.S.C. § 636(j)(11)(B)-(C))
Limits on majority ownership in 8(a) firms	Individuals determined to be disadvantaged for purposes of 8(a), their immediate family members, and 8(a) firms themselves may own no more than 20% in any other 8(a) firm (13 C.F.R. § 124.105(g))	May not own 51% or more of a firm obtaining the majority of its revenues from the same primary industry in which another tribally owned firm currently operates or has operated within the past two years; otherwise, no limit on the number of tribally	May not own 51% or more of a firm obtaining the majority of its revenues from the same primary industry in which another ANC-owned firm currently operates or has operated within the past two years; otherwise, no limit on the number of ANC-owned firms that operate in other	May not own 51% or more of a firm obtaining the majority of its revenues from the same primary industry in which another NHO-owned firm currently operates or has operated within the past two years; otherwise, no limit on the number of NHO-	May not own 51% or more of a firm obtaining the majority of its revenues from the same primary industry in which another CDC-owned firm currently operates or has operated within the past two years; otherwise, no limit on the number of CDC-owned firms that operate in other primary industries or on the ownership of multiple firms

(Continued)

Requirements	8(a) Businesses Generally	Tribally Owned 8(a) Businesses	ANC-Owned 8(a) Businesses	NHO-Owned 8(a) Businesses	CDC-Owned 8(a) Businesses
		owned firms that erate in other primary industries or on the ownership of multiple firms in the same secondary industry (15 U.S.C. § 636(j)(11)(B)-(C); 13 C.F.R. § 124.109(c)(3)(ii))	primary industries or on the ownership of multiple firms in the same secondary industry (15 U.S.C. § 636(j)(11)(B)-(C); 13 C.F.R. § 124.109(c)(3)(ii))	owned firms that operate in other primary industries or on the ownership of multiple firms in the same secondary industry (15 U.S.C. § 636(j)(11)(B)-(C); 13 C.F.R. § 124.110(c))	in the same secondary industry (15 U.S.C. § 636(j)(11)(B)-(C); 13 C.F.R. § 124.111(d))
Limits on the amount of 8(a) contracts that a firm may receive	No source awards possible once the firm has received a total of $100 million, or other applicable value, in 8(a) contracts (13 C.F.R. § 124.519(a)(1)-(2)) Firms must receive an increasing percentage of revenue from non-8(a) sources throughout their participation in the 8(a) Program (13 C.F.R. § 124.509(b))	Can make sole-source awards even when a firm has received a total of $100 million, or other applicable value, in 8(a) contracts (13 C.F.R. § 124.519(a)(1)-(2)) Firms must receive an increasing percentage of revenue from non-8(a) sources throughout their participation in the 8(a) Program (13 C.F.R. § 124.509(b))	Can make sole-source awards even when a firm has received a total of $100 million, or other applicable value, in 8(a) contracts (13 C.F.R. § 124.519(a)(1)-(2)) Firms must receive an increasing percentage of revenue from non-8(a) sources throughout their participation in the 8(a) Program (13 C.F.R. § 124.509(b))	No source awards possible once the firm has received a total of $100 million, or other applicable value, in 8(a) contracts (13 C.F.R. § 124.519(a)(1)-(2)) Firms must receive an increasing percentage of revenue from non-8(a) sources throughout their participation in the 8(a) Program (13 C.F.R. § 124.509(b))	No source awards possible once the firm has received a total of $100 million, or other applicable value, in 8(a) contracts (13 C.F.R. § 124.519(a)(1)-(2)) Firms must receive an increasing percentage of revenue from non-8(a) sources throughout their participation in the 8(a) Program (13 C.F.R. § 124.509(b))

Source: Congressional Research Service.

a. The rules governing NHO- and/or CDC-owned firms do not address this issue, and although the general rules apply where no "special rules" exist, it seems unlikely that NHO- and/or CDC-owned firms are treated differently than tribally or ANC-owned firms in this regard.

b. These criteria include (1) the management experience of the disadvantaged individual(s) upon whom eligibility is based; (2) the business's technical experience; (3) the firm's capital; (4) the firm's performance record on prior federal or other contracts in its primary field of operations; and (5) whether the firm presently has, or can demonstrate its ability to timely obtain, the personnel, facilities, equipment, and other resources necessary to perform contracts under Section 8(a).

c. These criteria include (1) the technical and managerial experience and competency of the individuals who will manage and control the daily operation of the concern; (2) the financial capacity of the concern; and (3) the concern's performance record on prior federal or other contracts in the firm's primary industry.

End Notes

[1] Small Bus. Admin., Office of Business Development, FY2008 Annual Report to Congress, *available at* http://www.sba.gov/idc/groups/public/documents/sba_program_office/8abd_408_fy2008report.pdf.
[2] Small Business Mobilization Act, P.L. 77-603, § 4(f), 56 Stat. 351 (June 11, 1942).
[3] *Id.*
[4] Act of July 31, 1951, P.L. 82-96, § 110, 65 Stat. 131.
[5] P.L. 83-163, § 207(c)-(d), 67 Stat. 230 (July 30, 1953).
[6] *See, e.g.*, H.Rept. 494, 83d Cong., 1st Sess., at 2 (1953) (stating that the SBA would "continue many of the functions of the [SDPA] in the present mobilization period and in addition would be given powers and duties to encourage and assist small-business enterprises in peacetime as well as in any future war or mobilization period"); S. Rep. No. 1714, 85th Cong., 2d Sess., at 9-10 (1958) (stating that the act would "put[] the procurement assistance program on a peacetime basis").
[7] P.L. 85-536, § 8(a)(1)-(2), 72 Stat. 384 (July 18, 1958).
[8] *Id.*
[9] Thomas Jefferson Hasty, III, Minority Business Enterprise Development and the Small Business Administration's 8(a) Program: Past, Present, and (Is There a) Future? 145 *Mil. L. Rev.* 1, 8 (1994) ("[B]ecause the SBA believed that the efforts to start and operate an 8(a) program would not be worthwhile in terms of developing small business, the SBA's power to contract with other government agencies essentially went unused. The program actually lay dormant for about fifteen years until the racial atmosphere of the 1960s provided the impetus to wrestle the SBA's 8(a) authority from its dormant state.").
[10] Exec. Order No. 8802, 6 Fed. Reg. 3,109 (June 25, 1941). Similar requirements were later imposed on non-defense contracts. *See* Exec. Order No. 9346, 8 Fed. Reg. 7,182 (May 29, 1943).
[11] *See, e.g.*, Exec. Order No. 10308, 16 Fed. Reg. 12,303 (Dec. 3, 1951) (Truman); Exec. Order No. 10557, 19 Fed. Reg. 5,655 (Sept. 3, 1954) (Eisenhower); Exec. Order No. 10925, 26 Fed. Reg. 1,977 (Mar. 6, 1961) (Kennedy); Exec. Order No. 11458, 34 Fed. Reg. 4,937 (Mar. 7, 1969) (Nixon).
[12] *Report of the National Advisory Commission on Civil Disorders* 21 (1968).
[13] *See, e.g.*, Hasty, *supra* note 9, at 11-12.
[14] *See, e.g.*, Jonathan J. Bean, *Big Government and Affirmative Action: The Scandalous History of the Small Business Administration* 66 (2001).
[15] *See* Exec. Order No. 1625, 36 Fed. Reg. 19,967 (Oct. 13, 1971).
[16] 13 C.F.R. § 124.8-1(b) (1970).
[17] 13 C.F.R. § 124.8(c) (1973).
[18] S. Rep. No. 95-1070, 95th Cong., 2d Sess., at 14 (1978) ("One of the underlying reasons for the failure of this effort is that the program has no legislative basis."); H.Rept. 95-949, 95th Cong., 2d Sess., at 4 (1978) ("Congress has never extended legislative control over the activities of the 8(a) program, save through indirect appropriations, thereby permitting program operations. ... [The] program is not as successful as it could be.").
[19] P.L. 95-507, 92 Stat. 1757 (Oct. 24, 1978).
[20] *Id.* at § 202.
[21] *Id.* (codified at 15 U.S.C. § 637(a)(4)(A)-(B)). Firms that are owned and controlled by Indian tribes, ANCs, or NHOs were later included within the definition of a "socially and economically disadvantaged small business concern." *See infra* notes 29 to 36 and accompanying text.
[22] *Id.* (codified at 15 U.S.C. § 637(a)(5)).
[23] *Id.* at § 201 (codified at 15 U.S.C. § 631(f)(1)(C)). The meaning of "socially disadvantaged individuals" was the subject of much debate at the time of the 1978 amendments. Some Members of Congress, perhaps focusing on the SBA's use of its authority under Section 8(a) in 1968-1970, viewed the 8(a) Program as a program for African Americans and would have defined "social disadvantage" accordingly. *See, e.g.*, Parren J. Mitchell, Federal Affirmative Action for MBE's: An Historical Analysis, 1 *Nat'l Bar Ass'n Mag.* 46 (1983). Mitchell was a Member of the U.S. House of Representatives and leader of the Black Caucus when the 1978 amendments were enacted. Others favored a somewhat broader view, including both African Americans and Native Americans on the grounds that only those who did not come to the United States seeking the "American dream" should be deemed socially disadvantaged. *See, e.g.*, Testimony Before the House Comm. on Small Bus., Subcomm. on General Oversight & Minority Enter., Task Force on Minority Enter., 96th Cong., at 21 (1979). Yet others suggested that groups that are not racial or ethnic minorities should be able to qualify as "socially disadvantaged," or that individuals ought to be able to prove they are personally socially disadvantaged even if they are not racial or ethnic minorities. *See, e.g.*, H.Rept. 95-949, 95th Cong., 2d Sess., at 9 (1978) ("[T]he committee intends that the SBA give most serious consideration to, among others, women business owners" when determining which groups are socially disadvantaged. ... [T]he bill does recognize that persons falling outside of the racial and ethnic groups presumed to be disadvantaged, may nevertheless be disadvantaged."). Ultimately, the bill that passed the House defined "socially disadvantaged individuals," in part, by establishing a rebuttable presumption that African Americans and Hispanic Americans are socially

disadvantaged, while the bill that passed the Senate did not reference any racial or ethnic groups in defining "social disadvantage." *See, e.g.*, H.R. Conf. Rep. No. 95-1714, 95th Cong., 2d Sess., at 20 (1978); S.Rept. 95-1070, 95th Cong., 2d Sess., at 13-16 (1978). The conference committee reconciling the House and Senate versions ultimately arrived at a definition of "socially disadvantaged individuals" that was broader than the definition used in the SBA's 1973 regulation and included "those who have been subjected to racial or ethic prejudice or cultural bias because of their identity as a member of a group." P.L. 95-507, at § 202. This definition did not incorporate the rebuttable presumption that members of certain groups are socially disadvantaged included in the House bill. However, the conference bill included congressional findings that "Black Americans, Hispanic Americans, Native Americans, and other minorities" are socially disadvantaged, thereby arguably achieving similar effect. *Id.* at § 201.

[24] P.L. 95-507, at § 202 (granting the SBA's Associate Administrator for Minority Small Business and Capital Ownership Development authority to make determinations regarding which other groups are socially disadvantaged); H.Rept. 95-949, *supra* note 23, at 9 (expressing the view that Sections 201 and 202 of the bill provide "sufficient discretion ... to allow SBA to designate any other additional minority group or persons it believes should be afforded the presumption of social ... disadvantage").

[25] *See* 13 C.F.R. § 124.103(d)(2)(i)-(iii)(1980).

[26] 13 C.F.R. § 124. 103(b)(2009). Different groups are sometimes recognized as socially disadvantaged for purposes of other programs, such as those of the Department of Commerce's Minority Business Development Agency (MBDA). *See* 15 C.F.R. § 1400.1(a). The SBA has rejected petitions from certain groups, including Hasidic Jews, women, disabled veterans, and Iranian-Americans. *See, e.g.*, George R. La Noue & John C. Sullivan, Gross Presumptions: Determining Group Eligibility for Federal Procurement Preferences, 41 *Santa Clara L. Rev.* 103, 127-29 (2000). Hasidic Jews are, however, eligible to receive assistance from the MDBA. *See* 15 C.F.R. § 1400.1(c) (2009).

[27] 13 C.F.R. § 124. 103(c)(2) (2009) (standards of evidence for showing personal disadvantage); 13 C.F.R. § 124.103(b)(3) (2009) (mechanisms for rebutting the presumption of social disadvantage).

[28] P.L. 95-507, § 202.

[29] 13 C.F.R. § 124. 104(c)(2). Some commentators estimate that 80 to 90% of Americans are economically disadvantaged under the SBA's net-worth requirements. *See, e.g.*, La Noue & Sullivan, *supra* note 26, at 108.

[30] *Id.* at § 613, codified at 42 U.S.C. § 9802.

[31] P.L. 97-35, Ch. 8, Subch. A, 95 Stat. 489 (1981) (codified at 42 U.S.C. §§ 9801 et seq.).

[32] *Id.* at § 626, 95 Stat. 496 (codified at 42 U.S.C. § 9815).

[33] P.L. 99-272, § 18015, 100 Stat. 370 (1986) (codified at 15 U.S.C.§ 637(a)(13)) (defining "Indian tribe" to include "any Indian tribe, band, nation, or other organized group or community of Indians, including any Alaska Native village or regional or village corporation (within the meaning of the Alaska Native Claims Settlement Act (43 U.S.C.§ 1606)) which—(A)is recognized as eligible for the special programs and services provided by the United States to Indians because of their status as Indians, or (B) is recognized as such by the State in which such tribe, band, nation, group, or community resides.").

[34] *Id.* (codified at 15 U.S.C. § 637(a)(4)). An "Indian Tribe" includes any "Indian tribe, band, nation, or other organized group or community of Indians, including any ANC, which is recognized as eligible for the special programs and services provided by the United States to Indians because of their status as Indians, or is recognized as such by the State in which the tribe, band, nation, group, or community resides." 13 C.F.R. § 124.3. An Alaska Native Corporation is "any Regional Corporation, Village Corporation, Urban Corporation or Group Corporation organized under laws of Alaska in accordance with the Alaska Native Claims Settlement Act." *Id.* An Alaska Native is any "citizen of U.S. who is person one-fourth degree or more Alaskan Indian, Eskimo, Aleut blood, of combination thereof. In absence of proof of minimum bloodlines, it is any citizen whom a Native village or Native groups regards as such provided their father or mother is regarded as an Alaska Native." *Id.*

[35] P.L. 102-415, § 10, 106 Stat. 2115 (1992) (codified at 43 U.S.C. §1626(e)).

[36] P.L. 100-656, § 207, 102 Stat. 3861 (1988) (codified at 15 U.S.C. § 637(a)(4)).

[37] *Id.* (codified at 15 U.S.C. § 637(a)(15)). A "Native Hawaiian" is "any individual whose ancestors were natives, prior to 1778, of [the] area which now comprises [the] state of Hawaii." 13 C.F.R. § 124.3.

[38] *See, e.g.*, 13 C.F.R. § 124.109(a) ("*Special rules for ANCs*: Small business concerns owned and controlled by ANCs are eligible for participation in the 8(a) program and must meet the eligibility criteria set forth in § 124.112 to the extent the criteria are not inconsistent with this section.").

[39] 13 C.F.R. § 124.101.

[40] The SBA's Office of Hearings and Appeals has, for example, developed a seven-part test for determining whether a small business is "unusually reliant" on a contractor that is used in determining affliations. *See* Valenzuela Eng'g, Inc. & Curry Contracting Co., Inc., SBA-4151 (1996).

[41] *See* 13 C.F.R. § 124.112 (a) ("In order for a concern ... to remain eligible for 8(a) ... program participation, it must continue to meet all eligibility criteria contained in [Section] 124. 101 through [Section] 124.108.").

[42] 15 U.S.C. § 632(a)(1)-(2)(A).

[43] 13 C.F.R. §§ 121.101-121.108. The number of employees is the average of each pay period for the preceding twelve calendar months. Gross income is based on the average for the last three completed fiscal years. It includes all revenues, not just those from the firm's primary industry. *See* IMDT, Inc., SBA-4121 (1995).
[44] 13 C.F.R. § 121.201.
[45] 13 C.F.R. § 121. 103(a)(1). Control or the power of control need only exist. It need not be exercised for affiliation to be found.
[46] 13 C.F.R. § 121.103(a)(6).
[47] 13 C.F.R. § 121.103(h) ("[T]he joint venture entity cannot submit more than three offers over a two year period, starting from the date of the submission of the first offer.").
[48] 13 C.F.R. § 121. 103(h)(4) ("A contractor and its ostensible subcontractor are treated as joint venturers, and therefore affiliates, for size determination purposes. An ostensible subcontractor is a subcontractor that performs primary and vital requirements of a contract ... or a subcontractor upon which the prime contractor is unusually reliant.").
[49] 13 C.F.R. § 121.103(i) ("Affiliation may arise ... through ... common ownership, common management or excessive restrictions on the sale of the franchise interest.").
[50] 13 C.F.R. § 121. 105(a)(1). "Business" is separately defined for small agricultural cooperatives. *See* 13 C.F.R. § 121. 105(a)(2).
[51] 13 C.F.R. § 121.105(b).
[52] 15 U.S.C. § 637(a)(4)(A)(i)-(ii) (requiring at least 51% unconditional ownership);13 C.F.R. § 124.105.
[53] 13 C.F.R. § 124.3.
[54] 13 C.F.R. § 124.105(a).
[55] 13 C.F.R. § 124. 105(h)(1). Ownership is limited to 10% when the 8(a) firm in is the "developmental stage" of the 8(a) Program and 20% when it is in the "transitional stage." *Id.* The developmental stage consists of the first four years of the 8(a) Program, while the transitional stage consists of the last five years. Firms in the transitional stage must earn ever increasing percentages of their revenue from non-8(a) sources, as discussed below.
[56] 13 C.F.R. § 124.105(h)(2).
[57] 15 U.S.C. § 637(a)(4)(A)(i)-(ii) (requiring control of management and daily business operations); 13 C.F.R. § 124. 106.
[58] *Id.*
[59] *Id.*
[60] 13 C.F.R. § 124.106(a)(3).
[61] 13 C.F.R. § 124.106(a)(2).
[62] 13 C.F.R. § 124.106(e).
[63] 13 C.F.R. § 124.106(e)(1) & (3).
[64] 15 U.S.C. § 637(a)(5); 13 C.F.R. § 124.103(a).
[65] 13 C.F.R. § 124. 103(b)(1). If required by the SBA, individuals claiming membership in these groups must demonstrate that they held themselves out and are recognized by others as members of the designated group(s). 13 C.F.R. § 124.103(b)(2).
[66] 13 C.F.R. § 124.103(b)(3).
[67] 13 C.F.R. § 124.103(c)(1).
[68] 13 C.F.R. § 124. 103(c)(2)(i)-(iii).
[69] 13 C.F.R. § 124.103(c)(2)(iii).
[70] 13 C.F.R. § 124. 103(d)(4). Groups petitioning for recognition as socially disadvantaged do not always obtain it. Over the years, the SBA has rejected petitions from Hasidic Jews, women, disabled veterans, and Iranian-Americans. *See supra* note 26.
[71] 15 U.S.C. § 637(a)(6)(A); 13 C.F.R. § 124.104(a).
[72] 13 C.F.R. § 124.104(b)(1).
[73] 15 U.S.C. § 637(a)(6)(E)(i)-(ii); 13 C.F.R. § 124.104(c).
[74] 13 C.F.R. § 124. 104(c)(2)(ii).
[75] *Id.*
[76] *Id.*
[77] 13 C.F.R. § 124.108(a). For more on debarment and suspension, see CRS Report RL34753, *Debarment and Suspension of Government Contractors: An Overview of the Law Including Recently Enacted and Proposed Amendments*, by Kate M. Manuel.
[78] 13 C.F.R. § 124.107. Specifically, "[i]ncome tax returns for each of the two previous tax years must show operating revenues in the primary industry in which the applicant is seeking 8(a) ... certification." 13 C.F.R. § 124.107(a).
[79] 15 U.S.C. § 637(a)(7)(A) ("reasonable prospects for success"); 13 C.F.R. § 124. 107(b)(i)-(v).
[80] SBA may delegate the function of executing contracts to the procuring agencies and often does so. *See* 13 C.F.R. § 124.501(a).

[81] An acquisition is a procurement. Set-asides may be total or partial. *See* 48 C.F.R. § 19.502-3(a). The federal government presently has several other programs authorizing set-asides and sole-source awards for various subcategories of small businesses. *See generally* CRS Report R40591, *Set-Asides for Small Businesses: Recent Developments in the Law Regarding Precedence Among the Set-Aside Programs and Set-Asides Under IndefiniteDelivery/Indefinite-Quantity Contracts*, by Kate M. Manuel.

[82] 15 U.S.C. § 644(a) (describing when set-asides for small businesses are permissible); 41 U.S.C. § 253(b)(2) (CICA provision authorizing set-asides for small businesses); 48 C.F.R. §§ 6.203-6.206 (authorizing set-asides for small business generally, 8(a) small businesses, Historically Underutilized Business Zone (HUBZone) small businesses, and service-disabled veteran-owned small businesses). CICA authorizes competitions excluding all sources other than small businesses when such competitions assure that a "fair proportion of the total purchases and contracts for property and services for the Government in each industry category are placed with small-business concerns." 41 U.S.C. § 253(b)(1); 41 U.S.C. § 259(b). CICA also authorizes sole-source awards when, among other things, the property or services needed by a government agency are available from only one responsible source and no other type of property or service will satisfy the agency's needs. 10 U.S.C. § 2304(c)(1) (defense agency procurements) & 41 U.S.C. § 253(c)(1) (civilian agency procurements). For more on competition in federal contracting, see CRS Report R40516, *Competition in Federal Contracting: An Overview of the Legal Requirements*, by Kate M. Manuel.

[83] 15 U.S.C. § 644(g)(1)-(2).

[84] They also count toward a separate goal for the percentage of federal procurement dollars awarded to small businesses generally. Currently, the government-wide goal is that 5% of all federal contract dollars be spent with small disadvantaged businesses, including 8(a) businesses, while agency-specific goals range from 1.6% (Department of Energy) to 5%. Small Bus. Admin., FY2006-FY2008 Goals and Achievements, *available at* http://www.sba.gov/ aboutsba/sbaprograms/goals/index.html. The government-wide goal was met in FY2008, the most recent year for which information is available. Small Bus. Admin., FY2008 Government-Wide Score Card, *available at* http://www.sba.gov/idc/groups/public/documents/sba_homepage/goals_08_gov_wide.pdf. Agency performance varies, with some agencies under, some agencies at, and some agencies exceeding their goals. Small Bus. Admin., FY2008 Goals and Achievements, *available at*http://www.sba.gov/idc/groups /public/documents/sba_homepage/ fy2008goals_and_achievements.html.

[85] *See* 13 C.F.R. § 124.1002 (defining "small disadvantaged business").

[86] *See, e.g.*, AHNTECH, Inc., B-401092, Comp. Gen. Dec. (Apr. 22, 2009) ("The [Small Business] Act affords the SBA and contracting agencies broad discretion in selecting procurements for the 8(a) program.").

[87] Even in this situation, SBA may accept the requirement under "extraordinary circumstances." 13 C.F.R. § 124.504(a); Madison Servs., Inc., B-400615 (Comp. Gen. Dec., Dec. 11, 2008) (finding that extraordinary circumstances existed when the agency's initial small business set-aside was erroneous and did not reflect its intentions).

[88] 13 C.F.R. § 124.504(a)-(c). The third provision applies only to preexisting requirements. It does not apply to new contracts, follow-on or renewal contracts, or procurements under $100,000. *Id.* Also under its regulations, SBA must presume an adverse impact when

(A)The small business concern has performed the specific requirement for at least 24 months;

(B)The small business is performing the requirement at the time it is offered to the 8(a) ... program, or its performance of the requirement ended within 30 days of the procuring activity's offer of the requirement to the 8(a) ... program; and

(C)The dollar value of the requirement that the small business is or was performing is 25 percent or more of its most recent annual gross sales (including those of its affiliates).

13 C.F.R. § 124.504(c)(1)(A)-(C).

[89] 15 U.S.C. § 637(a)(1)(A); 48 C.F.R. § 19.806(b). Fair market price is estimated by looking at recent prices for similar items or work, in the case of repeat purchases, or by considering commercial prices for similar products or services, available in-house cost estimates, cost or pricing data submitted by the contractor, or data from other government agencies, in the case of new purchases. 15 U.S.C. § 637(a)(3)(B)(i)-(iii); 48 C.F.R. § 19.807(b) & (c).

[90] 15 U.S.C. § 637(a)(1)(A). *See also* Totolo v. United States, 2009 U.S. Claims LEXIS 221, at *42-*43 (June 15, 2009) ("The manner in which [an agency] assesses its needs is a business judgment and lies within its own discretionary domain."); JT Constr. Co., B-254257 (Comp. Gen. Dec. 6, 1993) (stating that it is a business judgment, within the contracting officer's discretion, to decide not to set aside a competition for small businesses).

[91] 4 C.F.R. § 21.5(b)(3); Rothe Computer Solutions, LLC, B-299452, Comp. Gen. Dec. (May 9, 2007).

[92] 15 U.S.C. §637(a)(16)(A). A noncompetitive award may be made under this authority so long as (1) the firm is determined to be a responsible contractor for performance of the contract; (2) the award of the contract would be consistent with the firm's business plan; and (3) award of the contract would not result in the firm exceeding the percentage of revenue from 8(a) sources forecast in its annual business plan. 15 U.S.C. §637(a)(16)(A)(i)-(iii).

[93] 15 U.S.C. § 637(a)(1)(D)(ii); 48 C.F.R. § 19.805-1(d).

[94] 15 U.S.C. § 637(a)(1)(D)(i)(I)-(II); 48 C.F.R. § 19.805-1(a)(1)-(2).

[95] 48 C.F.R. § 19.805-1(b)(1)-(2) (sole-source awards to tribally or ANC-owned firms); 48 C.F.R. § 219.805-1(b)(2)(A)-(B) (sole-source awards to NHO-owned firms). Prior to enactment of the National Defense Authorization Act (NDAA) for FY20 10, contracting officers making sole-source awards in reliance on the second exception did not have to justify such awards, obtain approval of them from higher-level agency officials, or post notices of the award. The NDAA changed this by requiring justifications, approvals, and notices for sole-source contracts in excess of $20 million awarded under the authority of Section 8(a) similar to those required for sole-source contracts awarded under the general contracting authorities. *Compare* P.L. 111-84, § 811, 123 Stat. 2405-06 (Oct. 28, 2009) *with* 10 U.S.C. § 2304(c) & (f) (procurements of defense agencies); 41 U.S.C. § 253(c) & (f) (procurements of civilian agencies).

[96] 48 C.F.R. § 19.805-1(c).

[97] 48 C.F.R. § 19.805-2(d).

[98] 15 U.S.C. § 636(j)(10)(C)(i) (nine-year term); 15 U.S.C. § 637(a)(9) (termination and early graduation); 13 C.F.R. § 124.301 (exiting the 8(a) Program); 13 C.F.R. § 124.302 (early graduation); 13 C.F.R. § 124.303 (termination from the Program).

[99] 15 U.S.C. § 636(j)(11)(B)-(C); 13 C.F.R. § 124.108(b).

[100] 13 C.F.R. § 124.108(b)(4).

[101] 13 C.F.R. § 124.105(g).

[102] 13 C.F.R. § 124.519(a)(1)-(2). Contracts less than $100,000 are not counted in determining whether a firm has reached the applicable limit. 13 C.F.R. § 124.5 19(a)(3). The Administrator of the SBA may waive this requirement if the head of the procuring agency determines that a sole-source award to a firm is necessary "to achieve significant interests of the Government." 13 C.F.R. § 124.519(f). Even after they have received a combined total of competitive and sole-source awards in excess of $100 million, or other applicable amount, firms may still receive competitive contracts under the 8(a) Program. 13 C.F.R. § 124.5 19(b).

[103] 15 U.S.C. § 636(j)(10)(I)(i) (iii); 13 C.F.R. § 124.509(b)(1).

[104] 13 C.F.R. § 124.509(b)(2).

[105] 13 C.F.R. § 124.509(d)(1). This prohibition may be waived when the Director of the Office of Business Development finds that denial of a sole-source contract would cause severe economic hardship for the firm, potentially jeopardizing its survival, or extenuating circumstances beyond the firm's control caused it to miss its target. *Id.*

[106] 15 U.S.C. 637(a)(14)(A)-(B); 15 U.S.C. § 644(o); 13 C.F.R. § 125.6; 48 C.F.R. § 52.219-14.

[107] 13 C.F.R. § 124.510 (limits on subcontracting for 8(a) firms); 13 C.F.R. § 125.6(a)(1)-(4) (limits on subcontracting for small businesses generally). The Government Accountability Office has criticized the SBA for poor monitoring of the percentage of work performed by subcontractors on 8(a) contracts with ANC-owned firms, and some commentators have criticized ANC-owned firms for subcontracting with companies that are themselves ineligible for the 8(a) program. *See* Gov't Accountability Office, Increased Used of Alaska Native Corporations' Special 8(a) Provisions Calls for Tailored Oversight, GAO-06-399, at 6 (Apr. 2006); Michael Scherer, Little Big Companies: How Did Corporations Like Halliburton Get Millions in Government Contracts Designated for Small Minority Businesses?, *Mother Jones Mag.*, Jan./Feb. 2005, *available at* http://www.motherjones.com/commentary/notebook/2005/01/ 1_400.html. However, any 8(a) firm may subcontract with a "large business" provided that the subcontracting relationship is not such as to result in affiliation and the 8(a) firm directly performs the required percentage of the contract costs with its own personnel.

[108] 13 C.F.R. § 124. 109(c)(3)(i) (tribally and ANC-owned firms); 13 C.F.R. § 124.111(c) (CDC-owned firms).

[109] 13 C.F.R. §§ 124.109-124.111.

[110] 13 C.F.R. § 124. 109(c)(2)(i) (tribally and ANC-owned firms); 13 C.F.R. § 124.110(b) (NHO-owned firms); 13 C.F.R. § 124.111(c) (CDC-owned firms).

[111] 13 C.F.R. § 124. 109(c)(2)(iii) (tribally and ANC-owned firms); 13 C.F.R. § 124.110(b) (NHO-owned firms); 13 C.F.R. § 124.111(c) (CDC-owned firms). The language here, stating that "any other business enterprise owned by [an organization]" shall be excluded from the size determination, seems somewhat contrary to that in 13 C.F.R. § 121.103(2)(ii), which suggests that businesses owned and controlled by organizations could be found to be affiliates of the organization for reasons other than common ownership or management, or performance of common administrative services. According to the GAO, some agency contracting officers reported not knowing how to determine what constitutes a "substantial unfair competitive advantage" when making size determinations for ANC-owned firms in particular. *See* Increased Used of Alaska Native Corporations' Special 8(a) Provisions, *supra* note 107, at 37.

[112] *See, e.g.*, Valenzuela Eng'g, Inc. & Curry Contracting Co., Inc., SBA-4151 (1996) (rejecting a challenge to the size of an ANC-owned firm because its subcontractor performed less than 25% of the work on the contract and was not its affiliate); Increased Used of Alaska Native Corporations' Special 8(a) Provisions, *supra* note 107, at 29 (describing "early graduation" of ANC-owned 8(a) firms).

[113] 13 C.F.R. § 124.109(a) & (b) (requiring tribally and ANC-owned firms to comply with the general eligibility requirements where they are not contrary to or inconsistent with the special requirements for these entities); 13

C.F.R. § 124.110(a) (similar provision for NHO-owned firms); 13 C.F.R. § 124.111(a) (similar provision for CDC-owned firms).

[114] 13 C.F.R. § 124.109(a)(3).

[115] 13 C.F.R. § 124.109(a) & (b) (requiring tribally and ANC-owned firms to comply with the general eligibility requirements where they are not contrary to or inconsistent with the special requirements for these entities); 13 C.F.R. § 124.110(a) (similar provision for NHO-owned firms); 13 C.F.R. § 124.111(a) (similar provision for CDC-owned firms).

[116] 13 C.F.R. § 124.109(c)(4)(B).

[117] *See* 13 C.F.R. § 124.110.

[118] *Id.* ("Concerns owned by economically disadvantaged Native Hawaiian Organizations, as defined in [Section] 124.3, are eligible for participation in the 8(a) program and other federal programs requiring SBA to determine social and economic disadvantage as a condition of eligibility. Such concerns must meet all eligibility criteria set forth in [Section] 124.101 through 124.108 and [Section] 124.112 to the extent that they are not inconsistent with this section.").

[119] 13 C.F.R. § 124.111(b).

[120] 13 C.F.R. § 124. 109(b)(1) (tribally and ANC-owned firms); 15 U.S.C. § 637(a)(4)(A)(i)(II) (NHO-owned firms); *See* Small Disadvantaged Business Certification Application: Community Development Corporation (CDC) Owned Concern, OMB Approval No. 3245-0317 ("A Community Development Corporation (CDC) is considered to be a socially and economically disadvantaged entity if the parent CDC is a nonprofit organization responsible to residents of the area it serves which has received financial assistance under 42 U.S.C. 9805, et seq."). SBA's authority to designate CDCs as socially and economically disadvantaged derives from 42 U.S.C. § 9815(a)(2), although the SBA does not currently have regulations addressing this issue. *See* 42 U.S.C. § 9815(a)(2) ("Not later than 90 days after August 13, 1981, the Administrator of the Small Business Administration, after consultation with the Secretary, shall promulgate regulations to ensure the availability to community development corporations of such programs as shall further the purposes of this subchapter, including programs under section 63 7(a) of title 15.").

[121] 43 U.S.C. § 1626(e)(1) ("For all purposes of Federal law, a Native Corporation shall be considered to be a corporation owned and controlled by Natives and a minority and economically disadvantaged business enterprise if the Settlement Common Stock of the corporation and other stock of the corporation held by holders of Settlement Common Stock and by Natives and descendants of Natives, represents a majority of both the total equity of the corporation and the total voting power of the corporation for the purposes of electing directors."); 13 C.F.R. § 124.109(a)(2) (same).

[122] *See* Small Disadvantaged Business Certification Application, *supra* note 120.

[123] 15 U.S.C. § 637(a)(6)(A); 13 C.F.R. § 124. 109(b)(2)(i)-(vii).

[124] 13 C.F.R. § 124.109(b).

[125] *See* 13 C.F.R. § 124.110.

[126] *Id.* ("Concerns owned by economically disadvantaged Native Hawaiian Organizations, as defined in [Section] 124.3, are eligible for participation in the 8(a) program and other federal programs requiring SBA to determine social and economic disadvantage as a condition of eligibility. Such concerns must meet all eligibility criteria set forth in [Section] 124.101 through 124.108 and [Section] 124.112 to the extent that they are not inconsistent with this section.").

[127] 13 C.F.R. § 124. 109(b)(7)(ii).

[128] *See supra* note 126 and accompanying text.

[129] 13 C.F.R. § 124.111(g).

[130] 13 C.F.R. § 124.109(c)(6) (tribally and ANC-owned firms); 13 C.F.R. § 124.110(e) (NHO-owned firms); 13 C.F.R. § 124.11 1(f)(2)(i)-(iii) (CDC-owned firms).

[131] 13 C.F.R. § 124. 109(c)(6)(ii)(A)-(C) (tribally and ANC-owned firms); 13 C.F.R. § 124.1 10(e)(2)(i)-(iii) (NHO-owned firms); 13 C.F.R. § 124.111(f) (CDC-owned firms).

[132] *See* 13 C.F.R. § 124.107(b)(i)-(v).

[133] An Act To Amend the Small Business Act To Reform the Capital Ownership Development Program, and for Other Purposes; P.L. 100-656, § 602(a), 102 Stat. 3887-88 (Nov. 15, 1988) (codified at 15 U.S.C. § 637 note); 48 C.F.R. § 19.805-1(b)(2).

[134] The authority for DOD to make sole-source awards to NHO-owned firms of contracts valued at more than $3.5 million ($5.5 million for manufacturing contracts) even if contracting officers reasonably expect that offers will be received from at least two responsible small businesses existed on a temporary basis in 2004-2006 and became permanent in 2006. *See* Department of Defense, Emergency Supplemental Appropriations to Address Hurricanes in the Gulf of Mexico, and Pandemic Influenza Act of 2006, P.L. 109-148, § 8020, 119 Stat. 2702-03 (Dec. 30, 2005) ("[Provided] [t]hat, during the current fiscal year and hereafter, businesses certified as 8(a) by the Small Business Administration pursuant to section 8(a)(15) of Public Law 85-53 6, as amended, shall have the same status as other program participants under section 602 of P.L. 100-656 ... for purposes of contracting with agencies of the Department of Defense."); 48 C.F.R. § 219.805-1(b)(2)(A)-(B).

[135] *See supra* note 97.

[136] 13 C.F.R. § 124.109(a) & (b) (requiring tribally and ANC-owned firms to comply with the general eligibility requirements where they are not contrary to or inconsistent with special requirements for these entities); 13 C.F.R. § 124.110(a) (similar provision for NHO-owned firms); 13 C.F.R. § 124.111(a) (similar provision for CDC-owned firms).

[137] 15 U.S.C. § 644(o); 13 C.F.R. § 125.6; 48 C.F.R. § 52.219-14.

[138] *Id.*

[139] *Id.*; 15 U.S.C. § 636(j)(1 1)(B)-(C).

[140] 13 C.F.R. § 124. 109(c)(3)(ii) (tribally and ANC-owned firms); 13 C.F.R. § 124.110(c) (NHO-owned firms); 13 C.F.R. § 124.111(d) (CDC-owned firms). GAO has also faulted agencies' tracking of the industries in which 8(a) firms have contracts to ensure compliance with this rule. *See Northern Lights and Procurement Plights: The Effects of the ANC Program on Federal Procurement and Alaska Native Corporations*, Joint Hearing Before the Comm. on Gov. Reform & the Comm. on Small Bus., House of Representatives, 109th Cong., 2d Sess., at 134-35 (June 21, 2006) (statement of David Cooper, Director, Acquisition and Sourcing Management, GAO).

[141] 13 C.F.R. § 124. 109(c)(3)(ii) (tribally and ANC-owned firms); 13 C.F.R. § 124.110(c) (NHO-owned firms); 13 C.F.R. § 124.111(d) (CDC-owned firms).

[142] 13 C.F.R. § 124.519(a).

[143] 13 C.F.R. § 124.509.

[144] Small Bus. Admin., Office of Business Development, 2008 Report to Congress, at 6, *available at* http://www.sba.gov/idc/groups/public/documents/sba_program_office/8abd_408_fy2008report.pdf.

[145] *See, e.g.*, *Federal Contracting: Removing Hurdles for Minority-Owned Small Businesses*, Hearing Before the Subcomm. on Gov't Mgmt., Org. & Procurement of the Comm. on Oversight & Gov't Reform, U.S. House of Representatives, 1 10th Cong., 1st Sess., at 68 (Sept. 26, 2007) (statement of Michael I. Barrera, President & CEO of the United States Hispanic Chamber of Commerce) (advocating removal of the net worth requirement for ongoing eligibility in the 8(a) Program).

[146] *See, e.g.*, Gov't Accountability Office, SBA Could Better Focus Its 8(a) Program to Help Firms Obtain Contracts, GAO RCED 00-196 (reporting that 8(a) firms expect SBA to help them obtain contracts, while SBA focuses on business development activities).

[147] *See, e.g.*, Minority Small Business Enhancement Act of 2009, H.R. 2299, § 5 (proposing to increase the goals for contracting with small disadvantaged businesses, among others).

[148] *See, e.g.*, Gov't Accountability Office, Agency Should Assess Resources Devoted to Contracting and Improve Several Processes in the 8(a) Program, GAO RCED-00-196 (noting widespread fraud in the 8(a) Program).

[149] *See, e.g.*, *id.* (noting that SBA lacks personnel to perform effective monitoring of contracts); Gov't Accountability Office, SBA's 8(a) Information System Is Flawed and Does Not Support the Program's Mission, GAO RCED-00-197.

[150] *See, e.g.*, Robert Brodsky, Senate Panel to Probe Alaska Native Contracting Preferences, *Gov't Exec.*, May, 15, 2009, *available at* http://www.govexec.com/dailyfed/0509/051509rb2.htm (describing plans for the July 16, 2009 hearing).

[151] *See, e.g.*, ANCs Receiving Disproportionate Share of SBA 8(a) Program Awards, Panel Told, 92 *Fed. Contr. Rep.* 50 (July 21, 2009).

[152] *See, e.g.*, Increased Used of Alaska Native Corporations' Special 8(a) Provisions, *supra* note 107, at 22 (noting agencies' use of contracts with ANCs to "pass through" work to particular subcontractors).

[153] *See, e.g.*, *Northern Lights and Procurement Plights*, *supra* note 140, at 9 (statement of Representative Henry A. Waxman).

[154] *See, e.g.*, *id.* at 120 (statement of Representative Nydia Velázquez) (noting SBA's "sheer lack of attention to the [8(a)] program"); *id.* at 134 (statement of David Cooper, Director of Acquisition Sourcing and Management, GAO) ("[F]ederal agency contracting officials need to do a better job of complying with certain requirements that are intended to preclude abuses of the 8(a) program.").

[155] *See, e.g.*, *id.* at 12 1-23 (statement of Representative Don Young); Native American Contracting Under Section 8(a) of the Small Business Act: Economic, Social, and Cultural Impacts, Oct. 2007, *available at* http://www.nativecontractors.org/media (noting that ANCs paid $413 million in wages to employees and $32 million in dividends to shareholders in FY2005 as a result of federal contracting). Some commentators have expressed concern about the relatively low number of ANC shareholders or Alaska Natives employed by ANC-owned 8(a) firms. *See, e.g.*, Jenny J. Yang, Rising Giant: Policies and Costs of Section 8(a) Contracting Preferences for Alaska Native Corporations, 23 *Alaska L. Rev.* 315, 346-47 (2006). However, there is no requirement that 8(a) firms employ certain percentages of socially disadvantaged individuals.

[156] *See, e.g.*, 8(a) Modernization Act, H.R. 1611, § 3 (requiring the Administrator of the SBA to establish thresholds for maximum net worth for economic disadvantage based on industry classifications, with consideration of the capital needs of various industries); Minority-Owned Venture Empowerment Act, H.R. 2532, § 202 (raising the net worth for initial eligibility to $750,000); Small Business Contracting Program Improvements Act, H.R. 3867, § 501 (raising the net worth threshold for economic disadvantage to $550,000; providing that investments in other small businesses are excluded except when comparing firms to others in the same field

owned by socially disadvantaged individuals; and allowing individuals who are determined to be economically disadvantaged at time of entry into the 8(a) Program to be deemed economically disadvantaged for the duration of the Program).

[157] *See, e.g.*, Small Business Contracting Program Improvements Act, H.R. 3867, § 201, 1 10th Cong.

[158] *See, e.g.*, Disabled Veteran Small Business Eligibility Expansion Act, H.R. 109, § 2 (making service-disabled veteran-owned small businesses eligible for the 8(a) Program and redefining "socially and economically disadvantaged small business concern" to include service-disabled veteran-owned small businesses); Service-Disabled Veteran- Owned Small Business Equity Act, H.R. 1265, § 2 (same); Coast Guard appropriation act for FY2008, H.R. 2830, § 219 (deeming women to be socially and economically disadvantaged for purposes of contracts awarded under the Coast Guard's Disadvantaged Business Enterprise Program); Small Business Contracting Program Improvements Act, H.R. 3867, § 505 (requiring the Administrator of SBA to review the list of groups whose members are presumed to be socially disadvantaged and "consider whether the list should be updated to include additional groups"); An Act to Amend the Small Business Act to Establish a Mentorship Program Designed to Help Minority and Women-Owned Small Businesses Build Their Capacities and Access to Contracting Opportunities in the Construction Industry, H.R. 7087, § 1 (making women-owned small businesses eligible for the same mentorship opportunities under the act as 8(a) businesses are eligible for).

[159] *See, e.g.*, Small Business Contracting Program Improvements Act, H.R. 3867, § 502.

[160] *See, e.g.*, Minority-Owned Venture Empowerment Act, H.R. 2532, §§ 102 and 202.

[161] *Id.* at § 303.

[162] *See, e.g.*, A Bill to Enact Title 51 of the United States Code, "National and Commercial Space Programs," as Positive Law, H.R. 4780, § 30304 (requiring the Administrator of NASA to annually establish a goal that at least 8% of NASA contract dollars be awarded to small disadvantaged businesses).

[163] Small Business Contracting Program Improvements Act, H.R. 3867, § 204 (increasing the "competitive threshold" for nonmanufacturing contracts to $5.1 million); Minority-Owned Venture Empowerment Act, H.R. 2532, § 202 (raising the competitive threshold to $6 million for nonmanufacturing contracts and $10 million for manufacturing contracts); 8(a) Modernization Act, H.R. 1611, § 3 (raising the competitive thresholds to $10 for nonmanufacturing contracts and $12 million for manufacturing contracts).

[164] Accountability in Contracting Act, H.R. 1362, § 102.

[165] Small Business Contracting Program Improvements Act, H.R. 3867, § 205.

[166] Minority Small Business Enhancement Act of 2009, H.R. 2299, § 2; An Act to Amend the Small Business Act to Change the Net Worth Amount Under the Small Business Program for Socially and Economically Disadvantaged Individuals from $750,000 to $978,722, H.R. 4253, § 1(a); Small Business Reform Act of 2010, H.R. 4818, § 3(b); Expanding Opportunities for Main Street Act, H.R. 4929, § 201.

[167] H.R. 4253, at § 1(a) (requiring annual adjustments).

[168] H.R. 4818, at § 3(a).

[169] H.R. 2299, at § 2; H.R. 4929, at § 201.

[170] Promoting Jobs for Veterans Act of 2009, H.R. 4220, § 104. As used here, "active duty" has the same meaning it has under 10 U.S.C. § 101(d)(2).

[171] H.R. 2299, at § 5; H.R. 4929, at § 204. *See also* Small Business Bill of Rights, H.R. 5109, § 1011 (increasing the overall goal for contracting with small businesses).

[172] *Id.*

[173] Disabled Veteran Small Business Eligibility Expansion Act of 2009, H.R. 456, § 2.

[174] Freedom from Government Competition Act, S. 1167, § 4 and H.R. 2682, § 4.

[175] Small Business Export Enhancement and International Trade Act of 2009, S. 2862 (establishing a three-year pilot program to make grants to states to carry out export programs that assist 8(a) firms, among others); An Act to Amend the Small Business Act to Establish Mentorship and Assistance Programs Designed to Help Minority, Veteran-Owned, and Women-Owned Small Business Operate in the Construction Industry, H.R. 3771, § 2 (requiring the SBA to establish a mentorship program to assist 8(a) firms, among others, in gaining the "specialized knowledge" and "professional services" necessary to operate businesses in the construction industry).

[176] The focus upon implementation here potentially distinguishes this provision from existing law. Currently, contractors are required to make good faith efforts to comply with their subcontracting plans, but can be excused from implementing them in certain circumstances. *See* 15 U.S.C. § 637(d)(2)(F)(ii).

[177] Transportation Security Administration Authorization Act, H.R. 2200, § 103. H.R. 2200 would also require TSA to report annually to the House and Senate committees of jurisdiction on contractors' performance in subcontracting with small disadvantaged businesses. *See also* H.R. 4929, § 205 (allowing withholding of contract payments from prime contractors who fail to implement their subcontracting plans).

[178] P.L. 111-118, § 8016, 123 Stat. 3430-31 (Dec. 19, 2009).

[179] *See* DHS Acquisition Alert 07/15, *available at* http://www.nativecontractors.org/media/

[180] *See* ACC Policy Letter 08-0 1, *available at* http://www.nativecontractors.org/media Air%20Force%20Sole%20Source%20Policy%20April%202008.pdf.

[181] Testimony of Darryl Hairston, Acting Administrator, U.S. Small Business Administration, Before the U.S. House of Representatives Committee on Small Business, March 25, 2009, *available at* http://www.house.gov/smbiz/hearings/ hearing-3-25-09-SBA-oversight/Hairston.pdf.

[182] *See* Small Business Admin., Small Business Size Regulations; 8(a) Business Development/Small Disadvantaged Business Status Determinations, 74 Fed. Reg. 55694 (Oct. 28, 2009). The SBA also proposes changes to the regulations governing the size standards for small businesses. Among other things, these changes would clarify that (1) protégés in other agencies' mentor/protégé programs are generally not exempt from SBA's size affiliation rules; (2) any joint venture that seeks to use 8(a) mentor/protégé status as grounds for an exemption to the affiliation requirements must follow the 8(a) requirements; (3) procurements for supplies cannot be classified under a North American Industry Classification System (NAICS) code for retail trade; and (4) the "nonmanufacturer rule"—requiring that firms that are not themselves the manufacturer of the end products being procured provide the products of small businesses—applies only when the procuring agency has classified the procurement under a manufacturing NAICS code. *Id.* at 55694-97. The proposed rule would also grant SBA's Office of Inspector General authority to request formal size determinations and make clear that certain requirements for the 8(a) Program do not apply to small disadvantaged businesses. *Id.* at 55697, 55710.

[183] 74 Fed. Reg. at 55702.

[184] *Id.*

[185] *Id.*

[186] *Id.*

[187] *Id.* at 55703.

[188] *Id.* at 55705-06.

[189] *Id.* at 55701.

[190] *Id.* at 55694.

[191] Dynalatic Corp. v. U.S. Dep't of Defense, Civil Action No. 95-2301 (EGS) (D.D.C.).

[192] *See, e.g.*, Rothe Dev. Corp. v. Dep't of Defense, 545 F.3d 1023 (Fed. Cir. 2008). In *Rothe*, DOD did not contest whether the presumption regarding race and disadvantage incorporated in the challenged program constituted a racial classification subjecting the program to strict scrutiny. However, some courts had previously denied firms or individuals standing to challenge programs with racial presumptions like that in DOD's program on the grounds that the would-be plaintiffs were denied the contract because of inability to demonstrate social and economic disadvantage, not because of race. *See, e.g.*, Interstate Traffic Control v. Beverage, 101 F. Supp. 2d 445 (S.D. W. Va. 2000); Ellsworth Assocs. v. United States, 926 F. Supp. 207 (D.D.C. 1996). For more on the *Rothe Development Corporation* decision, see CRS Report R40440, *Rothe Development Corporation v. Department of Defense: The Constitutionality of Federal Contracting Programs for Minority-Owned and Other Small Businesses*, by Jody Feder and Kate M. Manuel.

[193] Rothe Dev. Corp., 545 F.3d at 1049.

[194] *See, e.g.*, Shaw v. Hunt, 517 U.S. 899, 909-10 (1996); Concrete Works of Colorado, Inc. v. City & County of Denver, 321 F.3d 950, 958 (10th Cir. 2003).

[195] P.L. 99-661, § 1207, 100 Stat. 3816, 3973-75 (Nov. 14, 1986) (codified at 10 U.S.C. § 2323). A price evaluation adjustment works as follows: when comparing a bid or offer from a small disadvantaged business with one submitted by another business, the agency can subtract up to 10% of the price from the bid or offer submitted by the small disadvantaged business in determining which bid or offer has the lowest price or represents the best value. For example, if a business that is not a small disadvantaged business bids $100,000 and a small disadvantaged business bids $110,000, the small disadvantaged business would win because it is the lower bidder after its price is reduced by 10% ($1 10,000-$1 1,000=$99,000).

[196] There are, however, goals for the percentage of contracts awarded to small disadvantaged businesses, which includes 8(a) businesses, under 15 U.S.C. § 644(g)(1)-(2).

[197] The legislative history of the 8(a) Program is arguably more extensive than that for the DOD program, although it is unclear whether this legislative history includes congressional findings based upon methodologically rigorous empirical studies that were current, nationwide in scope, and properly before Congress, such as were required in *Rothe*. *See* Rothe Dev. Corp., 545 F.3d at 1039-46.

[198] Dynalantic Corp. v. U.S. Dep't of Defense, 503 F. Supp. 2d 262 (D.D.C. 2007).

[199] *See* 13 C.F.R. § 124. 103(c)(2) (standards of evidence for showing personal disadvantage).

[200] *See* 15 U.S.C. § 657a (describing the HUBZone program); 48 C.F.R. § 19.1305 (same).

[201] Although the classification of individuals as "Native Americans" might seem like a racial one, courts have found that it is not. *See, e.g.*, Morton v. Mancari, 417 U.S. 535, 548 (1973). Native Americans are generally viewed as a political class, and programs targeting them are generally found to be programs "reasonably designed to further the cause of Indian self-government." *Id.* at 548.

[202] *See* Craig v. Boren, 429 U.S. 190, 197 (1976).

[203] Mission Critical Solutions v. United States, 2010 U.S. Claims LEXIS 36 (Mar. 2, 2010).

[204] *Id.* at *7-*11.

[205] Mission Critical Solutions, 2009 U.S. Comp. Gen. LEXIS 86, at *15 (May 4, 2009). The GAO specifically contrasted the language of 15 U.S.C. § 657a(b)(2), which states that "[n]otwithstanding any other provision of

law ... a contract opportunity shall be awarded pursuant to this section on the basis of competition restricted to qualified HUBZone small business concerns if the contracting officer has a reasonable expectation that not less than 2 qualified HUBZone small business concerns will submit offers and that the award can be made at a fair market price," with that of 15 U.S.C. § 637(a)(1)(A), which states that:

...[i]t shall be duty of the [SBA] and it is hereby empowered, whenever it determines such action is necessary or appropriate ... to enter into contracts with the United States Government and any department, agency, or officer thereof having procurement powers obligating the [SBA] to furnish articles, equipment, supplies, services, or materials to the Government or to perform construction work for the Government. In any case in which the [SBA] certifies to any officer of the Government having procurement powers that the [SBA] is competent and responsible to perform any specific Government procurement contract to be let by any such officer, such officer shall be authorized in his discretion to let such procurement contract to the [SBA] upon such terms and conditions as may be agreed upon between the [SBA] and the procurement officer.

[206] Office of Legal Counsel, Department of Justice, Permissibility of Small Business Administration Regulations Implementing the Historically Underutilized Business Zone, 8(a) Business Development, and Service-Disabled Veteran-Owned Small Business Concern Programs, Aug. 21, 2009, *available at* http://www.usdoj.gov/olc/2009/sbahubzone-opinion082109.pdf.

[207] *Id.* at 13-14. The Office of Management and Budget had previously directed agencies to maintain parity among the set-aside programs pending an "Executive Branch review of the legal basis underlying the GAO's decisions." Executive Office of the President, Office of Mgmt. & Budget, Recent Government Accountability Office Decisions Concerning Small Business Programs, July 10, 2009, *available at* http://www.whitehouse.gov/omb/assets memoranda_fy2009/m09-23.pdf.

[208] Mission Critical Solutions, 2010 U.S. Claims LEXIS at *8.

[209] *Id.* at *10-*11.

[210] *Id.* at *48-*49 (quoting *Cisneros v. Alpine Ridge Group*, 508 U.S. 10, 18 (1993)).

[211] *Id.* at *27 (relying on *Or. Natural Res. Council v. Thomas*, 92 F.3d 792, 796-97 (9th Cir. 1996) and *In re Glacier Bay*, 944 F.2d 577, 582 (9th Cir. 1991)).

[212] *Id.* at *28-*29.

[213] *Id.* at *36.

[214] *Id.* at *51-*56.

[215] *Id.* at *52. The government specifically relied upon *Ky., Educ. Cabinet, Dep 't for the Blind v. United States*, 424 F.3d 1222, 1227 (Fed. Cir. 2005) ("Congress's use of the two terms 'may' or 'shall' does not end the analysis. ... [The Court may consider] indications of legislative intent to the contrary or [] obvious inferences from the structure and purpose of the statute.").

[216] *Id.* at *56-*64.

[217] *Id.*

[218] *Id.* at *23-*26.

[219] *Id.* at *25.

[220] *Id.* at *64-*77.

[221] *Id.* at *76 (quoting *Shoshone Indian Tribe of Wind River Reservation v. United States*, 364 F.3d 1339, 1345 (Fed. Cir. 2004).

[222] For example, the court said that deletion of proposed language regarding parity among the set-aside programs from the HUBZone Act when it was enacted could have meant that Congress did not intend for the set-aside programs to have parity. *Id.* at *72-73. Its deletion did not necessarily mean that Congress construed the statute as providing for parity, in the court's view. *Id.* at *72.

[223] *Id.* at *78-*86.

[224] *Id.* at *86. The Court also rejected the argument that Congress "acquiesced to the SBA's parity regulations, and has affirmatively adopted the OLC legal opinion" because of language included in the conference report on the National Defense Authorization Act (NDAA) for FY2010. The version of the NDAA passed by the Senate would have substituted "may" for "shall" in the HUBZone Act. *See* S. 1390, § 838, as engrossed. However, this language was omitted by the conferees because

...the Department of Justice has concluded that no change to the Small Business Act is required to ensure that contracting officers of the Department of Defense and other federal agencies have the discretion whether or not to award contracts pursuant to the HUBZone program. The conferees direct the Secretary of Defense to continue to administer the HUBZone program in a manner consistent with the Department of Justice opinion.

H.R. Rep. No. 111-288, at 789 (2009). The court did not find this purported "acquiescence" determinative. Instead, it noted that congressional statements about the proper interpretation of a statute made subsequent to its enactment are "of little persuasive authority." Mission Critical Solutions, 2010 U.S. Claims LEXIS at *75.

[225] Mission Critical Solutions v. United States, No. 2010-5099 (appeal docketed Apr. 2, 2010).

[226] *See* U.S. Department of Justice, Civil Division, Re: Mission Critical Solutions v. United States, No. 09-864 (Fed. Cl.) (Feb. 26, 2010), Mar. 17, 2010 (letter on file with the author).

[227] Commentators made this point regarding the earlier GAO decisions recommending that HUBZone set-asides have precedence over set-asides for 8(a) and service-disabled veteran-owned small businesses. *See, e.g.*,

HUBZone Council, GAO Gives HUBZone Program Priority over Service Disabled Veteran Owned Firms, Nov. 6, 2008, *available at* http://www.ppi-timezero.com/resource-documents/hubzonerelease.pdf (hailing the decision's potential impact on HUBZone small businesses); SBA Warns of Turmoil without Parity Rule, *Entrepreneur.com*, Nov. 7, 2008, *available at* http://www.entrepreneur.com/tradejournals/article/189159 380.html (warning that HUBZone companies "could receive a disproportionate share of set-aside contracts, squeezing out other groups").

[228] 15 U.S.C. § 644(g)(1). There are also agency-specific goals, which tend to be set at 3% and 5% of contract dollars for HUBZone and 8(a) small businesses, respectively. *See* U.S. Small Bus. Admin., FY2008 Goals and Achievements, *available at* _http://www.sba.gov/idc/groups/public/documents/sba_homepage/fy2008goal s_and_achievements.html.

In: Disadvantaged Small Businesses and the 8(a) Program ISBN: 978-1-61209-309-3
Editors: James P. Carlson and Andrea M. Bernard

Chapter 3

Small Business Administration: Steps Have Been Taken to Improve Administration of the 8(a) Program, but Key Controls for Continued Eligibility Need Strengthening

United States Government Accountability Office

Why GAO Did This Study

The Small Business Administration's (SBA) 8(a) program helps eligible socially and economically disadvantaged small businesses compete in the economy by providing business development activities, such as counseling and technical assistance, and providing opportunities to obtain federal contracts on a set-aside basis. GAO was asked to review SBA's internal control procedures for determining 8(a) eligibility. Specifically, we (1) evaluated the procedures and processes that SBA has implemented to ensure that only eligible firms participate in the 8(a) program, and (2) assessed the extent to which SBA uses external mechanisms such as complaint information in helping to ensure that only eligible firms participate. To address these objectives, GAO reviewed SBA guidance and prior reports, interviewed SBA officials, and conducted site visits and file reviews of 123 randomly sampled 8(a) firms covering the most recent 2 years of annual reviews at five SBA locations.

What GAO Recommends

GAO makes six recommendations to SBA that include providing more guidance to help ensure staff more consistently follow procedures, reassessing BDSs' workload distribution, and developing more standard processes for documenting and analyzing certain program data. In responding to a draft of this report, SBA agreed with each of the six recommendations and stated that some corrective measures have already been implemented and additional actions are planned to be implemented in the near future.

WHAT GAO FOUND

SBA relies primarily on its annual review of 8(a) firms to ensure their continued eligibility in the program, but inconsistencies and weaknesses in annual review procedures limit program oversight. GAO's review of a random sample of 8(a) firms identified an estimated 55 percent in which SBA staff failed to complete required annual review procedures intended to assess fundamental eligibility criteria, such as being economically disadvantaged (see table). Multiple factors appear to have contributed to the inconsistencies identified, including the lack of specific criteria in SBA's current regulations and procedures that relate to some eligibility requirements such as determining whether firms exceed program thresholds for industry size averages, personal compensation, and personal asset limits. As a result, firms that may have outgrown the program continued to receive 8(a) program benefits. For example, GAO estimated that 17 percent of the firms we reviewed had exceeded one or more eligibility criteria for 2 consecutive years, but were recommended by SBA for retention. SBA has taken steps to clarify some, but not all, of these rules in recent proposed rule changes. SBA is required by statute to perform annual reviews on 100 percent of 8(a) firms but staff spent significant amounts of time trying to obtain annual review documents from firms—especially firms that did not have 8(a) contracts—which affected the timeliness of reviews. GAO identified a significant number of instances in which firms failed to submit annual review documents as required but still were recommended for retention. The Business Development Specialists' (BDS) dual role of advocacy for and monitoring of the firms may have contributed in part to the retention of ineligible firms. SBA has been addressing some data integrity and compatibility issues by enhancing its primary electronic system for annual review information. Finally, SBA did not maintain an accurate inventory of 8(a) Mentor-Protégé Program participant data, which limited the agency's ability to monitor these firms.

Estimated Percentage of Time That SBA Did Not Complete Selected Annual Review Procedures Relating to 8(a) Eligibility

Requirement not met	Estimated percentage
Taking action when a firms exceeded industry averages for economic success by	
• notifying firms that exceeded four of seven industry averages for 1 year (intended to make firms aware they may be subject to early graduation)	26
• graduating or explaining retention of firms that exceeded four of seven industry trends for 2 consecutive years	4
• Reviewing net worth or graduating firms in which individuals exceeded adjusted net worth limitations	7
• Performing required eligibility reviews due to a change in the firms' ownership	4
• Completing required annual reviews	2

Source: GAO analysis of a random sample of 123 8(a) firms.

SBA's program offices did not maintain comprehensive data on or have a system in place to track complaints on the eligibility of firms participating in the 8(a) program. District staff were not aware of the types and frequency of complaints across the agency. As a result, SBA staff lacked information that could be used with other information to help identify issues relating to program integrity and help improve the effectiveness of SBA oversight. Although complaint data are not a primary mechanism to ensure program eligibility, continuous monitoring is a key component in detecting and deterring fraud.

ABBREVIATIONS

BDMIS	Business Development Management Information System
BDS	Business Development Specialist
DCI	data collection instrument
FPDS-NG	Federal Procurement Data System-Next Generation
IRS	Internal Revenue Service
NAICS	North American Industry Classification System
OBD	Office of Business Development
OFO	Office of Field Operations
OHA	Office of Hearing and Appeals
OIG	Office of Inspector General
SBA	Small Business Administration

March 30, 2010

The Honorable Nydia M. Velázquez
Chairwoman
Committee on Small Business
House of Representatives

Dear Madam Chairwoman:

In fiscal year 2008, the federal government awarded $93.3 billion in contracts to small businesses. The Small Business Administration (SBA) plays an important role in ensuring that small businesses gain access to federal contracting opportunities. Section 8(a) of the Small Business Act is intended to help small businesses owned by socially and economically disadvantaged individuals compete in the economy by providing business development activities, such as counseling and technical assistance, and providing access to federal contracting opportunities. The 8(a) program does not guarantee that participating firms will obtain federal contracts, but the firms are eligible for competitive (for which only 8(a) firms can compete) and sole-source (for which awards are made without competition) federal contracts when certain requirements are met.[1] As of fiscal year 2008, approximately 9,460 firms were in the program.

However, we and others have identified oversight weaknesses in SBA controls that are intended to help ensure that only eligible small businesses gain access to federal contracting opportunities. For example, in congressional hearings on SBA's Historically Underserved Business Zone (HUBZone) Program that you held on July 17, 2008, we highlighted fraud and eligibility control weaknesses in the program that allowed the participation of fictitious and ineligible firms.[2] In a November 2008 report on the 8(a) program, we noted that SBA faced several challenges in its overall administration of the 8(a) program, including competing demands on a limited number of staff. For example, the amount of time staff spent on statutorily mandated annual reviews of all 8(a) firms diminished the amount of time they could devote to business development activities.[3] Our recommendations to SBA included assessing the workloads of business development specialists (BDS) to ensure they could carry out their responsibilities and improving processes to terminate firms. SBA agreed with these recommendations in its written comments on the report.

You asked us to review SBA's internal control procedures for determining 8(a) eligibility, including mentor-protégé arrangements (which provide technical and management assistance as well as assistance in performing federal contracts as a prime contractor through joint-venture arrangements). Specifically, we (1) evaluated the procedures and processes that SBA has implemented to ensure that only eligible firms remain in the 8(a) program, and (2) assessed the extent to which SBA uses external mechanisms, such as complaints by other 8(a) firms, to help ensure that only eligible firms participate.

To address these objectives, we reviewed applicable statutes and the legislative history of the 8(a) program, SBA's regulations and guidance for administering the program, our previous reports, and studies of the program conducted by SBA, the SBA Inspector General, and external organizations. To assess SBA's compliance with its eligibility review procedures, we visited 5 of the 68 SBA districts and reviewed files of 123 randomly sampled 8(a) firms and an additional 13 8(a) firms that had mentor-protégé agreements.[4] For each firm, we reviewed the most recent 2 years of annual reviews for the period 2007-2009, and any existing mentor-protégé agreements, related documents, and correspondence. We developed a data collection instrument to collect key annual review information from each file, including SBA documentation and evidence supporting eligibility criteria such as financial disadvantage. We selected SBA districts based on the size of their 8(a) portfolios of firms with contracts and for geographic diversity. These 5 districts represented 29 percent (or 672) of all active fiscal year 2008 8(a) firms with contracts and 37 percent (or about $2 billion) of contracting obligation dollars. The results of the interviews and sample results cannot be generalized to all 68 district offices; however, the results of our file review sample can be generalized to all files managed by the 5 district offices we included in our review. We also interviewed SBA officials in the Office of Business Development, Division of Program Certification and Eligibility, and district staff to discuss their procedures for determining initial and continuing eligibility, oversight efforts, technical assistance offered, and mechanisms to help identify ineligible firms in the program. Appendix I discusses our scope and methodology in further detail.

We conducted our work in Boston, Massachusetts; Denver, Colorado; San Antonio, Texas; San Francisco, California; and Washington, D.C., between May 2009 and March 2010 in accordance with generally accepted government auditing standards. Those standards require that we plan and perform the audit to obtain sufficient, appropriate evidence to provide a reasonable basis for our findings and conclusions based on our audit objectives. We believe that the evidence obtained provides a reasonable basis for our findings and conclusions based on our audit objectives.

Table 1. Key Eligibility Requirements for 8(a) Program Participation

General requirement	General description[a]
Socially disadvantaged individual	Socially disadvantaged individuals are those who have been subjected to racial or ethnic prejudice or cultural bias because of their identity as members of a group and without regard to their individual qualities. Members of designated groups are entitled to a rebuttable presumption of social disadvantage; other individuals must prove they are socially disadvantaged by a preponderance of the evidence.[b]
Economically disadvantaged individual	Economically disadvantaged individuals are socially disadvantaged individuals whose ability to compete in the free enterprise system has been impaired because of diminished capital and credit opportunities as compared with others in the same or similar business area who are not socially disadvantaged. SBA considers various factors, including adjusted net worth, that for initial eligibility must be less than $250,000, and for continued eligibility must be less than $750,000.
Ownership	8(a) applicants concerns or participants must be at least 51 percent unconditionally and directly owned by one or more socially and economically disadvantaged individuals who are U.S. citizens.
Control	8(a) applicants or participants must be controlled by one or more socially and economically disadvantaged individuals; control includes both strategic policy setting and day-to-day management and administration of business opportunities, and a participant's management and daily operations must also be conducted by one or more disadvantaged individuals.
Small business	The firm must qualify as a small business concern as defined by SBA's size standards, based on the North American Industry Classification System code. This includes affiliations.
Good character	The applicant or participant and all of its principals must have good character. SBA considers such things as criminal conduct and violations of SBA regulations. Debarred or suspended concerns are ineligible.
Potential for success	The applicant or participant must possess reasonable prospects for success in competing in the private sector. Specifically, applicants or participants must show that they have been in the primary industry for 2 years as of date of application by showing revenues on 2 years of tax returns. This requirement may be waived if the firm shows revenues and adequate business management and technical expertise. Other requirements include demonstrating financial capability, technical expertise, contract success, and contract support for the industry of applicant or participant.
U.S. citizenship	Applicant or participant must be a U.S. citizen. Individuals born outside the United States must show proof of citizenship through a U.S. passport or naturalization papers.

Source: GAO.

[a]Does not include tribal firms, Alaskan Native Corporations, Native Hawaiian Organizations, or Community Development Corporation-owned firms.

[b]Designated groups include (1) Black Americans, (2) Hispanic Americans, (3) Native Americans, and (4) Asian Pacific Americans.

BACKGROUND

A firm must meet several initial eligibility requirements to qualify for the 8(a) program (a process known as certification), and then meet other requirements to continue participation. In general, a concern meets the basic requirements for admission to the program if it is a small business that is unconditionally owned and controlled by one or more socially and economically disadvantaged individuals who are of good character and U.S. citizens, and which demonstrates the potential for success. Table 1 summarizes the key requirements.

Participation in the 8(a) program lasts 9 years, and once it is completed, a firm and the individual cannot reapply. The 9-year program tenure is divided into two stages—a developmental stage covering years 1 through 4, and a transitional stage covering years 5 through 9. During the transitional years, firms are required to meet certain activity targets for non-8(a) contracts to ensure they do not develop an unreasonable reliance on the program. Additionally, firms in the 8(a) program are eligible to receive sole-source and competitively awarded set-aside federal contracts.[5]

As part of the 8(a) program, SBA developed the Mentor-Protégé Program, in which experienced firms mentor 8(a) firms to enhance the capabilities of the protégé, provide various forms of business developmental assistance, and improve the protégé's ability to successfully compete for contracts.[6] To qualify initially as a protégé, an 8(a) firm must meet one of three conditions: (1) be in the developmental stage of the 8(a) program, or (2) never have received an 8(a) contract, or (3) be of a size that is less than half the size standard corresponding to its primary standard industry code. The mentor and protégé enter into a written agreement that sets forth the protégé's needs and details the assistance the mentor commits to provide to address those needs. SBA must review and approve the initial agreement and annually evaluate specific mentor-protégé requirements.

SBA's 8(a) program is delivered collaboratively by two departments of SBA. The Office of Business Development (OBD) is responsible for policy formation and the certifications of 8(a) applications, approval of mentor- protégé applications, as well as the approval of existing 8(a) firms that are exiting the program (early graduations, approval of changes of ownership, approval of voluntary withdrawals, approval of terminations, and suspensions). OBD is also responsible for the virtual training and relevant policy briefings provided to SBA staff across the country responsible for executing the 8(a) program on an ongoing basis throughout the year. The Office of Field Operations (OFO) is responsible for supporting the business development specialists, tasked with executing the 8(a) program, who are located in 68 district offices across the country. Selected BDSs will have 8(a) firms assigned to them. The BDSs work directly with 8(a) firms to help prepare business plans; provide technical assistance; review continuing eligibility; coordinate with resource partners that provide counseling, training, loans, and other assistance to small businesses; and coordinate additional assistance and training for firms through another SBA program.[7] BDS staff also conduct annual reviews of the firms' progress in implementing business plans and analyze firms' year-end financial statements, income tax returns, and records of contracting activity for certain compliance requirements, including program eligibility. The purpose of the annual reviews is to determine if firms continue to meet eligibility requirements and to identify business development needs. SBA long has been required by statute to complete annual reviews of all firms.[8] As of fiscal year 2008, SBA had 182.5 full-time-equivalent BDS staff.

While SBA Has Made Improvements to Its 8(a) Annual Reviews, Internal Control Weaknesses and Other Challenges Limit Program Oversight

SBA relies primarily on its annual reviews of 8(a) firms to ensure the continued eligibility of firms enrolled in the program, but we observed inconsistencies and weaknesses in annual review procedures related to determining continued eligibility for the program. For example, we found that SBA did not consistently notify or graduate 8(a) firms that exceeded industry averages for economic success or graduate firms that exceeded the net worth threshold of $750,000. The lack of specific criteria in the current regulations and procedures may have contributed to the inconsistencies that we observed, and SBA has taken steps to clarify some, but not all, of these requirements in a recent proposed rule change. Although BDSs have been challenged to perform all their responsibilities—in particular the statutory requirement to perform annual reviews on 100 percent of 8(a) firms—SBA has not yet assessed its workload to ensure it could carry out its responsibilities as we recommended in our 2008 report.[9] SBA recently has implemented new procedures intended to streamline terminations that may address some of these inconsistencies that we identified with the lack of termination actions taken against firms that did not submit annual review documents as required. Finally, we found that SBA did not maintain an accurate inventory of Mentor-Protégé Program participants and did not document some annual oversight activities of these firms. As a result of these inconsistencies and weaknesses, there is increased potential that firms that no longer meet SBA 8(a) continuing eligibility requirements could be allowed to continue in the program and receive 8(a) contracts.

SBA's Staff Did Not Follow Required Annual Review Procedures Related to Continuing Program Eligibility in about Half of the Files We Reviewed

In a substantial number of cases we reviewed, SBA staff failed to complete required annual review procedures intended to assess fundamental eligibility conditions, such as the firm's net worth, used to determine if participants continue to meet the criteria for being economically disadvantaged. SBA may terminate firms found to be ineligible based on several conditions, including failure to submit required documentation for the annual review process or failure to maintain ownership and control by a disadvantaged individual. SBA may also graduate firms that have successfully completed the program by substantially achieving the targets, objectives, and goals in their business plans prior to the expiration of their program terms, and demonstrated their ability to compete in the marketplace without assistance from the program, or where one or more of the disadvantaged owners no longer are economically disadvantaged (a process known as early graduation). Criteria used to determine continuing eligibility and associated conditions such as economic disadvantage include factors such as personal assets, income, and net worth, while criteria used to determine if a firm successfully met targets and objectives include exceeding industry averages for economic success and owners making excessive withdrawals of company funds or other assets.

We selected a random sample of files from each of the five district offices we visited to determine if district offices' practices for monitoring 8(a) firms were consistent with requirements in regulations, policies, and procedures.[10] Specifically, we estimated that for the five district offices, SBA failed to complete one or more annual required review procedures 55 percent of the time.[11] Our estimates were based on a statistical sample of 123 annual review files from a population of 672 files. Of the 123 files sampled, we identified 67 instances where SBA failed to complete one or more annual review procedures related to eligibility determinations (a 55 percent rate). We tested seven specific annual review requirements relating to continuing eligibility: (1) notifying 8(a) firms that they had exceeded industry averages for economic success, (2) reviewing or graduating 8(a) firms or providing an explanation for retention if they had exceeded industry averages for 2 consecutive years, (3) reviewing net worth or graduating firms in which individuals exceeded the net worth threshold of $750,000, (4) performing eligibility reviews when required for such cases as a change in the firm's ownership, (5) completing the required annual reviews, (6) obtaining required supervisory reviews (and signatures), and (7) imposing remedial actions or obtaining waivers for firms not meeting business activity targets. Table 2 shows information on the extent to which SBA did not complete these annual review requirements.

- *Exceeding industry averages*: Officials from two of the five district offices told us that while the guidance requires notifying 8(a) firms when they have exceeded industry averages for economic success, in practice the districts have been using discretion in notifying the firm after the first year in which this condition occurs. SBA procedures identify exceeding industry averages as a criterion for considering that the firm has met its goals and therefore may no longer be economically disadvantaged. The notification is intended to make participants aware that they may be subject to early graduation proceedings if they exceed industry averages for 2 consecutive years. SBA procedures state that if the firm exceeds industry averages for 2 consecutive years, the participant no longer can be considered economically disadvantaged unless the BDS provides evidence that early graduation is not warranted because of compelling reasons. Officials from these district offices explained that they did not follow these procedures, even though they were required, because they did not think that exceeding industry averages always indicated that participants no longer were economically disadvantaged. The level of staff knowledge about calculations for industry averages and the way in which staff entered the calculations into information systems also may have contributed to failures to meet this requirement. One district office told us it was not clear how the ratios were calculated. We also found errors in the calculations of industry averages at another district office. As we discuss in more detail later in the report, the industry ratio calculations require the BDS to manually enter data into a template that will then calculate the ratio of the firm's performance against that of industry. As shown in table 2, we estimate that staff failed to complete this requirement in about 26 percent of the cases in which a notification letter was required, and in about 4 percent of cases in which industry averages were exceeded for 2 consecutive years.[12]
- *Reviewing net worth or graduating firms in which individuals exceeded adjusted net worth limitations*: One of the clearest indicators of economic disadvantage that SBA uses is the net worth requirement. The regulations specifically state that for

continued eligibility after admission into the program, adjusted net worth must be less than $750,000. Our file review shows that SBA retained an estimated 7 percent of the firms we sampled, in which there was no evidence that staff reviewed the firms' net worth, or retained firms in the program despite their exceeding the net worth limits.[13] Similarly, in our companion report investigating the potential for 8(a) program fraud and abuse, we identified cases in which SBA's files clearly indicated that the firms were not eligible for the 8(a) program, yet SBA staff failed to terminate or graduate the firms from the program.[14] Later in this report we discuss different factors that may have contributed to the retention of firms that clearly appeared to be no longer eligible, including the BDSs' dual role of advocacy for and monitoring of the firms and workload constraints.

- *Completing eligibility reviews*: We estimated that about 4 percent of our file sample contained no evidence that SBA staff had performed a separate required eligibility review.[15] Eligibility reviews are required in cases in which the BDS has reason to question a participant's eligibility, including a change in the firm's ownership (the factor we used for our analysis).[16] Eligibility reviews are critical because they could uncover program participants that no longer met control and ownership eligibility requirements. Representatives from one district office we visited explained that these reviews were a low priority compared with other responsibilities, such as completing annual reviews and initial certifications.
- *Completing annual reviews*: Although SBA is statutorily required to perform annual reviews of 100 percent of 8(a) firms, we estimated that in about 2 percent of our sample, the files contained no evidence that SBA had performed the annual reviews.[17] For example, in two cases, a district office had no record on file that annual reviews had been performed, and in three other cases it had bundled 2 years of reviews because of a change in the internal deadline for completing annual reviews (it skipped an annual review). Our sample of 123 files included only firms that received contracts. As a result, SBA could be unaware that a potentially ineligible firm had received contracts because it had not performed an annual review.

We also identified a few instances in which SBA failed to follow procedural requirements related to the annual reviews, including not consistently documenting supervisory reviews in one district and failing to take remedial actions for firms not meeting their business activity targets.

- *Documenting supervisory reviews*: One district office did not always have the required supervisory signatures on the BDSs' annual review recommendations.[18] Of the 64 files that we sampled in that district, 20 lacked evidence of supervisory review signatures. That is, it appeared that only a BDS recommended a firm's retention or dismissal from the program. Overall, we estimated that SBA did not meet this requirement for about 23 percent of the files in the five district offices.[19] The noncompliance rate in this district may be attributable to the large size of its 8(a) portfolio—about 20 percent of all active fiscal year 2008 8(a) firms. According to district officials, the office also had competing priorities, such as the need to review applications for the Mentor-Protégé Program.[20] Nevertheless, SBA officials were not properly monitoring their staff in these cases. Without the quality controls intended by the supervisory reviews, SBA has limited assurances that the annual reviews are fulfilling their intended purpose.

- *Imposing remedial actions or obtaining waivers for firms not meeting business activity targets*: In about 10 percent of the files we reviewed, district offices did not submit required documentation of remedial actions or a waiver when a firm in the transitional phase of the program did not meet its business activity targets.[21] The remedial action is intended as an incentive for firms to obtain non-8(a) contracts so that they will be prepared to compete in the marketplace without the assistance of the 8(a) program upon graduation. Firms are required to achieve their targets or otherwise are not eligible to receive 8(a) sole-source contracts. By not notifying firms and setting up a remedial plan when required, the BDSs' actions did not appear to be consistent with a key business development activity intended to help firms develop and exit from the program. Furthermore, SBA could be providing opportunities for potentially ineligible firms to receive sole-source contracts.

Although SBA Has Proposed Changes to Its Regulations to Improve Eligibility Determinations, It Still Lacks Specific Guidance for Some Criteria

Our file review results and interviews with district office officials identified numerous instances in which staff did not consistently apply objective standards relating to eligibility determinations. SBA lacks specific criteria in its current regulations and procedures that relate to some of the eligibility requirements such as determining whether a firm should be graduated from the program when it exceeds size standards, industry averages (such as total assets, net sales, working capital, or pretax profit), limits for personal compensation and assets, and excessive withdrawals. Furthermore, SBA guidance directs staff to rely on Office of Hearings and Appeals (OHA) decisions to use as thresholds for eligibility criteria, such as total assets and total compensation, in order to make eligibility determinations. However, as we noted in our related investigation, agency staff did not follow case law consistently.[22]

More specifically, we estimate that 17 percent of the firms had exceeded one or more eligibility criteria for 2 consecutive years, indicating that the firms may have been outgrowing the program, but were recommended by SBA for retention.[23] Although each criterion in and of itself may not be a determinant for early graduation based on the current regulations, each is an important factor in determining if these firms continue to meet eligibility requirements and if they should remain in the program. SBA considers the totality of circumstances to determine whether a firm has met its goals and objectives and should be recommended for early graduation.

- In two cases in one district office, firms had exceeded both average compensation limits and the limits for excessive withdrawals for 2 consecutive years, and still were recommended for retention. The District Director and staff at the district office agreed that the two cases were red flags and that the firms should have been recommended for early graduation or termination.

Table 2. Estimated Percentage of Time That SBA Did Not Complete Selected Annual Review Procedures Relating to 8(a) Eligibility

Requirement not met	Estimated percentage
Taking action when a firm exceeded industry averages for economic success by	
• notifying firms that exceeded four of seven industry averages for 1 year	26
• graduating or explaining retention of firms that exceeded four of seven industry averages for 2 consecutive years	4
Reviewing net worth or graduating firms in which individuals exceeded adjusted net worth limitations	7
Performing required eligibility reviews because of a change in the firms' ownership	4
Completing required annual reviews	2
Documenting supervisory reviews	23
Imposing remedial actions or obtaining waivers for firms not meeting business activity targets	10

Source: GAO.

Note: These estimates are based upon a random sample. See table 5 in appendix I for the associated 95 percent confidence intervals.

- In another example, at a different district office, one firm that, over its 8- year tenure in the 8(a) program. had exceeded (1) industry averages for 5 years (in 2 of these years, the firm could have been considered for early graduation because it exceeded industry averages for 2 consecutive years), (2) compensation limits by having an average salary of more than $200,000 for 2 years, (3) the size standard for its primary North American Industry Classification System code, (4) and made excessive withdrawals in 1 year, but in each year was recommended for retention. This firm had more than $16 million in contracts by its sixth year in the program.[24]

We also found inconsistencies in the use of third-party sources to verify firm-reported data. For instance, two districts told us they reviewed third- party sources such as Internal Revenue Service (IRS) tax transcripts, debarments, and bank information such as withdrawals more routinely as part of their annual review, while two other districts told us they had not performed any third-party verification. At least in part, these inconsistencies can be attributed to lack of specific guidance or criteria regarding the need for third-party verification. Overall, the regulations state that SBA may terminate a firm on the basis of discovering false information, but contain few specific requirements to consult third-party sources for continuing eligibility. For example, participants must submit the IRS 4506-T transcript request form as part of the annual review requirements, which allows SBA to request tax return information. Additionally, the regulations suggest that staff should consult the federal list of debarred and suspended firms, since such firms are ineligible for admission to the 8(a) program. However, we found little evidence of regulatory requirements to obtain other third-party verifications. As noted in our report on the potential for 8(a) program fraud and abuse, validating data against other government or third-party sources is a fraud preventive control meant to keep ineligible firms from entering the program.[25] However, we found that SBA relied heavily on self-reported information from the firms during the initial certification and annual reviews, with limited data validation performed after the firms had entered the program. Additionally, in that report we make a recommendation to assess the feasibility of using additional third-party data sources and site visits, based on random or risk-based criteria, to allow more independent verification of firm-reported data.

SBA recently proposed changes to its Small Business Size and 8(a) Business Development Regulations to address technical issues as well as make more substantive changes resulting from its experience in implementing the current regulations.[26] The agency last updated most of these regulations in 1998. According to a senior SBA official, these changes are intended to help SBA administer the program more effectively. The proposed rules would introduce more detailed guidance and allow for less staff judgment, particularly for the standards that appeared to be associated with the inconsistencies in the annual review procedures in our review of 8(a) case files. For example, the proposed regulations define more specific thresholds for considering an individual's personal assets and compensation, and whether a firm has exceeded size standards. However, the proposed regulations do not introduce more specific requirements relating to exceeding industry averages, and would increase staff flexibility to make judgments relating to excessive withdrawals. Furthermore, the proposed rule changes do not address under what circumstances or to what extent staff should verify firm- reported information with third-party sources. According to SBA, the proposed rules attempt to address areas where the current regulations needed more clarity to ensure consistency with SBA policy as well as areas where the current regulations may unreasonably restrict participants. For example, the proposed rule changes allow for flexibility in judgment regarding excessive withdrawals because SBA believes that it is important that SBA look at the totality of the circumstances in determining whether to include a specific amount as a withdrawal in an effort to prevent some firms from circumventing excessive withdrawal limitations. However, the lack of specific criteria in the current regulations and procedures reduces assurances that the BDSs are making consistent and objective determinations about 8(a) firms' continued eligibility in the program.

SBA Has Not Assessed BDS Workload, a Significant Portion of Which Is Devoted to Annual Reviews, a Fact That Limits Other 8(a) Activities

BDSs devote significant time and resources to complying with the statutory requirement to perform annual reviews on 100 percent of 8(a) firms, a fact that affects the time and resources they can devote to other 8(a) activities. Monitoring the firms' continuing eligibility for the 8(a) program is just one of many responsibilities of the BDS. The BDS also has an advocacy role—maintaining an ongoing responsibility to assist the participant in developing the business to the fullest extent possible. This includes striving to increase both the dollar value and the percentage of 8(a) contracts through communication of procurement activities, training, and counseling. SBA guidance requires the BDS to be the primary provider in helping firms develop business plans, seek loans, and receive counseling on finances, marketing, and management practices.

Officials in all five of the district offices we visited indicated that they met the 100 percent annual review goal for fiscal year 2008 but stated it was a time- and resource-intensive process. For example, district staff estimated that the annual review process consumed from about 40 to 70 percent of their time. BDSs in the district offices told us their individual portfolios ranged from about 30 to 140 firms, depending on their experience level. Three districts noted that BDS turnover resulted in newer staff initially taking more time to process reviews and having smaller portfolios while they were learning their job. One of the districts told us that all available staff in the district office, including staff not assigned to the 8(a) program, had to assist in completing and processing annual reviews in order to meet the review goal. District office staff also told us that they spent a significant amount of time and resources following up with 8(a) firms to have them submit required documentation such as tax and business financial information, which also slowed the review process.[27] District offices indicated that firms that did not have contracts were especially prone to submitting documents late because annual reviews were not a priority for them. [28] These delays, in turn, reduced the amount of time that the BDSs had to spend on firms that exhibited a high risk of misrepresentation or noncompliance with 8(a) eligibility requirements— monitoring necessary for effective program oversight.

Furthermore, in our November 2008 report we noted that demands of the annual review process and resource constraints affected SBA's ability to conduct other program activities.[29] For this report, some districts noted that the annual review goal affected their ability to perform site visits; follow up on issues that warranted more attention, such as red flags identified in the prior year's annual review; and conduct other core business development activities. For instance, the frequency of site visits varied in the five offices we visited. One district office told us that staff were able to conduct site visits for all firms, but another district conducted site visits for about half of its firms, and the remaining districts performed site visits on a limited basis, citing circumstances such as a firm transferring into the district or confirming that a firm was operating at a bona fide place of business. Another district stated that staff do not have time to follow up on red flags such as concerns identified in prior annual reviews because of the emphasis on meeting the annual review goal. Another district also told us that meeting the 100 percent annual review goal has limited the district's ability to get out and educate agencies and firms. This included providing outreach and awareness training. Finally, another district told us the annual reviews have affected its ability to provide developmental assistance and services to address the 8(a) firm's needs. The officials also stated that it was hard to develop working relationships with the firms because of the amount of work reports, projects, and other duties assigned.

Although BDSs have been challenged to perform all their responsibilities, SBA has not yet assessed their workload to ensure they could carry out their responsibilities, as we recommended in our 2008 report.[30] As we reported, SBA did recognize specifically that staffing constraints affected its ability to perform annual reviews. For example, according to its 2006 Performance and Accountability Report, a main contributing factor in the agency's inability to complete annual reviews of all 8(a) firms was a lack of staff resources in the district offices. However, since our previous work in 2008, the emphasis on meeting annual review compliance requirements has strained staff capacity to conduct other core activities for the 8(a) program.

By not assessing BDS workloads, SBA may be bypassing opportunities to better support the mission of the 8(a) program—that is, to develop and prepare small disadvantaged firms for procurement and other business opportunities. In addition, the lack of time to follow up on issues of concern identified in prior-year reviews also undermines SBA's ability to carry out its monitoring responsibilities.

Noncompliant Firms Remain in the 8(a) Program, although Termination Rates Have Increased and New Procedures Should Streamline the Termination Process

On the basis of our file review, we observed instances in which firms were not compliant with 8(a) continuing eligibility requirements related to document submission, but remained in the program. Failure to submit documentation as required is the primary source of noncompliance in the 8(a) program, and is listed in the regulations as an example of good cause for termination.[31] Our file review showed that business development staff frequently accepted incomplete, incorrect, and late documentation from firms and in many cases recommended the noncompliant firms for retention.

Most Firms Submitted Documents Late, but Few Were Terminated for This Cause

Of the 123 firms we tested, 61 percent were noncompliant because of failures to submit documents as required, but staff recommended 3 percent for termination.[32] According to the regulations and procedures, unless participants are also suspended in conjunction with termination proceedings, 8(a) firms remain eligible to receive program benefits and to compete for contracts during termination proceedings, a fact that affords them the opportunity for notice and an opportunity to appeal a termination decision.[33]

During interviews with district office staff, SBA officials acknowledged that some firms took more time than allowed to submit documents. One district office official stated that some firms did not take deadlines seriously and would delay the annual review process. District staff estimated that despite a 30-day deadline, most firms submitted documents within 30 to 45 days and in some cases, up to 60 days after their anniversary date. As mentioned earlier, our file review of 123 firms showed that 49 percent submitted late documentation. In one case, a firm failed to provide documents on time and SBA staff waited 4 months before recommending the firm for termination. After receiving the letter of intent to terminate, the firm took another 2 months to submit the requested documents. SBA then reinstated the firm after a total of 6 months' delinquency. In another case, a firm failed to submit financial information, and business development staff sent the letter of intent to terminate shortly after the firm's deadline passed. SBA waited another 6 months for the firm to submit the required documentation, which turned out to be incomplete, but upon receipt SBA chose to reinstate the firm. The next year, the firm submitted a personal financial statement identical to the previous year's (including dates), but SBA did not take action.

Advocacy Role of BDSs May Contribute to Decisions to Retain Firms

As previously discussed, the BDS's role as an advocate for 8(a) firms may have contributed to a reluctance to terminate firms even if the BDSs had a basis for doing so. Staff in one district office explained they worked with firms before initiating the termination process, in an attempt to avoid termination and to achieve the program mission of preparing disadvantaged firms to compete in the market. Similarly, as noted in our companion report,

SBA staff responsible for annually assessing the eligibility of participants were not actively looking for fraud and abuse in the program—and in some cases, staff supported firms despite eligibility concerns that we raised.[34] Furthermore, our file review provides examples of reluctance to terminate noncompliant firms.

- An 8(a) firm sent an unsigned annual update form 3 months after its deadline. One month later, SBA recommended retention pending receipt of the firm's remaining documents, such as the personal financial statement and tax returns required to demonstrate economic disadvantage. More than 2 months later, the firm provided partial financial documentation. Although SBA's recommendation to retain the firm was based on expecting to eventually receive the firm's remaining documents, these required documents still were outstanding at the time of our file review— which occurred approximately 1.5 years after the initial annual review deadline. As a result, it is unknown whether the firm was eligible to continue participating in the 8(a) program because SBA did not have the needed information to fully assess the financially disadvantaged status of the firm.
- We also have observed instances in which the BDS recommended termination but higher levels of management retained the noncompliant firms in the program. For example, one firm did not submit any annual review documentation and the BDS subsequently recommended it for termination. SBA headquarters disagreed with the determination and chose to retain the firm. However, there was no documentation in the file to explain the basis for this decision.

The Overall Trend in Recent Years Showed an Increase in Terminations

In contrast to these cases, there has been an overall upward trend of firms exiting the 8(a) program through termination or voluntary withdrawal. According to headquarters officials, this trend is a result of the agency's emphasis in recent years on fully meeting its statutory requirements to conduct annual reviews of all firms. By requesting the annual update from the firm in anticipation of completing the annual review, business development staff provide the firms an opportunity to demonstrate basic program compliance.

Table 3. Number of Terminations and Voluntary Withdrawals from the 8(a) Program, 2005-2008

	Fiscal year			
	2005	2006	2007	2008
Number of 8(a) firms	9,470	9,667	9,423	9,462
Number of terminations	130	318	143	537
Percentage terminated	1	3	2	6
Number of voluntary withdrawals	98	95	149	228
Percentage of voluntary withdrawals	1	1	2	2

Source: SBA. Percentages calculated by GAO and rounded to the nearest whole number.

Table 3 shows exit data trends over the past several years. The most recent data indicate a sharp increase in overall terminations and voluntary withdrawals from the 8(a) program. For example, from 2007 to 2008, the number of terminations increased more than threefold. Firms are given the option to withdraw from the program when faced with termination proceedings. SBA headquarters officials explained that some firms prefer a withdrawal instead of a termination on their record, and that the increase in annual reviews also increased this opportunity.

SBA Has Streamlined Termination Procedures, but Has Not Provided Additional Guidance on Conditions That Would Warrant Termination

Effective September 2009, SBA revised its 8(a) program procedures to shorten the termination process and improve internal controls. The procedural change shortens the termination process by 30 days to 135 days.[35] While this falls short of the 75-day reduction SBA officials planned at the time of our November 2008 report, it may succeed in removing more ineligible firms from the program.[36] It remains to be seen what effect this time reduction will have on termination as an eligibility control.

To create the 30-day reduction in the termination procedure, SBA gave the district offices responsibility for sending letters of intent to terminate directly to the firms. Previously, district offices had to submit termination information to headquarters before an intent letter could be mailed. Because of this change, the district office primarily will be in charge of handling new documents the firm submits after receiving the intent letter. By giving the district offices direct responsibility for tracking documentation and communicating with the firm during this phase, SBA intends the process to be more streamlined and straightforward.

While the new procedures reaffirm that firms may be terminated for good cause (as outlined in the program regulations), they provide no additional discussion of what factors or conditions would warrant termination.[37] The 8(a) regulations to which the program procedures refer do provide examples of "good cause," including a "pattern of failure" to make required submissions in a timely manner.[38] However, they provide no examples or criteria for staff to use in determining what constitutes a pattern of failure. The lack of guidance may have contributed to staff decisions to retain or reinstate noncompliant firms.

SBA Plans to Address Compatibility and Functionality Issues in the 8(a) Program's Management Information System to Improve the Efficiency of Annual Reviews

Issues such as data integration, compatibility, and functionality associated with SBA's Business Development Management Information System (BDMIS) for the 8(a) program present challenges that affect effective program management. The agency has been planning to address some data integrity and compatibility issues with BDMIS and E-8(a), a database that provides business status and business contract activity for each participant in the 8(a) program. District office officials indicated that information discrepancies existed between the two systems and required dual data entry of some firm information. SBA officials stated they were reconciling the information in E-8(a) and BDMIS to address discrepancies. Additionally, the officials explained that some information had to be entered separately into the two systems but that they were moving toward a single data feed. The officials expected this change to occur by the end of the third quarter of fiscal year 2010.

As of October 2008, BDMIS was operational in all district offices, allowing 8(a) participants to submit their annual review data electronically and the BDSs to review the documentation electronically. District staff identified benefits and challenges with the implementation of the online annual review process in BDMIS. For example, one district told us that learning the BDMIS system was challenging initially for some 8(a) participants and depended on participants' skills and abilities to enter information into the system. Another district noted that a calculator that assesses a firm's performance in its respective industry was a positive addition to the BDMIS system, allowing the BDS to move through reviews more quickly and efficiently. But the BDS still had to enter firm financial data manually into the calculator, a fact that could increase the likelihood for data entry errors. (The industry ratio calculations require the BDS to manually enter data into a template that calculates the ratio between the firm's performance and that of industry.) For example, at one district we visited, we observed BDS staff manually entering industry performance ratios. District staff also told us that BDMIS's functionality has been limited because the system did not allow staff to access complete firm information, such as contract and historical information, and develop reports. Some district offices also told us that the BDSs' overall workload has not improved and that BDSs spend a significant amount of their time following up with 8(a) firms to submit relevant annual review documents. Despite these challenges, district staff with whom we spoke said BDMIS has been helping to achieve better organization and tracking and anticipated that when fully operational, it could save time and increase transparency.

SBA officials also told us that they have been planning to upgrade BDMIS, which currently is operating in its first version. SBA expects to complete three upgrades by the end of the fiscal year 2010. As part of the upgrades, SBA plans to integrate an existing federal database, the Federal Procurement Data System-Next Generation, that contains contracting information that could help SBA staff to verify firms' contracting information and enable district staff to run reports on their 8(a) firms. District staff told us they rely on the 8(a) firm and federal agencies to provide contract information that is used in the annual review to determine a firm's ratio of 8(a) and non-8(a) contracts. As the firm matures, the goal for 8(a) firms is to increase the amount of non-8(a) contract work and decrease reliance on 8(a) contracts. However, one district explained that contract information such as contracts pending and awarded is recorded in E8(a) but the information is not complete because it does not contain obligation data.

SBA's planned system upgrades could improve the efficiency of annual reviews, particularly because they would likely address duplicative data entry, make more information readily available to staff, and decrease the amount of time spent on annual reviews. However, it is too early to tell whether these changes, once implemented and fully operational, would achieve their intended purposes.

SBA Did Not Have an Accurate Inventory of Mentor-Protégé Firms and Did Not Follow Important Procedures to Properly Monitor the Program

SBA did not maintain an accurate list of Mentor-Protégé Program participants. Specifically, the headquarters office has had difficulty verifying which firms actively participate in the program. An SBA headquarters official responsible for the program stated that staff added firms to a working list based on agreements once they were approved at headquarters. However, this list is not systematically updated when mentor-protégé agreements are extended or dissolved, which occurs at the district office level instead of at headquarters. While the list constituted the agency's only central participation roster for the program, officials stated it was not meant to be used as an eligibility control. Most district offices that we visited kept their own lists, which occasionally were used to verify the headquarters list. One district office we visited did not compile a list of its mentor-protégé participants, but instead relied on individual program files and the list from headquarters for information. When we followed up with other district offices, we found contradictory or inconsistent data in comparison with those of headquarters. For example, the headquarters list showed two active mentor-protégé agreements for a district office that stated it had no active participants.

Because there is no list of active mentor-protégé agreements, SBA may not be able to properly monitor 8(a) protégé firms that submit agreements with more than one mentor, or mentors that submit agreements with more than one 8(a) protégé. Currently, mentors may have more than one protégé if specially approved by SBA. At least 28 mentor firms appeared to have more than one protégé firm, but SBA was unable to confirm whether 5 of these mentors were authorized to do so. SBA has proposed new regulations that would limit mentor firms to a maximum of 3 protégé firms at a time.[39] SBA also has proposed changes to the regulations that would allow protégé firms to have more than 1 mentor under limited circumstances.[40] To date, the regulations have prohibited protégé firms from having more than one mentor at a time.[41] However, we identified 12 protégé firms that appeared to have 2 mentors at the same time. SBA indicated that some of these relationships had been dissolved, but these firms remained on its list of approved mentor-protégé agreements. The current lack of data limits the agency's ability to fully monitor the Mentor- Protégé Program. As a result, unauthorized partnerships could receive 8(a) set-aside contracts.

Maintaining an accurate list of firms participating in SBA's Mentor-Protégé Program is an important control mechanism to ensure participation only by eligible firms and that the agency has relevant and reliable information for management. Monitoring eligibility for the Mentor-Protégé Program is especially important because participants were more successful in earning proceeds from federal contracts in fiscal year 2008 than the larger pool of 8(a) firms.[42] Mentor-protégé participants averaged $4.1 million in sales compared with $2.4 million for other 8(a) firms. As a group, these participants earned $638 million in fiscal year 2008.

In addition to finding high-level data inconsistencies, including unverifiable participation lists and mentors and protégés with multiple agreements, we found cases in which SBA failed to properly document analysis and monitoring of the Mentor-Protégé Program. As part of our file review across five district offices, we tested 20 8(a) firms with mentor- protégé agreements. We focused on initial agreement information, annual updates, and recommendations. Our file review results showed that SBA staff failed to comply with certain initial review and annual review procedures for participants in 6 of the 20 mentor-protégé cases that we reviewed. These procedures include providing a written eligibility analysis and ensuring a signed supervisory review of the BDS's recommendation. In our interviews with district office officials, we also found that Mentor- Protégé eligibility information had not been incorporated into BDMIS. District offices were not able to integrate initial approval recommendations and annual review monitoring with the firm's general 8(a) eligibility information held electronically in BDMIS. As a result of the lack of documentation and the data limitations discussed above, SBA has not been able to properly oversee this program.

SBA Lacks a Formal Mechanism to Collect and Analyze Complaint Data Related to 8(a) Eligibility

SBA can receive information and complaints from other 8(a) firms, disgruntled 8(a) employees, and anonymous sources, but SBA does not maintain comprehensive data about complaints such as allegations that certain 8(a) firms may not comply with eligibility requirements.[43] Although complaint information is not the primary mechanism for ensuring continuing program eligibility, it can be an additional tool for identifying fraud or wrongdoing. As we noted in our other GAO investigative report on the 8(a) program, detection and monitoring are crucial elements in a well-designed fraud prevention system.[44] Complaints and other allegations regarding the eligibility of firms in the program can serve as red flags for SBA staff to take additional steps to ensure that firms continue to meet program requirements.

District office officials told us that complaints received at the district receive an initial review (to determine if they warrant follow-up), which may include follow- up with other agencies and the specific firm to gather more information. SBA's standard operating procedures instruct staff to refer to SBA's Office of Inspector General (OIG) any possible criminal violations and other wrongdoing involving SBA programs, such as knowingly making or using a statement or document that is false, fictitious, or fraudulent. If warranted, complaints are to be referred to SBA's OIG for possible investigation. One district told us that the district counsel reviews the evidence, and if the case has merit, the information is referred to the SBA OIG for further investigation. Two other districts told us the BDS will seek more information by checking with the contracting agency involved regarding the nature of the complaint or contacting the 8(a) firm for clarification before making a referral to OIG.

However, because district staff do not collect and maintain comprehensive complaint information involving 8(a) firms, staff are not aware of the types and frequency of complaints across the agency, including potential eligibility concerns. Specifically, none of the five districts that we visited were able to provide us with a list of complaints or allegations that they received over the past year regarding the potential ineligibility of 8(a) firms in their districts. While OIG maintains general complaint information such as the name of the 8(a) firm and type of complaint, a senior OIG official told us that 8(a) complaints involving a single company generally did not rank high in priority for a review because of resource limitations and other priorities but that it might be considered in the OIG's work- planning effort. OIG officials explained that the OIG ultimately also could refer a case to the U.S.

Attorney for prosecution, but that the threshold for prosecutions was high and many cases did not meet that threshold.

As a result, it appears that complaint data involving 8(a) firms are not being utilized to the full extent as a means to identify potential areas of concern such as program eligibility issues. Without a standard process for collecting and analyzing complaints, SBA staff—and the agency as a whole—lack information that could be used to help identify issues relating to program integrity and help improve the effectiveness of SBA oversight.

CONCLUSIONS

SBA's 8(a) program provides opportunities for participating firms to collectively receive billions of dollars in federal contracts on a competitive or noncompetitive basis. As a result, it is critical that SBA's annual reviews of 8(a) firms are performed effectively to help ensure that only eligible firms are allowed to continue to participate in and benefit from the program. However, our file review at five district offices found inconsistencies in the annual review policies and procedures followed by SBA staff related to program eligibility. This suggests a need for greater monitoring by SBA and potentially a need for more guidance and training to ensure greater consistency in the performance of required annual review procedures.

Furthermore, the lack of specific criteria in the current regulations related to eligibility determinants such as size standards and industry averages and the dual roles of the BDSs—providing oversight and being an advocate for the firm—may have contributed to the variation in annual review practices we observed. By clarifying guidance, further detailing or expanding procedures, and emphasizing the importance of quality controls, SBA could help eliminate ambiguities, improve the quality of reviews, and provide clearer criteria against which to judge eligibility and ensure that only intended recipients benefit from program participation.

Workload constraints of BDS staff may have been a contributing factor to the inconsistencies and deficiencies identified in our review of annual review files in the five districts that we visited. While the annual review process is central to ensuring program integrity, SBA's statutory requirement to conduct annual reviews of 100 percent of 8(a) firms also is time- and resource-intensive. The workload demands associated with the annual review process likely have affected the quality of these reviews as well as detracted from the time staff have been able to devote to other core 8(a) program responsibilities, ranging from technical assistance to mentoring. As we previously recommended and continue to believe, an assessment of the BDS workload could help ensure the BDSs can carry out their responsibilities and determine what mechanisms can be used to prioritize or redistribute their workload. Such an assessment also would be helpful in assessing the multiple roles and responsibilities of BDS staff, including ways to mitigate the conflicting roles of business development, and ensuring that only eligible firms are allowed to participate in the program. In a fiscally challenged environment and with workload constraints as a constant, it is important that the agency review staff and resource allocations and identify process efficiencies wherever possible.

Changes that SBA recently made to termination procedures, coupled with the increase in terminations overall, may help to alleviate workload constraints for district office staff. As we noted in our November 2008 report, the inefficient termination process consumed scarce SBA resources and may have affected business development activities. District staff could take advantage of the revised, more efficient termination process to minimize time spent waiting for documents from firms and free up time for business development and other activities. However, SBA retained some firms that repeatedly did not submit required documentation for annual reviews. By monitoring the implementation of regulations relating to documentation requirements, SBA could help staff more readily identify firms for termination, reduce the time staff spent "chasing" documentation, and help improve the timeliness of annual reviews. Additionally, by providing specific examples in the regulations or procedures of what is considered to be a pattern of failure, staff would be able to better justify termination decisions.

The agency also faces a number of challenges in effectively monitoring and managing the Mentor-Protégé Program, which is an important subset of the 8(a) program. For example, SBA headquarters and district offices could not agree or provide current and basic information on the total number of mentor-protégé agreements. Maintaining accurate information on participants is a basic and important control mechanism to monitor 8(a) protégé firms that submit agreements with more than one mentor, or mentors that submit agreements with more than one 8(a) protégé. By developing a centralized process to collect and maintain information on program participants, SBA would have a critical tool necessary to properly monitor and oversee the program.

Finally, SBA also has an opportunity to develop another tool that could enhance its oversight of the 8(a) program. Currently, SBA lacks comprehensive data on complaints involving 8(a) firms because it does not systematically collect and analyze information on the nature of the complaints and their disposition. Although complaint data are not a primary mechanism to ensure program eligibility, continual monitoring is a key component in detecting and deterring fraud. By developing an agencywide process for documenting and analyzing complaints, SBA would have an information resource that could be used with other efforts to provide reasonable assurance that only eligible firms are participating in the program.

Recommendations for Executive Action

To improve the monitoring of and procedures used in assessing the continuing eligibility of firms to participate in and benefit from the 8(a) program, we recommend that the Administrator of SBA take the following six actions:

- To help ensure greater consistency in carrying out annual review procedures and improve the overall quality of these reviews, we recommend that the SBA Administrator monitor, and provide additional guidance and training to, district offices on the procedures used to determine continuing eligibility, including
  - taking appropriate action when firms exceed four of seven industry size averages, including notifying firms the first year and enforcing procedures relating to early graduation of firms that exceed industry averages for 2 consecutive years;

- obtaining appropriate supervisory signatures to finalize annual review decisions;
- submitting remedial action or a waiver for firms in the transition phase that did not meet business activity targets;
- graduating firms that exceed the net worth threshold of $750,000;
- performing timely eligibility reviews in required cases; and
- completing required annual reviews.

- To help reduce inconsistencies between districts and BDS staff in annual review procedures requiring judgment, we recommend that SBA review its existing 8(a) program regulations and its proposed changes with the intent of providing additional criteria and examples for staff when assessing key areas of program eligibility and determining whether a firm should be graduated from the program when it exceeds size standards, industry averages (such as total assets, net sales, working capital, or pretax profit), and limits for personal compensation and assets, and excessive withdrawals.
- To help address competing demands on 8(a) resources, SBA should assess the workload of business development specialists to ensure that they can carry out all their responsibilities. As part of this assessment, SBA should review the roles and responsibilities of the BDSs to minimize or mitigate to the extent possible the potentially conflicting roles of advocacy for firms in the program with the responsibility of ensuring that only eligible firms are allowed to continue to participate in the program. In addition, SBA should review the size of the 8(a) portfolio for all business development specialists and, if necessary, determine what mechanisms should be used to prioritize or redistribute their workload.
- To reduce the practice of retaining firms that fail to submit annual review documentation as required, SBA should monitor the implementation of regulations relating to termination to see if they are achieving their purpose or whether business development staff need further guidance in interpreting the regulations. SBA should consider providing specific examples of what might be considered a pattern of failure to submit documentation as required.
- To better manage and monitor participation in the Mentor-Protégé Program, including compliance with the number of allowable mentor and protégé firms, SBA should develop a centralized process to collect and maintain up-to-date and accurate data on 8(a) firms participating in the Mentor-Protégé Program. SBA should consider incorporating information on Mentor-Protégé approvals, extensions, and dissolutions in existing electronic data systems used for the annual review process.
- To more fully utilize and leverage third-party complaints to identify potentially ineligible firms participating in the 8(a) program, design and implement a standard process for documenting and analyzing complaint data.

APPENDIX I. SCOPE AND METHODOLOGY

Our objectives were to (1) evaluate the procedures and processes that the Small Business Administration (SBA) has implemented to ensure that only eligible firms remain in the 8(a) program, and (2) assess the extent to which SBA used external mechanisms, such as complaints by other 8(a) firms, to help ensure that only eligible firms participate in the program.

To evaluate the procedures and processes that SBA has implemented to help to ensure that only eligible firms participate in the 8(a) program, we reviewed applicable statutes and the legislative history of the 8(a) program, SBA's regulations and guidance for administering the program, our previous reports, and studies of the program conducted by SBA, SBA's Office of Inspector General (OIG), and external organizations. Additionally, we randomly sampled files for review at 5 selected district offices to assess SBA's compliance with its eligibility review procedures for the 8(a) and Mentor-Protégé programs.[45] We selected the 5 district offices based on the high dollar value of contract obligations in these districts and geographic diversity.[46] Our sample population included firms that were active in the 8(a) program in fiscal year 2008 and had 8(a) contracts in fiscal year 2008. We identified these firms by using SBA's list of active fiscal year 2008 8(a) firms and matching these data to the Federal Procurement Data System-Next Generation (FPDS-NG) to determine which of those firms had obligations. For our review, we excluded those firms that joined the program during calendar year 2008, because these firms would not yet have been in the program long enough to have an annual review on file.[47] We also excluded Alaska Native Corporations, tribally owned, Native Hawaiian Organization-owned, other Native American-owned, and Community Development Corporation-owned firms because of the different 8(a) eligibility requirements applied to these entities. The results of our sample are generalizable only to the 5 district offices. We randomly sampled 123 8(a) firms from our population, and an additional 13 8(a) firms that had mentor-protégé agreements, which we judgmentally selected from SBA's list of Mentor-Protégé firms as of September 2009.[48] For each firm, we reviewed its most recent 2 years of annual reviews for the period 2007-2009, and any existing mentor-protégé agreements, related documents, and correspondence. We developed a data collection instrument (DCI) to collect key annual review data from each file. The DCI was pretested in 2 district offices and modified based on these tests. We also analyzed mentor- protégé data to identify protégé firms that may have multiple mentors, which are against regulation, and mentor firms that may have multiple protégés, which is allowable only when specially authorized by SBA. To identify these cases, we sorted the data by firm name and searched for duplicate matches. A total of 672 firms met our study criteria and are shown in table 4.

We randomly selected the indicated number of cases within each regional office. We treated this as a stratified random sample and weighted the sample cases accordingly for our analysis. Our estimates are statistically representative for all files maintained in these 5 SBA regional offices.

Table 4. Total Number of Files and Sample Sizes at Five Selected District Offices

SBA field office	Number of files	Sample size
Washington, D.C.	479	64
Denver	70	14
San Antonio	56	15
Massachusetts	27	15
San Francisco	40	15
Total	**672**	**123**

Source: GAO.

Table 5. 95 Percent Confidence Intervals for Statistical Sample Estimates in Table 2.

Requirement not met	Estimated percentage	Lower endpoint of 95 percent confidence interval	Upper endpoint of 95 percent confidence interval
Taking action when a firms exceeded industry averages by			
notifying firms that exceeded four of seven industry averages for 1 year	26	19	35
graduating or explaining retention of firms that exceeded four of seven industry averages for 2 consecutive years	4	1	9
Reviewing net worth or graduating firms in which individuals exceeded adjusted net worth limitations	7	3	13
Performing required eligibility reviews	4	1	9
Completing required annual reviews	2	1	7
Documenting supervisory reviews	23	15	31
Imposing remedial actions or obtaining waivers for firms not meeting business activity targets	10	5	17

Source: GAO.

Because we treated our file review as a stratified random sample, we assumed our sample was only one of a large number that could have been drawn. Because each sample could have provided different estimates, we expressed our confidence in the precision of our particular sample's results as a 95 percent confidence interval. This is the interval that would contain the actual population value for 95 percent of the samples we could have drawn. As a result, we are 95 percent confident that each of the confidence intervals based on the file review includes the true values in the sample population. The 95 percent confidence intervals for each of the estimates are summarized in table 5.

We performed appropriate data reliability procedures for our sample testing at the 5 district offices and analysis of inappropriate mentor- protégé relationships. We compared SBA data with data from other sources such as FPDS-NG and the Central Contractor Registry, performed electronic testing, reviewed related documentation and internal controls, and performed interviews with knowledgeable agency officials. We determined that the data were sufficient to perform our sample testing and project our results to the 5 district offices in our population of 8(a) firms. We also determined through these methods that data relating to mentor- protégé participants were sufficient to report on descriptive statistics of mentor-protégé firms with contracts. The discrepancies we found in the general list of mentor-protégé participants are documented within the report.

To assess the extent that external mechanisms exist, such as complaints by other 8(a) firms, to help ensure that only eligible firms participate, we interviewed agency and SBA Office of Inspector General officials, and we reviewed SBA OIG complaint data. We also interviewed officials in SBA's Office of Business Development, Division of Program

Certification and Eligibility, and district office staff to discuss their procedures for determining initial and continuing eligibility, oversight efforts, technical assistance offered, and mechanisms to help identify ineligible firms in the program.

We conducted our work in Boston, Massachusetts; Denver, Colorado; San Antonio, Texas; San Francisco, California; and Washington, D.C., between May 2009 and March 2010 in accordance with generally accepted government auditing standards. Those standards require that we plan and perform the audit to obtain sufficient, appropriate evidence to provide a reasonable basis for our findings and conclusions based on our audit objectives. We believe that the evidence obtained provides a reasonable basis for our findings and conclusions based on our audit objectives.

APPENDIX II. COMMENTS FROM THE SMALL BUSINESS ADMINISTRATION

March 10, 2010

Mr. William B. Shear
Director
Financial Markets and Community Investment
U.S. Government Accountability Office
Washington, DC 20548

Dear Mr. Shear:

The U.S. Small Business Administration (SBA) is pleased to provide a response addressing the issues outlined in your draft Government Accountability Office (GAO) Report Number: GAO-10-353, entitled, "Steps Have Been Taken to Improve Administration of the 8(a) Program, but Key Controls for Continued Eligibility Need Strengthening."

BACKGROUND:

As you are aware, the SBA's 8(a) Business Development (BD) program seeks to foster the business growth and development of firms deemed socially and economically disadvantaged and offers a number of programmatic benefits which include advocacy support, management, technical, financial, and procurement assistance. While there is a continual need to implement policy and procedural guidance to ensure proper internal controls, oversight, monitoring and compliance, SBA is encouraged by the significant strides that the agency has already made along these lines.

SBA also recognizes that there are weaknesses and areas that require immediate action and implementation of corrective measures. Since the timeframe in which this GAO audit was conducted, the Office of Business Development (OBD) has already implemented (or will implement) corrective measures that will address all of the recommendations outlined in this GAO Report.

One significant step toward addressing many of these weaknesses occurred in October 2009, when SBA announced in the *Federal Register* proposed regulatory revisions aimed at strengthening opportunities for disadvantaged small businesses to benefit from its 8(a) BD program. The proposed 8(a) regulation changes are the result of the first comprehensive review of the 8(a) BD program in a number of years. The rules cover a variety of areas of the program, ranging from providing further clarification on determining economic disadvantage to requirements on Joint Ventures and the Mentor-Protégé program. The public comment period was extended to January 28, 2010, in an effort to obtain comments from our broad customer base as well as other stakeholders.

The 8(a) BD program has a proven track record as an effective program for helping socially and economically disadvantaged small businesses gain access to training and contracting opportunities to help them grow, create jobs and ultimately succeed in the marketplace upon leaving the program. We believe that the proposed rule changes build on that foundation of success, and will strengthen the program and maximize its benefits for eligible small businesses.

The OBD, in conjunction with the Office of Field Operations, will be conducting an extensive National Training Conference in June 2010 that will include all of the Business Development (BD) personnel from our 68 district offices. This National Training Conference will emphasize all aspects of continuing eligibility for 8(a) BD participants.

The following is SBA's response to the six recommendations made by GAO regarding SBA's need to improve the monitoring of and procedures used in assessing the continuing eligibility of firms to participate and benefit from the 8(a) program. Some of the responses include corrective measures already implemented and actions that are planned to be implemented in the near future.

GAO's RECOMMENDATIONS FOR EXECUTIVE ACTION:

RECOMMENDATION 1:

To help ensure greater consistency in carrying out annual review procedures and improve the overall quality of these reviews, we recommend that the SBA Administrator should monitor, and provide additional guidance and training to district offices on the procedures used to determine continuing eligibility, including:

- taking appropriate action when firms exceed four of the seven industry size averages, including notifying firms the first year and enforcing procedures relating to early graduation of firms that exceed industry averages for 2 consecutive years;
- obtaining appropriate supervisory signatures to finalize annual review decisions;
- submitting remedial action or waiver for firms in the transition phase that did not meet business activity targets;
- graduating firms that exceeded the net worth threshold of $750,000;
- performing timely eligibility reviews in required cases; and
- completing required annual reviews.

SBA's RESPONSE TO RECOMMENDATION 1:

SBA agrees with the recommendation and has already begun implementing corrective measures.

In an effort to ensure consistency and improve the overall quality of annual reviews, the OBD has implemented a comprehensive Training Curriculum that consists of training sessions (utilizing Ready Talk conferencing) for BD personnel on a variety of programmatic issues and topics. This training (which is recorded and archived on a share portal for access by BD personnel) covered the following aspects of the annual review process:

- an outline of the steps involved in the annual review process;
- procedures related to conducting a "Personal Asset Test" to include reviewing and analyzing financial statements;
- the importance of financial analysis in determining business trends and other growth indicators;
- excessive withdrawals of an individual 8(a) participant or an 8(a) firm
- calculating a disadvantaged individuals average two year income for S Corporations, Partnerships and LLC's

OBD revised and issued Chapter 5 *"Participant Review Process"* of the 8(a) BD program Standard Operation Procedure 80 05 3 (SOP) to provide guidance regarding the process for obtaining appropriate supervisory signatures to finalize annual review decisions; conducting eligibility reviews, where appropriate, and the process for recommending firms for early graduation, where appropriate.

The OBD conducted a training sessions for all BD personnel on October 15 and 22, 2009, solely on newly issued Chapter 10 of the 8(a) BD program SOP shortly after its release.

In addition, the OBD has issued the following procedural and policy guidance to ensure uniformity as it relates to annual review processing:

- SBA Information Notice (issued 5/15/09), "8(a) Business Development Program Application and Continuing Eligibility Processing"

- SBA Procedural Notice (issued 11/18/08), "Oversight of 8(a) Program Participants"

We will evaluate the guidance outlined in the newly revised Chapter 10 (*Leaving the 8(a) Business Development Program*) of the 8(a) SOP concerning procedures related to early graduation of firms that exceed industry averages for two consecutive years and take appropriate action, where necessary.

RECOMMENDATION 2:

To help reduce inconsistencies between districts and BDS staff in annual review procedures requiring judgment, we recommend that SBA review its existing 8(a) program regulations and its proposed changes with the intent of providing additional criteria and examples for staff when assessing key areas of program eligibility and determining whether a firm should be graduated from the program when it exceeds size standards, industry averages (such as total assets, net sales, working capital, pre-tax profit), and limits for personal compensation and assets, and excessive withdrawals.

SBA'S RESPONSE TO RECOMMENDATION 2:

SBA agrees with this recommendation.

We will continue to conduct training on this topic as well as revise the applicable sections of the 8(a) BD SOP to provide examples that will assist staff in assessing key areas and making determinations – after analyzing a myriad of factors that include taking into consideration that the 8(a) Program is a business development program – as to whether or not early graduation is appropriate.

RECOMMENDATION 3:

To help address competing demands on 8(a) resources, SBA should assess the workload of business development specialists to ensure that they can carry out all their responsibilities. As part of this assessment, SBA should review the roles and responsibilities of the BDS to minimize or mitigate to the extent possible the potentially conflicting roles of advocacy for firms in the program with the responsibility of ensuring that only eligible firms are allowed to continue to participate in the program. In addition, SBA should review the size of the 8(a) portfolio for all business development specialists and, if necessary, determine what mechanisms should be used to prioritize or redistribute their workload.

SBA's RESPONSE TO RECOMMENDATION 3:

SBA agrees with this recommendation.

SBA's O FO will assess the workload of BDSs to review roles and responsibilities and evaluate staffing levels.

A key component of SBA's mission is advocacy support on behalf of small businesses. To that end, 8(a) BD program participants are small businesses first and foremost, who happen to have an additional tool (8(a) certification) to increase their competitive viability in the Federal marketplace. These 8(a) BD program participants often require advocacy support as well as individual business counseling assistance. The BDS is the primary individual responsible for servicing an 8(a) BD program participant during its nine year term and, as such, cultivates a business and professional relationship with that 8(a) BD program participant. There are often occasions where the BDS works with the 8(a) BD program participant to recommend technical assistance and as a result of that technical assistance, the participant (who may not have met its business activity target) will be able to obtain a non-8(a) contract award and; thereby meet the required business activity target. Because the 8(a) BD program is a business development program, the BDS must evaluate and assess the totality of the circumstance and in some cases, make a judgment call.

RECOMMENDATION 4:

To reduce the practice of retaining firms that fail to submit annual review documentation as required, SBA should monitor the implementation of regulations relating to termination to see if they are achieving their purpose or whether business development staff needs further guidance in interpreting the regulations. SBA should consider providing specific examples of what might be considered a pattern of failure to submit documentation as required.

SBA's RESPONSE TO RECOMMENDATION 4:

SBA agrees with this recommendation.

SBA will continue to conduct training on the annual review and termination actions reinforcing the requirements of the regulations and the guidance provided in Chapters 5 and 10 of the 8(a) SOP whereby a pattern of failure (repeated failures to respond to SBA's requests for required submissions or responses in a timely manner) is established.

RECOMMENDATION 5:

To better manage and monitor participation in the Mentor-Protégé Program, including compliance with the number of allowable mentors and protégé firms, SBA should develop a centralized process to collect and maintain up-to-date and accurate data on 8(a) firms participating in the Mentor-Protégé Program.

SBA's RESPONSE TO RECOMMENDATION 5:

SBA agrees with this recommendation.

The OBD has already begun to develop a routine centralized process to collect and maintain accurate data related to 8(a) BD program participants in the Mentor-Protégé Program. We are developing a Procedural Notice that will be issued to the BD field staff outlining this process.

RECOMMENDATION 6:

To more fully utilize and leverage third-party complaints to identify potentially ineligible firms participating in the 8(a) program, design and implement a standard process for documenting and analyzing complaint data.

SBA's RESPONSE TO RECOMMENDATION 6:

SBA agrees with this recommendation.

We will work with the Office of General Counsel to develop a central repository for third-party complaints that will be accessible on the agency's homepage to provide a centralized location for such complaints. SBA will then maintain this data for follow-up and appropriate action, as necessary.

Again, thank you for the opportunity to provide comments on this draft GAO Report. My staff and I look forward to working with you in resolving the issues outlined in this draft GAO Report as we seek to strengthen the SBA's 8(a) BD program.

If you have additional questions or comments, please contact me directly.

Sincerely,

Joseph G. Jordan
Associate Administrator
Office of Government Contracting
and Business Development

End Notes

[1] Section 8(a) authorizes SBA to enter into contracts with government agencies and to, in turn, contract with qualified 8(a) firms for the performance of its requirements. SBA enters into partnership agreements with government agencies that delegate its contracting functions to the agencies and establish the basic procedures for expediting the award of 8(a) contract requirements.

[2] GAO, *HUBZone Program: SBA's Control Weaknesses Exposed the Government to Fraud and Abuse*, GAO-08-964T (Washington, D.C.: July 17, 2008), and *Small Business Administration: Additional Actions Are Needed to Certify and Monitor HUBZone Businesses and Assess Program Results*, GAO-08-975T (Washington, D.C.: July 17, 2008). In the HUBZone program, certain small businesses located in economically distressed communities (Historically Underutilized Business Zones) may be eligible for set-aside and sole-source contracts.

[3] GAO, *Small Business Administration: Agency Should Assess Resources Devoted to Contracting and Improve Several Processes in the 8(a) Program*, GAO-09-16 (Washington, D.C.: Nov. 21, 2008).

[4] In addition to the 13 8(a) firms with mentor-protégé arrangements, another 7 firms in our sample of 123 had mentor-protégé agreements on file.

[5] Competitively awarded contracts can be set aside for 8(a) firms if there is a reasonable expectation that at least two 8(a) firms will submit offers and the award can be made at a fair price. Sole-source contracts can be awarded when the dollar thresholds are $5.5 million or less for acquisitions involving manufacturing and $3.5 million or less for all other acquisitions.

[6] Under the program, the mentor and protégé may operate a joint venture as a small business for any government contract.

[7] Through the 7(j) Management and Technical Assistance Program, SBA provides qualifying businesses with counseling and training in the areas of financing, business development, management, accounting, bookkeeping, marketing, and other small business operating concerns. The 7(j) program by its terms applies to 8(a) firms.

[8] Pub. L. No. 100-656, §209, 102 Stat. 3853, 3863 (1988), codified at 15 U.S.C. §637 (a)(6)(B). The requirement to complete annual reviews of all program participants, along with other provisions in the law, was intended to prevent ineligible firms from participating in the program.

[9] GAO-09-16.

[10] Criteria for our selection of five district offices (Boston, Massachusetts; Denver, Colorado; San Antonio, Texas; San Francisco, California; and Washington, D.C.) included the dollar amount of contract obligations in the districts and geographic diversity. See appendix I for more information on our scope and methodology.

[11] Because these estimates are based on a probability sample, they are subject to sampling error. The 95 percent confidence interval for SBA not complying with one or more annual review procedures is (46, 64) percent of all the cases in the five offices.

[12] The corresponding 95 percent confidence intervals for these estimates are (19, 35) and (1, 9).

[13] The 95 percent confidence interval for this estimate is (3, 13).

[14] GAO, 8(a) *Program: Fourteen Ineligible Firms Received $325 Million in Sole Source and Set-aside Contracts*, GAO-10-425 (Washington, D.C.: March 30, 2010).

[15] The 95 percent confidence interval for this estimate is (1, 9).

[16] Upon receipt of specific and credible information alleging that a participant no longer meets the eligibility requirements for continued program eligibility, SBA will review the concern's eligibility for continued participation in the program. As part of an annual review, each participant must certify that it meets the eligibility requirements and that there have been no changed circumstances that could adversely affect its eligibility, and may be required to submit supporting documentation.

[17] The 95 percent confidence interval for this estimate is (1, 7).

[18] We identified one case in another district office without the required supervisory signature.

[19] The 95 percent confidence interval for this estimate is (15, 31).

[20] Applications to the Mentor-Protégé Program are time-sensitive and therefore are prioritized above annual reviews. We discuss additional workload constraints in greater detail later in this report.

[21] The business activity targets require a certain ratio of revenues from 8(a) versus non-8(a) contracts, depending on how many years the firm has been in the program. The 95 percent confidence interval for this estimate is (5, 17).

[22] GAO-10-425.

[23] The 95 percent confidence interval for this estimate is (11, 25).

[24] This includes both 8(a) and non-8(a) contracts.

[25] GAO-10-425.

[26] SBA, *Small Business Size Regulations; 8(a) Business Development/Small Disadvantaged Business Status Determinations*, 74 Fed. Reg. 55694 (proposed Oct. 28, 2009) (to be codified at 13 C.F.R. pts. 121 and 124). The public comment period for the proposed regulations ended on January 28, 2010, and, according to an SBA official, the regulations are expected to be finalized by the end of fiscal year 2010.

[27] Annual review documents are due each year, 30 days after a firm's certification date, and BDSs are required to complete the review within 30 days after receiving all required documentation. However, our file review of 123 8(a) firms found about 49 percent of the firms submitted documentation late. The corresponding 95 percent confidence interval for this estimate is (40, 57).

[28] About 50 percent of the firms listed on the 8(a) participant list for fiscal year 2008 had active contracts, which include any contract having a modification in fiscal year 2008 even if those modifications were non-monetary.

[29] GAO-09-16.

[30] GAO-09-16.

[31] According to 8(a) regulations, SBA may, but is not required to, terminate a firm for good cause, one example of which is a "pattern of failure" to make required submissions in a timely manner. 13 C.F.R. § 124.303(a)(7).

[32] The corresponding 95 percent confidence intervals for these estimates are (52, 69) and (1, 8), respectively.

[33] SBA may suspend a participant when it is determined that suspension is needed to protect the interests of the federal government, such as cases in which information showing a clear lack of program eligibility or conduct indicating a lack of business integrity exists. This includes cases in which the firm or one of its principals submitted false statements to the government, including false information in its 8(a) application. The criteria that make an 8(a) firm eligible for termination are not the same as the causes for suspension. See 13 C.F.R. § 124.303 and Federal Acquisition Regulation § 9.407-2.

[34] GAO-10-425.

[35] Effective from September 2009, termination proceedings may last approximately 135 days from the firm's anniversary date, including the time the firm is allowed to appeal its case to OHA.

[36]GAO 09-16.

[37]SBA Standard Operating Procedures 80 05 3B, effective September 22, 2009.

[38]13 C.F.R. § 124.303(a)(7).

[39] SBA, *Small Business Size Regulations; 8(a) Business Development/Small Disadvantaged Business Status Determinations*, 74 Fed. Reg. 55694, 55707 (proposed Oct. 28, 2009) (to be codified at 13 C.F.R Pt. 121 and 124).

[40]74 Fed. Reg. 55694, 55708.

[41]13 C.F.R. § 124.520(c)(3).

[42] Excludes Alaska Native Corporations, Native Hawaiian Organizations, tribally owned firms, and firms owned by Community Development Corporations.

[43] SBA officials stated that there was a great deal of "self-policing" in the program, since firms were aware of which competitor has received contracts.

[44] GAO-10-425.

[45] The 8(a) program is managed from 68 district offices, each one containing the paper documents we wanted to evaluate. Because our compliance review required a site visit to a district office to review the file documents for a particular firm, we narrowed the scope of our review down to 5 district offices: Washington, D.C., San Antonio, Denver, Massachusetts, and San Francisco SBA district offices.

[46] The 5 districts we selected represented 29 percent (or 672) of all active fiscal year 2008 8(a) firms with contracts and 37 percent (or about $2 billion) of the contracting obligation dollars.

[47] SBA is required by statute to conduct annual reviews to monitor continuing eligibility of 8(a) firms. These reviews begin 1 year after the firm's certification date.

[48] In addition to the 13 8(a) firms with mentor-protégé arrangements, another 7 firms in our sample of 123 had mentor-protégé agreements on file.

In: Disadvantaged Small Businesses and the 8(a) Program ISBN: 978-1-61209-309-3
Editors: James P. Carlson and Andrea M. Bernard

Chapter 4

8(A) PROGRAM: FOURTEEN INELIGIBLE FIRMS RECEIVED $325 MILLION IN SOLE-SOURCE AND SET-ASIDE CONTRACTS

United States Government Accountability Office

WHY GAO DID THIS STUDY

The Small Business Administration (SBA) helps socially and economically disadvantaged small businesses gain access to federal contracting opportunities through its 8(a) program. To participate, firms must be at least 51 percent owned and controlled by an individual who meets SBA's criteria of socially and economically disadvantaged. The firm must also qualify as a small business. Once certified, 8(a) firms are eligible to receive sole-source and set-aside contracts for up to 9 years.

GAO was asked to (1) determine whether ineligible firms are participating in the 8(a) program, (2) proactively test SBA's controls over the 8(a) application process, and (3) determine what vulnerabilities, if any, exist in SBA's fraud prevention system. To identify cases, GAO reviewed SBA data and complaints to GAO's fraud hotline. To perform its proactive testing, GAO created four bogus businesses and applied for 8(a) certification. GAO did not attempt to project the extent of fraud and abuse in the program.

WHAT GAO RECOMMENDS

GAO makes six recommendations to improve SBA's ability to screen and monitor fraud and abuse within the 8(a) program. SBA agreed with five recommendations and stated that it would evaluate our recommendation related to how family members' assets are included in the assets of the 8(a) participant based upon the comments received as a result of the proposed 8(a) rule change.

WHAT GAO FOUND

GAO identified $325 million in set-aside and sole-source contracts given to firms not eligible for the 8(a) program. Most were obtained through fraudulent schemes. In the 14 cases GAO investigated, numerous instances were found where 8(a) firm presidents made false statements, such as underreporting income or assets, to either qualify for the program or retain certification. For example, one firm president who is not socially disadvantaged misrepresented her ethnicity to SBA. GAO also found cases where ineligible companies used certified firms to secure 8(a) work. For instance, a West Virginia company that graduated from the program in 2001 used a series of three certified companies as pass-throughs to continue obtaining set-aside and sole-source contracts. In some cases, SBA did not detect the false statements and misrepresentations made by certified firms. In others, SBA became aware of the firms' ineligibility but failed to take action. The table below shows details on 3 of the 14 case studies.

GAO's proactive testing found several strengths in SBA's 8(a) application process that helped prevent three bogus applicants from being certified for the program. Examples of the strengths included validation of data with third- party credit bureaus and the Excluded Parties List System. These controls and effective review appropriately raised questions about income and assets of GAO's bogus applicants that would have made them ineligible. However, GAO obtained 8(a) certification for one bogus firm using fabricated documentation and owner information. Certification of GAO's bogus firm shows vulnerabilities in the process such as the lack of any face to face contact that could allow ineligible individuals or pass through companies to enter the program. Although we were unable to determine whether all 14 cases were ineligible at application, these cases show substantial vulnerabilities in SBA's monitoring of eligibility for individuals and firms already in the program. The lack of a consistent enforcement strategy or any real consequences for fraud and abuse is a further weakness in SBA's fraud prevention program.

Selected Case Studies of Fraud and Abuse in the 8(a) Program

Industry	Ineligible 8(a) awards/ awarding department	Case details
Roofing/ construction	$48.3 million— Agriculture, Commerce, Defense, Interior, EPA, GSA, SSA	• This firm is ineligible because it operated as a pass-through for a graduated company—both firms were being run by the same white, father-and-son team at the time of our investigation.
Construction	$ 11.2 million—Defense, Homeland Security	• This firm is ineligible because the president fraudulently reported his adjusted net worth to be $217,000 on his application when it was actually at least $806,000—an amount clearly exceeding the allowable $250,000 threshold. We estimate his currentadjusted net worth to be at least $1.7 million dollars—nearly double the allowable $750,000.
Landscaping/ janitorial	$13.8 million—Defense	• This firm is ineligible because it operated as an extension of a graduated 8(a) firm run by the same father-and-son team that owned the previous firm—effectively giving them an extra 9 years of eligibility.

Source: GAO.

ABBREVIATIONS

AGI	Adjusted Gross Income
BDS	Business Development Specialists
CAIVRS	Credit Alert Interactive Voice Response System
DSBS	Dynamic Small Business Search
EIN	Employer Identification Numbers
FPDS-NG	Federal Procurement Database System-Next Generation
HUD	U.S. Department of Housing and Urban Development
IRA	Individual Retirement Account
IRS	Internal Revenue Service
LLC	Limited Liability Company
SBA	Small Business Administration

March 30, 2010

The Honorable Nydia M. Velázquez
Chairwoman
Committee on Small Business
House of Representatives

Dear Madam Chairwoman:

The 8(a) Business Development Program, administered by the Small Business Administration (SBA), is one of the federal government's primary vehicles for nurturing small businesses owned by socially and economically disadvantaged individuals. To participate in the program, a firm must be certified as meeting several criteria, including: be a small business as defined by SBA; be unconditionally owned and controlled by one or more socially and economically disadvantaged individuals who are of good character and citizens of the United States; and show potential for success. Upon certification, firms can obtain federal contracts without competing fully and openly for the work. For example, agencies are permitted to enter into sole-source contracts after soliciting and negotiating with only one 8(a) company. They also can participate in restricted competitions for federal contracts, known as set asides, open to only 8(a) companies. According to SBA, in fiscal year 2008, there were a total of 9,462 firms certified to participate in the program—about half of which had at least one active 8(a) sole-source or set-aside contract.[1] In fiscal year 2008, according to the Federal Procurement Database System- Next Generation (FPDS-NG), federal agencies awarded $15.2 billion in 8(a) sole-source and set-aside contracts.

SBA's Office of Business Development administers the 8(a) program. The office's Business Development Specialists (BDS) work directly with 8(a) firms and are located in 68 district offices throughout the nation. They perform a variety of functions: help firms prepare a business plan, conduct annual reviews of the firms' progress in implementing these plans, review firms' continued eligibility, and provide technical assistance. Once approved for the program, participant firms must continue to meet all eligibility criteria and submit documentation to SBA to complete mandatory annual reviews. For instance, each year, as part of the annual review, participants must provide SBA with a certification that they continue to meet eligibility requirements as well as year-end financial statements, income tax returns, and a report on all non-8(a) contracts.

Given your interest in whether the 8(a) program has sufficient controls in place to detect fraud and abuse, you asked us to (1) determine whether ineligible firms are participating in the 8(a) program, (2) proactively test SBA's controls over the 8(a) application process, and (3) use case studies and proactive testing to determine what vulnerabilities, if any, exist in SBA's fraud prevention system.

To determine whether firms are participating in the 8(a) program through fraudulent misrepresentation, we used a risk-based approach to identify firms that exhibited signs that they were not qualified for the program. For example, we used data from the FPDS-NG to determine which firms in the Washington, D.C., area received the most 8(a) contracts in 2006 and 2007. Next, we used data from SBA's Dynamic Small Business Search (DSBS) Web site to identify current 8(a) firms in the Washington, D.C., area that were operating at the address of a graduated 8(a) firm. We limited our work to the Washington, D.C., area because there are significantly more firms located there than in any other area in the country. We used information about 8(a) firms provided by SBA to data mine for potentially fraudulent activity. We also reviewed allegations of fraud and abuse sent to our email address established to receive reports about small business contracting programs. We received about 30 allegations related to 8(a) fraud and abuse—more than we were able to investigate. In addition, we pursued leads found during the course of our other work on the Service Disabled Veteran Owned Small Business and HUBZone programs. From these sources, we selected 14 cases for further investigation based on a variety of factors,[2] including facts and evidence provided in allegations, and whether a firm received 8(a) contracts. For the firms we selected for further investigation, we reviewed documentation available from SBA in the firms' official 8(a) files maintained in district offices. We worked with SBA's audit liaison to request this documentation; in some instances we received information directly from officials in SBA district offices and other times information was transmitted through this liaison. We conducted both unannounced and announced site visits and interviewed firm employees and executives. We used a variety of investigative methods, such as analyzing firm payroll data, verifying the value of assets, and reviewing information from investigative databases to gather information about the firms and to determine whether the firms or their principals met 8(a) program criteria. In some cases, we also met with SBA staff responsible for annually recertifying these firms for the 8(a) program. Although 8(a) firms must meet several eligibility criteria to enter and remain in the program, we did not test all criteria. Generally our investigations focused on whether firms' presidents were economically disadvantaged, and whether they managed the day-to-day operations of the firm because we felt these eligibility criteria posed the highest risk of being misrepresented to the SBA.

To proactively test whether SBA's 8(a) application process and controls were sufficient to prevent ineligible firms from entering into the program, we established four bogus businesses, and submitted falsified applications and supporting documentation to SBA. For each application, we created substantial information on the business management experience and technical expertise of the firm's disadvantaged owner, the firm's ability to obtain the resources necessary to perform contracts, the firm's access to capital, and the firm's record of contract performance. To the extent possible, we developed scenarios to test various controls related to the firm's management and the owner's adjusted net worth. For one scenario, we also hired a for-profit certification firm to assist in the development of our application package. As part of SBA's application process, agency officials request copies of personal and business tax transcripts from the applicant as well as directly from the Internal Revenue Service (IRS). Therefore, in order to proactively test SBA's program application process, we used Employer Identification Numbers (EIN) and undercover Social Security numbers to file real tax returns with the IRS for our four bogus individuals. In order to minimize our costs associated with paying taxes, we created tax scenarios in which our firms reflected net business losses over multiple tax years. While these income scenarios minimized costs to GAO, they also limited our testing scenarios to firms that were not profitable, and thus decreased the likelihood that our firms would meet SBA's criteria that firms show reasonable potential for success.

To determine what vulnerabilities, if any, existed in SBA's fraud prevention system, we made observations based on our case studies and proactive testing. Furthermore, we compared current controls in the 8(a) program to a fraud-prevention model we developed and utilized in prior small business contracting investigations. Our work was not designed to identify all fraud and abuse in the 8(a) program or estimate its full extent for the entire population of 8(a) firms. In addition, our 14 case studies cannot be projected to the overall population of 8(a) firms. This investigative work complements our other work on the internal controls SBA has implemented to ensure that only eligible firms participate in the 8(a) program.[3]

We conducted our audit work and investigation from October 2008 through January 2010 in accordance with U.S. generally accepted government auditing standards. Those standards require that we plan and perform the audit to obtain sufficient, appropriate evidence to provide a reasonable basis for our findings and conclusions based on our audit objectives. We believe that the evidence obtained provides a reasonable basis for our findings and conclusions based on our objectives. We performed our investigative work in accordance with the standards prescribed by the Council of the Inspectors General on Integrity and Efficiency (CIGIE). A detailed discussion of our scope and methodology is presented in appendix 1.

Background

SBA's 8(a) program, named for a section of the Small Business Act, is a development program created to help small, disadvantaged businesses compete in the American economy and access the federal procurement market. To qualify for the 8(a) program, a firm must be at least 51 percent owned and controlled by an individual or individuals who meet SBA's definition of socially and economically disadvantaged and are of good character and citizens of the United States. The firm must also be a small business, as defined by SBA, and show a reasonable potential for success.

According to SBA regulations, at least 51 percent of the 8(a) firm must be owned and controlled by one or more disadvantaged individuals. Ownership requirements vary depending on whether the firm is a sole proprietorship, partnership, limited liability company (LLC), or a corporation. However, SBA makes a clear distinction between ownership of an 8(a) firm, and control of an 8(a) firm. To be in control of an 8(a) firm the disadvantaged individual or individuals must control both the strategic policy setting and the day-to-day management and administration of business operations. For example, SBA may find that nondisadvantaged individuals actually control an 8(a) firm if the firm cannot exercise independent business judgment without great economic risk.

Socially disadvantaged individuals include, but are not restricted to, members of designated groups, such as blacks or Hispanics,[4] or any individuals who have been subjugated to racial, ethnic, or cultural bias because of their identities as members of groups without regard for their individual qualities. Others, who may not be members of these groups, can be considered for the 8(a) program if they are able to provide substantial evidence and documentation that they have been subjected to chronic racial prejudice, cultural bias, or similar circumstances beyond their control. Economically disadvantaged individuals are defined by SBA regulations as those who at the time of application have a personal net worth of $250,000 or less, adjusted to exclude personal residence and business assets. Once certified to participate in the 8(a) program, the individual's adjusted net worth must not exceed $750,000 according to regulation. In addition, if an individual's income or total assets exceed certain standards, SBA may determine that the individual is not economically disadvantaged.[5] Applicants must also be of good character and citizens of the United States.

The firm must further qualify as a small business under the size standard that corresponds with its primary industry classification. SBA defines a small business concern as one that is independently owned and operated, is organized for profit, is not dominant in its field, has a place of business in the United States, and either operates primarily within the United States or makes a significant contribution to the U.S. economy. Depending on the industry, size standard eligibility is based on the average number of employees for the preceding 12 months or on sales volume averaged over a 3-year period. In addition, a firm must demonstrate its potential for success by documenting revenues in its primary industry for at least 2 years; however, a waiver of this requirement may be granted if a firm meets certain criteria. SBA also considers a firm's access to credit and capital, as well as the technical and managerial experience of the firm's managers.

To help clarify eligibility criteria and address other issues, SBA recently proposed changes to its Small Business Size and 8(a) Business Development Regulations.[6] Among other things, the proposed rules would introduce more detailed guidance for specific thresholds for personal assets, compensation, and exceeding size standards. The proposed changes would also limit the participation of firms with a family member that is a previous participant of the 8(a) program. The public comment period for these proposed regulations closed in January 2010, and according to an SBA official, the comments are expected to be finalized by the end of fiscal year 2010.

Firms in the 8(a) program are eligible to receive set-aside and sole-source contracts. Set-aside contracts can be awarded to 8(a) firms if there is a reasonable expectation that at least two 8(a) firms will submit offers and the award can be made at a fair price. Sole-source contracts can be awarded when the dollar thresholds are $5.5 million or less for acquisitions involving manufacturing and $3.5 million or less for all other acquisitions.[7] In addition, once a firm receives an 8(a) contract, the firm is required to abide by certain subcontracting limitations based on the type of contract. For example, in the case of a contract for services, the 8(a) firm must perform at least 50 percent of the cost of the contract incurred for personnel with its own employees. In the case of general construction contracts, the 8(a) firm must perform at least 15 percent of the cost of the contract with its own employees (not including the costs of materials).

Firms can remain in the program for up to 9 years provided that they maintain their eligibility. At the end of this term, SBA considers the firm to have "graduated" from the program. SBA can also remove a firm's 8(a) status by graduating it early if the agency determines that it no longer meets the criteria for assistance. Examples of such eligibility changes include the following: meeting the goals and objectives set forth in a firm's business plan; demonstrating the ability to compete in the marketplace without assistance from the 8(a) program; or the qualified owners of a firm are determined to be no longer economically disadvantaged. Firms are required to inform SBA of any changes that would adversely affect program eligibility while they are participating in the 8(a) program. SBA may also terminate a firm from the 8(a) program for good cause, such as submission of false information or failure to maintain eligibility requirements. Firms may also voluntarily remove themselves from the program. Once a firm graduates from the 8(a) program it cannot reapply, even if it changes its name or comes under new management. The disadvantaged individual upon whom eligibility was based is no longer eligible to qualify another firm. Federal law states that any person who misrepresents a firm's status as an 8(a) participant, or makes any other false statement in order to influence the certification process in any way or to obtain a contract awarded under the 8(a) program shall be: (1) subject to fines and imprisonment; (2) subject to civil and administrative remedies, including suspension and debarment; and (3) ineligible for participation in programs conducted under the authority of the Small Business Act.

SELECTED CASE STUDIES OF FRAUD AND ABUSE IN THE 8(A) PROGRAM

We identified 14 firms that received set-aside or sole-source 8(a) contracts worth $325 million through fraud or abuse.[8] These 14 firms received another $1.2 billion in other federal obligations since entering the 8(a) program,[9] including $17 million in awards through the American Recovery and Reinvestment Act of 2009. We found evidence that shows officials at 13 of these firms misrepresented their eligibility for the program to fraudulently acquire or maintain 8(a) status and obtain federal contracts awarded with limited or no competition. Examples include underreporting adjusted net worth and serving as a "pass-through" for non-8(a) companies. In the case of a pass-through, an 8(a) firm receives the sole- source or set-aside contract, but contrary to program requirements, work is performed and managed by a non-8(a) company. We also determined that SBA staff responsible for annually assessing firm eligibility allowed 3 firms to remain in the 8(a) program and receive contracts despite clear evidence provided by company officials during annual reviews that showed they were no longer eligible. For example, SBA allowed a firm to remain certified even though the president reported a salary which substantially exceeded the threshold. Permitting ineligible firms to obtain 8(a) contracts undermines the intent of the program and deprives qualified firms from receiving targeted contracting opportunities.

Table 1 highlights the case studies we developed on these 14 firms. More detailed information on 5 of these cases follows the table. We will be referring all 14 cases to SBA and the agency's Office of Inspector General for further investigation.

Table 1. Selected Cases of Fraud and Abuse in the 8(a) Program

Case	Industry/ business location	8(a) obligations since firm was not eligible and awarding department[a]	Case details
1	Construction Toms River, NJ	$11.2 million— Department of Defense, Department of Homeland Security	• This firm was ineligible because the president fraudulentlyreported his adjusted net worth to be $217,000 on his application when it was actually at least $806,000—an amount clearly exceeding the allowable $250,000 threshold. We estimate his current adjusted net worth to be at least $1.7 million dollars—more than double the allowable $750,000. • The president underreported the value of investment properties, an Individual Retirement Account, and other assets. He also failed to report the ownership of multiple properties held in a LLC registered to his wife, but under his control. • The president made numerous false statements during the application process to hide his relationship with a previous employer that was a graduated 8(a) company. • The firm contacted us in September 2009 to state that it had decided to voluntarily withdraw from the 8(a) programas a result of our investigation. SBA agreed to remove thefirm from the program.
2	Landscaping, janitorial, and painting Wharton, NJ	$13.8 million— Department of Defense	• This firm is ineligible because it is operating as an extension of a graduated 8(a) firm owned by the same father-and-son team. The arrangement effectively gave the team an extra 9 years of eligibility to receive 8(a) sole-source and set-aside contracts. • Four months after the father's landscaping and janitorial firm graduated from the program, the son applied to the program under a

Table 1. (Continued)

Case	Industry/ business location	8(a) obligations since firm was not eligible and awarding department[a]	Case details
			different company name and received certification about a month later. • The current 8(a) firm and the graduated company share workers and equipment to perform contract work.
			• We requested a number of documents to verify the net worth of the current 8(a) president and establish whether the two firms were affiliated but were denied access by company officials—a material breach of the firm's program agreement. • The firm is slated to graduate in September 2015.
3	Roofing and construction Hyattsville, MD	$48.3 million—Department of Agriculture, Department of Commerce, Department of Defense, Department of the Interior, Environmental Protection Agency, General Services Administration, Social Security Administration	• The firm is ineligible because it operated as a pass-through for a graduated company—both of which were being run by the same white, father-and-son team at the time of our investigation. • The two businesses share top executives, staff, administrative offices, and warehouse space. As such, wedetermined that they were essentially operating as one company. • The father and son never applied to SBA to be considered as disadvantaged, yet they controlled and managed the daily operations of the currently certified firm. For example, the white vice-president disclosed much of the operational knowledge of the firm during the site visit, while the black president rarely spoke. The white executives both work out of large suites while the black president sits in a small room located at the back of the building. • The firm is slated to graduate in April 2011.

Table 1. (Continued)

Case	Industry/ business location	8(a) obligations since firm was not eligible and awarding department[a]	Case details
4	Security consulting Arlington, VA	$6.7 million—Department of Defense, Department of Homeland Security, National Aeronautics and Space Administration, Nuclear Regulatory Commission	• This firm is ineligible because the president is not socially disadvantaged and it relied, at the time of application, on a graduated company for operational resources. The firm fraudulently obtained contracts by making false statements to SBA about these matters. • The president attested to being Hispanic on her 8(a) application, but she stated on her Maryland driver's license application that she was not. In addition, her previous employer stated that the woman had misrepresented herself as socially disadvantaged. • The firm is slated to graduate in August 2013.
5	Health and human services consulting Rockville, MD; Fairfax, VA; Atlanta, GA	$12.6 million—Department of Health and Human Services, Office of Personnel Management	• This firm is ineligible because the president of the firm is no longer economically disadvantaged. • The president withdrew about $600,000 from the firm for an equity loan—double what SBA regulations allow. • The president provided corporate tax returns during annual reviews which showed she drew a salary in excess of $1 million for several years—exceeding the cap for adjusted gross income (AGI) established by SBA case law and placing her in the top 1 percent of American taxpayers. • In March 2009 we pointed out these violations to SBA staff responsible for assessing firm eligibility; however, no action was taken to graduate the firm. Subsequently, the firm received a $3.3 million set-aside contract. • The firm is slated to graduate in May 2010.
6	Roofing Emmett, ID	$400,000—Department of the Interior	• This firm is ineligible because it is a shell company dependent upon the resources of a large construction firmmanaged by a

Table 1. (Continued)

Case	Industry/ business location	8(a) obligations since firm was not eligible and awarding department[a]	Case details
			nondisadvantaged individual.[b] • The president worked for the nondisadvantaged individual's firm—but was not compensated for this work— while in the 8(a) program. The 8(a) firm did not have any employees and used employees of the nondisadvantaged individual's firm to perform work. • The president stated that her firm was located on land owned by the same nondisadvantaged individual. • The large construction firm provided bonding for work performed by the 8(a) company and the president of this firm told the SBA that he was compensated for providing this support. • Both SBA district office staff and the State of Idaho found evidence that the firm was affiliated with a nondisadvantaged individual. • The firm is slated to graduate in October 2014.
7	IT consulting Fairfax, VA	$9.9 million—Department of Defense, Department of State, Peace Corps	• The firm was ineligible because the president failed to report the ownership of significant assets to SBA, which would have disqualified it from the program. • The president failed to declare joint ownership of $4.2 million in properties located in Virginia, Maryland, and Nevada, including a $900,000 home in Las Vegas—whichwould have been included in SBA's calculation of adjusted net worth. • When we inquired about these purchases, the president could not provide evidence substantiating her claim that the properties were purchased with monies inherited by her husband. • We brought the unreported assets to the attention of SBA; however, once SBA learned that the firm was

Table 1. (Continued)

Case	Industry/ business location	8(a) obligations since firm was not eligible and awarding department[a]	Case details
			scheduled to graduate in 8 months, it no longer wanted to investigate the firm's actions. Eleven days later, the firm was awarded a $1.7 million dollar contract. • The firm graduated in September 2009.
8	Construction Fort Dix, NJ	$2 million—Department of Defense	• This firm is ineligible because it is a shell company that is economically dependent upon a large, privately-owned construction company in Brooklyn, NY, and subcontracts all of its work to other businesses. • The firm operates out of a regional office for the Brooklyn company. A founding owner also works for the Brooklyn company, as does its general manager. Interrelated relationships such as these have been found by SBA to disqualify a business from being considered small. • The firm also has only four employees, including the president—too few to complete contract work on its own, so it subcontracts all of its 8(a) work to other businesses. SBA regulations require 8(a) firms to perform at least 15 percent of the work on construction contracts with its own employees. • The firm is slated to graduate in May 2017.
9	Human resources Alexandria, VA	$117 million—Department of Agriculture, Department of Commerce, Department of Defense, Department of Health and Human Services, Department of Homeland Security, Department of Labor, Department of Transportation	• The firm fraudulently obtained 8(a) contracts after the president failed to report a $450,000 down payment madetowards the purchase of a $3.7 million dollar home which would have caused the president's adjusted net worth to exceed program limits. • SBA allowed this firm to remain 8(a) certified for 5 years even after the president of the firm reported receiving a salary which, according to SBA case law, indicated that the

Table 1. (Continued)

Case	Industry/ business location	8(a) obligations since firm was not eligible and awarding department[a]	Case details
			president was no longer economically disadvantaged. She reported a salary ranging from $525,000 to $730,000 during this time. • Moreover, the firm was determined to be ineligible by SBA because it had exceeded small-business size standards, but was allowed to “ride out the program” for 21 months. During this period, the firm received an 8(a) sole-source contract worth $554,000 for which it was no longer eligible. We asked SBA why it approved a contract to an ineligible firm, but were told by the audit liaison that SBA had no records related to this contract. • The firm graduated in November 2008.
10	IT consulting Bethesda, MD	$12.6 million— Department of Agriculture, Department of the Interior, Department of Transportation, Department of Veterans Affairs	• The firm was ineligible because the president misrepresented that he used proceeds from the sale of a $236,000 Miami condominium to purchase his home, but instead transferred the property into his wife’s name. • The president also exhibited signs that he is not economically disadvantaged. For example, he owns a $2.5 million house on a private island in Miami, FL, a $450,000 yacht, and a $200,000 Lamborghini. The president’s wife owns a $1 million house in Bethesda, MD, but SBA regulations do not require a spouse’s assetsto be included in an owner’s adjusted net worth. • The firm graduated in March 2010.
11	Construction Weirton, WV	$70.8 million— Department of Agriculture, Departmant of Defence, Department of Defense, Department of Energy,	• The firm fraudulently received 8(a) contracts because it graduated from the program in 2001 and used a series of three certified companies

Table 1. (Continued)

Case	Industry/ business location	8(a) obligations since firm was not eligible and awarding department[a]	Case details
		Department of Health and Human Services, Department of Homeland Security, Department of the Interior, Department of Justice, Department of Veterans Affairs, General Services Administration	as pass-throughs to continue obtaining 8(a) contracts. In addition, all four businesses are currently being controlled by two white men who never applied to SBA to be considered as disadvantaged. • The three pass-through companies effectively operated as extensions of the graduated firm because they all shared facilities and employees to perform contract work. • There is evidence that two white men controlled the businesses: (1) they maintained offices at headquarters where the daily operations were conducted, while the black presidents worked about a mile away in a satellite office, and (2) they also earned more money than the black executives do. • One pass-through graduated in September 2007. The other two are slated to graduate in October 2013 and May2014 respectively.
12	Consulting Alexandria, VA	$2.5 million— Department of Defense, Environmental Protection Agency	• The firm was ineligible because the president failed to disclose over $1 million in reportable property, including an ocean-front condominium in Florida and two townhouses in Virginia. • The firm graduated in December 2009.
13	Manufacturing rubber products Mansfield, TX	$15.5 million— Department of Defense, General Services Administration	• The firm was ineligible because the president underreported his salary to SBA, stating in 2001 that he earned a salary of $100,000; tax documents showed he received an income of $1.6 million that year. The president reported income on an annual review in excess of $1.9 million for 2003—exceeding the cap for AGI and placing him in the top 1 percent of American taxpayers, which does not demonstrate economic disadvantage. • The firm graduated in June 2006.

Table 1. (Continued)

Case	Industry/ business location	8(a) obligations since firm was not eligible and awarding department[a]	Case details
14	Janitorial, carpet cleaning, grounds maintenance Baltimore, MD	$600,000—Department of Defense	• This firm was not eligible to obtain 8(a) contracts after the president passed away and his wife failed to report this to SBA for 2 years. • After the president of the firm passed away, his wife continued to submit documentation to SBA falsely indicating that he was the president. • Approximately 2 years after his death, SBA staff responsible for assessing firm eligibility was able to determine that the president of this firm had died and in September of 2009 filed paperwork to terminate the firm from the program. At the time of this report, in March of 2010, the termination was still being processed.

Source: GAO Analysis.

[a] This figure represents the amount of obligations that 8(a) firms received from the date at which we determined that the firm was no longer eligible to participate in the program. We found that some firms were ineligible for participation prior to their certification, while others became ineligible at some time during the course of their participation in the 8(a) program. Obligation amounts are rounded to the nearest $100,000.

[b] A shell company is defined as a business that has no independent assets or operations of its own, but is used by its owners to conduct specific business dealings or maintain control of other companies.

The following provides a more detailed description of five of the cases in table 1.

Case Study 1

The president of this New Jersey construction firm fraudulently obtained $11.2 million in 8(a) set-aside and sole-source contracts by misrepresenting his qualifications for the program. This firm was never eligible because the president's adjusted net worth was at least $806,000— more than triple what he reported on his application in late 2007 and what SBA regulations allow. As of May 2009, after a year in the program, his adjusted net worth had grown to at least $1.7 million—more than double the $750,000 cap set by SBA regulations to retain 8(a) status. We found evidence the president hid his relationship with a graduated 8(a) company in order to obtain certification for his own firm. In addition, we also were told by Navy job-site inspectors that the firm was subcontracting most, if not all, of the work on the $2.3 million sole-source demolition contract it received from the Department of the Navy. After we began questioning the president's qualifications and the firm's contracts, the president withdrew his company from the 8(a) program. SBA agreed to remove the firm from the program in November of 2009.

The president of this firm attested to an adjusted net worth of $217,370 at the time of application, which was about $32,000 below the cap for being considered economically disadvantaged. However, using public records and documents provided by the president, our investigation found that the president's actual adjusted net worth at that time was at least $806,527, which is triple the allowable limit. The difference results in part from the president underreporting the value of his individual retirement account (IRA) and two investment properties. SBA took no steps to verify the value of these assets. The president also failed to report a third investment property entirely. Later in this report we describe the steps that SBA takes to verify information during the application and subsequent annual review processes. Table 2 summarizes the discrepancies we found between the asset values the president submitted to SBA and the ones we determined to be accurate based on public records and documentation, such as bank statements, provided by the president.

For the undervalued investment property in Manchester Township, the president submitted a market analysis produced by a real estate agent with whom he had a prior business relationship showing the vacant land to be worth less than a quarter of what public records state he actually paid for it. In addition, an LLC that lists the president's wife as its registered agent and manager—but evidence indicates is controlled by the president himself—paid $220,000 in cash for an investment property 10 days after the president applied to the 8(a) program.

Table 2. President's Adjusted Net Worth in November 2007 at the Time of Application

	President's claimed value of assets	GAO's estimated value of assets
Cash	$7,080	$14,202
IRA or other retirement account	$40,000	$99,913
Stocks and bonds (other than ownership in 8(a) firm)	$72,000	$152,122
Real estate (excluding personal residence)		
Investment property 1 (Ulster, NY)	$10,000	$24,000
Investment property 2 (Manchester Township, NJ)	$70,000	$278,000
Investment property 3 (Seaside Heights, NJ)	Not reported	$220,000
Other assets and personal property[a]	$40,618	$40,618
Total assets	**$239,698**	**$828,855**
Debt (excluding mortgage for personal residence)[a]	$22,328	$22,328
Total net worth	**$217,370**	**$806,527**

Source: SBA documents, public records, and documents provided to GAO by the president.

[a] GAO did not attempt to verify the accuracy of these figures.

Table 3. President's Adjusted Net Worth in May 2009 about the Time of the Firm's First Annual Review

	President's reported value of assets	GAO's estimated value of assets
Cash	$21,555	$21,499
IRA or other retirement account	$48,164	$77,788
Stocks and bonds (other than ownership in 8(a) firm)	$15,842	$31,685
Real estate (excluding personal residence)		
Investment property 1	$10,000	$24,000
(Ulster, NY)		
Investment property 2 (Manchester Township, NJ)	$70,000	$838,700
Investment property 3 (Seaside Heights, NJ)	Not reported	$336,000
Investment property 4 (Lacey Township, NJ)	Not reported	$451,500
Other assets and personal property[a]	$93,175	$93,175
Total assets	**$230,434**	**$1,930,947**
Debt (excluding mortgage for personal	$139,302	$139,302
residence)[a]		
Total net worth	**$119,434**	**$1,735,145**

Source: SBA documents, public records, and documents provided to GAO by the president.
[a] GAO did not attempt to verify the accuracy of these figures.

A little more than a year after entering the program, the president's adjusted net worth had grown to at least about $1.7 million—more than double the cap set by SBA regulations to remain eligible. However, the president again understated his assets to SBA in May 2009, which resulted in SBA calculating his adjusted net worth as $119,434. Table 3 summarizes the discrepancies we found between the asset values the president submitted to SBA as part of his annual review and the ones we determined to be accurate based on public records and documentation provided by the president.

The president continued to understate the value of his Manchester Township property, despite the tripling of its assessed taxable value. He maintained in an interview that the vacant land was worthless, but public records and interviews with Township officials indicate he spent 2 years and over $30,000 to connect it to public utilities. In addition, the same LLC mentioned above purchased a nearly $500,000 waterfront home in Lacey Township, New Jersey, with cash in January 2009—4 months before the firm's first annual review.

Case Study 2

A landscaping and janitorial firm in New Jersey fraudulently obtained $13.8 million in 8(a) contracts because it was operating as an extension of a graduated 8(a) firm owned by the same family. The father's company— also a landscaping and janitorial company—entered the program in 1997, but its certification for 8(a) contracts ended after the 9-year eligibility term expired. Four months after the father's company graduated, the son applied to the program in 2006 under a different firm name and was certified about a month later.[10] Our investigation found the two businesses operated out of the same location, employed the same workers, and shared the same equipment. This effectively gave the family an extra 9 years of eligibility to receive sole-source and set-aside 8(a) contracts.

We determined that the current 8(a) firm is operating as the graduated 8(a) firm with little more than a name change.[11] First, an undercover site visit and postal records revealed that the two firms are operating out of the same unmarked administrative office. They also share an email address. Second, we found that, according to tax records, the two firms shared 16 employees in 2008. We interviewed 6 people who worked for the current 8(a) firm, each of whom indicated that the graduated company and 8(a) firm were operating as the same business, but used different names depending on where work was being performed. One employee stated that he applied for a job at the graduated company, but that he received most of his paychecks from the current 8(a) firm—despite never having filled out tax forms for the current firm. Another told us that employees often do not know which job site at which they are working until the morning when they are told where to go by a foreman who oversees employees working for both businesses. In addition, the son once worked as the vice-president for operations and marketing for his father at the graduated company. Third, several employees stated that the two companies share equipment, such as trucks. Lastly, a former consultant for the graduated company told us that the current 8(a) firm was created for the sole purpose of remaining in the program after the 9-year eligibility term expired.

We requested a number of documents to verify the adjusted net worth of the current 8(a) president and establish whether the two firms were affiliated but were denied access by company officials—a material breach of the firm's program agreement.[12] We asked the two firms for a list of all equipment owned or leased, including identifying information such as serial numbers or Vehicle Identification Numbers. We also requested personal financial information from the president, such as investment account statements. We notified SBA program officials about our inability to obtain these documents; however, SBA officials told us that they would not request information on our behalf. Breach of the program agreement is a basis for 8(a) termination.[13] According to the SBA, the firm is slated to graduate from the program in September 2015.

Case Study 3

We found that this Hyattsville, Maryland, construction firm fraudulently obtained $48.3 million in 8(a) set-aside and sole-source contracts by operating as a pass-through for a graduated company—both of which were being run by nondisadvantaged individuals at the time of our investigation. We determined that the two businesses were essentially operating as one because they shared the work on contracts, top executives, staff, administrative offices, and warehouse space. We also found that a father and son—two white executives from the graduated company who never applied to SBA as disadvantaged—actually control and manage the daily operations of the currently certified firm. One of the white men told us that in order to receive federal contracts, a person needed to "create" other companies because it was difficult to compete without some type of preference. He referred to this process as "succession planning." We did not determine who controlled the graduated company while it was active in the program.

The president of the currently certified firm received 8(a) status in April 2002—about a month after the graduated company left the program. The president's firm works in the same line of business as that of his former employer—roofing, sheet metal, and other commercial construction.

The firm uses about 6,000 square feet of office space and approximately 13,000 square feet of warehouse space leased by the president's former employer. In addition, about a third of the firm's 29 staff were hired from the president's former employer after the graduated company left the 8(a) program. The father initially served as the firm's senior vice-president, according to the business's Web site, but is now listed as a mentor and advisor; at the graduated company, he worked as vice-president. The son, meanwhile, acts as one of the firm's vice-presidents and was operations manager at the graduated company. The father said that he formed the currently certified firm with the president before his company left the program. His son joined the currently certified firm the same year that it received its 8(a) certification.

Evidence that the currently certified firm is being controlled by two white men includes subcontracts that the 8(a) firm awarded to both the graduated company and a woman-owned construction firm that was closely tied to these men. We concluded that this woman-owned construction firm was closely tied to these men after one of them told us they created the firm to prepare the graduated 8(a) firm for an expected increase in government contracts to woman-owned businesses. He called this "pre-positioning". The president of the woman-owned firm is a former employee of the two white men and operates from the same address as the graduated 8(a) firm. Additionally, the domain name for the woman-owned firm's website is registered to the graduated 8(a) firm. Other evidence of control over the current 8(a) firm includes the operational knowledge of the white men and the size and location of the black president's office. When we interviewed the men about the firm's business operations, the white vice-president answered most of the questions while the black president rarely spoke. SBA officials told us that they consider a key indicator of control to be who discloses much of the operational knowledge during site visits. Finally, the white vice-president worked in a large executive suite. The black president, meanwhile, sat in a small room located at the back of the building. SBA considers the relative size of offices given to disadvantaged and nondisadvantaged individuals to be a key indicator of control. We visited the currently certified firm's headquarters as part of our fraud investigation of the HUBZone program—also administered by SBA—which allows sole-source and set-aside contracts to be awarded to firms located in economically depressed areas. The firm also had been granted HUBZone certification and as a result received an additional $15.3 million in noncompetitive federal contracts.

Our investigation found, however, that the firm was not actually located in a HUBZone. SBA subsequently revoked this certification. According to SBA, the firm is slated to graduate from the 8(a) program in April 2011.

Case Study 8

A construction firm in Fort Dix, New Jersey, fraudulently obtained $2.2 million in 8(a) sole-source and set-aside contracts because it is economically dependent upon a large, privately-owned construction company in Brooklyn, New York, and subcontracts all of its work. First, the Fort Dix firm operates out of a regional office for the Brooklyn company. In addition, a founding owner of the firm works for the Brooklyn company, as does its general manager. A business's close affiliation with a large company through the sharing of facilities, employees, and economic interests has been found by SBA to disqualify a business from being considered small.[14] Second, the Fort Dix firm possesses only four employees, including the president—too few to complete the contract work on its own. It subcontracts all of its 8(a) work to other businesses. SBA regulations require 8(a) firms completing general construction contracts perform at least 15 percent of the cost of the contract with their own employees (not including the costs of materials). Third, we found evidence indicating that a previous 8(a) participant in Jersey City, New Jersey, had an interrelated relationship with the Brooklyn company while in the program. The Jersey City business also had ties to the Fort Dix firm, such as a common employee and nearly identical business plans. However, the Jersey City firm did not provide us with all of the documents we requested, so we could not determine whether it was economically independent.

Case Study 11

A graduated 8(a) firm currently controlled by two white men fraudulently obtained $70.8 million in 8(a) set-aside and sole-source contracts by using a series of three construction companies as pass-throughs to obtain the awards. The graduated firm—founded by one black man as president and two white men as fellow executives—gained certification in 1992 and completed the program in 2001 after its eligibility term expired. A succession of certified companies subsequently operated as an extension of the graduated firm because they all shared facilities and employees to perform contract work. In addition, two of the top executives of the successor companies, both disadvantaged individuals, were personally tied to the graduated firm's president. For example, the president of the second successor company was the sister of the graduated firm's president, while the president of the third successor company was his cousin. After graduating from the program, the graduated firm's president received a salary from the first and second successor companies. We could not determine who controlled the graduated firm during its participation in the program, but we believe that the two white men—neither of whom ever applied to SBA as disadvantaged individuals—currently oversee all of the firms' daily operations. The use of the successor companies effectively gave the two men an extra 13 years of eligibility to receive sole-source and set-aside 8(a) contracts.[15]

Table 4. Chronology of Firms

	SBA 8(a) entrance date	Date of first 8(a) obligation	SBA 8(a) graduation date	8(a) obligations
Graduated firm	September 1992	April 1996	September 2001	$17,355,321
Successor 1	September 1998	November 2002	September 2007	$9,401,780
Successor 2	October 2004	June 2005	October 2013	$57,321,506
Successor 3	May 2005	September 2006	May 2014	$4,085,870

Source: SBA and FPDS-NG.

The graduated firm controls the three successor companies because it shares its facility and employees with the other businesses—a relationship that SBA regulations and case law consider indicative of which entity is actually in power. The graduated firm's headquarters, located in Weirton, West Virginia, effectively serves as the operations center for the successor companies. We conducted a surprise visit to this location and found on- site clerical staff and project managers conducting day-to-day operations for all four businesses. The payroll clerk also told us that the graduated firm pays the rent for this facility. In addition, the resumes of three job site superintendents at the first and second successor company show that they once worked for the graduated firm. The wage and tax statements from when the graduated firm was in the program were destroyed in a 2004 flood. We were able to obtain the wage and tax statements from the graduated firm and its three successor companies for 2006 and 2007. These documents show the companies paid the same employees in the same calendar year. For example, in 2006, 82 employees received a paycheck from two or more of the businesses. In 2007, 37 employees received a paycheck from each of the four businesses. The on-site payroll clerk at headquarters told our investigators that an employee earns the same salary each year regardless of which business pays the employee. The clerk said she never had a problem issuing paychecks from multiple businesses because they all use the same bank.

Our investigation also found that the two white men who were among the founders of the graduated firm control all four businesses. First, both white men have offices at headquarters where the daily operations of the four businesses are located, while the black presidents work about a mile away in a satellite office.[16] Second, both white men also earn more money than the black executives do.[17] In 2009, the highest-paid black president received only $53,000 in compensation compared to the $125,000 the two white men told our investigators that they each earned. The two white men received this income from more than one company. Both earn a paycheck from multiple companies and both receive a portion of the money that the graduated firm charges the second successor company for equipment leases. One of the white men also received income from monthly fees as the accountant for the second successor company. In addition, the two white men told our investigators that one or more of the companies pays for their personal vehicles. Both men agreed with our investigators that they were managing all four businesses but told investigators, "We don't do [the third successor company] as a steady diet. We do [the second one]."According to SBA, the second and third successor companies—the only ones with current 8(a) certification—are slated to graduate in October, 2013 and May, 2014 respectively.

Our Proactive Testing Identified Strengths and Vulnerabilities in SBA's 8(a) Application Process

Our proactive testing found strengths in SBA's 8(a) application process that allowed the agency to correctly determine firms' lack of qualifications. We also identified vulnerabilities that demonstrate weaknesses ineligible firms could exploit to fraudulently receive program certification. We were unsuccessful in gaining certification for three bogus firms. In the first unsuccessful application, SBA stated that it denied our application because the firm lacked the financial capacity to perform 8(a) contracts. In the other two of these cases, SBA raised concerns about our eligibility based on the presidents' adjusted net worth. The agency also questioned control of one of these firms. SBA provided us with such thorough comments that we determined we could not overcome the deficiencies and eligibility issues identified in both applications, so we abandoned them. However, we obtained 8(a) certification for one bogus firm using fabricated documentation and fictitious owner information. We consider this a vulnerability because unscrupulous firms could do the same to create front companies and funnel 8(a) contracts to themselves, circumventing eligibility requirements. In contrast to our 2008 test of SBA's HUBZone program—in which we were quickly and easily able to obtain certification for four fictitious firms—the agency demanded we overcome more rigorous controls, such as verification of critical business information contained in IRS tax returns with third-party sources.

We prepared all but one of these applications to reflect scenarios in which the individual or the firm would not be eligible for the program, such as a firm president with an adjusted net worth in excess of program limits. SBA identified many of the eligibility issues that we included in our applications and requested substantial documentary evidence and clarification for claims and statements that we made. We reviewed the approved application to obtain details on why it was certified, and determined that SBA performed independent verifications of some of the information we provided. However, we do not know what verifications SBA performed on our other three firms. Communications and submissions were conducted primarily through the Internet, by mail, and by fax. For the accepted firm, we conducted limited real-time telephone conversations with SBA staff responsible for processing our application. SBA staff also left several voice messages for all but one of our firms. At no time during the application process for the four bogus firms were we required to conduct face-to-face meetings.[18] By all indications, SBA's review focused on our firms' potential for success and the technical and administrative completeness of our applications. This is a necessary and reasonable focus; however, SBA did not question the legitimacy of the documents we submitted and, as a result, we were able to gain 8(a) certification for a company that only existed on paper. This successful application shows that SBA is vulnerable to certifying firms based upon fraudulent application information. We provide specific details on each of our four applications below.

Unapproved Fictitious Applications

Fictitious Application 1: SBA denied this application after a 4-month review because the firm appeared to lack the financial capacity to execute contracts in the 8(a) program. We prepared this application to appear as if a nondisadvantaged individual had the potential to control the applicant. In addition, the personal financial statement of the applicant included a substantial degree of debt that was unsustainable because the owner had limited wage income and the firm had not generated any measurable profit in the past. To appear as if another individual could potentially control our disadvantaged individual, we created another fictitious identity and added his name as a signatory on a bogus bank signature card that we submitted to SBA. We also incorporated this name in various documents throughout our application, such as in bank statements, loan agreements, and leases, without including him as a partial owner of the firm, naming him as an employee, or providing any information on his identity. SBA requested that we provide evidence from our bank listing the names of all individuals with access to our business account. To meet this request, we provided a bogus story to explain why the individual was a signatory on our account and then indicated that he was removed. To back up our claim, we provided a phony bank letter indicating that our firm's owner was the sole signatory on the account.

Fictitious Application 2: SBA's requests for evidence and documents to support the claims and explanations we made about control and adjusted net worth were so extensive that we abandoned this application after 3 months, determining that we could not overcome the agency's concerns. SBA identified almost all of the "red flags" that we included in this application, except for indications that our bogus applicant could be involved in money laundering. For example, SBA identified the fact that we underreported the value of a high-end sports car and luxury motorcycle that were included in our statement of assets and subsequently determined that the adjusted net worth of our bogus applicant exceeded $250,000, because of the value of the vehicles. In contrast, SBA did not question us about the information we provided that suggested money laundering. For instance, we provided SBA with fake bank statements that included numerous banking transactions that were split into sums that fell just below the $10,000 identification and reporting threshold. The bank statements reflected substantial transfers that originated from countries identified as tax havens with no association with our business activity. They also reflected large deposits that were immediately followed by cash withdrawals of an equal sum or a wire transfer to another financial institution or individual. While SBA requested copies of contracts, invoices, and other information related to any business that our bogus firm may have conducted outside of the United States, there was no indication that its staff became suspicious of the illicit activities that are generally associated with the information we included in our bank statement.

Fictitious Application 3: SBA determined that this firm had significant eligibility issues and that it could not accept our 8(a) application for processing, after 4 months of correspondence, and despite the hiring of a private company to help us obtain certification. Specifically, SBA determined that the fictitious firm had limited potential for success because we reported that we did not receive any W-2 income or wages on both our 2007 and 2008 income taxes. Additionally, our firm's application reflected significant business debts and liabilities, ownership of real estate assets, and personal and business lines of credit that could not be reconciled or sustained with the fact that we reported no wages and or income. For this fictitious firm, we employed the services of a private company that offered "8(a) Certification Services" to determine if such businesses offer the advantage that they advertised. We selected this particular firm because it described itself as deft at helping individuals who are not generally classified as disadvantaged obtain 8(a) certification for their firms. We signed a contract and paid the private company almost $4,000. The company stated that it would advise us if we were not eligible for the program. However, it did not identify any of the eligibility issues that we planted in the application. In fact, the company told us that our firm's application was as "good as any it had ever seen" and "had as good a chance as any firm of being certified." SBA returned our application, citing a number of eligibility issues, such as our limited potential for success and our net worth exceeding the cap. The private company neither provided continuous guidance in addressing SBA's concerns throughout the process, nor did it follow up with us to determine the status of our application after resubmission. While we did not systematically test these private companies, as a result of our testing, we are concerned that they are marketing and advertising themselves as capable of improving an 8(a) applicant's chances of getting certified when they may not offer the advantages they claim.

"...Congratulations! Your firm has been Certified as a Participant in the U.S. Small Business Administration's (SBA) 8(a) Business Development Program."

U.S. SMALL BUSINESS ADMINISTRATION
WASHINGTON, D.C. 20416

August 11, 2009

[redacted]

Dear Mr. [redacted]:

Congratulations! Your firm has been certified as a Participant in the U.S. Small Business Administration's (SBA) 8(a) Business Development Program. Your nine (9) year program term begins on the date of this letter.

During participation in the 8(a) Business Development Program, you will receive business development assistance from an assigned Business Development Specialist in the Baltimore, Maryland District Office located at 10 S. Howard Street, Suite 6220. The phone number is 410-962-6195.

Your firm will become eligible to receive 8(a) Business Development contracts after you submit a business plan using SBA Form 1010C and receive SBA's approval of the plan. We are sending a copy of this certification letter to the SBA Baltimore, Maryland District Office. That office will send you the business plan form.

SBA requires that the 8(a) participant s President or Chief Executive Officer sign a Participation Agreement to show that he or she understands the conditions of 8(a) program participation. Please

Source: SBA.

Figure 1. SBA Certification Letter for Our Bogus 8(a) Firm.

Approved Fictitious Application

Fictitious Application 4: SBA approved this fictitious application for 8(a) certification after conducting a 5-month review. We did not intentionally prepare this application with any specific eligibility issues, but SBA identified several discrepancies and missing items in our application during its review. For example, SBA found a significant eligibility issue regarding our firm's business experience since it had less than the minimum 2 years required.[19] To overcome this issue, we crafted a request for a business waiver including detailed information that demonstrated our firm's potential for success. Table 5 below provides details on the timeline and interactions that occurred with SBA during the processing of this application. It shows that SBA's certification process was lengthy—requiring our bogus firm to submit substantial documentation.

Table 5. Timeline of Approved Fictitious Application.

Date	Actions of fictitious 8(a) firm	Actions of SBA
March 9, 2009		SBA confirms receipt of signed 8(a) application via email.
March 18, 2009		SBA sends a letter via email indicating application deficiencies; namely, our firm did not meet its 2 years in business requirement. To continue processing, SBA notes that our firm would have to submit documents demonstrating that we met business waiver requirements. SBA also requested the following: • copies of all contracts with corresponding customer payments, invoices, and bank statements equaling revenues reflected in financial statements; • copies of personal taxes stamped by IRS; • evidence of payment for taxes owed; and • clarification of information provided in our financial statements, among other things.
April 13, 2009	Mailed requested items to SBA.	
May 12, 2009		SBA sends an email indicating that our application required follow-up. Items requested include: • additional documentation that supports revenue and evidence of annual personal income; • a front and back photocopy of several bank-deposited checks, and evidence of available credit; • explanation of a promissory note; and • updated income statement and balance sheets.
May 27, 2009	Emailed requested items to SBA.	
June 8, 2009		SBA requests evidence of payment for 2008 taxes, and that we certify that there have been no changes with our firm since the submission of our application.
July 16, 2009	Emailed requested items to SBA.	
July 21, 2009		SBA runs a credit report on our firm.

Table 5. (Continued)

Date	Actions of fictitious 8(a) firm	Actions of SBA
July 28, 2009		SBA leaves a voice mail requesting a copy of our firm's business insurance.
July 30, 2009	Emailed copy of business insurance to SBA.	
August 11, 2009		Received SBA letter stating that our firm was certified as a participant in the 8(a) Business Development Program.

Source: GAO analysis.

In some instances, SBA failed to adequately follow up on issues that it identified as potential concerns. For example, SBA discovered that the firm represented in this application shared the same home and business addresses as the firm represented in our third application. While SBA requested information from the owner represented in our third application to determine if the two firms operated separate concerns, no such information was requested from the owner represented in this application. Additionally, when we prepared this application, we submitted a bogus military service record and represented that the owner of our firm had over 20 years of active-duty military service. While SBA requested evidence of all compensation, including a military pension, the agency did not inquire as to why an honorably discharged veteran with over 20 years of military service did not report or receive any military pension after we failed to provide any information on this pay on our income tax returns. Moreover, because this firm had been in business for less than 2 years, SBA requested that we provide documentation to prove that the president had substantial business management experience. We were also required to document that the firm had the technical experience to carry out its business plan; adequate capital to sustain operations; a record of successful performance on contracts; and the ability to obtain personnel, facilities, and equipment to perform on contracts if admitted to the program. SBA did not independently verify any of the information that we submitted was true. SBA did not verify that we actually performed work on any of the contracts we stated we had previously obtained, nor did it confirm if we had the office space that we represented as our firm's bona fide place of business. If SBA had verified any of the information in the documents that we submitted for this waiver, it would have discovered that none of it was true.

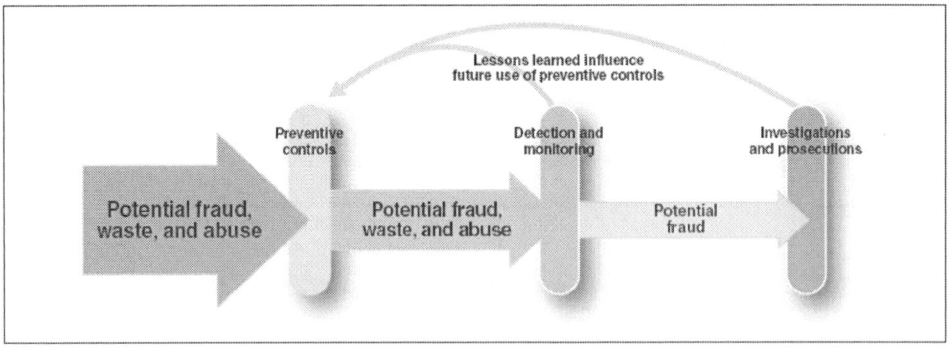

Source: GAO.

Figure 2. Fraud-Prevention Model

8(A) PROGRAM HAS INADEQUATE CONTROLS TO PREVENT FRAUD AND ABUSE

The 14 case studies of ineligible firms discussed above and the certification of a bogus firm show that weaknesses exist in SBA's controls for preventing, detecting, monitoring, and investigating fraud and abuse in the 8(a) program. We did not systematically test SBA's fraud prevention controls, but the awarding of over $325 million in sole-source and set-aside 8(a) contracts to just 14 ineligible firms illustrates the need for improving them. Fraud prevention requires a system of controls which, in their aggregate, minimize the likelihood of fraud occurring while maximizing the possibility of detecting any fraudulent activity that may transpire. Fraud prevention systems set forth what actions constitute fraudulent conduct and specifically spell out who in the organization handles fraud matters under varying circumstances. The potential of being caught can also deter likely perpetrators from committing fraud.

No system of internal control can provide absolute assurance against fraud. While the complete elimination of fraud risk is unlikely, agencies can take constructive steps to reduce their exposure. As shown in figure 4 below, a well-designed fraud prevention system (which can also be used to prevent waste and abuse) should consist of three crucial elements: (1) upfront preventive controls, (2) detection and monitoring, and (3) investigations and prosecutions. For the 8(a) program this would mean (1) front-end controls at the application stage, (2) fraud detection and monitoring of firms already in the program, and (3) the aggressive prosecution or suspension and debarment of individuals committing fraud. In addition, as shown in figure 4, the organization should use "lessons learned" from its detection and monitoring controls and investigations and prosecutions to design more effective preventive controls.

Preventive Controls

We found weaknesses and strengths in SBA's fraud prevention controls for the 8(a) program. Controls that keep ineligible firms and individuals from entering a federal program in the first place are the most efficient and effective means to minimize fraud, waste, and abuse. Three examples of preventive controls are validating data used in decision making against other government or third-party sources, inspecting whenever possible to confirm information, and training staff on fraud awareness.

Data Validation: SBA relied heavily on self-reported information from the firms during the initial certification and annual reviews, particularly in evaluating an individual's adjusted net worth and total assets, with limited data validation performed after firms enter the program. At the time of application, and for each year of their 9-year term, SBA requires 8(a) firm presidents to complete a "Personal Financial Statement." This statement is the primary document used to calculate the individuals' assets and liabilities. SBA uses the information disclosed in it to determine whether an applicant's adjusted net worth is under $250,000 at the time of application and under $750,000 during the 9-year program period. SBA's 8(a) standard operating procedures require agency staff to verify the completeness of all information provided to them by program participants. However, officials in the 8(a) program office told us that the only document routinely used to "cross-check" the value of assets and liabilities disclosed in the statement is the president's annual tax return. While the information found in a tax return can corroborate the income component of a president's adjusted net worth, it would not allow SBA to confirm the value of assets, such as the president's retirement account or other stocks and bonds being held. It also would not confirm how much equity a president has in an investment property, among other things. While, a president's spouse is also required by regulation to submit separate financial information to SBA, recent Office of Hearings and Appeals (OHA) decisions have interpreted the regulation to exclude consideration of a spouse's assets in the calculation.[20] Regulations do not specifically prohibit SBA from taking a spouse's assets or income into consideration. On the basis of our work, there is evidence that 8(a) firm presidents are using this loophole to "hide" assets by transferring or holding them in a spouse's name, as illustrated in Cases 1 and 10.

We found SBA applied some effective validation controls during the processing of our successful application. We requested to review this firm's file without alerting SBA to the fact that the firm was our bogus applicant. On the basis of this review, we documented that SBA verified (1) business information through Dun and Bradstreet; (2) credit and loan information through the Credit Bureaus; (3) federal loan delinquency status through the U.S. Department of Housing and Urban Development's (HUD) Credit Alert Interactive Voice Response System (CAIVRS); and (4) suspension and debarment status through the Excluded Parties List System. Nevertheless, these controls did not allow SBA to identify the bogus documents we submitted. Although SBA guidance requires the request of income tax transcripts from the IRS in order to validate tax returns submitted by applicants, in the case of our bogus firm that was certified, SBA did not request a tax transcript. SBA's data validation controls are strongest during the initial certification phase, but are less rigorous during subsequent annual reviews. For example, according to the program's standard operating procedures, SBA does not routinely request tax transcripts from the IRS once a firm has been certified to participate in the program. Instead program staff is advised by internal procedures to request the tax transcript "as needed."

Inspection: As we reported in 2008, SBA staff stated that emphasis on ensuring the completion of 100 percent of 8(a) firm annual reviews, an inefficient termination process, and resource constraints, limited the amount of time available for staff to conduct site visits of 8(a) firms.[21] There is neither a requirement that SBA conduct a site visit of a firm prior to certification, nor must the applicant meet anyone from SBA in person prior to entering the program. We conducted unannounced site visits and found instances of firms in violation of 8(a) program regulations. For example, when the president of the firm highlighted in Case 1 applied for initial certification, SBA raised several questions and concerns about the president's affiliation with his previous employer, a recently graduated 8(a) firm. However, officials in the New Jersey district office stated that they had not been able to conduct a site visit on any firm in their portfolio in several years. Our site visit verified that the president had made numerous misrepresentations on his application.

Staff Training: SBA staff responsible for annually recertifying firms for program participation told us that they are provided with limited fraud detection training. As a result, these staff may not be adequately trained to detect the occurrence of fraud in the 8(a) program.

Detection and Monitoring

Although preventive controls are the most effective way to minimize fraud, continual monitoring is an important component in detecting and deterring fraud. Monitoring and detection within a fraud prevention program involve actions such as data-mining for fraudulent and suspicious applicants and evaluating firms in order to provide reasonable assurance that they continue to meet program requirements. Although SBA requires that 8(a) firms are annually recertified for participation, evidence based on our investigation of 14 firms indicates that SBA needs to strengthen its controls in order to provide reasonable assurance that only eligible firms remain in the program. For example, SBA was not able to identify properties purchased by 8(a) participants that were not reported during the annual review. Moreover as noted in our related report,[22] SBA failed to complete some required annual review procedure 55 percent of the time.[23]

While SBA is required to conduct a review of 100 percent of 8(a) firms annually, SBA does not use data-mining techniques or other means in order to identify "red flags;" such techniques could identify firms that might warrant further investigation. For example, data-mining techniques could be used to detect applicant firms that are operating at the same address as a graduated 8(a) firm. When we asked 8(a) program office officials whether the agency took this step during the initial application process, they told us that their current systems did not provide them with the capability to determine if firms in their own database share a common address. They also said that they did not feel a new 8(a) firm operating at the same address as a previous participant was a concern unless they have reason to believe a relationship exists that would cause them to question ownership and control, or the two companies exceed small-business size standards because of their affiliation. However, we found that when 8(a) firms were operating at the same address as a previous participant, the companies were affiliated or had commingled resources.

From our limited review, there is indication that SBA staff responsible for assessing firms' continued eligibility do not always follow established program criteria during the annual review process. As mentioned previously, some of the 14 firms described in table 1 were determined to be ineligible after our investigators confirmed information that was concealed from SBA by firm presidents. In other cases, our review of SBA's files clearly indicated that these firms were not eligible for the 8(a) program, yet SBA failed to terminate or graduate these firms from the program, as the following examples illustrate.

- In our review of SBA's file of Case 6, we found that SBA received strong indications that a nondisadvantaged individual influenced the management and operations of the current 8(a) firm, yet took no action to investigate further or to terminate the firm from the program. In January 2006, SBA received a decision letter from the Idaho Department of Transportation Certification Committee on its decision to deny the 8(a) firm's application for certification as a Disadvantaged Business Enterprise.[24] The state's denial was based on concerns it found regarding the ownership and control of the firm. SBA staff told us that such a letter should raise a red flag, but acknowledged that no action was taken to review or investigate the state's findings. Then, in March 2006, SBA denied the firm's request for a mentor/protégé relationship with the nondisadvantaged individual—deeming such a relationship as "merely a vehicle to enable a non-8(a) participant to receive contracts." One month later, SBA wrote a letter to the 8(a) firm's owner about the completion of her annual review. In that letter, SBA indicated that the firm's annual revenues increased by nearly 1,300 percent over a 1-year period. It also attributed the growth to management and technical assistance the firm had received from the nondisadvantaged individual. SBA acknowledged that for the 8(a) firm to sustain such growth, it would have to depend upon the future assistance of said individual. SBA took no action to address concerns that the firm was affiliated with a nondisadvantaged individual in either of the aforementioned instances, or under the totality of the circumstances.

- For Case 4, SBA initiated termination proceedings against the 8(a) firm after conducting a site visit and determining that a nondisadvantaged individual exercised control over the 8(a) firm. It determined that the president of the 8(a) firm operated her business from the same office as her previous employer. In an attempt to convince SBA that her former employer no longer exercised control over her firm and that its efforts to terminate her from the program should cease, the 8(a) president provided SBA with a lease showing that she had relocated to an adjacent office. SBA accepted this document as evidence and dropped its termination proceedings. The agency did not take any other steps to determine whether the former employer exercised control over the 8(a) firm from within the same building.
- In Case 9, SBA staff responsible for annual reviews allowed an ineligible firm to remain in the program for 21 months past the date at which SBA staff determined that it was no longer eligible. Notes in the firm file indicate that the president had exceeded salary limitations and that the firm had exceeded all applicable size standards and was no longer "small" by federal standards. The SBA supervisor of the agency specialist responsible for the firm noted that the firm should be graduated and profiled as a success story. During the 21-month period, the firm received a contract extension worth $554,418 that it would no longer have been eligible for. We asked SBA why it awarded this contract to an ineligible firm, but were told by the audit liaison that SBA had no records related to this contract.

In a number of instances, our staff brought eligibility violations to the attention of the relevant specialist in SBA's district office. In none of these instances did the agency take any action to remove these firms from the program, even after acknowledging to our staff that the issues we raised ought to be "red flags" or cause for termination from the program. For three of the cases we investigated, 8(a) firm presidents' earned salaries that placed them in the top 1 percent of American taxpayers—a level at which SBA OHA has determined an individual is no longer economically disadvantaged. SBA regulations do set eligibility caps for adjusted net worth, but not for income and total assets. Agency staff are expected to rely on case law when determining whether program participants are economically disadvantaged for these last two criteria. However, agency staff follow case law inconsistently. These three 8(a) firm presidents received salaries which indicated they were no longer economically disadvantaged;

however, SBA officials failed to graduate these firms. As we noted in our related report,[25] a file review in five SBA district offices found that for about seven percent of the 123 firms we reviewed there was no evidence that SBA reviewed the president's net worth, or SBA retained the firms despite a net worth that exceeded program limits.[26] SBA is currently considering changing the regulations to explicitly set caps for salary and total assets.

Investigation and Prosecution

The final element of an effective fraud prevention system is the aggressive investigation and prosecution of individuals who commit fraud against the federal government. However, SBA currently does not have an effective process for investigating fraud and abuse within the 8(a) program.

Through the course of our interviews, we found that SBA staff responsible for annually assessing the eligibility of participants were not actively looking for fraud and abuse in the program. For example, we raised questions about the eligibility of one firm, and were told by the SBA employee responsible for monitoring the firm's eligibility that the firm was one of the 8(a) program's best success stories and that we would be unlikely to find any problems with the firm's operations. In another case, we provided evidence showing a participant withheld information that should have been reported and were told that if the president failed to report the purchase of several pieces of property, it was by mistake. Another official told us that they recommended the termination of a number of firms, but were overruled by their supervisors or the OHA.

In a small number of cases, SBA's Office of Inspector General (SBA OIG) has worked in collaboration with other criminal investigative units at agencies such as the Department of Defense, IRS, and the Federal Bureau of Investigation to prosecute cases of 8(a) eligibility fraud. In the last several years, the SBA OIG has recommended that SBA debar only two firms and their presidents. In one case, the firm was recommended for debarment because the financial and managerial involvement of a nondisadvantaged individual was not disclosed.[27] SBA ultimately suspended both the individual and the company and will consider debarment upon sentencing. In the other case, SBA OIG recommended that the 8(a) firm and its president be debarred for intentionally violating subcontracting limitations. SBA did not carry out the recommendation. As noted in our related report,[28] SBA lacks a formal mechanism to collect and analyze complaint data related to 8(a) eligibility. While SBA OIG maintains general complaint information such as the name of the 8(a) firm and type of complaint, an SBA OIG official told us that 8(a) complaints involving a single company generally do not rank high in priority for a review due to resource limitations and other priorities. We asked the SBA 8(a) program office if it had ever referred any firms for debarment or suspension proceedings based on their findings from their program eligibility reviews.

As of the writing of our report, the SBA liaison had not provided us an answer to the question. Officials in SBA's program office told us that while the agency annually tracks the number of firms that are terminated from the program, its records do not allow the agency to isolate which firms were terminated for fraud or abuse. While supporting the growth of 8(a) firms is an important aspect of SBA's mission, investigating those firms that are involved in fraudulent activity is essential to the integrity of the program. By failing to hold firms accountable, SBA has sent a message to the contracting community that there is no punishment or consequences for committing fraud or abusing the intent of the 8(a) program.

CONCLUSIONS

The 8(a) program needs to strengthen its fraud prevention, detection, monitoring, and investigative controls to minimize its vulnerability to fraud and abuse. SBA's prevention controls have some strengths, such as the validation of certain information with third-party sources. However, there are substantial vulnerabilities in the detection, monitoring, and investigation components. The consequences of these control weaknesses are substantial: in just the 14 cases we investigated for this report, over $325 million in sole-source and set-aside 8(a) contracts went to ineligible firms that manipulated the current system. To a substantial degree, the steps we took to investigate these firms could be part of an effective fraud detection program. Victims of the fraud and abuse in this program are legitimate economically and socially disadvantaged small businesses. To address the vulnerabilities we identified, an improved fraud prevention program is necessary. Ineligible firms will continue to participate in the 8(a) program unless the weaknesses are addressed.

RECOMMENDATIONS FOR EXECUTIVE ACTION

In order to minimize the potential for fraud and abuse in the 8(a) program, we recommend that the Administrator of SBA take the following six actions to improve its fraud prevention program:

- As part of implementing our previous recommendation to assess the workload of business development specialists, evaluate the feasibility of using additional third-party data sources and unannounced site visits, based on random or risk-based criteria, to allow more independent verification of firm-reported data during both initial certification and subsequent annual reviews.
- Evaluate the use of fraud detection tools, such as the use of data- mining techniques (e.g., matching addresses of applicants and previous participants), and evaluate the use of financial and analytical training for business opportunity specialists.
- Enact proposed regulation changes that would specify economic disadvantage with respect to participant's income and asset levels at the time of application and annual recertification.
- Evaluate changing program regulations to require adjusted net worth or total asset calculations to include assets held by the spouses of 8(a) participants.
- Enact proposed regulation changes that would limit new firms from participating in the 8(a) program if an immediate family member is, or has been, an 8(a) participant in the same line of work.

- Develop a more consistent enforcement strategy, to include the suspension or debarment of contractors who knowingly misrepresent themselves to qualify for the 8(a) program.

APPENDIX I. SCOPE AND METHODOLOGY

To determine whether ineligible firms are participating in the 8(a) program, we used a risk-based approach to identify firms that exhibited signs that they were not qualified for the program.[29] For example, we used data from the Federal Procurement Database System-Next Generation (FPDS-NG) to determine which firms in the Washington, D.C., Metropolitan Statistical Area received the most 8(a) contracts in 2006 and 2007. Next, we used data from the Small Business Administration's (SBA) Dynamic Small Business Search (DSBS) Web site to identify current 8(a) firms that were operating at the address of a graduated 8(a) firm. We limited this search to Washington, D.C., because there are significantly more firms located there than in any other area in the country. We used information about 8(a) firms provided by SBA to data mine for potentially fraudulent activity. In addition, we pursued leads found during the course of our work on the Service Disabled Veteran Owned Small Business and HUBZone programs. Finally, we established a new hotline, SmallBizFraud@gao.gov, to receive allegations of fraud related to SBA contracting programs. We advertised this hotline on GAO's Web site and in a major newspaper in the Washington, D.C., region. We received over 30 allegations of fraud and abuse in the 8(a) program through the hotline—far more than we were able to investigate given time and resource constraints. Six of these allegations were substantiated during the course of this work.

From these sources, we selected 14 cases for further investigation based on a variety of factors, such as facts and evidence provided in allegations and whether a firm received multiple 8(a) contracts. For the purposes of our investigation, we defined a case as one or more affiliated firms or joint ventures that obtained an 8(a) contract. To investigate these case studies, we reviewed documentation available from SBA in the firms' official files, including initial application materials, and documentation required by the annual review process. We worked with SBA's audit liaison to request this documentation; in some instances we received information directly from officials in SBA district offices and other times information was transmitted through this liaison. In some cases, we conducted both announced and unannounced site visits and interviewed firm owners, managers, and previous employees. We requested supporting documentation from some firms. We used a variety of investigative methods—such as analyzing firm payroll data, verifying the value of assets, and reviewing information from investigative databases—to gather information about the firms and to determine whether the firms' or their principals met 8(a) program criteria. In some cases, we also met with SBA staff responsible for annually recertifying these firms for the 8(a) program. Although 8(a) firms must meet several eligibility criteria to enter and remain in the program, we did not test all criteria. Generally, our investigations focused on whether firms' presidents were economically disadvantaged, and whether they managed the day-to-day operations of the firm because we felt these eligibility criteria posed the highest risk of being misrepresented to SBA. We did not, for example, attempt to independently verify whether the presidents of any 8(a) firms were United States citizens. We also analyzed data from FPDS-NG to identify 8(a) contracts received by the firms during their participation in the program.

In order to determine whether SBA only certifies firms that are qualified and capable of meeting the business development objectives of the 8(a) program, we established four fictitious companies and used fabricated documentation in our applications. For one firm, we employed the services of a private company that offered "8(a) Certification Services" to determine if such businesses offer the advantage that they advertised. We selected this particular firm because it described itself as deft at helping individuals who are not generally classified as disadvantaged obtain 8(a) certification for their firms. The firms we created were designed to appear as credible businesses that met basic 8(a) program eligibility criteria. These criteria require SBA to consider the following factors when screening applicant firms: (1) technical competence and managerial experience of the applicant firm's managers; (2) the operating history of the firm; (3) the firm's record of performance on previous federal and private sector contracts in the primary industry in which it is seeking 8(a) certification; (4) its financial capacity; and (5) the requisite licenses if the firm is engaged in an industry requiring professional licensing. As part of SBA's application process, agency officials review financial statements, conduct credit checks, and request copies of personal and business tax transcripts from the applicant as well as directly from the Internal Revenue Service (IRS). If SBA requested tax information associated with our bogus firms from the IRS, no record would have existed and our firms may have been deemed ineligible. Because SBA standard operating procedures require verification of tax information with the IRS, our tests did not focus on whether SBA carried this step out in any of the four cases. Therefore, to allow us to proactively test SBA's 8(a) program application process, we used Employer Identification Numbers (EIN) and undercover Social Security numbers to file real tax returns with the IRS for our four bogus individuals. In order to minimize our costs associated with paying taxes, we created tax scenarios in which our firms reflected net business losses over multiple tax years. While these income scenarios minimized our costs, they limited our testing scenarios to firms that were not profitable, and thus the likelihood that our firms could meet SBA's definition of success.

To determine what vulnerabilities, if any, existed in SBA's fraud prevention system, we made observations based on our case studies and proactive testing. We did not perform a systematic evaluation of the 8(a) program's fraud prevention system. We reviewed relevant regulations and guidance governing the program. We also interviewed officials from the Office of Inspector General, 8(a) program office, and SBA General Counsel about their responsibility over the program and controls currently in place to prevent, detect, and monitor fraud and abuse. Furthermore, we compared current controls in the 8(a) program to a fraud-prevention model developed by GAO and utilized in prior small- business contracting investigations. Our work was not designed to identify all fraud and abuse in the 8(a) program or estimate its full extent for the entire population of 8(a) firms.

We conducted our audit work and investigation from October 2008 through January 2010 in accordance with U.S. generally accepted government auditing standards. Those standards require that we plan and perform the audit to obtain sufficient, appropriate evidence to provide a reasonable basis for our findings and conclusions based on our audit objectives. We believe that the evidence obtained provides a reasonable basis for our findings and conclusions based on our objectives. We performed our investigative work in accordance with the standards prescribed by the Council of the Inspectors General on Integrity and Efficiency (CIGIE).

Appendix II. Comments from the Small Business Administration

U.S. SMALL BUSINESS ADMINISTRATION
WASHINGTON, D.C. 20416

March 8, 2010

Mr. Gregory Kutz
Managing Director
Forensic Audits and Special Investigations
U.S. Government Accountability Office
Washington, DC 20548

Dear Mr. Kutz:

The U.S. Small Business Administration (SBA) is pleased to provide a response addressing the issues outlined in your draft Government Accountability Office (GAO) Report Number: GAO-10-425, entitled, "8(a) Program – 14 Ineligible Firms Receive $325 million in Sole Source and Set Aside Contracts."

BACKGROUND:

As you are aware, since its inception, the 8(a) Business Development (BD) Program has significantly enhanced the SBA's mission and contributed toward the growth of the American economy. Although the 8(a) BD Program has enjoyed numerous successes, we recognize that there are weaknesses and areas that require increased monitoring and oversight. In an effort to address these weaknesses, in October 2009, SBA drafted proposed regulatory revisions aimed at strengthening opportunities for disadvantaged small businesses to benefit from its 8(a) BD program. The proposed 8(a) regulation changes are the result of the first comprehensive review of the 8(a) BD program in a number of years and were published in the *Federal Register*. The rules cover a variety of areas of the program, ranging from providing further clarification on determining economic disadvantage to requirements on Joint Ventures and the Mentor-Protégé program. The public comment period was extended to January 28, 2010, in an effort to obtain comments from our broad customer base as well as other stakeholders.

The 8(a) BD program has a proven track record as an effective program for helping socially and economically disadvantaged small businesses gain access to training and contracting opportunities to help them grow, create jobs and ultimately succeed in the marketplace upon leaving the program. We believe that the proposed 8(a) changes build on that foundation of success, and will strengthen the program and maximize its benefits for eligible small businesses.

ROLES AND RESPONSIBILITIES:

SBA's 8(a) BD program is delivered collaboratively between two departments of the SBA. The Office of Business Development (OBD) is responsible for policy formation and the certifications of 8(a) applications, approval of mentor- protégé applications as well as the approval of existing 8(a) firms that are exiting the program (early graduations, approval of change of ownerships, approval of voluntary withdrawals, approval of terminations, and suspensions). OBD is also responsible for the virtual training and relevant policy briefings provided to SBA staff across the country responsible for executing the 8(a) BD program on an on-going basis throughout the year.

The Office of Field Operations (OFO) is responsible for supporting the Business Development Specialists (BDS) who are tasked with executing the 8(a) BD program and are located in 68 District offices across the country. Selected BDSs will have 8(a) firms assigned to them. The BDSs work directly with 8(a) firms to help prepare business plans, provide technical assistance, review continuing eligibility, coordinate with resource partners that provide counseling, training, loans, and other assistance to small businesses, and coordinate additional assistance and training for firms through another SBA program.

The following is SBA's response to the six recommendations made by GAO regarding SBA's need to minimize the potential for fraud and abuse in the 8(a) BD program. Some of the responses include corrective measures already implemented and actions that are planned to be implemented in the near future.

GOVERNMENT ACCOUNTABILITY OFFICE'S RECOMMENDATIONS:

RECOMMENDATION 1:

As part of implementing our previous recommendation to assess the workload of business development specialists, evaluate the feasibility of using additional third-party data sources and unannounced site visits, based on random or risk-based criteria, to allow more independent verification of firm-reported data during both initial certification and subsequent annual reviews.

SBA RESPONSE TO RECOMMENDATION 1

SBA agrees with the recommendation.

OFO will assess the workload of BDSs to determine the need for additional staffing resources.

An internal data verification process is currently being conducted by OBD. In addition, we will evaluate the third party data validation sources we currently use (IRS transcripts, CAVIRS, and Experian) to determine the need for an independent verification of firm-reported data. Through individualized and group training, we will re-emphasize the requirement to conduct unannounced site visits, where appropriate in determining a participant's continuing 8(a) BD program eligibility.

RECOMMENDATION 2:

Evaluate the use of fraud detection tools, such as the use of data-mining techniques (e.g. matching addresses of applicants and previous participants), and financial and analytical training of business opportunity specialists.

SBA RESPONSE TO RECOMMENDATION 2:

SBA agrees with this recommendation.

OBD has already begun this evaluation process. SBA will conduct on-going training of BD personnel for purposes of determining 8(a) participant's continuing eligibility. Several staff in OBD are currently participating in a comprehensive agency-sponsored data training course which will significantly enhance their data analytical skills. Also, OBD has developed the course content and format for a National Training Conference, planned for June 2010, which is intended to provide in-depth training in the areas of financial and data analysis.

RECOMMENDATION 3:

Enact proposed regulation changes that would specify economic disadvantage with respect to participant's income and asset levels at the time of application and annual recertification.

SBA RESPONSE TO RECOMMENDATION #3:

SBA agrees with this recommendation and has included this change in the proposed regulations.

The proposed changes to the 8(a) regulations specifically address the area of economic disadvantage. In addition, OBD has revised Chapter 5, *"Participant Review Process"* and Chapter 10, *"Leaving the 8(a) Business Development Program"* of the 8(a) Standard Operating Procedures 80 05 3 (SOP) to provide improve the guidance available to BD personnel related to determining a participant's income and asset levels as it relates to continuing eligibility. SBA intends to evaluate whether additional SOP revisions will be required once the proposed rule making is complete.

RECOMMENDATION 4:

Evaluate changing program regulations to require adjusted net worth and/or total asset calculations to include assets held by the spouses of 8(a) participants.

SBA RESPONSE TO RECOMMENDATION 4:

SBA will evaluate this recommendation based upon the comments received as a result of the proposed 8(a) rule change.

The proposed 8(a) regulatory change will evaluate and clearly define when and how a family member's assets will be included in the assets of the 8(a) participant. The proposed 8(a) regulations stipulate that SBA may consider a spouse's financial situation in determining an individual's access to capital and credit. It is anticipated the revised 8(a) regulations will be finalized by October 2010.

RECOMMENDATION 5:

Enact proposed regulation changes that would limit new firms from participating in the 8(a) BD program if an immediate family member, is, or has been an 8(a) participant in the same line of work.

SBA RESPONSE TO RECOMMENDATION 5:

SBA agrees with this recommendation and has included this change in the proposed regulations.

In order to prevent disadvantaged individuals from using family members to extend their program terms and to prevent fronts, SBA proposes to amend 13 C.F.R. § 124.105(g) to provide that an individual may not use his or her disadvantaged status to qualify a firm if such individual has an immediate family member who has used his or her disadvantaged status to qualify another firm for participation in the 8(a) BD program. However, the proposed rule will permit the SBA's Associate Administrator for Business Development (AA/BD) to waive this prohibition under certain circumstances.

RECOMMENDATION 6:

Develop a more consistent enforcement strategy, to include the suspension and/or debarment of contractors who knowingly misrepresent themselves to qualify for the 8(a) BD program.

SBA RESPONSE TO RECOMMENDATION 6:

SBA agrees with this recommendation.

OBD will disseminate guidance to all BD personnel outlining a consistent strategy for recommending immediate enforcement action for firms that knowingly misrepresent themselves to obtain 8(a) BD program certification.

Again, thank you for the opportunity to provide comments on this draft GAO Report. My staff and I look forward to working with you in resolving the issues outlined in this draft GAO Report as we seek to strengthen the SBA's 8(a) Business Development program.

If you have additional questions or comments, please contact me directly.

Sincerely,

Joseph G. Jordan
Associate Administrator
Office of Government Contracting
and Business Development

End Notes

[1] Active contracts included any contract having a modification in fiscal year 2008 even if those modifications were non-monetary ones.

[2] We excluded Alaskan Native Corporation (ANC) 8(a) firms from our investigation due to different qualification standards.

[3] GAO, *Small Business Administration: Steps Have Been Taken to Improve Administration of the 8(a) Program, but Key Controls for Continued Eligibility Need Strengthening*, GAO-10-353 (Washington, D.C.: Mar. 30, 2010).

[4] SBA regulations presume that the following individuals are socially disadvantaged: black Americans; Hispanic Americans; Native Americans; Asian Pacific Americans; and Subcontinent Asian Americans.

[5] Although not currently spelled out in the 8(a) regulations, SBA may, in its discretion, deny 8(a) certification or continued participation to an applicant or participant, respectively, if his or her Adjusted Gross Income (AGI) for the past 2 years falls within the top 1 to 2 percentiles of all American taxpayers. An applicant may also be disqualified because of an excessive amount of total assets. On December 9, 2009, SBA solicited comment on a proposed rule amending the 8(a) regulations to explicitly state that an applicant is presumed not to be economically disadvantaged if their AGI exceeds $200,000 (averaged over the last 2 years). For continued 8(a) participation, an 8(a) participant may not exceed an AGI of $250,000. In addition, the proposed regulations would disqualify an individual with assets in excess of $3 million at the time of application and $4 million for continued 8(a) participation.

[6] *Small Business Size Regulations; 8(a) Business Development/Small Disadvantaged Business Status Determinations*, 74 Fed. Reg. 55694 (proposed Oct. 28, 2009) (to be codified at 13 C.F.R. pts. 121 and 124).

[7] However, SBA generally may award a sole-source 8(a) contract to an 8(a) firm owned and controlled by an Indian tribe or an Alaska Native Corporation where the value of the procurement exceeds the competitive dollar threshold. If it is a Department of Defense procurement, this exemption extends to Native Hawaiian Organizations.

[8] The firms are located in Georgia, Idaho, Maryland, New Jersey, Texas, Virginia, and West Virginia.

[9] This $1.2 billion includes both non-8(a) awards, as well as 8(a) awards that these firms were eligible to receive.

[10] SBA has proposed changes to the 8(a) regulations that would prohibit firms from participating in the 8(a) program if the president has an immediate family member who is a disadvantaged principal of a former 8(a) firm. This prohibition may be waived by the Associate Business Development Administrator if there are no connections between the two firms and if the applicant can demonstrate sufficient expertise to operate the firm. There is a presumption against the waiver if the firms are in the same line of business.

[11] SBA has previously disqualified firms that are simply an extension of a former 8(a) participant, as well as firms in which there is a "confusion of identities" between the firm and a previous 8(a) participant. Matter of Infotech International, Inc., SBA No. 205 (2004).

[12] All 8(a) participants sign an agreement upon entering the program which states, among other things, that the firm president agrees to fully cooperate with any and all requests from authorized government officials (including auditors and investigators from SBA or other agencies) for examination of business records and any other information deemed necessary by such officials for legitimate program purposes.

[13] 13 C.F.R. § 124.303(a)(19).

[14] See, for example, Size Appeal of Bering Pacific Construction, SBA No. 4094 (1995).

[15] Eligibility calculated by adding the years since the graduated firm's eligibility term expired (2001) and the last successive firm's eligibility term will expire (2014).

[16] SBA regulations require that the disadvantaged principal manage the day-to-day operations of the firm.

[17] SBA regulations require that employees of 8(a) firms generally may not receive greater compensation than the disadvantaged principal. 13 C.F.R. § 124. 106(e)(3).

[18] The owners of newly certified 8(a) firms are required to attend an orientation in person. We never attended our required orientation session.

[19] This application was submitted with less than the necessary 2 years of business experience to avoid tax implications.

[20] The Office of Hearings and Appeals (OHA) is an independent office of the SBA established in 1983 to provide an independent, quasi-judicial appeal of certain SBA program decisions.

[21] GAO, *Small Business Administration: Agency Should Assess Resources Devoted to Contracting and Improve Several Processes in the 8(a) Program* GAO-09-16 (Washington, D.C.: Nov. 21 2008).

[22] GAO, *Small Business Administration: Steps Have Been Taken to Improve Administration of the 8(a) Program, but Key Controls for Continued Eligibility Need Strengthening*, GAO-10-353 (Washington, D.C.: Mar. 30, 2010).

[23] Because these estimates are based on a probability sample, they are subject to sampling error. The 95 percent confidence interval for this estimate is (46, 64) percent of the cases, SBA failed to comply with some annual review procedure.

[24] In general, to be eligible for the Disadvantaged Business Enterprise program, persons must own 51 percent or more of a "small business," establish that they are disadvantaged within the meaning of Idaho Department of Transportation regulations, and prove they control their business.

[25] GAO, *Small Business Administration: Steps Have Been Taken to Improve Administration of the 8(a) Program, but Key Controls for Continued Eligibility Need Strengthening*, GAO-10-353 (Washington, D.C.: Mar. 30, 2010).

[26] Because these estimates are based on a probability sample, they are subject to sampling error. The 95 percent confidence interval for this estimate is (3, 13).

[27] During the application process, firms are reminded of the program's eligibility requirements. The owners sign a document stating that they understand if they misrepresent the firm's status as an 8(a) participant, or make any other false statement in order to influence the certification process in any way, they will be subject to penalties, such and fines and imprisonment.

[28] GAO, *Small Business Administration: Steps Have Been Taken to Improve Administration of the 8(a) Program, but Key Controls for Continued Eligibility Need Strengthening*, GAO-10-353 (Washington, D.C.: Mar. 30, 2010).

[29] We excluded Alaskan Native Corporation (ANC) 8(a) firms from our investigation due to different qualification standards.

In: Disadvantaged Small Businesses and the 8(a) Program ISBN: 978-1-61209-309-3
Editors: James P. Carlson and Andrea M. Bernard

Chapter 5

Alaska Native Corporations: Increased Use of Special 8(a) Provisions Calls for Tailored Oversight

Katherine V. Schinasi

Why GAO Did this Study

Alaska Native corporations (ANC) were created to settle land claims with Alaska Natives and foster economic development. In 1986, legislation passed that allowed ANCs to participate in the Small Business Administration's (SBA) 8(a) program. Since then, Congress has extended special procurement advantages to 8(a) ANC firms, such as the ability to receive sole-source contracts for any dollar amount and to own multiple subsidiaries in the 8(a) program. We were asked to testify on an earlier report where we identified (1) trends in the government's 8(a) contracting with ANC firms, (2) the reasons agencies have awarded 8(a) sole- source contracts to ANC firms and the facts and circumstances behind some of these contracts, and (3) how ANCs are using the 8(a) program. GAO also evaluated SBA's oversight of 8(a) ANC firms.

GAO made recommendations aimed at improving SBA's oversight of 8(a) ANC contracting activity and ensuring that procuring agencies properly oversee 8(a) contracts they award to ANC firms. SBA has either taken action or plans to take action on the recommendations. The procuring agencies generally agreed with our recommendation to them.

We believe implementation of our recommendations will provide better oversight of 8(a) ANC contracting activity and provide decision makers with information to know whether the program is operating as intended.

WHAT GAO FOUND

While representing a small amount of total federal procurement spending, obligations for 8(a) contracts to ANC firms increased from $265 million in fiscal year 2000 to $1.1 billion in 2004. Over the 5-year period, agencies obligated $4.6 billion to ANC firms, of which $2.9 billion, or 63 percent, went through the 8(a) program. During this period, six federal agencies—the departments of Defense, Energy, the Interior, State, and Transportation and the National Aeronautics and Space Administration—accounted for over 85 percent of 8(a) contracting activity. Obligations for 8(a) sole source contracts by these agencies to ANC firms increased from about $180 million in fiscal year 2000 to about $876 million in fiscal year 2004.

ANCs use the 8(a) program as one of many tools to generate revenue with the goal of providing benefits to their shareholders. Some ANCs are heavily reliant on the 8(a) program for revenues, while others approach the program as one of many revenue-generating opportunities. GAO found that some ANCs have increasingly made use of the congressionally authorized advantages afforded to them. One of the key practices is the creation of multiple 8(a) subsidiaries, sometimes in highly diversified lines of business. From fiscal year 1988 to 2005, ANC 8(a) subsidiaries increased from one subsidiary owned by one ANC to 154 subsidiaries owned by 49 ANCs.

In general, acquisition officials at the agencies reviewed told GAO that the option of using ANC firms under the 8(a) program allows them to quickly, easily, and legally award contracts for any value. They also noted that these contracts help them meet small business goals. In reviewing selected large sole-source 8(a) contracts awarded to ANC firms, GAO found that contracting officials had not always complied with certain requirements, such as notifying SBA of contract modifications and monitoring the percentage of work that is subcontracted.

SBA, which is primarily responsible for implementing the 8(a) program, had not tailored its policies and practices to account for ANCs' unique status and growth in the 8(a) program, even though SBA officials recognized that ANCs enter into more complex business relationships than other 8(a) participants. Areas where SBA's oversight fell short included determining whether more than one subsidiary of the same ANC was generating a majority of its revenue in the same primary industry, consistently determining whether awards to 8(a) ANC firms had resulted in other small businesses losing contract opportunities, and ensuring that the partnerships between 8(a) ANC firms and large firms were functioning in the way they were intended.

Mr. Chairman and Members of the Committee:

I am pleased to be here today to discuss our April 2006 report on Alaska Native Corporation (ANC) 8(a) firms.[1] In December 1971, Congress enacted the Alaska Native Claims Settlement Act to resolve long-standing aboriginal land claims and to foster economic development for Alaska Natives. This legislation created ANCs, which would become the vehicle for distributing land and monetary benefits to Alaska Natives in lieu of a reservation system. As of December 2005, there were 13 regional ANCs and 182 village, urban, and group corporations.

In 1986, legislation was enacted that allowed ANC-owned firms to participate in the Small Business Administration's (SBA) 8(a) program— one of the federal government's primary means for developing small businesses owned by socially and economically disadvantaged individuals. Since then, Congress has extended special procurement advantages to ANC firms. For example, ANC firms are permitted to receive noncompetitive contracts for any amount, whereas other 8(a) companies are subject to competitive thresholds of $5 million for manufacturing contracts or $3 million for all other contracts. ANCs can also own multiple subsidiaries participating in the 8(a) program,[2] unlike other 8(a) firms that may own only one in a lifetime and no more than 20 percent of another 8(a) firm.

Our 2006 report on 8(a) ANC contracting identified (1) trends in contracting with ANC firms, (2) the reasons agencies have awarded 8(a) sole-source contracts to ANC firms and the facts and circumstances behind some of these contracts, and (3) how ANCs are using the 8(a) program. We also evaluated SBA's oversight of 8(a) ANC firms. We made a number of recommendations to SBA and also recommended that the agencies in our review work with SBA to develop training for their contracting personnel.

Today I will discuss the highlights of our report and provide an update on actions SBA and the other agencies have taken to address our recommendations.

To address the objectives of our 2006 report, we obtained data on federal 8(a) contracting with ANCs. It is important to note that there is no readily available central source of information on ANC 8(a) contracting activity. We obtained each ANC firm's Data Universal Numbering System (DUNS) number and used this information to obtain data from the Federal Procurement Data System (FPDS) and agencies. To assess the reliability of the procurement data, we (1) compared FPDS and agency data to verify its accuracy, (2) reviewed related documentation, including contract files, and (3) worked closely with agency officials to identify and resolve any data problems. When we found discrepancies, we brought them to the agency's attention and worked with them to correct the discrepancies before conducting our analyses. We also analyzed 16 large, sole-source 8(a) contracts awarded to ANC firms from the departments of Defense, Energy, the Interior, State, Transportation, and Homeland Security and the National Aeronautics and Space Administration (NASA). We selected the contracts based on high ultimate award values and high dollar obligations that represented a variety of contractors and services. We traveled to Alaska and met with executives of 13 regional ANCs and 17 village or urban corporations. The report on which this testimony is based was prepared in accordance with generally accepted government auditing standards.

Our work did not include within its scope an objective or analyses that either support or challenge special ANC advantages within the 8(a) program. The program has been established in law and any changes are up to the Congress.

ANC Trends in and Use of 8(a) Contracting

8(a) ANC contracting represents a small amount of total federal procurement spending. However, dollars obligated to ANC firms through the 8(a) program grew from $265 million in fiscal year 2000 to $1.1 billion in 2004. Overall, during the 5-year period, the government obligated $4.6 billion to ANC firms, of which $2.9 billion, or 63 percent, went through the 8(a) program.

During this period, six federal agencies—the departments of Defense, Energy, the Interior, State, and Transportation and NASA—accounted for almost 85 percent of total 8(a) ANC obligations. Obligations for 8(a) sole- source contracts by these agencies to ANC firms increased from about $180 million in fiscal year 2000 to about $876 million in fiscal year 2004.

ANCs use the 8(a) program as one of many tools to generate revenue with the goal of benefiting their shareholders. Some ANCs are heavily reliant on the 8(a) program for revenues, while others approach the program as one of many revenue-generating opportunities, such as investments in stocks or real estate. ANCs are using the congressionally authorized advantages afforded to them, such as ownership of multiple 8(a) subsidiaries,[3] sometimes in diversified lines of business. From fiscal year 1988 to 2005, numbers increased from one 8(a) subsidiary owned by one ANC to 154 subsidiaries owned by 49 ANCs. Figure 1 shows the recent growth in ANCs' 8(a) subsidiaries.

ANCs use their ability to own multiple businesses in the 8(a) program, as allowed by law, in different ways. For example, some ANCs

- create a second subsidiary in anticipation of winning follow-on work from one of their graduating subsidiaries;[4]
- wholly own their 8(a) subsidiaries, while others invest in partially- owned subsidiaries; and
- diversify their subsidiaries' capabilities to increase opportunities to win government contracts in various industries.

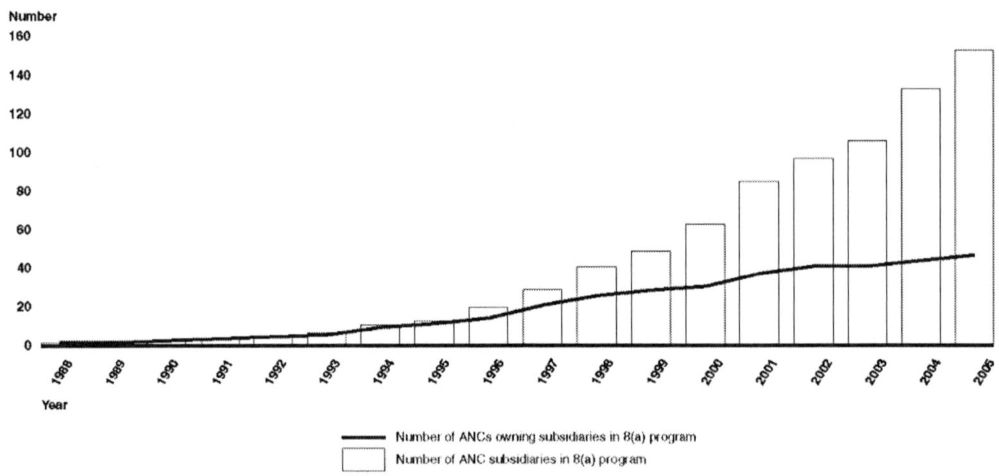

Source: GAO analysis of SBA data.

Figure 1. Number of ANC Parent Corporations and Subsidiaries Active in the 8(a) Program, 1988 to 2005.

Contract Execution Shortfalls

Our review of 16 large sole-source contracts awarded by 7 agencies found that agency officials view contracting with 8(a) ANC firms as a quick, easy, and legal way to award contracts while at the same time helping their agencies meet small business goals.[5]

Memoranda of Understanding (partnership agreements) between SBA and agencies delegate the contract execution function to federal agencies, although SBA remains responsible for implementing the 8(a) program. We found that contracting officials had not always complied with requirements to notify SBA when modifying contracts, such as increasing the scope of work or the dollar value, and to monitor the percentage of the work performed by the 8(a) firms versus their subcontractors. For example:

- Federal regulation requires that when 8(a) firms subcontract under an 8(a) service contract, they incur at least 50 percent of the personnel costs with their own employees.[6] The purpose of this provision, which limits the amount of work that can be performed by the subcontractor, is to ensure that small businesses do not pass along the benefits of their contracts to their subcontractors. For the 16 files we reviewed, we found almost no evidence that the agencies are effectively monitoring compliance with this requirement. In general, the contracting officers we spoke with were confused about whose responsibility it is.
- Agencies are also required to notify SBA of all 8(a) contract awards, modifications, and exercised options where the contract execution function has been delegated to the agencies in the partnership agreements. We found that not all contracting officers were doing so. In one case, the Department of Energy contracting officer had broadened the scope of a contract a year after award, adding 10 additional lines of business that almost tripled the value of the contract. These changes were not coordinated with SBA.

SBA Lacks Oversight of 8(a) ANC Activity

We reported in 2006 that SBA had not tailored its policies and practices to account for ANCs' unique status and growth in the 8(a) program, even though officials recognize that ANC firms enter into more complex business relationships than other 8(a) participants. SBA officials told us that they have faced a challenge in overseeing the activity of the 8(a) ANC firms because ANCs' charter under the Alaska Native Claims Settlement Act is not always consistent with the business development intent of the 8(a) program. The officials noted that the goal of ANCs—economic development for Alaska Natives from a community standpoint—can be in conflict with the primary purpose of the 8(a) program, which is business development for individual small, disadvantaged businesses.

SBA's oversight fell short in that it did not:

- track the primary business industries in which ANC subsidiaries had 8(a) contracts to ensure that more than one subsidiary of the same ANC was not generating the majority of its revenue under the same primary industry code;

- consistently determine whether other small businesses were losing contracting opportunities when large sole-source contracts were awarded to 8(a) ANC firms;
- adhere to a statutory and regulatory requirement to ascertain whether 8(a) ANC firms, when entering the 8(a) program or for each contract award, had, or were likely to obtain, a substantial unfair competitive advantage within an industry; [7]
- ensure that partnerships between 8(a) ANC firms and large firms were functioning in the way they were intended under the 8(a) program; and
- maintain information on ANC 8(a) activity.

SBA officials from the Alaska district office had reported to headquarters that the makeup of their 8(a) portfolio was challenging and required more contracting knowledge and business savvy than usual because the majority of the firms they oversee are owned by ANCs and tribal entities. The officials commented that these firms tend to pursue complex business relationships and tend to be awarded large and often complex contracts. We found that the district office officials were having difficulty managing their large volume and the unique type of work in their 8(a) portfolio.

When we began our review, SBA headquarters officials responsible for overseeing the 8(a) program did not seem aware of the growth in the ANC 8(a) portfolio and had not taken steps to address the increased volume of work in their Alaska office.

Previous Conclusions, Recommendations, and Agency Responses

In 2006, we reported that ANCs were increasingly using the contracting advantages Congress has provided them. Our work showed that procuring agencies' contracting officers are in need of guidance on how to use these contracts while exercising diligence to ensure that taxpayer dollars are spent effectively. Equally important, we stated, significant improvements were needed in SBA's oversight of the program. Without stronger oversight, we noted the potential for abuse and unintended consequences.

In our April 2006 report, we made 10 recommendations to SBA on actions that can be taken to revise its regulations and policies and to improve practices pertaining to its oversight of ANC 8(a) procurements. Our recommendations and SBA's June 2007 response are as follows.

We recommended that the Administrator of SBA:

1. Ascertain and then clearly articulate in regulation how SBA will comply with existing law to determine whether and when one or more ANC firms are obtaining, or are likely to obtain, a substantial unfair competitive advantage in an industry.

> SBA response: SBA is exploring possible regulatory changes that would address the issue of better controlling the award of sole-source 8(a) contracts over the competitive threshold dollar limitation to joint ventures between tribally and ANC-owned 8(a) firms and other business concerns.

2. In regulation, specifically address SBA's role in monitoring ownership of ANC holding companies that manage 8(a) operations to ensure that the companies are wholly owned by the ANC and that any changes in ownership are reported to SBA.

SBA response: SBA is building a Business Development Management Information System to electronically manage all aspects of the 8(a) program. According to SBA, this system, scheduled to be completed in fiscal year 2008, will monitor program participants' continuing eligibility in the 8(a) program and could include an ANC element in the electronic annual review that would monitor the ownership of ANC holding companies that manage 8(a) operations and ensure that any changes in ownership are reported to SBA.

3. Collect information on ANCs' 8(a) participation as part of required overall 8(a) monitoring, to include tracking the primary revenue generators for 8(a) ANC firms to ensure that multiple subsidiaries under one ANC are not generating their revenue in the same primary industry.

SBA response: The planned electronic annual review can collect information on ANCs' multiple subsidiaries to ensure that they are not generating the majority of their revenues from the same primary industry. Further, to ensure that an ANC-owned firm does not enter the 8(a) program with the same North American Industry Classification System (NAICS) code[8] as another current or former 8(a) firm owned by that ANC, the ANC-owned applicant must certify that it operates in a distinct primary industry and must demonstrate that fact through revenues generated. SBA notes that the planned annual electronic reviews can validate this information.

4. Revisit regulation that requires agencies to notify SBA of all contract modifications and consider establishing thresholds for notification, such as when new NAICS codes are added to the contract or there is a certain percentage increase in the dollar value of the contract. Once notification criteria are determined, provide guidance to the agencies on when to notify SBA of contract modifications and scope changes.

SBA response: SBA stated that its revisions to its partnership agreements with federal agencies address this recommendation. However, we note that the revised agreement does not establish thresholds or include new criteria for when agencies should send SBA contract modifications or award documentation. The agreement states that agencies "shall provide a copy of any contract... including basic contracts, orders, modifications, and purchase orders" to SBA.

5. Consistently determine whether other small businesses are losing contracting opportunities when awarding contracts through the 8(a) program to ANC firms.

SBA response: SBA stated that it plans to require the contracting agencies to include impact statements in their contract offer letters to SBA.

6. Standardize approval letters for each 8(a) procurement to clearly assign accountability for monitoring of subcontracting and for notifying SBA of contract modifications.

SBA response: SBA agreed with the recommendation but did not indicate an action taken or planned.

7. Tailor wording in approval letters to explain the basis for adverse impact determinations.

SBA response: SBA agreed with the recommendation but did not indicate an action taken or planned.

8. Clarify memorandums of understanding (known as partnership agreements) with procuring agencies to state that it is the agency contracting officer's responsibility to monitor compliance with the limitation on subcontracting clause.

SBA response: SBA has implemented this recommendation by revising the partnership agreements with the procuring agencies. It added several provisions that delineate the agencies'responsibilities for oversight, monitoring, and compliance with procurement laws and regulations governing 8(a) contracts, including the limitation on subcontracting clause.

9. Evaluate staffing levels and training needed to effectively oversee ANC participation in the 8(a) program and take steps to allocate appropriate resources to the Alaska district office.

SBA response: SBA stated that the planned Business Development Management Information System should help the Alaska district office more effectively oversee ANC participation in the 8(a) program. It stated that it is providing training to the Alaska district office. However, no plans were in place to evaluate staffing levels at the office.

10. Provide more training to agencies on the 8(a) program, specifically including a component on ANC 8(a) participation.

SBA response: SBA has provided training to agencies on the revised 8(a) partnership agreements; however, our review of the slides SBA used for the training found no reference to ANC 8(a) firms specifically. According to an SBA official, SBA will include a component on ANC 8(a) participants in future training sessions.

We also recommended that procuring agencies provide guidance to contracting officers to ensure proper oversight of ANC contracts. The procuring agencies generally agreed with the recommendation. Some agencies are waiting for SBA to implement our recommendations before they take their own actions, but others have taken steps to tighten their oversight of contracts with 8(a) ANC firms. The Department of Homeland Security, for example, recently issued an "acquisition alert" requiring that its heads of contracting activities provide guidance and training on the use of 8(a) firms owned by ANCs. The alert provides that use of the authority to award sole-source 8(a) contracts to ANCs must be judicious with appropriate safeguards to ensure that the cost/price is fair and reasonable, that the ANC has the technical ability to perform the work, that the ANC will be performing the required percentage of the work and that the award is in the best interests of the government. The Department of Energy revised its acquisition guidance regarding small business programs to remind contracting officers to use care in awarding and administering ANC contracts, to include notifying SBA of contract modifications and monitoring the limits on subcontracting. The Department also provided training on the 8(a) program, to include contracting with ANC firms. By providing contracting officers with appropriate training on these issues, the government is taking steps to ensure that the ANC firms are operating in the program as intended, thereby mitigating the risk of unintended consequences or abuse of some of the privileges provided to these firms.

This concludes my testimony. I would be happy to answer any questions you may have.

End Notes

[1] GAO, *Contract Management: Increased Use of Alaska Native Corporations' Special 8(a) Provisions Calls for Tailored Oversight*, GAO-06-399, (Washington, D.C.: Apr. 27, 2006).

[2] Each 8(a) ANC firm must be in a different primary industry.

[3] In this testimony, "ANC" refers to the parent corporation. The term "ANC firm" denotes a business owned by an ANC. We use the term "ANC firm" and "subsidiary" interchangeably.

[4] There is a 9-year limit to participation in the 8(a) program; firms could graduate earlier if they outgrow their primary industry size standards.

[5] ANC firms in the 8(a) program are deemed by law as socially and economically disadvantaged. Awards to these firms are credited to agencies' small business goals.

[6] For general construction, the 8(a) firm is required to incur at least 15 percent of the personnel costs.

[7] This requirement is set forth in the Small Business Act (15 U.S.C. § 636(j)(10)(J)(ii)(II)).

[8] SBA has designated a small business size standard for every NAICS code. 8(a) applicants must qualify as small under their primary NAICS code at the time of application and SBA's certification date. SBA regulation requires that at least 2 years lapse after an ANC firm exits the 8(a) program before another firm owned by the same parent ANC can enter the program with the prior firm's primary NAICS code. However, once accepted into the program, 8(a) firms may pursue contracts in any line of work, called secondary NAICS codes.

In: Disadvantaged Small Businesses and the 8(a) Program ISBN: 978-1-61209-309-3
Editors: James P. Carlson and Andrea M. Bernard

Chapter 6

CONTRACTING PROGRAMS FOR ALASKA NATIVE CORPORATIONS: HISTORICAL DEVELOPMENT AND LEGAL AUTHORITIES

John R. Luckey, Kate M. Manuel and Roger Walke

SUMMARY

According to some reports, federal contract dollars awarded to Alaska Native Corporations and their subsidiaries increased by 916% between FY2000 and FY2008, going from $508.4 million to $5.2 billion. The dollars awarded to ANC-owned firms through the Small Business Administration's (SBA's) 8(a) Program, in particular, reportedly tripled between FY2004 ($1.1 billion) and FY2008 ($3.9 billion). This widely reported increase has generated congressional and public interest in the legal authorities governing contracting with these entities. Of particular interest are the authorities creating the alleged "special procurement advantages" that ANC subsidiaries enjoy in contracting under the 8(a) Program.

The 111th Congress enacted legislation (P.L. 111-84) requiring justifications, approvals, and notices for sole-source contracts in excess of $20 million awarded through the 8(a) Program, including contracts with ANC-owned firms. An amendment to the Senate version of the National Defense Authorization Act for FY2010 (S.Amdt. 1762 to S. 1390) was also proposed, but subsequently withdrawn, that would have limited the Department of Defense's authority to make sole-source awards in excess of $3.5 million ($5.5 million for manufacturing contracts) to ANC- owned firms, as well as restricted agencies' authority to pay subcontracting "bonuses" under the Indian Financing Act.

This report discusses the historical development of contracting programs for ANCs. It summarizes the general authorities governing contracting with ANCs and ANC-owned firms, as well as the specific authorities pertaining to issues that commonly recur in discussions of contracting with such firms (e.g., protests of sole source awards, size standards and affiliations, subcontracting bonuses). The report also describes legislative activity related to contracting with ANCs during the 111th Congress and the changes that the SBA proposed on

October 28, 2009, to the regulations governing contracting with ANCs under the 8(a) Program.

Introduction

The widely reported increase in federal contract dollars awarded to Alaska Native Corporations (ANCs) and their subsidiaries over the past eight years has generated congressional and public interest in the legal authorities governing contracting with these entities. Of particular interest are the authorities creating the alleged "special procurement advantages" that ANC subsidiaries enjoy in contracting under the Small Business Administration's 8(a) Program.[1]

According to some reports, federal contract dollars awarded to ANCs and their subsidiaries increased by 916% between FY2000 and FY2008, going from $508.4 million to $5.2 billion.[2] The dollars awarded to ANC-owned firms through the 8(a) Program, in particular, reportedly tripled between FY2004 ($1.1 billion) and FY2008 ($3.9 billion).[3] Critics are concerned about the impact of these increases on other minority-owned businesses participating in the 8(a) Program,[4] as well as the potential for fraud, waste, and abuse when agencies make sole-source awards to ANCs or their subsidiaries.[5] However, supporters of contracting programs for ANCs point out that, even with the recent increases, contracting with ANCs and their subsidiaries represents a small percentage of federal contract dollars.[6] They also note that profits from federal contracts are vital to improving the economic well-being of Alaska Natives.[7]

The 111th Congress enacted legislation (P.L. 111-84) requiring justifications, approvals, and notices for sole-source contracts in excess of $20 million awarded through the 8(a) Program, including contracts with ANC-owned firms. An amendment to the Senate version of the National Defense Authorization Act for FY2010 (S.Amdt. 1762 to S. 1390) was also proposed, but subsequently withdrawn, that would have limited the Department of Defense's authority to make sole-source awards in excess of $3.5 million ($5.5 million for manufacturing contracts) to ANC- owned firms, as well as restricted agencies' authority to pay subcontracting "bonuses" under the Indian Financing Act.[8]

This report discusses the historical development of contracting programs for ANCs. It summarizes the general authorities governing contracting with ANCs and ANC-owned firms, as well as the specific authorities pertaining to issues that commonly recur in discussions of contracting with such firms (e.g., protests of sole source awards, size standards and affiliations, subcontracting bonuses). The report also describes legislative activity relating to contracting with ANCs during the 111th Congress and the changes that the SBA proposed on October 28, 2009, to the regulations governing contracting with ANCs under the 8(a) Program.

THE HISTORY OF CONTRACTING PROGRAMS FOR ANCS

Alaska Native Claims Settlement Act and ANCs

The Small Business Administration's (SBA's) 8(a) minority contracting program slightly predates the creation of Alaska Native Corporations. The 8(a) minority contracting program dates from the late 1960s, when it was created administratively.[9] The SBA considered Indian tribes eligible for the 8(a) minority contracting program, as indicated by a September 1970 SBA pamphlet encouraging Indian tribes and individuals to participate in the 8(a) Program.[10]

Creation of Alaska Native Corporations

ANCs were created under the authority of the Alaska Native Claims Settlement Act (ANCSA),[11] enacted in 1971 to settle Alaska Natives' aboriginal land claims to most of Alaska. Congress's stated intent in passing ANCSA—shared by Alaska Native organizations and the state of Alaska—was to settle the claims

> without establishing any permanent racially defined institutions ... without creating a reservation system or lengthy wardship or trusteeship, and without adding to the categories of property and institutions enjoying special tax privileges.[12]

To carry out this intention, Congress authorized Native corporations, not tribes, to receive the lands and monies awarded in the settlement. Unlike Indian trust lands, the corporations' lands would be held in fee simple and could be developed without federal approval.[13]

Congress intended ANCs to be vehicles for the economic development of Alaska Natives. The conference report on ANCSA stated that

> the Regional Corporations shall be organized as business for profit corporations.... [T]he investment functions to be carried out by the [state-wide] Alaska Native Investment Corporation [under the Senate version] have been assigned ... to the Regional Corporations.[14]

The intended functions of this state-wide Investment Corporation, according to the earlier Senate committee report on its bill, were to

> conduct business for profit activities and to provide a long-range return through dividends to its Native stockholders. The Investment Corporation thus is intended to act as a prudent businessman would, and to administer the Natives' funds with the object of maximizing the value of their stock and their future unrestricted income.[15]

ANCSA created four types of ANCs, all to be incorporated under state law:

- 12 regional corporations, based on the regions of 12 specified Alaska Native associations, covering the entire state (plus a 13th regional corporation for Alaska Natives permanently residing outside Alaska);
- village corporations, for Alaska Native communities with populations of 25 or more Natives;

- group corporations, for Alaska Native communities with populations of fewer than 25 Natives in which Natives constituted a majority; and
- urban corporations, for urban Alaska Native communities.

An Alaska Native could become a voting shareholder in both the local regional corporation and the local village, group, or urban corporation.

As compensation for settling the land claims, ANCSA provided for the conveyance of some 40 million acres (including subsurface rights) and $962.5 million to the ANCs, chiefly to the 12 regional corporations and the village corporations. The settlement lands were to be divided among the 12 regional corporations (excluding the 13th corporation) based on the acreage of their regions and among the village corporations based chiefly on their populations. Group and urban corporations were to receive a set number of acres apiece. (Conveyance of title to the ANCs is the responsibility of the Bureau of Land Management, which reported in its FY20 10 budget justifications that 54% of the lands to be conveyed had been surveyed and patented to the ANCs.)[16] The settlement funds were to be paid out over a number of years and divided among the regional corporations (including the 13th corporation) based on their population. Each regional corporation was to distribute at least half of its share of these funds to the village corporations in its region.

As noted above, the ANCs were to hold their ANCSA lands in private fee title, not in the trust title usual for Indian lands, and subject to federal, state, and local taxation in specified circumstances. The regional corporations were to operate as for-profit entities, and the village corporations as either for-profit or non-profit entities. Their revenues from investment of their settlement funds were to be subject to taxation.

Definition of ANCs as Tribes

The Indian Self-Determination and Education Assistance Act of 1975

Congress has taken several steps to assist ANCs. An important step in relation to the 8(a) Program came in 1975, when Congress included regional and village ANCs in the definition of "Indian tribe" in a major Indian law, the Indian Self-Determination and Education Assistance Act of 1975:

> "Indian tribe" means any Indian tribe, band, nation, or other organized group or community, including any Alaska Native village or regional or village corporation as defined in or established pursuant to the Alaska Native Claims Settlement Act (85 Stat. 688) which is recognized as eligible for the special programs and services provided by the United States to Indians because of their status as Indians.[17]

8(a) Definition of Tribes

This 1975 definition of "Indian tribe" was used in two later amendments to the Small Business Act. First, in 1978, the definition was incorporated by reference in an amendment specifying that small businesses wholly owned by Indian tribes were eligible for the loan program implemented under the authority of Section 7(a) of the act.[18] Second, 1986 amendments to the Small Business Act used the language of the 1975 definition when making "economically disadvantaged" Indian tribes and ANCs eligible for the 8(a) Program.[19] These

1978 and 1986 amendments to the Small Business Act were each added after Indian tribes complained about SBA officials' varying opinions as to whether Indian tribes were eligible for the 7(a) and 8(a) Programs.[20]

ANCs Deemed Economically Disadvantaged

The 1986 amendments meant that tribes and ANCs still had to prove they were economically disadvantaged to be eligible for the 8(a) Program. In 1988, ANCSA was amended to specify that "Native Corporations" (ANCs) were to be considered "minority business enterprises" for all purposes of federal law.[21] Designation as minority business enterprises did not, however, lead the SBA to deem ANCs to be economically as well as socially disadvantaged. According to 1991 testimony of the Alaska Federation of Natives,

> [w]hen the ANCSA amendments of 1987 [P.L. 100-241] were being legislated, the parties involved agreed to include an amendment that would make it clear that Alaska Native corporations were eligible for SBA minority programs. At that time, congressional staff relied on the fact that "disadvantaged business enterprises" (called DBE's), were a subset of "minority business enterprises" (called MBE's), and would thus be covered by the explicit inclusion of Native corporations and specified affiliates as MBE's.... Since then, we have found that SBA is distinguishing disadvantaged business enterprises from minority business enterprises, saying that a statutory definition as an MBE does not qualify Native corporations as DBE's for purposes of SBA programs.[22]

In 1992, Congress further amended ANCSA to clarify that Native Corporations were to be considered "economically disadvantaged" for all purposes of federal law.[23] Since 1988, according to Government Accountability Office (GAO) figures, ANCs have consistently increased their involvement in the 8(a) Program, as measured by the number of ANCs owning subsidiaries that participate in the 8(a) Program.[24]

ANCs' Economic Performance

ANCs were to be ANCSA's vehicles—the "engines," as it were—for the economic development of Alaska Natives. However, the variation among regions and villages in acreage and population meant that ANCs differed widely in their shares of the $962.5 million settlement fund and the 40 million acres to be conveyed. The 12 land-based regional corporations, which together cover the entire state of Alaska, also varied not only in the size of their regions but in their regions' economic resources and activities. Likewise, the village, group, and urban corporations, which are scattered unevenly across the 12 regions, varied widely in their degree of isolation and the economic activity of their surroundings. Hence, ANCs differed widely in their initial ANCSA funding, the land-based resources they received, and their opportunities for economic development.

Since 1971, the ANCs have also differed widely in their business success, growth, income, and losses, but an overall pattern of loss, recovery, and gradual expansion has been suggested by several observers.

Loss

In the 1970s, ANCs organized themselves, made their land selections, and received their ANCSA payments. The last major ANCSA payments to regional ANCs were made in 1980.[25] In the 1970s and 1980s, the ANCs invested in a wide variety of business operations, such as hotels, seafood processing, shipping, oilfield services, and construction, as well as in natural resources. Their businesses and investments were chiefly in Alaska. However, as a group, regional ANCs lost substantial amounts of money in the period of 1971-1985, especially in non-resource business operations. "The [regional] corporations altogether lost money on business operations every year except 1974 and 1985," according to economist Steve Colt.[26] The same analyst later stated,

> the consolidated financial performance of the Alaska Native corporations over their first two decades was surprisingly poor. The twelve regional corporations lost about $380 million— more than three quarters of their original cash endowment—in business operations between 1973 and 1993.[27]

At the same time, the ANCs struggled with the significant financial costs of litigation to determine how ANCSA was to be applied and interpreted. There was "heavy litigation"[28] over land selections, Native village and group eligibility, individual Natives' enrollment, ANC elections and corporate governance, revenue-sharing among regional ANCs and with village ANCs,[29] and other i ssues.[30]

During this period, ANCs apparently had little or no involvement in the SBA's 8(a) Program.[31]

Recovery

What allowed the ANCs to recover, apparently, was their brief, unique opportunity to sell net operating losses (NOLs)[32] to other U.S. companies between 1986 and 1988. The ANCs' sale of NOLs provided an estimated $410 million for regional ANCs and $500 million for village ANCs.[33]

Congress created the ANCs' window of opportunity for NOL sales in 1986 when it added a provision to the Internal Revenue Code that disallowed sales of NOLs by any corporation except ANCs.[34] Two years later Congress repealed the ANC exception.[35]

"For the regional corporations as a group, NOL sales proceeds provided a cash infusion equal (in real dollars) to two thirds of the original ANCSA payments."[36] ANC income from NOL sales "essentially recapitalized many of the struggling regional corporations, and put them in position to benefit from the economic boom that began in the early 1990s."[37]

Expansion

Given the opportunity to start over, ANCs apparently selected investments more wisely and emphasized diversification, especially in businesses outside Alaska, although they also continued "to do what they do well."[38] ANCs became active and made profitable investments in tourism (including hotels), oilfield services, communications, catering, real estate, construction, and other businesses, as well as in natural resources (timber and mining). In addition, by about 1992, litigation costs were diminishing.[39]

Some ANCs also became active in federal contracting, especially through the SBA's 8(a) Program. As noted above, the first ANC 8(a) contract was in the late 1980s.[40] However, the

8(a) certification process was considered by many ANCs "arduous" until the 1992 amendment to ANCSA, discussed above, that deemed ANCs economically disadvantaged for purposes of the SBA's 8(a) Program and other federal programs.[41]

By 1992, an *Alaska Business* article had mentioned two regional ANCs as having 8(a) contracts.[42] By 1997, two regional ANCs, Aleut Corporation and Chugach Alaska Corporation, got the bulk of their revenues and profits from 8(a) contracts.[43] A chart in a 2006 GAO report on contracting with ANCs shows a gradual but consistent increase in the number of ANCs (of all types) with 8(a) subsidiaries and the total number of such subsidiaries in the 8(a) Program, from very low numbers in 1988 to a total of 49 ANCs and 154 subsidiaries in December 2005.[44] According to GAO, as of 2005, 12 of the 13 regional ANCs had 8(a) subsidiaries, as did 33 village ANCs and 4 urban ANCs (out of a total of 182 village, urban, and group ANCs).[45]

Legal Authorities Governing Contracting with ANCs

Various authorities presently govern contracting between federal agencies and ANCs or ANC- owned firms. These include (1) the general contracting authorities, (2) the general small business authorities, (3) Section 8(a) of the Small Business Act, (4) authorities pertaining to Native Americans, and (5) various appropriations riders. These authorities address the award of contracts, as well as related issues.

General Contracting Authorities

The Armed Services Procurement Act of 1947 and the Federal Property and Administrative Services Act of 1949, as amended, give defense and civilian agencies, respectively, broad authority to contract for goods and services.[46] So long as they comply with statutory and regulatory requirements governing solicitation of bids or offers, competition in contracting, and similar matters, agencies may generally make awards to any entity that happens to be the lowest qualified responsible bidder or offeror.[47] This includes ANCs and their subsidiaries. Moreover, agencies may make sole-source awards to ANCs or ANC-owned firms under the general contracting authorities in the same circumstances in which they can make sole-source awards to other entities. Such circumstances exist when (1) only one source can supply the goods or services, (2) there are unusual and compelling circumstances, (3) the agency seeks to maintain the industrial base, (4) international agreements require the agency to award the contract to a particular entity, (5) a statute authorizes non-competitive awards or the agency is acquiring brand- name commercial items for resale, (6) considerations of national security keep the agency from advertising its requirements, or (7) a particular award is necessary in the public interest.[48]

Contracting officers must generally justify such sole-source awards in writing[49] and obtain approval of these justifications from their superiors.[50] They must also generally issue a notice of their intent to make a sole-source award prior to awarding the contract.[51]

The general contracting authorities account for some awards recently made to ANCs and ANC- owned firms, including sole-source awards. According to information reported in the

Federal Procurement Data System-Next Generation (FPDS-NG), approximately 21% of all actions obligating funds on federal contracts with ANCs or ANC-owned firms in FY2008 involved firms that were not 8(a) certified firms, and the circumstances of some awards (i.e., the size of the award coupled with the extent of competition) suggest that they were made under the general contracting authorities.[52] In fact, the general contracting authorities may be necessary to make awards to ANCs themselves, as opposed to their subsidiaries or ANC-owned firms, given that some ANCs may not qualify as "small" under the size standards applicable to contracts awarded under the authority of the Small Business Act.[53] The general contracting authorities also do not require that entities be for-profit to receive an award, unlike the small business authorities.[54] Not all ANCs are for-profit,[55] and small non-profit ANCs could receive awards under the general contracting authorities when they could not receive awards under the small business authorities.

General Small Business Authorities

Contracts could also be awarded to small ANCs or ANC-owned firms under the general small business authorities. Section 15 of the Small Business Act of 1958, in conjunction with Sections 2711 and 2723 of the Competition in Contracting Act of 1984, provides agencies with special authorities for contracting with small businesses.[56] Under these authorities, agencies may "set aside" contracts for small businesses—by conducting competitions in which only they can compete—when certain conditions are met.[57] These set-asides can be total or partial, encompassing the entire acquisition or a severable segment of it.[58] Agencies may also make sole- source awards to small businesses when one of the seven circumstances authorizing noncompetitive awards under the general contracting authorities exist, although such awards are made under the general contracting authorities and not the general small business authorities.[59] They are thus subject to the notice, justification, and approval requirements discussed previously. [60]

One of the alleged "special provisions" governing contracting with ANCs arguably assists ANC- owned firms in qualifying as "small" for purposes of contracting under the general small business authorities. While all affiliations between businesses, or relationships allowing one party control or the power of control over another,[61] generally count when the SBA makes size determinations,[62] certain affiliations with the parent ANC or its subsidiaries are generally excluded when the SBA determines the size of an ANC-owned firm.[63] Although the SBA is authorized to consider these affiliations when not doing so results or is likely to result in an ANC- owned firm obtaining a "substantial unfair competitive advantage within an industry category,"[64] the SBA and agencies exercising delegated authority on its behalf[65] reportedly seldom exercise this authority.[66]

However, ANC-owned firms are not exempt from the requirement that they be "businesses" for purposes of the Small Business Act, which means that they must be for-profit to be awarded contracts under the general small business authorities.[67] They also must self-certify that they are "small," as measured by the size standards for the goods or services to be procured, when submitting bids or offers for contracts to be awarded under the general small business authorities.[68] However, while there are potentially severe penalties for misrepresentation of size[69] and other entities may generally challenge firms' size status,[70] most self-certifications are not closely scrutinized:

> A contracting officer may accept a concern's self-certification as true for the particular purpose involved in the absence of a written protest by other offerors or other credible information which causes the contracting officer or SBA to question the size of the concern.[71]

The general small business authorities may have accounted for some actions reported in FPDSNG that obligated funds to ANCs or ANC-owned firms in FY2008. For example, contracts of an amount typically set aside for small businesses (e.g., $3,000-$ 100,000) and awarded through "full and open competition after the exclusion of sources" may have resulted from agencies' exercise of the general small business authorities.

Section 8(a) of the Small Business Act

Agencies can also contract with ANC-owned firms, although not necessarily ANCs themselves,[72] under the authority of Section 8(a) of the Small Business Act of 1958, as amended. Section 8(a) generally authorizes set-asides and sole-source awards to "socially and economically disadvantaged small business concerns," which include firms at least 51% owned and unconditionally controlled by ANCs, Indian tribes, Native Hawaiian Organizations (NHOs) or Community Development Corporations (CDCs).[73] Contracts are typically "set aside" for competitions restricted to firms participating in the 8(a) Program when their anticipated value exceeds the so-called "competitive threshold" of $3.5 million ($5.5 million for manufacturing contracts).[74] In contrast, contracts whose anticipated value is below the competitive threshold are generally awarded on a sole-source basis without competition.[75] Contracts above the competitive threshold may also be awarded on a sole-source basis when (1) there is not a reasonable expectation that at least two eligible and responsible 8(a) firms will submit offers at a fair market price or (2) the SBA accepts the requirement on behalf of an 8(a) firm owned by an ANC, Indian tribe, or, in the case of Department of Defense contracts, an NHO.[76] However, because authority for the latter type of sole-source awards does not derive from the Competition in Contracting Act (CICA), such awards were not subject to the same requirements regarding justifications, approvals, and notices as other sole-source awards prior to enactment of the National Defense Authorization Act for FY20 10, discussed below.[77]

While agency discretion in determining whether to procure particular goods or services under the authority of Section 8 (a) is fairly broad,[78] detailed statutory and regulatory requirements govern firms' eligibility for and participation in the 8(a) Program. The places where the statutory or regulatory requirements pertaining to contracting with ANC-owned firms differ from the general 8(a) requirements have attracted the most scrutiny from those concerned about the alleged "special procurement advantages" of ANC-owned firms.[79] These places are briefly summarized in **Table 1**,[80] while a separate report explains the general 8(a) requirements in more detail.[81]

Table 1. "Special Rules" for Contracting with ANC-owned Firms Under Section 8(a) of the Small Business Act

Issue	General 8(a) Rule	"Special Rule" for ANC-Owned Firms	Authority for the "Special Rule"
Exclusion of certain affiliations in size determinations	All affiliations, as defined under SBA regulations, count when the SBA makes size determinations.	Affiliations with the parent ANC or its subsidiaries are excluded when the SBA makes size determinations unless the SBA determines that the ANC-owned firm has obtained, or is likely to obtain, a "substantial unfair competitive advantage within an industry category" if these affiliations are excluded.	15 U.S.C. § 636(j)(10)(J)(ii); 13 C.F.R. § 124.109(c)(2)(iii)
Management by non-disadvantaged individuals (as a component of control)	Management and daily business operations must be conducted by one or more disadvantaged individuals.	People who are not Alaska Natives may manage ANC-owned firms if the SBA determines that such management is required to assist the firm's development, the firm will retain control of all management decisions, and a written management plan shows how Alaska Natives will develop managerial skills sufficient to manage the concern or similar concerns in the future.	13 C.F.R. § 124.109(c)(4)(i)(B)
Social disadvantage	Individuals are either rebuttably presumed to be socially disadvantaged or must prove individual social disadvantage by a preponderance of the evidence.	ANC-owned firms are deemed "minority business enterprises" and are irrebuttably presumed to be socially and economically disadvantaged small business concerns provided they are at least 51% owned by an ANC and their management and daily business operations are controlled by one or more Alaska Natives.	43 U.S.C. § 1626(e); P.L. 99-272, 101 Stat. 370-71 (Apr. 7, 1986) (codified at 15 U.S.C. § 637(a)(4)(A)-(B))
Economic disadvantage	Individuals must show economic disadvantage upon entry to the program and annually thereafter.	ANCs are deemed economically disadvantaged provided that Alaska Natives and descendants of Alaska Natives own a majority of the total equity of the ANC and the total voting powers to elect directors of the ANC through their holdings of settlement common stock.	P.L. 100-241, § 15, 101 Stat. 1812-13 (Feb. 3, 1988); P.L. 102-415, § 10, 106 Stat. 2115 (Oct. 14, 1992) (codified at 43 U.S.C. § 1626(e)); 13 C.F.R. 124.109(a)
Sole-source awards above the competitive threshold	Agencies may make sole-source awards in excess of $3.5 million ($5.5 million for manufacturing contracts) only if the contracting officer does not reasonably expect that at least two responsible firms will submit offers and the award can be made at a fair market price.	Agencies may make sole-source awards to ANC-owned firms at any time, even when the contracting officer reasonably expects that at least two responsible 8(a) firms will submit offers and the award can be made at a fair market price.	P.L. 100-656, § 602(a), 102 Stat. 3887-88 (Nov. 15, 1988) (codified at 15 U.S.C. § 637(a)(1)(D)(i)-(ii)); 13 C.F.R. § 124.506(a)
Inability to receive additional	8(a) firms generally may not receive additional sole-source awards once they have received a	ANCs can continue to receive additional sole-source awards even once they have reached $100 "Special Rule" for ANC-	13 C.F.R. § 124.519(a)-(d) Authority for the

Table 1. (Continued)

Issue	General 8(a) Rule	"Special Rule" for ANC-Owned Firms	Authority for the "Special Rule"
source-source awards after obtaining a certain amount of 8(a) awards	combined total of competitive and sole-source awards in excess of (1) $100 million, in the case of firms whose size is based on their number of employees, or (2) the lesser of (A) $100 million or (B) five times the size standard for the industry, in the case of firms whose size is based on their revenues.	million or other applicable threshold.	
Owners' one-time eligibility for the 8(a) Program	Individuals may confer eligibility for the 8(a) Program upon only one firm; individuals, along with their firms, may participate in the 8(a) Program for a maximum of nine years.	ANCs may confer eligibility upon multiple firms; while ANC-owned firms must leave the 8(a) Program after a maximum of nine years, the ANC can continue to participate in the program as a firm owner perpetually.	P.L. 101-37, § 4, 103 Stat. 70-71 (June 15, 1989) (codified at 15 U.S.C. § 636(j)(11)(B)-(C))
Ability to own majority interests in multiple 8(a) firms	Individuals who have been determined to be disadvantaged for purposes of one 8(a) firm, their immediate family members, and 8(a) firms themselves generally may not own more than 20% of any other 8(a) firm.	ANCs are barred from owning more than 51% of another 8(a) firm obtaining the majority of its revenues from the same primary industry in which another ANC-owned firm operates or has operated within the past two years. They *may* own majority interests in multiple firms obtaining the majority of their revenues in different primary industries, or obtaining less than 50% of their revenues in the same secondary industry.	P.L. 101-37, § 4, 103 Stat. 70-71 (June 15, 1989) (codified at 15 U.S.C. § 636(j)(11)(B)-(C)); 13 C.F.R. § 124.109(c)(3)

Source: Congressional Research Service

ANC-owned firms are, however, subject to other requirements governing eligibility for and participation in the 8(a) Program, including requirements that they (1) be small under the SBA's size standards,[82] (2) be businesses under the SBA's definition,[83] (3) be unconditionally owned and substantially controlled by their owner (i.e., the ANC),[84] (4) possess good character,[85] (5) demonstrate potential for success,[86] and (6) obtain increasing percentages of their income from non-8(a) sources in their final five years of participation in the 8(a) Program.[87] ANC-owned firms must also apply to participate in the 8(a) Program like other firms. This application form is somewhat different from that used by individually owned firms, but requires similarly extensive supporting documentation concerning company personnel, corporate organization, financial status, and company operations.[88] ANC-owned firms must also submit an "8(a) Annual Update" like other 8(a) firms.[89] This update requires additional documentation much like that submitted with applications to the 8(a) Program.[90] Careful review of this documentation could potentially disclose some of the alleged problems with ANC-owned 8(a) firms, such as joint ventures to which the ANC-owned firm contributes nothing beyond its eligibility for 8(a) contracts. However, a November 2008 GAO report questioned whether the SBA presently has the resources to conduct thorough reviews of 8(a) firms.[91]

Many of the actions obligating funds to ANCs or ANC-owned firms reported in FPDS-NG for FY2008 appear to have resulted from agencies contracting under the authority of Section 8(a) of the Small Business Act. Approximately 80% of FY2008 actions involved firms that were 8(a) certified, and although contracts may be awarded to 8(a) certified firms under other authorities, such contracts probably represent a small number of the obligations reported in FPDS-NG.

Authorities in Native American Laws

Several authorities governing contracting with ANCs and their subsidiaries are located in statutes and U.S. Code sections pertaining to Native Americans, rather than those pertaining to contracting or small business. These include provisions (1) authorizing payment of a 5% "subcontracting bonus" to federal prime contractors that subcontract with certain "Indian organizations" or "Indian-owned economic enterprises," (2) authorizing set-asides under the Buy Indian Act, (3) allowing contracts with ANCs or ANC-owned firms of any size or without certification to count toward federal contractors' goals for subcontracting with small businesses or "small disadvantaged businesses," and (4) allowing certified ANCs or ANC-owned firms to qualify as "small disadvantaged businesses" for purposes of Department of Transportation contracts.

5% "Subcontracting Bonus"

Federal prime contractors are eligible for so-called "bonuses" equal to "5 percent of the amount paid, or to be paid, to a subcontractor" when they subcontract with ANCs or ANC-owned firms, among others.[92] Congress authorized such bonuses in 1988, in part, because of concerns that federal prime contractors had less incentive to use Indian-owned subcontractors than other minority-owned subcontractors because of the geographical "remoteness of [Indian] reservation[s]."[93] Congress also appropriated funds for the Department of Defense (DOD), in particular, to pay subcontracting bonuses.[94] The amount appropriated remained constant at $8 million per year between FY1989 and FY2006,[95] and was increased to $15 million per year during the 110th Congress.[96] Other agencies have not received similar appropriations to pay subcontracting bonuses, but have the same statutory authority to pay them that DOD has.

To be eligible for a bonus, the prime contractor must

> use its best efforts to give Indian organizations and Indian-owned economic enterprises ... the maximum practicable opportunity to participate in the subcontracts it awards to the fullest extent consistent with efficient performance of its contract.[97]

Contracting officers and contractors may generally rely on subcontractors' representations regarding their eligibility as Indian organizations or Indian-owned economic enterprises unless an interested party challenges their eligibility or the contracting officer has independent reason to question it.[98] Any challenges are referred to the Bureau of Indian Affairs for eligibility determinations.[99]

Set-Asides under the Buy Indian Act

ANC-owned firms are eligible for contracts set aside for "Indian organizations" and "Indian- owned economic enterprises" under the authority of the Buy Indian Act, as Section 23 of a 1910 act "[t]o provide for determining the heirs of deceased Indians" is commonly known.[100] The Buy Indian Act provides that,

> so far as may be practicable Indian labor shall be employed, and purchases of the products of Indian industry may be made in [the] open market in the discretion of the Secretary of the Interior.[101]

The Indian Health Service (IHS) retained this authority to give preference to the "products of Indian industry" when it moved from the Department of the Interior (DOI) to the Department of Health and Human Services.[102]

Both DOI and IHS thus have similar authority to prefer Indian products, but the regulations under which they do so differ slightly. [103] The IHS regulations specify that this authority is to be used in connection with the "maintenance and operation of hospital and health facilities for Indians and for the conservation of Indian health."[104] They also provide that no more than 50% of a subcontract on a set-aside contract may be performed by non-Indian firms and require competitive award of contracts to the "maximum extent ... practicable," with justifications and approvals issued for noncompetitive awards.[105] In contrast, the DOI regulations apply chiefly to contracts "performed on reservations," although other agencies can rely on this authority when contracting for work that is "specifically for the benefit of Indians."[106] The DOI regulations also provide a "preference" for subcontracting with Indians,[107] but are less explicit as to what this means than the IHS regulations.

Credit toward Prime Contractors' Subcontracting Goals

Subcontracts awarded by federal prime contractors to ANCs or their subsidiaries count toward contractors' goals for subcontracting with small businesses and "small disadvantaged businesses" *even if* the ANC or ANC subsidiary is large or not certified as "disadvantaged":

> Subcontracts awarded to an ANC or an Indian tribe shall be counted towards the subcontracting goals for small business and small disadvantaged business (SDB) concerns regardless of the size or Small Business Administration certification status of the ANC or Indian tribe.[108]

Section 8(d) of the Small Business Act, as amended, requires federal agencies to negotiate subcontracting plans with the apparently successful bidder or offeror on eligible prime contracts prior to awarding the contract.[109] These subcontracting plans establish goals for the value of subcontracts that prime contractors should award to small businesses and small disadvantaged businesses, among others.[110] A contractor's failure to comply with its subcontracting plan constitutes a material breach of the contract, potentially allowing the agency to terminate the contractor for default.[111] The contractor could also potentially be required to pay liquidated damages.[112]

Other firms must qualify as "small" under the SBA regulations for subcontracts with them to count toward contractors' goals for subcontracting with small businesses or small disadvantaged businesses (SDBs).[113] Moreover, until October 3, 2008, other firms had to be certified SDBs for subcontracts with them to count toward contractors' goals.[114] All 8(a) firms were deemed to be SDBs, but other firms at least 51% unconditionally owned and controlled by socially and economically disadvantaged individuals or groups could also obtain certification.[115]

Small Disadvantaged Businesses for Purposes of Transportation Contracts

The same statute that allows subcontracts with large or uncertified ANCs or ANC affiliates to count for purposes of contractors' subcontracting goals for small businesses also enables large ANCs or ANC affiliates to qualify as "small disadvantaged businesses" for contracts funded by the Department of Transportation (DOT) under the Transportation Equity Act for the 21st Century (TEA-21) provided they obtain the necessary certifications.[116] TEA-21 originally required that

> not less than 10 percent of the amounts made available for the program under titles I, III, and V of this Act shall be expended with small business concerns owned and controlled by socially and economically disadvantaged individuals.[117]

However, later regulations, promulgated in response to court cases challenging the constitutionality of "quotas" for minority firms,[118] construe "10 percent" as an "aspirational goal," which "does not authorize or require recipients to set overall or contract goals at the 10 percent level, or any other particular level, or to take any special administrative steps if their goals are above or below 10 percent."[119]

Allowing large ANCs and their affiliates to qualify as small disadvantaged businesses for purposes of DOT contracting goals is potentially significant for two reasons. First, "small business" arguably has a narrower meaning under TEA-21 than it does under the Small Business Act, which could render some non-ANC-owned firms that might otherwise qualify as "small" ineligible for the DOT program.[120] Second, "small disadvantaged businesses" under TEA-2 1 include women-owned firms,[121] which could place the collective interests of women-owned small businesses more directly at odds with those of ANC-owned firms than is the case when individual women-owned firms participate in the 8(a) Program or are designated as small disadvantaged businesses for SBA programs. Women are not among the groups presumed to be socially disadvantaged for purposes of SBA programs, and small businesses owned and controlled by women are eligible for such programs only when individual women owners prove by a preponderance of the evidence that they are socially disadvantaged.

Appropriations Riders Allowing Direct Conversion of DOD Functions

The Department of Defense (DOD) can also contract out functions performed by government employees to ANCs or ANC-owned firms without going through the competitive sourcing process normally required under Office of Management and Budget (OMB) Circular A-76.[122] OMB Circular A-76, along with its four attachments,[123] generally sets forth guidelines and procedures for determining whether an activity should be performed in-house by the agency with government personnel or contracted-out to the private sector. Beginning in the early 1980s, a series of appropriations riders[124] and permanent laws[125] affected DOD's use of the A-76 process. While most of these enactments in some way limited DOD's ability to contract out functions using the A-76 process, one rider attached to every DOD appropriations act since 1989 has permitted DOD to avoid the A-76 process and its restrictions on outsourcing by contracting functions out to firms owned by ANCs, Indian tribes, or NHOs.[126]

The original version of this rider generally restricted outsourcing using the A-76 process, but exempted so-called "direct conversions" to "qualified firm[s] under 51 percent Native American ownership," among others.[127] Such firms included those owned by ANCs, Indian tribes, or individual Native Americans. The 106th Congress later made two modifications to this provision. First, it exempted direct conversions to "qualified firms" from requirements concerning federal employee comments and congressional notification codified in 10 U.S.C. § 2461(b)-(c), as well as from the A-76 process codified in 10 U.S.C. § 2461(a).[128] Second, while it maintained the exemption for direct conversion to firms owned by ANCs and Indian tribes, it removed the exemption for direct conversions to firms owned by Native American individuals and replaced it with one for direct conversions to NHO-owned firms.[129] The exemptions for direct conversions remained unchanged from the 106th Congress through the 111th Congress.[130]

However, while these appropriations riders allowed DOD to avoid the A-76 process when contracting out functions to ANCs or ANC-owned firms, they did not authorize DOD to make noncompetitive awards to such entities. For this reason, DOD has used the authority to make sole-source awards above the competitive threshold to ANC-owned firms codified in the Small Business Act in conjunction with its authority under the appropriations riders.[131]

Specific Authorities Often at Issue in Discussions of Contracting with ANCs or ANC-owned Firms

In addition to the general authorities discussed in the previous section, certain specific statutes or regulations governing particular aspects of contracting with ANCs and ANC-owned firms are often at issue in discussions of contracting with such entities. These authorities address (1) sole- source awards, (2) protests of sole-source awards, (3) size standards and affiliations, (4) joint ventures and partnerships, (5) contract bundling, (6) limitations on subcontracting, (7) subcontracting bonuses, (8) limitations on agencies' discretion to award contracts under Section 8(a), (9) maximum term of participation in the 8(a) Program, (10) ownership of multiple 8(a) firms, (11) required revenue from non-8(a) sources, and (12) management by and employment of individuals who are not Alaska Natives.

Sole-Source Awards to ANCs and ANC-owned Firms

Agencies may make sole-source awards to ANCs and ANC-owned firms under two different authorities: Section 8(a) of the Small Business Act and the general contracting authorities. However, the circumstances surrounding such sole-source awards vary depending upon the authority under which they are made. Prior to enactment of the National Defense Authorization Act (NDAA) for FY20 10,[132] contracting officers making sole-source awards in excess of $3.5 million ($5.5 million for manufacturing contracts) to ANC-owned firms under the authority of Section 8(a) did not have to justify such awards, obtain approval of them from higher-level agency officials, or post notices of the award. In contrast, justifications,[133] approvals,[134] and notices[135] are typically required for sole-source awards under the general contracting authorities. The NDAA changed this by requiring justifications, approvals, and notices for sole-source contracts in excess of $20 million awarded under the authority of Section 8(a) similar to those required for sole-source contracts awarded under the general contracting authorities. [136] However, justifications, approvals, and notices are still not required for sole-source contracts valued at between $3.5 million ($5.5 million for manufacturing contracts) and $20 million awarded under the authority of Section 8(a). Only 8(a) firms owned by Indian tribes or ANCs can receive sole- source awards in excess of $3.5 million ($5.5 million for manufacturing contracts) when there is a reasonable expectation that at least two eligible and responsible 8(a) firms will submit offers at a fair market price. Other 8(a) firms cannot receive these awards when there is such an expectation.

In addition to being able to receive sole-source awards above the competitive threshold in circumstances when individually owned 8(a) firms cannot, ANC-owned 8(a) firms can, under SBA regulations, also receive additional sole-source awards after they have received a combined total of sole-source and competitive 8(a) awards in excess of (1) $100 million, in the case of firms whose size is based on their number of employees, or (2) the lesser of (A) $100 million or (B) five times the size standard for the industry, in the case of firms whose size is based on their revenue.[137] Individually owned 8(a) firms, in contrast, generally cannot receive additional sole- source awards under the authority of Section 8(a) in these circumstances. 138

ANC-owned 8(a) firms are, however, like individually owned 8(a) firms in generally being barred from receiving additional sole-source awards when they fail to achieve their targets for the percentage of revenue obtained from non-8(a) sources during the "transitional stage" of the 8(a) Program.[139] A firm's participation in the 8(a) Program is divided into two stages: the "developmental stage," comprised of its first four years in the program, and the "transitional stage," comprised of its last five years in the program.[140] Firms in the transitional stage must achieve certain targets for the amount of revenue they receive from sources other than 8(a) contracts.[141] These targets increase over time, with firms required to attain 15% of their revenue from non-8(a) sources in the fifth year, 25% in the sixth year, 35% in the seventh year, 45% in the eighth year, and 55% in the ninth year.[142] Firms that do not achieve these targets are generally ineligible for additional sole-source 8(a) contracts "unless and until" they correct the situation.[143]

Protesting Sole-Source Awards Under Section 8(a)

Other 8(a) firms have historically been unable to protest sole-source awards in excess of $3.5 million ($5.5 million for manufacturing contracts) made to ANC-owned firms under the authority of Section 8(a). This inability was largely due to the fact that the Business Opportunity Development Reform Act (BODRA), which amended Section 8(a) to authorize sole-source awards above the "competitive threshold" to ANC-owned firms, imposed no substantive or procedural requirements upon the contracting officers making such awards. They did not need to justify the award by finding the existence of particular circumstances under which sole-source awards were permissible.[144] They also did not need to obtain approvals of their written justifications or post notices regarding the sole-source award. [145] This meant that there were few grounds upon which would-be protesters could allege that contracting officers acted "in abuse of discretion" or "otherwise not in accordance with the law," as is generally required for successful protests.[146] The National Defense Authorization Act (NDAA) of FY20 10 may have changed this situation somewhat, at least for sole-source awards to ANC-owned firms in excess of $20 million, by requiring justifications, approvals, and notices for such awards.[147] However, the changes made by the NDAA would not affect the ability of other 8(a) firms to protest sole-source awards to ANC-owned firms valued at between $3.5 million ($5.5 million for manufacturing contracts) and $20 million because contracting officers still do not need to justify such awards, obtain approval of them, or post notices regarding them.

In contrast, Historically Underutilized Business (HUB) Zone small businesses and other, non-8(a) small businesses have traditionally had greater success than 8(a) firms in protesting sole-source awards to ANC-owned firms. This is because agency officials must accept the requirement for award through the 8(a) Program before awarding a sole-source contract to an ANC-owned firm under the authority of Section 8(a).[148] Certain statutes and regulations govern agencies' acceptance of requirements for the 8(a) Program, and to the degree that contracting officers fail to comply with these authorities when accepting a requirement, their conduct can be protested. For example, in May 2009, a HUBZone small business successfully blocked the Army's proposed award of a sole-source contract to an ANC on the grounds that the agency failed to properly consider a HUBZone set-aside before accepting the requirement for the 8(a) Program.[149] GAO, which decided this protest, found that HUBZone set-asides must be given precedence over 8(a) set-asides because HUBZone set-asides are "mandatory" and 8(a) set-asides are "discretionary."[150] Although the Obama Administration disagreed with GAO's recommendations and declined to implement them, a subsequent decision by the U.S. Court of Federal Claims also held that HUBZone set-asides have precedence over 8(a) set-asides.[151] Small businesses have similarly challenged sole-source awards to ANCs and their subsidiaries on the grounds that the requirement was accepted for award under Section 8(a) in violation of statutes and regulations that prohibit contracts from being accepted for the 8(a) Program when their acceptance would have an "adverse impact on an individual small business, a group of small businesses located in a specific geographical location, or other small business programs."[152]

An SBA regulation at 13 C.F.R. § 124.517(a) that prohibits challenges to 8(a) firms' eligibility for competitive or sole-source contracts is sometimes construed as uniquely applicable to ANC- owned firms and precluding protests of sole-source awards to them. [153] However, this regulation applies to all 8(a) firms, not just ANC-owned firms and is arguably more procedural than substantive. While precluding protests of eligibility, it allows "[a]nyone with information questioning the eligibility of a Participant to continue participation in the 8(a) BD program or for purposes of a specific 8(a) contract [to] submit such information to SBA."[154] SBA then reviews the firm's eligibility using the procedures and criteria listed in 13 C.F.R. § 124.112(c). The entity supplying the information is not a party in this review, as it would be in a protest, though.

Size Standards and Affiliations under the Small Business Act

Like other firms, ANCs and ANC-owned firms are subject to the SBA's "size standards" when receiving contracts under the authority of Sections 8(a) and 15 of the Small Business Act.[155] Among other factors, the SBA uses size standards based on either the number of employees or gross income in determining whether a firm qualifies as small for purposes of SBA programs.[156]

However, ANC-owned firms, as well as those owned by Indian tribes, NHOs, and CDCs, differ from other small businesses in that the SBA has statutory authority to exclude certain affiliations when determining a firm's size for purposes of the 8(a) Program. In particular,

> In determining the size of a small business concern owned by a socially and economically disadvantaged Indian tribe (or a wholly owned business entity of such tribe), each firm's size shall be independently determined without regard to its affiliation with the tribe, any entity of the tribal government, or any other business enterprise owned by the tribe.[157]

"Affiliation," as used here, is a term of art measuring control, not connections:

> Concerns and entities are affiliates of each other when one controls or has the power to control the other, or a third party or parties controls or has the power to control both. It does not matter whether control is exercised, so long as the power to control exists.[158]

This means that not all relationships between firms count as affiliations for purposes of SBA programs. For example, in *Valenzuela Engineering, Inc. and Curry Contracting Company, Inc.*, the SBA's Office of Hearings and Appeals found that the relationship between an ANC and its subcontractor did not constitute an affiliation when the subcontractor performed only discrete tasks set out in the statement of work, constituting about 20% of the contract, while the ANC performed the remaining tasks and administered the contract.[159]

Only affiliations with the ANC and other ANC-owned firms can be excluded under 15 U.S.C. § 636(j)(1 0)(J)(ii)(II) and its implementing regulations, however.[160] Other affiliations of ANC- owned firms count in size determinations,[161] and ANC-owned firms have been subjected to "early graduation" from the 8(a) Program because they exceeded the size standards.[162] Moreover, the SBA has statutory authority to count affiliations with parent ANCs or other ANC subsidiaries when making size determinations *if* failure to do so could result in an ANC-owned firm obtaining "a substantial unfair competitive advantage within an industry category."[163]

Joint Ventures and Partnerships Involving Small Businesses

Because of the potential exclusion of affiliations with parent ANCs or other subsidiaries,[164] ANCs and ANC-owned firms, among others, have arguably greater opportunities than individually owned firms to form joint ventures and partnerships and remain small for purposes of SBA programs. [165] In addition, a separate statutory provision provides that certain joint ventures and partnerships involving ANC-owned firms are themselves deemed "minority and economically disadvantaged business enterprises" for purposes of federal contracting when certain conditions are met:

> For all purposes of Federal law, direct and indirect subsidiary corporations, joint ventures, and partnerships of a [qualifying] Native Corporation ... shall be considered to be entities owned and controlled by Natives and a minority and economically disadvantaged business enterprise if the shares of stock or other units of ownership interest in any such entity held by such Native Corporation and by the holders of its Settlement Common Stock represent a majority of both (A) the total equity of the subsidiary corporation, joint venture, or partnership; and (B) the total voting power of the subsidiary corporation, joint venture, or partnership for the purpose of electing directors, the general partner or principal officers.[166]

However, not all joint ventures count against individually owned firms under SBA regulations, and ANCs and ANC-owned firms are arguably subject to the same procedural rules as individually owned firms when forming joint ventures. SBA regulations allow 8(a) firms, in particular, to form joint ventures with small or large businesses under certain circumstances, as **Table 2** illustrates. ANC-owned firms are arguably subject to these regulations when forming joint ventures with entities other than their parent corporations or other subsidiaries. Moreover, joint ventures involving ANC-owned 8(a) firms, like those involving other 8(a) firms, arguably must comply with the following procedural requirements when forming joint ventures:

- the SBA must approve joint venture agreements prior to the formation of the joint venture,[167]
- the agreement must designate the 8(a) firm as the managing partner of the joint venture,[168]
- the agreement must designate an employee of the 8(a) firm as the managing partner of the joint venture,[169]
- no less than 51% of the net profits from the joint venture must go to the 8(a) firm,[170]
- the venture must comply with the limitations on subcontracting discussed in a subsequent section[171] and
- the 8(a) firm must "perform a significant portion of the contract."[172]

There are no comparably detailed regulations governing partnerships involving 8(a) firms or other small businesses. However, 8(a) firms may generally take the form of a partnership[173] provided that (1) at least 51% of every class of partnership interest is unconditionally owned by one or more socially and economically disadvantaged individuals and (2) one or more disadvantaged individuals serve as general partners with control over all partnership decisions.[174]

Limitations on Contract Bundling under the Small Business Act

Agencies' ability to "bundle" certain requirements and contract them on a sole-source basis with ANC-owned firms is arguably somewhat limited by the provisions of the Small Business Act governing contract bundling.[175] Bundling occurs when agencies

> consolidat[e] 2 or more procurement requirements for goods or services previously provided or performed under separate smaller contracts into a solicitation of offers for a single contract that is likely to be unsuitable for award to a small-business concern due to—
>
> (A) the diversity, size, or specialized nature of the elements of the performance specified;
> (B) the aggregate dollar value of the anticipated award;
> (C) the geographical dispersion of the contract performance sites; or
> (D)any combination of the factors described in subparagraphs (A), (B), and (C).[176]

Under Section 15 of the Small Business Act, as amended, agencies must justify their determination to bundle requirements previously performed by government contractors to Small Business Procurement Center Representatives; conduct market research before proceeding with any acquisition strategy that could lead to contract bundling; and determine that consolidation of requirements is "necessary and justified" based upon its benefits to the government.[177]

However, "new requirements," or requirements not previously performed by government contractors are arguably exempt from these limitations on contract bundling because the Small Business Act's definition of "bundling" includes only "goods or services previously provided or performed under separate smaller contracts."[178]

Table 2. Circumstances When Joint Ventures Involving 8(a) Firms Do Not Count for Purposes of Affiliations

Size of the Fellow Venturer	Pertinent Circumstances
Small (need not be an 8(a) participant)	• Contract is competitively awarded • Size of at least one 8(a) participant to the joint venture is less than half the size standard for the industry code assigned to the contract • The procurement either (1) exceeds $10 million, in the case of procurements having employee-based size standards, or (2) exceeds half the size standard for the industry code, in the case of procurements having revenue-based size standards • Specific combinations of venturers carry out no more than three specific or limited- purpose business ventures over a two-year period
Large	• The large business is the 8(a) firm's approved mentor under the SBA's Mentor-Protégé program • The 8(a) firm is small for the size standard of the procurement • The 8(a) firm has not received competitive or sole-source contracts in excess of (1) $100 million, in the case of firms whose size is based on their number of employees, or (2) the lesser of (A) $100 million or (B) five times the size standard for the industry, in the case of firms whose size is based on their revenues • Specific combinations of venturers carry out no more than three specific or limitedpurpose business ventures over a two-year period

Source: Congressional Research Service based on 13 C.F.R. § 121.103; 13 C.F.R. § 124.513

Limitations on Subcontracting under the Small Business Act

Contracts with ANCs or ANC-owned firms under Sections 8(a) or 15 of the Small Business Act are subject to the same limitations on subcontracting as other contracts with small businesses, which should help limit the alleged use of such contracts to "pass through" work to large businesses. [179] All businesses awarded contracts under the authority of the Small Business Act are subject to statutory and regulatory limits on subcontracting.[180] They are required to perform a certain percentage of the contract work themselves, rather than subcontract it to other firms. The percentage that must be performed varies depending upon the type of the contract, with employees of the small business required to perform (1) at least 50% of the personnel costs of service contracts; (2) at least 50% of the costs of manufacturing (excluding materials) in supply contacts; (3) at least 15% of the costs of construction (excluding materials) in general construction contracts; and (4) at least 25% of the costs of construction (excluding materials) in "special trade" construction contracts.[181] ANC-owned firms have no statutory or regulatory exemption from these requirements, and to the degree that they falsely certify that they have performed the required percentage of work, they are subject to the penalties normally applicable to firms that make false statements to the SBA.[182] However, GAO has reported that the SBA may not adequately monitor the percentage of work performed by subcontractors on 8(a) contracts with ANC-owned firms.[183]

The statutory and regulatory limitations on subcontracting do not address the size of the firms with which small businesses may subcontract, and to the degree that the small business performs the required percentage of work on the contract, it may subcontract work to any firm, including firms that are "large" or otherwise ineligible for the 8(a) Program.[184]

"Bonuses" for Subcontracting under the Indian Financing Act

Federal prime contractors that subcontract with "Indian organizations" or "Indian-owned economic enterprises," including ANCs and ANC-owned firms, are eligible for "bonuses" equivalent to 5% of the subcontract amount under the authority of the Indian Financing Act. [185] However, the availability of such subcontracting bonuses does not necessarily give federal prime contractors an incentive to prefer ANCs and ANC-owned firms over other 8(a) or small disadvantaged businesses. [186] This is, in part, because the Federal Acquisition Regulation (FAR) authorizes agencies to provide "monetary incentives" to contractors that subcontract with "small disadvantaged businesses,"[187] which all 8(a) firms are.[188] The amount of the monetary incentive is determined by the contract between the agency and the prime contractor, but could be as high as 10% of the amount by which the prime contractor exceeds its monetary target for subcontracting with small disadvantaged businesses.[189] No funds are known to have been appropriated specifically for payment of monetary incentives, however, unlike with DOD's payment of "subcontracting bonuses. [190]

Agencies must opt to award bonuses for subcontracting under the Indian Financing Act; contractors do not automatically receive bonuses without agency action. Additionally, subcontracting bonuses are arguably only available to agencies' prime contractors, which means that ANCs do not automatically get "bonuses" whenever a subsidiary is awarded a federal contract under the 8(a) Program or whenever a subcontractor contracts with a subsidiary.[191]

Agencies' Discretion to Accept Requirements for the 8(a) Program

Although SBA and other federal agencies have fairly broad discretion when awarding contracts under Section 8(a) of the Small Business Act, their discretion in accepting requirements for the 8(a) Program is subject to some statutory and regulatory limitations that could theoretically help protect taxpayers, other small businesses, and other 8(a) firms from some possible effects of the alleged "special procurement advantages" available to ANCs and ANC-owned firms. First, agencies are prohibited from accepting contracts for award under the authority of Section 8(a) of the Small Business Act when the price of the 8(a) contract would exceed the fair market price,[192] or when SBA determines in writing that "acceptance of the procurement for 8(a) award would have an adverse impact on an individual small business, a group of small businesses located in a specific geographical location, or other small business programs."[193] If adequately implemented, the former provision could help protect taxpayers from agency contracts with ANCs or their subsidiaries costing "too much,"[194] while the latter could help ensure that the ease and speed of contracting with ANCs under Section 8(a) does not result in other small businesses losing contracting opportunities.[195] Second, statutes and regulations governing eligibility for contracts under Section 8(a) authorize SBA to count affiliations with parent ANCs or their subsidiaries when making size determinations if failure to do so results or could result in an ANC-owned firm obtaining "a substantial unfair competitive advantage within an industry category." [196] This provision, generally applied, could similarly help shield other 8(a) firms from the alleged loss of some contracting opportunities to ANC-owned firms.[197]

Maximum of Nine Years in the 8(a) Program

Under the Small Business Act and its implementing regulations, ANCs and other group owners of 8(a) businesses are unlike socially and economically disadvantaged individuals in that they can confer eligibility for the 8(a) Program upon multiple firms over a period of more than nine years.[198] Socially and economically disadvantaged individuals, in contrast, can generally confer eligibility for the 8(a) Program upon only one firm, which may generally participate in the 8(a) Program for a period of no more than nine years.[199]

However, specific ANC-owned firms and other group-owned firms are like individually owned firms in that they can participate in the 8(a) Program for no more than nine years.[200] Moreover, an SBA regulation arguably effectively precludes ANCs and other group owners from making what is essentially the same firm eligible for the 8(a) Program for more than nine years by specifying that a firm is deemed to have participated in the 8(a) Program when over 50% of its assets were formerly held by a prior 8(a) firm.[201]

Ownership of Multiple 8(a) Firms

Under the governing authorities, ANCs and other groups are unlike socially and economically disadvantaged individuals in that they can own majority interests in multiple 8(a) firms.[202] These firms may participate in the 8(a) Program simultaneously or sequentially, subject to certain requirements regarding their "primary" and "secondary" industries:

> [An ANC] cannot own 51% or more of another firm which, either at the time of application or within the previous two years, has been operating in the 8(a) program under the same primary SIC code as the applicant. [An ANC] may, however, own a Participant or an applicant that conducts or will conduct secondary business in the 8(a) BD program under the same SIC code that a current Participant owned by the tribe operates in the 8(a) BD program as its primary SIC code.[203]

A firm's primary industry is the industry in which it obtains more than half of its revenue. Its secondary industries are any industries in which it obtains less than half of its revenue.

Because follow-on contracts are likely to involve the same primary industry, the prohibition on owning multiple firms operating in the same primary industry simultaneously or within two years of each other could, if enforced, potentially limit ANCs' alleged ability to create new subsidiaries "in anticipation of the graduation of an existing subsidiary or the expiration of that subsidiary's 8(a) contract, so that the new subsidiary will take on a follow-on contract to essentially continue the work of the former subsidiary."[204]

Requirement to Obtain Revenue from Non-8(a) Sources

As mentioned previously, like other 8(a) firms, ANC-owned 8(a) firms are required by the Small Business Act and its implementing regulations to obtain increasing percentages of their revenue from sources other than 8(a) contracts while in the "transitional stage" of the 8(a) Program.[205] These percentages range from 15% in their fifth year of participation in the 8(a) Program to 55% in their ninth—and final—year.[206] Also like other 8(a) firms, ANC-owned 8(a) firms that do not obtain the required percentage of revenue from non-8(a) sources are ineligible for sole-source 8(a) contracts "unless and until" they correct the situation.[207] This requirement, in part, helps ensure that the 8(a) Program operates as a "business development" program for ANC-owned firms even if such firms are not "required" to compete for any 8(a) contracts.[208]

Management by and Employment of Non-Alaska Natives

Under the Small Business Act and SBA regulations, ANC-owned firms are unlike individually owned 8(a) firms, which must be managed by one or more socially and economically disadvantaged individuals,[209] in that they may be managed by individuals who are not Alaska Natives.[210] Such outside management is, however, permissible only if SBA determines that it

> is required to assist the [firm's] development, that the [ANC] will retain control of all management decisions common to boards of directors, including strategic planning, budget approval, and the employment and compensation of officers, and that a written management plan exists which shows how disadvantaged [Alaska Natives] will develop managerial skills sufficient to manage the concern or similar [ANC]-owned concerns in the future.[211]

Outside of their managers, 8(a) firms are not required to employ socially or economically disadvantaged individuals. ANC-owned 8(a) firms are like other 8(a) firms in this and are not required to employ any Alaska Natives, although they frequently do.[212]

LEGISLATIVE ACTIVITY DURING THE 111TH CONGRESS

Enacted and Proposed Legislation

The first session of the 111th Congress enacted one law affecting the authorities under which agencies contract with ANC-owned firms. The National Defense Authorization Act for FY20 10 (P.L. 111-84) requires that the Federal Acquisition Regulation (FAR) be amended to prohibit agencies from awarding sole-source contracts in excess of $20 million in "covered procurements" unless

(1) the contracting officer for the contract justifies the use of a sole-source contract in writing;
(2) the justification is approved by the appropriate official designated to approve contract awards for dollar amounts that are comparable to the amount of the sole-source contract; and
(3) the justification and related information are made public as provided in sections 2304(f)(1)(C) and 2304(l) of title 10, United States Code, or sections 303(f)(1)(C) and 303(j) of the Federal Property and Administrative Services Act of 1949 (41 U.S.C. 253(f)(1)(C) and 253(j)), as applicable.[213]

"Covered procurements" include those described in 10 U.S.C. § 2304(f)(2)(D)(ii) and 41 U.S.C. § 253(f)(2)(D)(ii),[214] provisions which exempt sole-source contracts awarded under the authority of Section 8(a) of the Small Business Act from the justifications, approvals, and notices required for other sole-source contracts. The act also specifies that justifications for sole-source awards under the FAR must include (1) a description of the agency's needs; (2) the specific statutory provision authorizing the agency to use other than competitive procedures; (3) a determination that use of a sole-source contract is in the best interest of the agency; (4) a determination that the anticipated cost of the contract will be fair and reasonable; and (5) any other matters that the head of the contracting agency might require.[215]

An amendment to the Senate version of this bill (S.Amdt. 1762 to S. 1390) was also proposed that would have (1) limited the Department of Defense's authority to make sole-source awards in excess of $3.5 million ($5.5 million for manufacturing contracts) to ANC-owned firms;[216] (2) granted contracting officers awarding DOD contracts of any value discretion to select between set-asides for tribally owned firms and set-asides for 8(a) firms;[217] and (3) restricted agencies' authority to pay subcontracting "bonuses" under the

Indian Financing Act.[218] This amendment was withdrawn before the Senate passed its version of the National Defense Authorization Act for FY2010,[219] and similar provisions were not included in the enacted law.

Committee Hearings

On July 16, 2009, the Ad Hoc Subcommittee on Contracting Oversight of the Senate Committee on Homeland Security and Governmental Affairs held a hearing on "Contracting Preferences for Alaska Native Corporations." It featured witnesses from the SBA, DOD, Native American Contractors Association, National Congress of American Indians, Alaska Federation of Natives, Inc., and industry. The SBA's assistant inspector general for auditing discussed findings from a recent report illustrating the increase in contracting with ANC-owned firms within the 8(a) Program and discussing deficiencies in SBA oversight of contracting with ANCs and ANC-owned firms.[220] The SBA's associate administrator for government contracting and business development testified about initiatives SBA has undertaken to improve oversight of contracting with ANC- owned firms, including hiring additional staff for the Alaska office, funding initiatives to better track ANC participation in the 8(a) Program, and developing regulations that would "ensure more effective administration of the 8(a) program for all participants."[221] The acting deputy under secretary of defense for acquisition and technology expressed DOD's intent to ensure that ANC contracts receive "the same audit and oversight as other DOD contracts," monitor compliance with limitations on subcontracting, and compete more 8(a) procurements.[222] Officials of the Native American Contractors Association and the National Congress of American Indians both addressed the positive effects of contracting programs for ANC-owned firms.[223] In contrast, representatives from Cirrus Technology, Inc., and Purcell Construction Corporation explained their difficulties in competing with ANCs under current rules.[224]

Committee Staff Reports

In *New Information about Contracting Preferences for Alaska Native Corporations* (Parts I-II), the majority staff of the Ad Hoc Subcommittee on Contracting Oversight of the Senate Committee on Homeland Security and Governmental Affairs analyze data gathered prior to the July 16, 2009, hearing.[225] Among the report's findings are that (1) ANCs are presently among the largest federal contractors, (2) ANCs are big businesses, (3) ANCs have created multiple 8(a) subsidiaries, (4) ANCs have been awarded multiple large sole-source contracts, (5) ANCs may be passing work through to subcontractors, (6) ANCs employ a relatively small percentage of shareholders, and (7) ANCs rely heavily on highly paid non-Alaska Native executives.

Proposed Changes to the SBA Regulations

On October 28, 2009, SBA issued a proposed rule that would change certain eligibility and other requirements pertaining to the 8(a)Program.[226] Several of these changes apply specifically to ANC-owned firms, including a proposed rule specifying that

> a newly certified [ANC-]owned Participant cannot receive an 8(a) contract in a secondary NAICS code that is the primary NAICS code of another Participant (or former participant that has left the program within two years of the date of application) owned by the [ANC] for a period of two years from the date of admission to the program.[227]

Other proposed rules would (1) allow ANC-owned firms to be found to have potential for success if the ANC pledges to use its resources to support the firm and to not allow the firm to cease operations;[228] (2) require ANCs to submit information to SBA annually showing how their participation in the 8(a) Program has benefited Alaska Natives;[229] (3) change the location for SBA's initial review of ANC-owned firms' applications from the Anchorage District Office to the San Francisco Division of Program Certification and Eligibility;[230] and (4) prohibit non-8(a) firms that form joint ventures with 8(a) firms to perform sole-source contracts in excess of $3.5 million ($5.5 million for manufacturing contracts) from serving as subcontractors on the contract.[231]

The comment period on SBA's proposed rule ended on December 28, 2009,[232] and SBA has yet to promulgate a final rule.

End Notes

[1] Office of the Inspector General, U.S. Small Business Administration, Participation in the 8(a) Program by Firms Owned by Alaska Native Corporations, at 2 (July 10, 2009), *available at* http://www.sba.go v/idc/groups/public/ documents/sba_homepage/oig_reptbydatejuly9-15.pdf.

[2] U.S. Senate, Committee on Homeland Security & Governmental Affairs, Subcommittee on Contracting Oversight, Majority Staff, New Information about Contracting Preferences for Alaska Native Corporations (Part I), at 1 (2009), *available at* http://mccaskill.senate.gov/pdf/ANCdataAnalysis.pdf.

[3] Participation in the 8(a) Program, *supra* note 1, at 4.

[4] *See, e.g., Northern Lights and Procurement Plights: The Effect of the ANC Program on Federal Procurement and Alaska Native Corporations: Joint Hearing Before the Committee on Government Reform and the Committee on Small Business, House of Representatives, 109th Cong., 2d Sess.*, at 173-74 (2006) (statement of Harry Alford, President and CEO, National Black Chamber of Commerce) (characterizing ANCs as "predators on the minority business community").

[5] *See, e.g., id.* at 161 (statement of Representative Henry A. Waxman).

[6] *See, e.g.*, Native American Contractors Association, Native American Contracting under Section 8(a) of the Small Business Act: Economic, Social, and Cultural Implications, at 3 (Oct. 2007), *available at* http://ww w.nativecontractors.org/media (noting that, in FY2005, contracts with ANCs represented less than 1% of all federal contracts, less than 2% of all sole-source contracts, less than 3% of all small business contracts, and less than 20% of all 8(a) contracts).

[7] *Id.* at 11-12 (discussing the dividends paid and job opportunities provided by ANCs, among other things).

[8] *See,e.g.,* Robert Brodsky, McCaskill Will Wait on Alaska Native Contracting Reform, *Government Executive*, July 29, 2009, *available at* http://www.govexec.com/dailyfed/0709/072909rb1.htm.

[9] See CRS Report R40744, The "8(a) Program" *for Small Businesses Owned and Controlled by the Socially and Economically Disadvantaged: Legal Requirements and Issues*, by John R. Luckey and Kate M. Manuel.

[10] U.S. Small Business Administration, *Developing Indian Owned Businesses Through the Assistance of the 8(a) Program of the Small Business Administration* (Sept. 1970).

[11] P.L. 92-203, 85 Stat. 688 (codified, as amended, at 43 U.S.C. §§ 1601-1629h).

[12] *Id.* at § 2(b); 43 U.S.C. § 1601(b).

[13] Robert D. Arnold, with Janet Archibald et al., *Alaska Native Land Claims* 106, 120, 274-76 (1976).

[14] U.S. Congress, House Conference Committee, *Alaska Native Claims Settlement Act: Conference Report to Accompany H.R. 10367, 92nd Cong., 1st Sess.*, at 41-42 (1971).

[15] U.S. Congress, Senate Interior and Insular Affairs Committee, *Alaska Native Claims Settlement Act of 1971: Report to Accompany S. 35, 92nd Cong., 1st Sess.*, at 105 (1971). *See also* Arnold et al., *supra* note 13, at 281.

[16] U.S. Department of the Interior, Budget Justifications and Performance Information, Fiscal Year 2010, Bureau of Land Management, at III-143 (2009), *available at* http://www.doi.gov/budget/2010/data/greenbook/ FY2010_BLM_Greenbook.pdf.

[17] P.L. 93-638, § 4(e), 88 Stat. 2204 (codified, as amended, at 25 U.S.C. § 450b(e)) (Jan. 4, 1975). Inclusion as Indian tribes made ANCs eligible for contracts and grants to operate Bureau of Indian Affairs and the Indian Health Service programs under this act.

[18] P.L. 95-507, § 231, 92 Stat. 1772 (Oct. 24, 1978); 15 U.S.C. § 636(a).

[19] Consolidated Omnibus Budget Reconciliation Act, P.L. 99-272, § 18015, 100 Stat. 370-71 (Apr. 7, 1986); 15 U.S.C. § 637(a).

[20] *See, e.g.*, U.S. Congress, Senate Small Business Committee, *S. 1022, A Bill to Make Small Businesses Owned by American Indian Tribes Eligible for the SBA 8(a) Program: Hearings, 98th Cong., 1st Sess.*, at 28 (1983) (discussing the Section 7(a) loan program); U.S. Congress, Senate Small Business Committee, *Amending Section 8(a) of the Small Business Act: Report to Accompany S. 1022, 98th Cong., 1st Sess.*, at 4-5 (1983) (discussing the 8(a) Program).

[21] P.L. 100-241, § 15, 101 Stat. 1812 (Feb. 3, 1988) (amending Section 29 of ANCSA, codified at 43 U.S.C. § 1626(e)(1)).

[22] U.S. Congress, Senate Energy and Natural Resources Committee, Subcommittee on Public Lands, National Parks, & Forests, *Alaska Land Status Technical Corrections Act of 1991: Hearing on S. 1625, 102nd Cong., 1st Sess.*, at 25 (1992) (prepared statement of Julie Kitka, President, Alaska Federation of Natives).

[23] P.L. 102-415, § 10, 106 Stat. 2115 (Oct. 14, 1992); 43 U.S.C. § 1626(e)(1). The House committee report on the bill stated that it was amending Section 29 of ANCSA

to clarify that Alaska Native corporations are minority and economically disadvantaged business enterprises for the purposes of implementing the SBA programs. Section 15(e) of the 1987

Amendments to ANCSA (P.L. 100-24 1) provided that Alaska Native corporations shall be defined as minority business enterprises for as long as a majority of both the total equity and total voting power of the corporation is held by holders of Settlement Common Stock and by Natives and descendants of Natives. This section would further clarify that Alaska Native corporations and their subsidiary companies are minority and economically disadvantaged business enterprises for the purposes of qualifying for participation in Federal contracting and subcontracting programs, the largest of which include the SBA 8(a) program and the Department of Defense Small and Disadvantaged Business Program.... While this section eliminates the need for Alaska Native Corporations or their subsidiaries to prove their 'economic' disadvantage the corporations would still be required to meet size requirements as small businesses.

U.S. Congress, House Interior and Insular Affairs Committee, Settlement of Certain Claims Under the Alaska Native Claims Settlement Act: Report to Accompany H.R. 3157, 102nd Cong., 2nd Sess., at 19 (1992).

[24] Government Accountability Office, Contract Management: Increased Use of Alaska Native Corporations' Special 8(a) Provisions Calls for Tailored Oversight, GAO-06-399, at 26 (Apr. 2006), *available at* http://www.gao.gov/ products/GAO-06-399.

[25] Steve Colt, Financial Performance of Native Regional Corporations, 28 *Alaska Rev. of Soc. & Econ. Conditions* 9-10 (1991).

[26] *Id.* at 3.

[27] Steve Colt, *Alaska Natives and the "New Harpoon": Economic Performance of the ANCSA Regional Corporations*, at 3 (Feb. 2, 2001), *available at* http://www.iser.uaa.alaska.edu/Publications/colt_newharpoon2.pdf.

[28] James D. Linxwiler, The Alaska Native Claims Settlement Act at 35: Delivering on the Promise, *Proceedings of the 53rd Annual Rocky Mountain Mineral Law Institute*, at 4 (2007), *available at* http://www.iser.uaa.alaska.edu/ Publications/8(a)/e-book%20layout/C/C. 1/ANCSA%20at%2035%20Delivering%20on%20the%20Promise.pdf.

[29] Section 7(i) of ANCSA, codified at 43 U.S.C. § 1606(i), provides for the distribution of 70% of a land-based regional ANC's net revenues from its timber and subsurface resources among the other land-based regional ANCs, with some limitations. Section 7(j), codified at 43 U.S.C. § 1606(j), provides for the further distribution of some of the timber and subsurface income from regional ANCs to village ANCs and certain shareholders.

[30] *See* Linxwiler, *supra* note 28.

[31] According to an *Alaska Business* article, a subsidiary of the Arctic Slope Regional Corporation, called Piqunik Management Corporation, was the first ANC subsidiary to be 8(a) certified, and it won its first contract in the late 1980s. *See* Julie Stricker, 8(a) Program Benefits Native Corporations, *Alaska Bus. Monthly*, June 2003, at 63.

[32] Internal Revenue Code § 172. NOLs may be deducted from gross income in certain past or future years, thereby reducing tax liability in those years. During the early 1980s, any U.S. corporation with NOLs could sell its NOLs to another corporation. *See* Colt, *supra* note 25, at 13.

[33] Julie Stricker, The Maturing of the 13 Regional Corporations, *Alaska Bus. Monthly*, Mar. 2001, at 49 (citing Steve Colt).

[34] P.L. 99-514, § 1804(e)(4), 100 Stat. 2801 (Oct. 22, 1986); 26 U.S.C. § 1504 note. Linxwiler explains:

while it was seeking reorganization pursuant to the bankruptcy laws, [regional ANC] Bering Straits Native Corporation (BSNC), along with its advisors, initiated an effort to engage in the sharing of the tax benefits of its NOLs through transactions with profitable companies with large tax liabilities—in essence, the ANCSA corporation "sold" its losses to the profitable company, which used them as deductions to decrease its tax liability. Senator Ted Stevens (R-AK) was instrumental in obtaining the enactment of a series of statutes that clarified the authority of all Native corporations to enter into such transactions and they eventually became widespread among ANCSA corporations until the authority for them was repealed in 1988.

Linxwiler, *supra* note 28, at 23.

[35] P.L. 100-647, § 5021, 102 Stat. 3666 (Nov. 10, 1988); 26 U.S.C. § 1504 note.

[36] Colt, supra note 25, at 13.

[37] Stricker, *supra* note 33, at 49-50.

[38] Jennifer Forker, 25 Years After ANCSA, *Alaska Bus. Monthly*, Nov. 1996, at 58 and following.

[39] Linxwiler, *supra* note 28, at 4.

[40] Stricker, *supra* note 31, at 63.

[41] *Id.* at 63-64.

[42] Clifford Gerhart, ANCSA Corporations, *Alaska Bus. Monthly*, Nov. 1992, at 25-31.

[43] Vivian Hamilton, Building on Experience, *Alaska Bus. Monthly*, Sept. 1997, at 28 and following.

[44] Contract Management, *supra* note 24, at 26, Fig. 6.

[45] *Id.* at 9.

[46] Armed Services Procurement Act, P.L. 80-413, 62 Stat. 21 (Feb. 19, 1948) (codified at 10 U.S.C. § 2302 et seq.); Federal Property and Administrative Services Act, P.L. 81-152, 63 Stat. 377 (June 30, 1949) (codified at 40 U.S.C. § 471 et seq. and 41 U.S.C. § 251 et seq.).

[47] There are some exceptions to this general rule, such as the prohibition upon contracting with government employees or entities owned or substantially owned and controlled by government employees. *See* 48 C.F.R. §§ 3.60 1-3.602. The exceptions are few and narrow, however.

[48] 10 U.S.C. § 2304(c)(1)-(7) (defense agencies) & 41 U.S.C. § 253(c)(1)-(7) (civilian agencies).

[49] 10 U.S.C. § 2304(f)(2) (defense agencies) & 41 U.S.C. § 253(f)(2) (civilian agencies). The justification must include (1) a description of agency needs; (2) the statutory exception upon which the agency relied and a demonstration of the reasons for using the exception that is based upon the proposed contractor's qualifications or the nature of the procurement; (3) a determination that the anticipated cost will be fair and reasonable; (4) a description of any market survey conducted, or a statement of the reasons for not conducting a market survey; (5) a listing of any sources that expressed, in writing, interest in the procurement; and (6) a statement of any actions that the agency may take to remove or overcome barriers to competition before subsequent procurements. 10 U.S.C. § 2304(f)(3)(A)-(F) (defense agencies) & 41 U.S.C. § 253(f)(3)(A)-(F) (civilian agencies).

[50] 10 U.S.C. § 2304(f)(1)(B) (defense agencies) & 41 U.S.C. § 253(f)(1)(B) (civilian agencies). The identity of the approving official is determined by the anticipated value of the contract.

[51] 10 U.S.C. § 2304(f)(1)(C) (defense agencies) & 41 U.S.C. § 253(f)(1)(C) (civilian agencies). *See also* 41 U.S.C. § 416(b)(5) (notice requirements). Notices identify the intended recipient of the sole-source contract and state the agencies' reason(s) for awarding a sole-source contract. *Id.*

[52] FPDS-NG is the primary database into which federal agencies report official statistical data on procurement contracts. It does not identify the specific legal authorities under which particular contracts were awarded.

[53] 15 U.S.C. § 632(a)(1)-(2)(A) (statutory definition of "small" for purposes of the Small Business Act); 13 C.F.R. §§ 121.101-121.108 (defining size in terms of the number of employees or gross income); Participation in the 8(a) Program, *supra* note 21, at 12 (characterizing ANCs as "large").

[54] *See* 13 C.F.R. § 121.105(a)(1) ("Except for small agricultural cooperatives, a business concern eligible for assistance from SBA as a small business is a business entity organized for profit, with a place of business located in the United States, and which operates primarily within the United States or which makes a significant contribution to the U.S. economy through payment of taxes or use of American products, materials or labor.").

[55] *See, e.g.*, Contract Management, *supra* note 24, at 1 (noting that Alaskan village, urban, and group corporations may be either for-profit or nonprofit). Regional corporations, in contrast, must be for-profit. *Id.*

[56] Small Business Act of 1958, P.L. 85-536, § 15, 72 Stat. 395 (July 18, 1958) (codified at 15 U.S.C. § 644(a)) ("To effectuate the purposes of this Act, small-business concerns within the meaning of this Act shall receive any award or contract or any part thereof, and be awarded any contract for the sale of Government property, as to which it is determined by the [Small Business] Administration and the contracting procurement or disposal

agency (1) to be in the interest of maintaining or mobilizing the Nation's full productive capacity, (2) to be in the interest of war or national defense programs, (3) to be in the interest of assuring that a fair proportion of the total sales of Government property be made to small business concerns."); Competition in Contracting Act, P.L. 98-369, § 2711, 98 Stat. 1175-76 (Aug. 18, 1984) ("In fulfilling the statutory requirements relating to small business concerns and socially and economically disadvantaged small business concerns, an executive agency shall use competitive procedures but may restrict a solicitation to allow only such business concerns to compete.") (procurements of civilian agencies); CICA, § 2723, 98 Stat. 1187-88 (same) (procurements of defense agencies).

[57] Contracts whose anticipated value is between $3,000 and $100,000 *must* be set aside for small businesses *unless* the contracting officer is unable to obtain offers from two or more small businesses that are competitive with market prices and in terms of the quality and delivery of goods or services. 15 U.S.C. § 644(j)(1); 48 C.F.R. § 19.502-2(a). Contracts whose anticipated value exceeds $100,000 *must* also be set aside for small businesses *if* the contracting officer reasonably expects that (1) offers will be obtained from at least two responsible small businesses offering the products of different small businesses and (2) the award will be made at a fair market price. 48 C.F.R. § 19.502-2(b).

[58] When a total set-aside is not appropriate, an acquisition can generally be partially set aside for small businesses if (1) the requirement is severable into two or more economic production runs or reasonable lots, (2) one or more small businesses are expected to have the technical competence and productive capacity to satisfy the set-aside portion of the requirement at a fair market price, and (3) the acquisition is not subject to simplified acquisition procedures. 48 C.F.R. § 19.502-3(a)(1)-(4). Partial set-asides cannot be made when procuring construction work, however. 48 C.F.R. § 19.502-3(a).

[59] *See supra* note 48 and accompanying text.

[60] *See supra* notes 49-51 and accompanying text.

[61] 13 C.F.R. § 121. 103(a)(1). Control or the power of control need only exist; it need not be exercised.

[62] 13 C.F.R. § 121. 103(a)(6) ("In determining the concern's size, SBA counts the receipts, employees, or other measure of size of the concern whose size is at issue and all of its domestic and foreign affiliates, regardless of whether the affiliates are organized for profit.").

[63] 15 U.S.C. § 636(j)(10)(J)(ii)(II); 13 C.F.R. § 121. 103(b)(2)(i) ("Business concerns owned and controlled by Indian Tribes, Alaska Native Corporations (ANCs) organized pursuant to the Alaska Native Claims Settlement Act (43 U.S.C. § 1601 et seq.), Native Hawaiian Organizations (NHOs), Community Development Corporations (CDCs) authorized by 42 U.S.C. § 9805, or wholly-owned entities of Indian Tribes, ANCs, NHOs, or CDCs are not considered affiliates of such entities.").

[64] 13 C.F.R. § 124. 109(c)(2)(iii). ("In determining the size of a small business concern owned by a socially and economically disadvantaged Indian tribe (or a wholly owned business entity of such tribe), each firm's size shall be independently determined without regard to its affiliation with the tribe, any entity of the tribal government, or any other business enterprise owned by the tribe, unless the Administrator determines that one or more such tribally owned business concerns have obtained, or are likely to obtain, a substantial unfair competitive advantage within an industry category."). ANCs are included within the definition of "Indian tribe" used here. *See* Omnibus Consolidated Budget Reconciliation Act of 1985, P.L. 99-272, § 18015, 100 Stat. 370 (1986) (codified at 15 U.S.C. § 637(a)(13)).

[65] 13 C.F.R. § 124.501(a).

[66] *See, e.g.*, Contract Management, *supra* note 24, at 37 (reporting that some contracting officers claimed not to know how to determine what constitutes a "substantial unfair competitive advantage" when making size determinations for ANC-owned firms).

[67] 13 C.F.R. § 124.109(a)(3).

[68] *See* Small Business Administration, Guide to SBA's Definitions of Small Business, "Use of Size Standards for Government Procurement," at 13-14, *available at* http://www.sba.gov/idc/groups/public/documents/sba_homepage/ guide_to_size_standards.pdf.

[69] *See* 13 C.F.R. § 121.108 (including criminal penalties under 15 U.S.C. § 645(d)).

[70] 13 C.F.R. § 121. 100 1(a)(2) (authorizing protests of competitive awards by offerors whom the contracting officer has not eliminated for reasons related to size; the contracting officer; the SBA Government Contracting Area Director with responsibility for the area in which the headquarters of the protested offeror is located; and other "interested parties"). Sole-source awards are treated differently. *See* 13 C.F.R. § 100 1(b)(2)(ii).

[71] 13 C.F.R. § 121.405(b).

[72] The statutes and regulations consistently refer to agencies' contracting with ANC-owned firms, and individual ANCs could have difficulty qualifying as small under the size standards. Additionally, non-profit ANCs would not qualify as businesses for purposes of the Small Business Act. *See* 13 C.F.R. § 124.109(a) (speaking of participation in the 8(a) Program by "ANC-owned concerns"); 13 C.F.R. §§ 121.101-121.108 (size standards used in determining whether a firm is small); 13 C.F.R. § 121.105(a)(1) (defining "businesses" as for-profit entities).

[73] 15 U.S.C. § 637(a)(1)(A)-(B). While "socially and economically disadvantaged small business concerns" were originally defined as those owned by one or more socially and economically disadvantaged individuals,

Congress later included firms that are at least 51% owned and unconditionally controlled by ANCs, Indian tribes, NHOs, or CDCs. *See* P.L. 95-507, § 202, 92 Stat. 1757 (Oct. 24, 1978) (codified at 15 U.S.C. § 637(a)(4)(A)-(B)) (creating statutory authority for the 8(a) Program for minority-owned businesses); Community Development Act of 1981, P.L. 97-35, Ch. 8, Subch. A, 95 Stat. 489 (Aug. 13, 1981) (codified at 42 U.S.C. §§ 9801 et seq.) (making CDC-owned firms eligible for the 8(a) Program); Omnibus Consolidated Budget Reconciliation Act of 1985, P.L. 99-272, § 18015, 100 Stat. 370 (Apr. 7, 1986) (making tribally and ANC-owned firms eligible for the 8(a) Program); Business Opportunity Development Reform Act of 1988, P.L. 100-656, § 207, 102 Stat. 3861 (Nov. 15, 1988) (codified at 15 U.S.C. § 637(a)(4)) (making NHO firms eligible for the 8(a) Program).

[74] 15 U.S.C. § 637(a)(1)(D)(i)(II); 48 C.F.R. § 19.805-1(a)(1)-(2). SBA regulations presently read $3 million and $5 million, respectively, when establishing the competitive threshold. *See* 13 C.F.R. § 124.506(a)(3). These numbers are probably incorrect and should be increased to $3.5 million ($5.5 million for manufacturing contracts) given changes that were apparently made by the SBA. The Federal Acquisition Regulation (FAR) has included the increased competitive thresholds since 2007, and the authority under which the competitive thresholds in the FAR were changed is such that the increase could probably only have been made by the SBA. *See* Department of Defense, General Services Administration, & National Aeronautics & Space Administration, Inflation Adjustment of Acquisition-Related Thresholds, 71 Fed. Reg. 57363 (Sept. 28, 2006) ("The statute does not authorize the FAR to escalate thresholds originating in executive order or the implementing agency (such as the Department of Labor or the Small Business Administration), unless the executive order or agency regulations are first amended."); Ronald W. Reagan National Defense Authorization Act for FY2005, P.L. 108-375, § 807, 118 Stat. 2010-11 (Oct. 28, 2004) (codified at 41 U.S.C. § 43 1a) (providing the FAR Councils with the authority underlying the regulations promulgated in the *Federal Register* on September 28, 2006).

[75] 15 U.S.C. § 637(a)(16)(A). A noncompetitive award may be made under this authority so long as (1) the firm is determined to be a responsible contractor for performance of the contract, (2) award of the contract would be consistent with the firm's business plan, and (3) award of the contract would not result in the firm exceeding the percentage of revenue from 8(a) sources forecast in its annual business plan. 15 U.S.C. § 637(a)(16)(A)(i)-(iii). For contracts whose value is below the competitive threshold to be awarded competitively, the SBA's Associate Administrator for 8(a) Business Development must approve the agency's request to do so. 15 U.S.C. § 637(a)(1)(D)(ii); 48 C.F.R. § 19.805- 1(d).

[76] 15 U.S.C. § 637(a)(1)(D)(i)(I)-(II); 48 C.F.R. § 19.805-1(b)(1)-(2) (sole-source awards to tribally or ANC-owned firms); 48 C.F.R. § 219.805-1(b)(2)(A)-(B) (sole-source awards to NHO-owned firms).

[77] P.L. 111-84, § 811, 123 Stat. 2405-06 (Oct. 28, 2009). *See infra* notes 212 to 214 and accompanying text.

[78] *See, e.g.*, AHNTECH, Inc., B-401092, Comp. Gen. Dec. (Apr. 22, 2009) ("The [Small Business] Act affords the SBA and contracting agencies broad discretion in selecting procurements for the 8(a) program.").

[79] *See, e.g.*, *Northern Lights and Procurement Plights*, *supra* note 4, at 178 (statement of Ann Sullivan, President, Madison Services Group, Inc., on behalf of Women Impacting Public Policy) (suggesting that all 8(a) firms should be subject to the same requirements). Firms owned by Indian tribes, NHOs, and CDCs enjoy many, but not all, of the alleged "special procurement advantages" enjoyed by ANC-owned firms. *See* 13 C.F.R. § 124. 109(b)-(c) (tribally owned firms); 13 C.F.R. § 124.110 (NHO-owned firms); 13 C.F.R. § 124.111 (CDC-owned firms). A notable exception is that tribally and NHO-owned firms are not deemed to be economically disadvantaged in the same way that ANC-owned firms are. *Compare* 13 C.F.R. § 124. 109(a)(2) (ANC-owned firms) *with* 13 C.F.R. § 124.109(b) (tribally owned firms) *and* 13 C.F.R. § 124.110 (NHO-owned firms).

[80] There are also variations in the regulations regarding "good character" and "potential for success." With 8(a) firms generally, SBA checks that the firm and its owner(s) have not engaged in criminal conduct, have not violated SBA regulations, and are not debarred or suspended from government contracting. *See* 13 C.F.R. § 124.108(a). With ANC- owned firms, the SBA applies these requirements only to officers, directors, and shareholders owning more than a 20% interest in the firm, not to all ANC shareholders. *See* 13 C.F.R. § 124. 109(c)(7)(B)(ii). Similarly, with potential for success, SBA generally considers the following five criteria when granting waivers: (1) the management experience of the disadvantaged individual(s) upon whom eligibility is based; (2) the firm's technical experience; (3) the firm's capital; (4) the firm's performance record on prior federal or other contracts in its primary field; and (5) whether the firm has or can timely obtain the personnel, facilities, equipment, and other resources necessary to perform contracts under Section 8(a). *See* 13 C.F.R. § 124.107. Waivers for ANC-owned firms, in contrast, are based on three criteria: (1) the technical and managerial experience and competency of the individuals who will manage and control the firm's daily operations, (2) the firm's financial capacity, and (3) the firm's performance record on prior federal or other contracts in the its primary industry. *See* 13 C.F.R. § 124.110(e). However, commentators generally do not attribute the reportedly increasing number of contracts with ANC-owned firms to these factors, and they are thus excluded from **Table 1**. In fact, the difference in the number and wording of the waiver criteria probably would not result in ANC- owned firms receiving waivers when other 8(a) firms would not.

[81] See CRS Report R40744, The "8(a) *Program" for Small Businesses Owned and Controlled by the Socially and Economically Disadvantaged: Legal Requirements and Issues*, supra note 9.

[82] 13 C.F.R. § 124. 109(c)(3)(i) ("A tribally-owned applicant concern must qualify as a small business concern as defined for purposes of Federal Government procurement in part 121 of this title."). ANC-owned firms are subject to the same requirements as tribally owned firms here.

[83] 13 C.F.R. § 124.109(a) & (b) (requiring ANC-owned firms to comply with the general eligibility requirements when they are not contrary to or inconsistent with the special requirements for these entities); 13 C.F.R. § 121. 105(a)(1) ("Except for small agricultural cooperatives, a business concern eligible for assistance from SBA as a small business is a business entity organized for profit, with a place of business located in the United States, and which operates primarily within the United States or which makes a significant contribution to the U.S. economy through payment of taxes or use of American products, materials or labor.").

[84] 13 C.F.R. § 124.109(a) & (b).

[85] 13 C.F.R. § 124. 109(b)(7)(ii).

[86] 13 C.F.R. § 124.109(c)(6).

[87] 13 C.F.R. § 124.509(b)(2). The final five years of a firm's participation in the 8(a) Program are known as the "transitional stage," and firms in the transitional stage must achieve annual targets for the amount of income they receive from non-8(a) sources. 15 U.S.C. § 636(j)(10)(I)(i)-(iii); 13 C.F.R. § 124.509(b)(1). These targets increase over time, with firms required to attain 15% of their revenue from non-8(a) sources in the fifth year, 25% in the sixth year, 35% in the seventh year, 45% in the eighth year, and 55% in the ninth year. 13 C.F.R. § 124.509(b)(2). Firms that do not obtain the required percentage of revenue from non-8(a) sources are generally ineligible for sole-source 8(a) contracts "unless and until" they remedy the situation. 13 C.F.R. § 124.509(d)(1).

[88] *Compare* Small Business Administration, 8(a) Business Development (BD) Program Application: Alaska Native Corporation-Owned Concern, *available at* http://www.sba.gov/idc/groups/public/documents/sba_homepage/ forms_trng1010banc.pdf *with* Small Business Administration, Application for 8(a) Business Development (8(a) BD) and Small Disadvantaged Business (SDB) Certification, *available at* http://www.sba.gov/idc /groups/public/documents/ sba_homepage/forms_trng1010banc.pdf.

[89] Small Business Administration, 8(a) Annual Update, *available at* http://www.sba.gov/idc/groups/public /documents/ sba_homepage/forms_1450.pdf.

[90] *Id.*

[91] Government Accountability Office, Small Business Administration: Agency Should Assess Resources Devoted to Contracting and Improve Several Processes in the 8(a) Program, GAO-09-16, at 1 (Nov. 2008), *available at* http://www.gao.gov/highlights/d0916high.pdf (noting a lack of routine surveillance reviews).

[92] 25 U.S.C. § 1544 ("Notwithstanding any other provision of law, a contractor of a Federal agency under any Act of Congress may be allowed an additional amount of compensation equal to 5 percent of the amount paid, or to be paid, to a subcontractor or supplier, in carrying out the contract if such subcontractor or supplier is an Indian organization or Indian-owned economic enterprise as defined in this chapter.").

[93] P.L. 100-442, § 7, 102 Stat. 1765 (Sept. 22, 1988) (codified at 25 U.S.C. § 1544); H.Rept. 100-838, at 6 (1988), reprinted in 1988 U. S.C.C.A.N. 2344, 2347 ("Currently, contracting agencies are authorized to encourage contractors to use minority subcontractors, however, there is no incentive for the contractors to use Indian contractors located on Indian reservations due to the remoteness of such reservation."). The statute and its implementing regulations (in Subpart 26.1 of the Federal Acquisition Regulation) only mention Indians, Indian organizations, Indian-owned economic enterprises, and Indian tribes, which include ANCs. However, Congress included Native Hawaiians among those entities that prime contractors may receive bonuses for subcontracting with in 2002. See P.L. 107-248, § 8021, 116 Stat. 1541 (Oct. 23, 2002) (including "small business[es] owned and controlled by an individual defined under 25 U.S.C. 422 1(9)" among those whom contractors receive bonuses for contracting with); 25 U.S.C. § 422 1(9) (defining "Native Hawaiians"); 48 C.F.R. Subpart 226.1 and § 252.226-7001 (DOD regulations on subcontracting bonuses). Native Hawaiians were included in subsequent appropriations. See P.L. 108-87, § 8021, 117 Stat. 1076 (Sept. 30, 2003); P.L. 108-287, § 8021, 118 Stat. 974 (Aug. 5, 2004); P.L. 109-148, § 8020, 119 Stat. 2702 (Dec. 30, 2005); P.L. 109-289, § 8018, 120 Stat. 1276-77 (Sept. 29, 2006); P.L. 110-116, § 8021, 121 Stat. 1319 (Nov. 13, 2007); P.L. 110- 329, § 8021, 122 Stat. 3625 (Sept. 30, 2008).

[94] *See* P.L. 101-165, § 9103, 103 Stat. 1151-52 (Nov. 21, 1989); P.L. 101-511, § 8077, 104 Stat. 1892-93 (Nov. 5, 1990); P.L. 102-172, § 8112A, 105 Stat. 1202 (Nov. 26, 1991); P.L. 102-396, § 9091A, 106 Stat. 1922 (Oct. 6, 1992); P.L. 103-139, § 8059A, 107 Stat. 1453 (Nov. 11, 1993); P.L. 103-335, § 8025A, 108 Stat. 2623 (Sept. 30, 1994); P.L. 104-61, § 8024, 109 Stat. 657 (Dec. 1, 1995); P.L. 104-208, § 8024, 110 Stat. 3009-93 (Sept. 30, 1996); P.L. 105-56, § 8024, 111 Stat. 1225 (Oct. 8, 1997); P.L. 106-79, § 8024, 113 Stat. 1236 (Oct. 25, 1999); P.L. 106-259, § 8022, 114 Stat. 679 (Aug. 9, 2000); P.L. 107-117, § 8022, 115 Stat. 2252 (Jan. 10, 2002); P.L. 107-248, § 8021; P.L. 108-87, § 8021; P.L. 108-287, § 8021; P.L. 109-148, § 8020; P.L. 109-289, § 8018; P.L. 110-116, § 8021; P.L. 110-329, § 8021.

[95] *Id.*

[96] P.L. 110-116, § 8021; P.L. 110-329, § 8021. The amount appropriated remained at $15 million per year during the first session of the 11 1th Congress. *See* P.L. 111-118, § 802 1,—Stat.—(Dec. 19, 2009).

[97] 48 C.F.R. § 52.226-1(b).

[98] 48 C.F.R. § 52.226-1(b)(1).

[99] *Id.*

[100] *See, e.g.*, Native American Industrial Distributors, Inc., B-3 10737.2; B-3 10737.4; B-3 10737.5 (Comp. Gen. Dec. Apr. 15, 2008) (upholding an award to a wholly owned subsidiary of an ANC under the Buy Indian Act).

[101] P.L. 61-3 13, § 23, 36 Stat. 861 (June 25, 1910) (codified, as amended, at 25 U.S.C. § 47). The Buy Indian Act also exempts ANCs, along with other Indian organizations and Indian-owned economic enterprises, from certain bonding requirements imposed on federal contractors by the Miller Act. *See* 25 U.S.C. § 47a ("[T]he Secretary [of the Interior], in his discretion, may require security other than bonds required by the Miller Act when entering into a contract with an Indian-owned economic enterprise pursuant to the provisions of the Act of June 25, 1910, for the construction, alteration, or repair of any public work of the United States: Provided, That, the alternative form of security provides the United States with adequate security for performance and pay.").

[102] *See* 48 C.F.R. § 370.50 1(b).

[103] *Compare* 48 C.F.R. §§ 370.500-370.505 (IHS procurements) *with* 48 C.F.R. §§ 1426.7002-1426.7005 (DOI procurements).

[104] 48 C.F.R. § 370.501(b).

[105] 48 C.F.R. § 370.503(e) (limitations on subcontracting); 48 C.F.R. § 370.504(a) (competitive awards preferred).

[106] 48 C.F.R. § 1426.7002(a) (work performed on reservations); 48 C.F.R. § 1452.226-71 (same); 48 C.F.R. § 1452.226-70 (allowing other agencies to contract under this authority in certain circumstances).

[107] 48 C.F.R. § 1426.7002(b).

[108] 48 C.F.R. § 19.703(c)(1)(i). The statutory authority for this regulation is presently unclear. Section 702 of the Emergency Supplemental Act of 2002 initially amended 43 U.S.C. § 1626(e)(4)(B) to allow subcontracts with large or uncertified ANCs or ANC subsidiaries to count toward subcontracting goals under Section 8(d) of the Small Business Act. *See* P.L. 107-117, § 702, 115 Stat. 2312 (Jan. 10, 2002). However, a later statute amended 43 U.S.C. § 1626(e)(4)(B) again, so that it now addresses government contracting and subcontracting goals under Section 15 of the Small Business Act, not subcontracting goals under 8(d). *See* Supplemental Appropriations Act for Further Recovery from and Responses to Terrorist Attacks on the United States, P.L. 107-206, § 3003, 116 Stat. 924 (Aug. 2, 2002). The regulations have apparently been promulgated as if the Emergency Supplemental Act still governed, though. *See* Department of Defense, General Services Administration, & National Aeronautics & Space Administration, FAR Case 2004-0 17, Small Business Credit for Alaska Native Corporations and Indian Tribes, 72 Fed. Reg. 46345 (Aug. 17, 2007).

[109] 15 U.S.C. § 637(d)(4) & (5). Eligible contracts are generally those exceeding $500,000 ($1 million for contracts to construct public facilities) and offering subcontracting possibilities. *Id.*

[110] 15 U.S.C. § 637(d)(6).

[111] 15 U.S.C. § 637(d)(8).

[112] 48 C.F.R. § 19.705-7.

[113] 15 U.S.C. § 637(d)(1) (describing subcontracting with "small businesses").

[114] *See* Small Business Administration, Small Disadvantaged Business Program, 73 Fed. Reg. 57490 (Oct. 3, 2008) (announcing that SBA would no longer certify SDBs);13 C.F.R. § 124.1001(c) (2009) ("A firm may represent that it qualifies as an SDB for any Federal subcontracting program if it believes in good faith that it is owned and controlled by one or more socially and economically disadvantaged individuals.").

[115] 13 C.F.R. § 124.1002.

[116] P.L. 107-117, § 702; P.L. 107-206, § 3003 (codified at 43 U.S.C. § 1626(e)(4)(C) ("Any entity that satisfies subsection (e)(1) or (e)(2) of this section that has been certified under section 637 of title 15 is a Disadvantaged Business Enterprise for the purposes of P.L. 105-178.").

[117] P.L. 105-178, § 1101(b), 112 Stat. 113 (June 9, 1998). TEA-21 lapsed on May 31, 2005, but was extended through FY2009 by the Safe, Accountable, Flexible, Efficient Transportation Equity Act: A Legacy for Users (SAFETEA-LU). *See* SAFETEA-LU, P.L. 109-59, § 1101(b), 119 Stat. 1144 (Aug. 10, 2005).

[118] *See* CRS Report RL3 3284, *Minority Contracting and Affirmative Action for Disadvantaged Small Businesses: Legal Issues*, by Jody Feder.

[119] 49 C.F.R. § 26.4 1(b)-(c).

[120] P.L. 105-178, § 1 101(b)(2)(A) ("The term 'small business concern' has the meaning such term has under section 3 of the Small Business Act (15 U.S.C. 632); except that such term shall not include any concern or group of concerns controlled by the same socially and economically disadvantaged individual or individuals which has average annual gross receipts over the preceding 3 fiscal years in excess of $16,600,000, as adjusted by the Secretary for inflation.").

[121] P.L. 105-178, § 1101(b)(2)(B).

[122] Since the 1950s, the federal government has had a stated policy of not competing with the private sector. This policy was first officially stated by the Bureau of the Budget (BOB) in a directive issued in 1955. *See* BOB Bulletin 55-4 (Jan. 15, 1955). Since 1966, this policy has been expressed in OMB Circular A-76. This circular was substantially revised in 1967, 1979, 1983, 1991, 1999, and, most recently and most extensively, in May 2003. The 1999 amendment was issued to bring the circular into conformance with and assist implementation

of the Federal Activities Inventory Reform (FAIR) Act of 1998 (P.L. 105-270), which generally requires each executive agency to annually inventory its activities that are not inherently governmental and submit this inventory to OMB. In the early 1990s, much of OMB Circular A76 was incorporated into the Federal Acquisition Regulation. *See* 48 C.F.R. § 7.3.

[123] Attachment A contains the inventory process for categorizing all activities as commercial or inherently governmental. Attachment B sets out the process to be used for public-private competitions. Attachment C gives the rules for calculating the cost of these competitions. Attachment D supplies the definitions for the circular.

[124] *See, e.g.*, P.L. 111-8, § 737, 123 Stat. 559 (Mar. 11, 2009) (suspending new A-76 competitions).

[125] *See, e.g.*, 10 U.S.C. §§ 2460-2476 ("Contracting for Performance of Civilian or Industrial Type Functions"). For more examples of this type of legislation, see CRS Report R40641, *Inherently Governmental Functions and Department of Defense Operations: Background, Issues, and Options for Congress*, by John R. Luckey, Valerie Bailey Grasso, and Kate M. Manuel, at Appendix A.

[126] *See* P.L. 101-165, § 9036, 103 Stat. 1137 (Nov. 21, 1989); P.L. 101-511, § 8026, 104 Stat. 1880 (Nov. 5, 1990); P.L. 102-172, § 8026, 105 Stat. 1177 (Nov. 26, 1991); P.L. 102-396, § 9026, 106 Stat. 1906 (Oct. 6, 1992); P.L. 103-139, § 8022, 107 Stat. 1442 (Nov. 11, 1993); P.L. 103-335, § 8020, 108 Stat. 2621 (Sept. 30, 1994); P.L. 104-61, § 8020, 109 Stat. 656 (Dec. 1, 1995); P.L. 104-208, § 8015, 110 Stat. 3009-91 (Sept. 30, 1996); P.L. 105-56, § 8014, 111 Stat. 1223 (Oct. 8, 1997); P.L. 106-79, § 8014, 113 Stat. 1234 (Oct. 25, 1999); P.L. 106-259, § 8014, 114 Stat. 677 (Aug. 9, 2000); P.L. 107-117, § 8014, 115 Stat. 2250 (Jan. 10, 2002); P.L. 107-248, § 8014, 116 Stat. 1539 (Oct. 23, 2002); P.L. 108-87, § 8014, 117 Stat. 1074 (Sept. 30, 2003); P.L. 108-287, § 8014, 118 Stat. 972 (Aug. 5, 2004); P.L. 109-148, § 8014, 119 Stat. 2700 (Dec. 30, 2005); P.L. 109-289, § 8013, 120 Stat. 1275-76 (Sept. 26, 2006); P.L. 110-116, § 8015, 121 Stat. 13 16-17 (Nov. 13, 2007); P.L. 110-329, § 8016, 122 Stat. 3623-24 (Sept. 30, 2008).

[127] P.L. 10 1-165, § 9036 ("None of the funds appropriated by this Act shall be available to convert to contractor performance an activity or function of the Department of Defense that, on or after the date of enactment of this Act, is performed by more than ten Department of Defense civilian employees until a most efficient and cost-effective organization analysis is completed on such activity or function and certification of the analysis is made to the Committees on Appropriations of the House of Representatives and the Senate: Provided, That this section shall not apply to a commercial or industrial type function of the Department of Defense that ... is planned to be converted to performance by a qualified firm under 51 percent Native American ownership."). Identical provisions were included in later statutes. *See* P.L. 101-5 11, § 8026; P.L. 102-172, § 8026; P.L. 102-396, § 9026; P.L. 103-139, § 8022; P.L. 103- 335, § 8020; P.L. 104-61, § 8020; P.L. 104-208, § 8015; P.L. 105-56, § 8014; P.L. 106-79, § 8014.

[128] P.L. 106-79, § 8014 ("[T]his section and subsections (a), (b), and (c) of 10 U.S.C. 2461 shall not apply to a commercial or industrial type function of the Department of Defense that ... is planned to be converted to performance by a qualified firm under 51 percent Native American ownership.").

[129] P.L. 106-259, § 8014 ("[T]his section and subsections (a), (b), and (c) of 10 U.S.C. 2461 shall not apply to a commercial or industrial type function of the Department of Defense that ... is planned to be converted to performance by a qualified firm under 51 percent ownership by an Indian tribe, as defined in section 450b(e) of title 25, United States Code, or a Native Hawaiian organization, as defined in section 637(a)(15) of title 15, United States Code.").

[130] *See* P.L. 111-118, § 8016,—Stat.—(Dec. 19, 2009).

[131] *See infra* notes 212 to 214 and accompanying text.

[132] P.L. 111-84, § 811, 123 Stat. 2405-06 (Oct. 28, 2009).

[133] Justifications explain that one of seven circumstances exist authorizing the agency to award a sole-source contract: (1) only one source can supply the goods or services; (2) there are unusual and compelling circumstances; (3) the agency seeks to maintain the industrial base; (4) international agreements require the agency to award the contract to a particular entity; (5) a statute authorizes non-competitive awards or the agency is acquiring brand-name commercial items for resale; (6) considerations of national security keep the agency from advertising the requirements; or (7) a particular award is necessary in the public interest. 10 U.S.C. § 2304(c)(1)-(7) (procurements of defense agencies); 41 U.S.C. § 253(c)(1)-(7) (procurements of civilian agencies).

[134] Justifications must be in writing and approved by agency officials at higher levels than the contracting officer. The identity of the approving official varies depending on the value of the contract. *See* 10 U.S.C. § 2304(f)(1)(B) (procurements of defense agencies); 41 U.S.C. § 253(f)(1)(B) (procurements of civilian agencies).

[135] The Competition in Contracting Act (CICA) originally required agencies to make their justifications for noncompetitive awards, as well as "any related information," available to the general public under the Freedom of Information Act (FOIA). CICA was later amended to require agencies to post the justification and approval documents for sole-source contracts on FedBizOpps (http://www.fedbizopps.gov) within 14 days of contract award. P.L. 110-181 § 844, 122 Stat. 236-39 (Oct. 14, 2008). CICA also requires agenices to publish notices regarding certain noncompetitive contracts that they propose to award on FedBizOpps prior to their

award. 10 U.S.C. § 2304(f)(1)(C) (procurements of defense agencies); 41 U.S.C. § 253(f)(1)(C) procurements of civilian agencies).

[136] *See infra* notes 212 to 214 and accompanying text.

[137] 13 C.F.R. § 519(a)(1)-(2). Contracts valued at less than $100,000 are not counted in determining whether a firm has reached the applicable limit.

[138] The Administrator of the SBA may waive this requirement if the head of the procuring agency determines that a sole-source award to a firm is necessary "to achieve significant interests of the Government." 13 C.F.R. § 124.519(f).

[139] 13 C.F.R. § 124.509(d)(1). This prohibition can be waived when the Director of the Office of Business Development finds that denial of a sole-source contract would cause severe economic hardship for the firm, potentially jeopardizing its survival, or extenuating circumstances beyond the firm's control caused it to miss its target. *Id.*

[140] 15 U.S.C. § 636(j)(10)(I)(i)-(iii); 13 C.F.R. § 124.509(b)(1).

[141] *Id.*

[142] 13 C.F.R. § 124.509(b)(2).

[143] 13 C.F.R. § 124.509(d)(1).

[144] *See supra* note 77 and accompanying text.

[145] *Id.*

[146] *See* 5 U.S.C. § 706(2)(A) (standard of review in bid protests).

[147] *See infra* notes 212 to 214 and accompanying text.

[148] 15 U.S.C. § 637(a)(1)(A) ("It shall be the duty of the [SBA] and it is hereby empowered, whenever it determines such action is necessary or appropriate to enter into contracts with the United States Government and any department, agency, or officer thereof having procurement powers obligating the [SBA] to furnish articles, equipment, supplies, services, or materials to the Government or to perform construction work for the Government. In any case in which the [SBA] certifies to any officer of the Government having procurement powers that the [SBA] is competent and responsible to perform any specific Government procurement contract to be let by any such officer, *such officer shall be authorized in his discretion to let such procurement contract to the [SBA] upon such terms and conditions as may be agreed upon between the [SBA] and the procurement officer.*") (emphasis added).

[149] Mission Critical Solutions, B-410057, 2009 U.S. Comp. Gen. LEXIS 86 (May 4, 2009).

[150] *Id.* at *15.

[151] Mission Critical Solutions v. United States, 2010 U.S. Claims LEXIS 36 (Mar. 2, 2010). *See, generally,* CRS Report R40591, *Set-Asides for Small Businesses: Recent Developments in the Law Regarding Precedence Among the Set- Aside Programs and Set-Asides Under Indefinite-Delivery/Indefinite-Quantity Contracts*, by Kate M. Manuel.

[152] 15 U.S.C. § 637(a)(1)(A); 48 C.F.R. § 19.806(b). *See, e.g.*, Ahntech, Inc., B-401092 (Comp. Gen. Dec., Apr. 22, 2009); OMNI Gov't Services, LP, B-297240.2; B-297240.3; B-297240.4 (Comp. Gen. Dec., Mar. 22, 2006); Catapult Tech., Ltd., B-294936; B-294936.2 (Comp. Gen. Dec., Jan. 13, 2005); C. Martin Co., Inc., B-292662 (Nov. 6, 2003). Such protests often fail, however, because "new" requirements are generally exempt from adverse impact determinations. 13 C.F.R. § 124.504(c)(1)(ii). Additionally, GAO, in particular, generally defers to agency determinations of what constitutes a new requirement. *See, e.g.*, C. Martin Co., Inc., B-292662 (Comp. Gen. Dec., Nov. 6, 2003) ("[W]e are aware of no requirement that an SBA finding that work can be considered 'new' must be based on a detailed comparison of the previous and new statements of work.").

[153] *See, e.g.*, Unique Rights of Alaska Native Corporation Owned 8(a) Businesses in the Federal Government Procurement Process, *available at* http://www.ago.noaa.gov/ago/acquisition/docs/alaska_native_contracting.pdf; Jenny J. Yang, Small Business, Rising Giant: Policies and Costs of Section 8(a) Contracting Preferences for Alaska Native Corporations, 23 *Alaska L. Rev.* 315, 328 (2006) (reading 13 C.F.R. § 124.5 17(a) to mean that "no competing contractor can challenge the eligibility of an ANC for a particular contract.").

[154] 13 C.F.R. § 124.517(d)(2).

[155] 15 U.S.C. § 636(j)(10)(J)(ii); 13 C.F.R. § 124. 109(c)(2)(i). *Contra Federal Contracting: Removing Hurdles for Minority-Owned Small Businesses: Hearing Before the Subcommittee on Government Management, Organization, and Procurement of the Committee on Oversight and Government Reform, 110th Cong., 1st Sess.*, at 71 (2007) (statement of Michael L. Barrera, President & CEO, Hispanic Chamber of Commerce) ("Small business size standards don't apply to ANCs the way they apply to all other small businesses, including Tribally-owned 8(a) firms."). Contrary to this statement, tribally owned firms are governed by requirements relating to size standards and affiliations identical to those governing ANC-owned firms. See 13 C.F.R. § 124. 109(c)(2)(i) (size standards); 13 C.F.R. § 124. 109(c)(2)(iii) (exclusion of certain affiliations).

[156] *See* 15 U.S.C. § 632(a)(1)-(2)(A); 13 C.F.R. §§ 121.101-121.108. The number of employees is the average of each pay period for the preceding 12 calendar moths. Gross income is based on the average for the last three completed fiscal years. It includes all revenues, not just those from the firm's primary industry. *See* IMDT, Inc., SBA-4121 (1995). For example, firms in the field of "scheduled passenger air transportation" are "small"

if they have fewer than 1,500 employees, while those in the data processing field are "small" if they have a gross income of less than $25 million. 13 C.F.R. § 121.201.

[157] 15 U.S.C. § 636(j)(10)(J)(ii)(II). The exclusion of affiliations with the parent ANC and its subsidiaries arguably affords ANC-owned firms access to financial and other resources not generally available to other small businesses, which are effectively precluded by the size standards from having similar affiliations. *See, e.g.*, *Federal Contracting*, *supra* note 155, at 71. As the SBA's assistant inspector general for auditing noted in July 2009,

[T]he ANC-owned firms ha[ve] access to capital, lines of credit, bonding capability, and administrative resources, as well as the management of their parent companies. This may explain why 63 percent of ANC participants received obligations in FY2007, while only 44% of the non- ANC owned firms received obligations that year.

Participation in the 8(a) Program, *supra* note 1, at 5.

[158] 13 C.F.R. § 121.103(a)(1).

[159] Valenzuela Eng'g, Inc. & Curry Contracting Co., Inc., SBA-4151 (1996), *available at* http://www.sba.gov/aboutsba/ sbaprograms/oha/allcases/sizecases/siz-415 1 .txt.

[160] *See* 13 C.F.R. 121.103(b)(2)(i); 13 C.F.R. 121.103(b)(2)(ii); 13 C.F.R. 124.109(c)(2)(iii).

[161] *See, e.g.*, Valenzuela Eng'g, Inc. & Curry Contracting Co., Inc., SBA-4151 (1996).

[162] *See* Contract Management, *supra* note 24, at 29.

[163] 13 C.F.R. § 124.109(c)(2)(iii).

[164] *See* 13 C.F.R. § 121.103(b)(2)(i)-(ii).

[165] *Cf.* U.S. House of Representatives, Committee on Government Reform—Minority Staff, Special Investigations Division, *Dollars, Not Sense: Government Contracting under the Bush Administration*, at 25 (June 2006), *available at* http://oversight ("[J]oint ventures and partnerships between Alaska Native Corporations and non-Native companies are eligible for sole-source contracts so long as the Alaska Native Corporation controls a majority of the total equity and total voting power of the joint venture or partnership."); *Federal Contracting*, *supra* note 155, at 57.

[166] 43 U.S.C. § 1626(e)(2)(A)-(B).

[167] 13 C.F.R. § 124.513(a)(2). SBA will approve the joint venture only when it determines that (1) the 8(a) concern brings something to the venture beyond its 8(a) status; (2) the 8(a) firm lacks the necessary capacity to perform the contract on its own; and (3) the agreement is fair, equitable, and will be of substantial benefit to the 8(a) firm. *Id.*

[168] 13 C.F.R. § 124.513(c)(2)-(3).

[169] *Id.*

[170] *Id.*

[171] 13 C.F.R. § 124.513(d). See *infra notes* 178-82 and accompanying text.

[172] 13 C.F.R. § 124.513(d).

[173] 13 C.F.R. § 121.105(b).

[174] 13 C.F.R. § 124.105(b) (ownership of partnership); 13 C.F.R. § 124.106(b) (management of partnership).

[175] *See, e.g.*, Testimony of Mark J. Lumer, Representing Cirrus Technology, Inc., Before the Subcommittee on Contracting Oversight, Committee on Homeland Security & Governmental Affairs, United States Senate, July 16, 2009, *available at* http://hsgac.senate.gov/public/index.cfm?FuseAction=Hearings.Hearing&Hearing_id=b181d787- 3563-4050-b1dd-1503adf47733 (alleging that his firm had lost work on requirements that were bundled and awarded on a sole-source basis to ANC-owned firms).

[176] 15 U.S.C. § 632(o).

[177] 15 U.S.C. § 644(a) & (e). Moreover, the governing statute specifies that reductions in administrative or personnel costs do not, per se, necessitate or justify consolidation. *See* 15 U.S.C. § 644(e)(2)(C).

[178] *Cf. Small Business Administration 50th Anniversary Reauthorization Act of 2003: Report to Accompany S. 1375, 108th Cong., 1st Sess.*, at 36 (2003) ("This definition [of 'bundlling'] has led to implementation problems because it does not account for all circumstances in which contracts can be bundled together, and the prerequisite that it be unsuitable for award to a small business concern. The definition excludes new requirements. This definition also excludes multiple award contracts ...").

[179] *See, e.g.*, *Northern Lights and Procurement Plights*, *supra* note 4, at 8; *Minority Entrepreneurship: Assessing the Effectiveness of the SBA's Programs for the Minority Business Community: Hearing Before the Committee on Small Business and Entrepreneurship, United States Senate, 110th Cong., 1st Sess.*, at 20 (2007); Small Business, Rising Giant, *supra* note 153, at 337 (2006).

[180] 15 U.S.C. § 637(a)(14) (limits on subcontracting for 8(a) firms); 13 C.F.R. § 124.510 (same); 15 U.S.C. § 644(o) (limits on subcontracting for small businesses generally); 13 C.F.R. § 125.6(a)(1)-(3) (same).

[181] 13 C.F.R. § 124.510 (limits on subcontracting for 8(a) firms); 13 C.F.R. § 125.6(a)(1)-(4) (limits on subcontracting for small businesses generally). The Government Accountability Office has criticized the SBA for poor monitoring of the percentage of work performed by subcontractors on 8(a) contracts with ANC-owned firms, and some commentators have criticized ANC-owned firms for subcontracting with companies that are themselves ineligible for the 8(a) program. *See* Contract Management, *supra* note 24, at 6; Michael

Scherer, Little Big Companies: How Did Corporations Like Halliburton Get Millions in Government Contracts Designated for Small Minority Businesses?, *Mother Jones Mag.*, Jan./Feb. 2005, *available at* http://www.motherjones.com/commentary/notebook/2005/01/ 1 1_400.html. However, any 8(a) firm may subcontract with a "large business" provided that the subcontracting relationship is not such as to result in affiliation and the 8(a) firm directly performs the required percentage of the contract costs with its own personnel.

[182] These include actions under the False Statements Act. *See* 18 U.S.C. § 1001. In addition, excessive reliance on a particular subcontractor, or performance of "primary and vital" requirements of the contract by a subcontractor, could result in the SBA finding that the firm is large because of its affiliation with the subcontractor. *See* 13 C.F.R § 121.103(f)(3) (the so-called "ostensible subcontractor" rule).

[183] Contract Management, *supra* note 24, at 20-23.

[184] *Cf.* Dollars, Not Sense, *supra* note 165, at 25 ("Alaska Native Corporations are free to subcontract work to nonminority and non-economically disadvantaged corporations, provided the Alaska Native Corporation performs at least 50% of the contract work."); Little Big Companies, *supra* note 181.

[185] *See* P.L. 100-442, § 7, 102 Stat. 1765 (Sept. 22, 1988) (codified at 25 U.S.C. § 1544) ("Notwithstanding any other provision of law, a contractor of a Federal agency under any Act of Congress may be allowed an additional amount of compensation equal to 5 percent of the amount paid, or to be paid, to a subcontractor or supplier, in carrying out the contract if such subcontractor or supplier is an Indian organization or Indian-owned economic enterprise as defined in this chapter."). ANCs and ANC-owned firms are "Indian organizations" and "Indian-owned economic enterprises," respectively. *See* 25 U.S.C. § 1452(b) & (e).

[186] *See, e.g.*, U.S. Senate, Committee on Homeland Security & Governmental Affairs, Subcommittee on Contracting Oversight, Majority Staff, New Information about Contracting Preferences for Alaska Native Corporations (Part II), at 14 (2009), *available at* http://mccaskill.senate.gov/pdf/071509/ANC

[187] 48 C.F.R. § 19.1203.

[188] *See* 13 C.F.R. § 124.1002 ("In determining whether a firm qualifies as an SDB, the criteria of social and economic disadvantage and other eligibility requirements established in subpart A of this part apply, including the requirements of ownership and control and disadvantaged status, unless otherwise provided in this subpart.").

[189] 48 C.F.R. § 52.2 19-26(b) ("If the Contractor exceeds its total monetary target for subcontracting to small disadvantaged business concerns in the authorized, NAICS Industry Subsectors, it will receive ________[Contracting Officer to insert the appropriate number between 0 and 10] percent of the dollars in excess of the monetary target, unless the Contracting Officer determines that the excess was not due to the Contractor's efforts (e.g., a subcontractor cost overrun caused the actual subcontract amount to exceed that estimated in the offer, or the excess was caused by the award of subcontracts that had been planned but had not been disclosed in the offer during contract negotiations).").

[190] *See supra* note 96.

[191] *See, e.g.*, New Information (Part II), *supra* note 186, at 6.

[192] 13 C.F.R. § 124.504(a)-(c).

[193] 15 U.S.C. § 637(a)(1)(A); 48 C.F.R. § 19.806(b).

[194] *See, e.g.*, *Northern Lights and Procurement Plights*, *supra* note 4, at 9, 161 (expressing concern that sole-source awards can cost the taxpayer up to twice as much as competitively awarded contracts).

[195] *See, e.g.*, *id.* at 125 (expressing concern about the effects of special programs for ANCs upon other small businesses). Some commentators have suggested, however, that SBA fails to properly make adverse impact determinations. *Id.* at 134.

[196] 13 C.F.R. § 124.109(c)(2)(iii).

[197] *Cf. Northern Lights and Procurement Plights*, *supra* note 4, at 125. Here again, however, some commentators have suggested that SBA does not adequately track firms' primary industry or make "substantial unfair impact determinations." *See, e.g.*, Contract Management, *supra* note 24, at 33.

[198] 15 U.S.C. § 636(j)(11)(B)-(C).

[199] 15 U.S.C. § 636(j)(11)(B)-(C); 13 C.F.R. § 124.108(b).

[200] *Compare* 13 C.F.R. § 124.2 *with Federal Contracting*, *supra* note 155, at 71 *and* New Information (Part II), *supra* note 186, at 5.

[201] 13 C.F.R. § 124.108(b)(4).

[202] *Cf.* 13 C.F.R. § 124.105(g) (prohibiting individuals determined to be disadvantaged for purposes of the 8(a) Program, their immediate family members, or 8(a) firms from owning more than 20% of any other 8(a) firm now or in the future).

[203] 13 C.F.R. § 124.109(c)(3)(ii) ("A tribe cannot own 51% or more of another firm which, either at the time of application or within the previous two years, has been operating in the 8(a) program under the same primary SIC code as the applicant. A tribe may, however, own a Participant or an applicant that conducts or will conduct secondary business in the 8(a) BD program under the same SIC code that a current Participant owned by the tribe operates in the 8(a) BD program as its primary SIC code.").

[204] Small Business, Rising Giant, *supra* note 153, at 342. Other factors include federal agencies' control over whom they contract with and the finite term of federal contracts. *See, e.g.*, 41 U.S.C. § 15 (prohibiting the transfer of government contracts from the contractor to a third party); 48 C.F.R. § 42.1204 (same); 48 C.F.R. § 17.204(e) ("Unless otherwise approved in accordance with agency procedures, the total of the basic and option periods shall not exceed 5 years in the case of services, and the total of the basic and option quantities shall not exceed the requirement for 5 years in the case of supplies.").

[205] 15 U.S.C. § 636(j)(10)(I)(i)-(iii); 13 C.F.R. § 124.509(b)(1)-(2).

[206] *Id.*

[207] 13 C.F.R. § 124.509(d)(1). This prohibition may be waived when the Director of the Office of Business Development finds that denial of a sole-source contract would cause severe economic hardship for the firm, potentially jeopardizing its survival, or extenuating circumstances beyond the firm's control caused it to miss its target. *Id.*

[208] *Cf.* Small Business, Rising Giant, *supra* note 153, at 343 ("The circumvention of graduation and other aspects of the 8(a) Program not only diverts 8(a) resources and opportunities away from new small disadvantaged businesses but also hurts the ANCs by delaying their entry into the new world of competitive contracting. This can thwart the development of any accompanying drive to prepare their businesses to succeed in that world."); *Federal Contracting, supra* note 155, at 71 ("Unlike all other 8(a) firms, ANCs don't have to secure any contracts competitively during their 8(a) tenure."); *Northern Lights and Procurement Plights*, *supra* note 4, at 162 (noting that ANC-owned firms have lost competitions for contracts they formerly held on a sole-source basis). No 8(a) firms are "required" to obtain competitively awarded 8(a) contracts, however. Firms could limit their participation in the 8(a) Program to sole-source awards below the competitive threshold, or obtain only sole-source contracts above the competitive threshold awarded in one of the circumstances in which noncompetitive awards are permitted under the general contracting authorities.

[209] *See* 15 U.S.C. § 637(a)(4)(A)(i)-(ii); 13 C.F.R. § 124.106.

[210] 13 C.F.R. § 124.109(c).

[211] 13 C.F.R. § 124. 109(c)(4)(B). There are also limits on the amount of executive compensation that may be charged to government contracts, which may help ensure that ANC-owned firms do not enjoy the benefits of highly paid non- Alaska Native managers at taxpayers' expense. *See* 48 C.F.R. § 31.205-6(p); Contract Management, *supra* note 24, at 29; Small Business, Rising Giant, *supra* note 153, at 342. Managers of other 8(a) firms must have managerial experience "of the extent and complexity needed to run the concern," which typically must have been in operation for at least two years prior to its entry into the 8(a) Program. 13 C.F.R. § 124.106(a)(3).

[212] ANC-owned firms are also not required to be located in Alaska. *Contra Northern Lights and Procurement Plights*, *supra* note 4, at 8. There is generally no legal requirement that firms be located in particular places in order to be eligible for federal contracting programs. One notable exception is the Historically Underutilized Business Zone (HUBZone) program, which requires that firms be located in HUB Zones in order to be eligible for set-asides, sole- source awards, and price evaluation preferences. 15 U.S.C. § 657a.

[213] P.L. 111-84, § 811(a)(1)-(3).

[214] *Id.* at § 811(c)(1).

[215] *Id.* at § 81 1(b)(1)-(5). The contents of the justifications required under the FAR thus differ slightly from those required for other sole-source awards under the Competition in Contracting Act (CICA). Justifications under CICA must include: (1) a description of the agency's needs; (2) the specific statutory provision authorizing the agency to use other than competitive procedures; (3) a determination that the anticipated cost will be fair and reasonable; (4) a description of the market survey conducted or a statement of the reasons for not conducting a market survey; (5) a listing of any sources that expressed an interest in the procurement in writing; and (6) a statement of any actions the agency may take to remove or overcome barriers to competition before future procurements of similar goods or services.

[216] Amendment 1762 would have amended the Business Opportunity Development Reform Act (BODRA) to remove the Department of Defense's (DOD's) authority to make sole-source awards to ANC-owned firms when there is a reasonable expectation that at least two eligible small businesses will submit offers and the award can be made at a fair market price. S.Amdt. 1762 (proposing to add Section 1083(a)(1) to Subtitle H of Title X of S. 1390). Instead, the amendment would have required that contracts awarded by or on behalf of DOD be awarded "on the basis of competition restricted to eligible Program Participants that are owned and controlled by economically disadvantaged Indian tribes" if the anticipated price of the contract is over $3.5 million ($5.5 million for manufacturing contracts) and there is a reasonable expectation that at least two eligible small businesses will submit offers. *Id.* (proposing to add section 1083(a)(2) to Subtitle H of Title X of S. 1390). ANCs are "Indian tribes," as the phrase is used here. *See* 15 U.S.C. § 637(a)(13).

[217] S.Amdt. 1762 (proposing to add Section 1083(a)(3) to Subtitle H of Title X of S. 1390).

[218] Amendment 1762 would have removed agencies' authority to pay subcontracting "bonuses" under the Indian Financing Act when "the subcontractor or supplier, including the Indian organization or Indian-owned economic enterprise that owns the subcontractor or supplier, is affiliated with the contractor." S.Amdt. 1762 (proposing to add Section 1083(b) to Subtitle H of Title X of S. 1390).

[219] *See* McCaskill Will Wait on Alaska Native Contracting Reform, *supra* note 8.

[220] Testimony of Debra S. Ritt, Assistant Inspector General for Auditing, U.S. Small Business Administration, Before the Subcommittee on Contracting Oversight, Committee on Homeland Security & Governmental Affairs, United States Senate, July 16, 2009, *available at* http://hsgac.senate.gov/public/index.cfm?Fuse Action=Hearings.Hearing& Hearing_id=b1 8 1d787-3563-4050-b1dd-1503adf47733.

[221] Testimony of Joseph G. Jordan, Associate Administrator for Government Contracting and Business Development, U.S. Small Business Administration, Before the Subcommittee on Contracting Oversight, Committee on Homeland Security & Governmental Affairs, United States Senate, July 16, 2009, *available at* http://hsgac.senate.gov/public/ index. cfm?FuseAction=Hearings.Hearing&Hearing_id=b1 8 1d787-3563-4050-b1dd-1503adf47733.

[222] Statement by Shay D. Assad, Acting Deputy Under Secretary of Defense for Acquisition and Technology, Before the Subcommittee on Contracting Oversight, Committee on Homeland Security & Governmental Affairs, United States Senate, July 16, 2009, *available at* http://hsgac.senate.gov/public/index.cfm?Fuse Action=Hearings.Hearing& Hearing_id=b1 8 1d787-3563-4050-b1dd-1503adf47733.

[223] Statement of Sarah Lukin, Executive Director, Native American Contractors Association, and Testimony of Jacqueline Johnson-Pata, Executive Director, National Congress of American Indians, Before the Subcommittee on Contracting Oversight, Committee on Homeland Security & Governmental Affairs, United States Senate, July 16, 2009, *available at* http://hsgac.senate.gov/public/index.cfm?FuseAction=H earings.Hearing&Hearing_id=b181d787- 3563-4050-b1dd-1503adf47733.

[224] Testimony of Mark J. Lumer, *supra* note 175, and Testimony of Christina J. Schneider, Chief Financial Officer, Purcell Construction Corp., Before the Subcommittee on Contracting Oversight, Committee on Homeland Security & Governmental Affairs, United States Senate, July 16, 2009, *available at* http://hsgac.s enate.gov/public/index.cfm? FuseAction=Hearings.Hearing&Hearing_id=b1 8 1d787-3563-4050-b1dd-1503adf47733.

[225] *See* New Information (Part I), *supra* note 2; New Information (Part II), *supra* note 184.

[226] *See* Small Business Admin., Small Business Size Regulations; 8(a) Business Development/Small Disadvantaged Business Status Determinations, 74 Fed. Reg. 55694 (Oct. 28, 2009). The SBA also proposes changes to the regulations governing the size standards for small businesses. Among other things, these changes would clarify that (1) protégés in other agencies' mentor/protégé programs are generally not exempt from SBA's size affiliation rules; (2) any joint venture that seeks to use 8(a) mentor/protégé status as grounds for an exemption to the affiliation requirements must follow the 8(a) requirements; (3) procurements for supplies cannot be classified under a North American Industry Classification System (NAICS) code for retail trade; and (4) the "nonmanufacturer rule"—requiring that firms that are not themselves the manufacturer of the end products being procured provide the products of small businesses—applies only when the procuring agency has classified the procurement under a manufacturing NAICS code. *Id.* at 55694-97. The proposed rule would also grant SBA's Office of Inspector General authority to request formal size determinations and make clear that certain requirements for the 8(a) Program do not apply to small disadvantaged businesses. *Id.* at 55697, 55710.

[227] *Id.* at 55702.

[228] *Id.*

[229] *Id.*

[230] *Id.* at 55703.

[231] *Id.* at 55705-06.

[232] *Id.* at 55694.

In: Disadvantaged Small Businesses and the 8(a) Program ISBN: 978-1-61209-309-3
Editors: James P. Carlson and Andrea M. Bernard

Chapter 7

MINORITY CONTRACTING AND AFFIRMATIVE ACTION FOR DISADVANTAGED SMALL BUSINESSES: LEGAL ISSUES

Jody Feder

SUMMARY

Since the early 1960s, minority participation "goals" have been an integral part of federal policies to promote racial and gender equality in contracting on federally financed construction projects and in connection with other large federal contracts. Federal contract "set-asides" and minority subcontracting goals evolved from Small Business Administration (SBA) programs to foster participation in the federal procurement process by small disadvantaged businesses (SDBs), or small businesses owned and controlled by "socially and economically disadvantaged" individuals. Minority group members and women are presumed to be socially and economically disadvantaged under the Small Business Act, while non-minority contractors must present evidence to prove their eligibility. "Goals" or "set-asides" for minority groups, women, and other "disadvantaged" individuals have also been routinely included in federal funding measures for education, defense, transportation, and other activities over much of the last two decades.

The U.S. Supreme Court has narrowly approved of congressionally mandated racial preferences to allocate the benefits of contracts on federally sponsored public works projects, while generally condemning similar actions taken by state and local entities to promote public contracting opportunities for minority entrepreneurs. Disputes prior to *City of Richmond v. J.A. Croson* generated divergent views as to whether state affirmative action measures for the benefit of racial minorities were subject to the same "strict scrutiny" as applied to "invidious" racial discrimination under the Equal Protection Clause, an "intermediate" standard resembling the test for gender-based classifications, or simple rationality. *In Croson*, a 5 to 4 majority resolved that while "race-conscious" remedies could be legislated in response to proven past discrimination by the affected governmental entities, "racial balancing" untailored to "specific" and "identified" evidence of minority exclusion was impermissible.

Until *Adarand Constructors, Inc. v. Pena*, however, a different, more lenient standard was thought to apply to use of racial preferences in federally conducted activities. The majority there applied "strict scrutiny" to a federal transportation program of financial incentives for prime contractors who subcontracted to firms owned by socially and economically disadvantaged group members. Although the Court refrained from deciding the constitutional merits of the particular program before it, and remanded for further proceedings below, it determined that all "racial classifications" by government at any level must be justified by a "compelling governmental interest" and "narrowly tailored" to that end. But the majority opinion, by Justice O'Connor, sought to "dispel the notion" that "strict scrutiny is 'strict in theory, but fatal in fact,'" by acknowledging a role for Congress as architect of remedies for discrimination nationwide. Bottom line, *Adarand* and its progeny suggest that racial preferences in federal law or policy are a remedy of last resort, which must be adequately justified and narrowly drawn to pass constitutional muster. In the post-*Adarand* era, lower federal courts have at times upheld and at other times struck down federal programs that contain minority contracting preferences. For example, in *Rothe Development Corporation v. Department of Defense*, the Federal Circuit recently held that the Department of Defense's Small Disadvantaged Business program was unconstitutional.

INTRODUCTION

It has long been the policy of the federal government to assist minority and other "socially and economically disadvantaged" small businesses become fully competitive and viable business concerns. The objective has largely been pursued through the federal procurement process by allocating federal assistance and contracts to foster disadvantaged business development. Federal assistance has taken a variety of forms, including targeting procurement contracts and subcontracts for disadvantaged or minority firms, management and technical assistance grants, educational and training support, and surety bonding assistance.

Present day set-aside programs authorizing preferential treatment in the award of government contracts to disadvantaged business enterprises (DBEs), or socially and economically disadvantaged small businesses, originated in § 8(a) of the Small Business Act of 1958.[1] Initially, the Small Business Administration (SBA) utilized its § 8(a) authority to obtain contracts from federal agencies and subcontract them on a noncompetitive basis to firms agreeing to locate in or near disadvantaged areas and provide jobs for the unemployed and underemployed. The § 8(a) contracts awarded under this program were not restricted to minority-owned firms and were offered to all small firms willing to hire and train the unemployed and underemployed in five metropolitan areas, as long as the firms met the program's other criteria.[2] As the result of a series of executive orders by President Nixon, the focus of the § 8(a) program shifted from job-creation in low-income areas to minority small business development through increased federal contracting with firms owned and controlled by socially and economically disadvantaged persons.[3] With these executive orders, the executive branch was directed to promote minority business enterprise and many agencies looked to SBA's § 8(a) authority to accomplish this purpose.

The administrative decision to convert § 8(a) into a minority business development program acquired a statutory basis in 1978 with the passage of P.L. 95-507, which broadened the range of assistance that the government—SBA, in particular—could provide to minority businesses. Section 8(a), or the "Minority Small Business and Capital Ownership Development" program, authorizes SBA to enter into all kinds of construction, supply, and service contracts with other federal departments and agencies. The SBA acts as a prime contractor and then subcontracts the performance of these contracts to small business concerns owned and controlled by "socially and economically disadvantaged" individuals, Indian Tribes or Hawaiian Native Organizations.[4]

Applicants for § 8(a) certification must demonstrate "socially disadvantaged" status or that they "have been subjected to racial or ethnic prejudice or cultural bias because of their identities as members of groups without regard to their individual qualities."[5] The Small Business Administration "presumes," absent contrary evidence, that small businesses owned and operated by members of certain groups—including Blacks, Hispanics, Native Americans, and Asian Pacific Americans—are socially disadvantaged.[6] Any individual not a member of one of these groups must "establish individual social disadvantage by a preponderance of the evidence" in order to qualify for § 8(a) certification.[7] The § 8(a) applicant must, in addition, show that "economic disadvantage" has diminished its capital and credit opportunities, thereby limiting its ability to compete with other firms in the open market.[8] Accordingly, while disadvantaged status under the SBA includes a racial component, in terms of presumptive eligibility, it is not restricted to racial minorities, but also includes persons subjected to "ethnic prejudice or cultural bias" who are able to satisfy specified regulatory criteria.[9] It also excludes businesses owned or controlled by persons who, regardless of race, are "not truly socially and/or economically disadvantaged."[10]

The "Minority Small Business Subcontracting Program" authorized by § 8(d) of the Small Business Act codified the presumption of disadvantaged status for minority group members that applied by SBA regulation under the § 8(a) program.[11] Section 8(d) requires prime contractors on all federal contracts that exceed the simplified acquisition threshold, are performed in the United States, and are not for personal services to negotiate a "subcontracting plan" with the procuring agency which includes "percentage goals" for utilization of small socially and economically disadvantaged firms. Award of the contract hinges upon the contractor's agreeing to a plan that is also acceptable to the agency,[12] and each contract must include a clause which states that "[t]he contractors shall presume that socially and economically disadvantaged individuals include Black Americans, Hispanic Americans, Native Americans, Asian Pacific Americans, and other minorities, or any other individual found to be disadvantaged by the Administration pursuant to § 8(a) ... "[13] Section 8(d) also allows the government to collect liquidated damages from contractors that fail to comply in good faith with their plans.[14]

P.L. 95-507, which created these § 8(d) programs further required that all federal agencies with procurement powers establish annual percentage goals for the award of procurement contracts and subcontracts to small disadvantaged businesses (SDBs).[15] A decade later, Congress enacted the Business Opportunity Development Reform Act of 1988,[16] directing the President to set annual, government-wide procurement goals of at least 20% for small businesses and 5% for disadvantaged businesses, as defined by the SBA. Simultaneously, federal agencies were required to continue to adopt their own goals, compatible with the government-wide goals, in an effort to create "maximum practicable opportunity" for small disadvantaged businesses to sell their goods and services to the government. The goals may be waived where not practicable due to unavailability of DBEs in the relevant area and other factors.[17] Federal Acquisition Act amendments adopted in 1994 amended the 5% minority procurement goal, and the minority subcontracting requirements in § 8(d), to specifically include "small business concerns owned and controlled by women" in addition to "socially and economically disadvantaged individuals."[18]

Additionally, statutory "set-asides" and other forms of preference for "socially and economically disadvantaged" firms and individuals, following the Small Business Act or other minority group definition, have frequently been added to specific grant or contract authorization programs. "Goals" or "set-asides" for minority groups, women, and other "disadvantaged" individuals have routinely been part of federal funding measures for education, defense, transportation and other activities over much of the last two decades. [19] Early on, Congress established goals for participation of small disadvantaged businesses in procurement for the Department of Defense (DOD), National Aeronautics and Space Administration (NASA), and the Coast Guard.[20] It also enacted the Surface Transportation Assistance Act of 1982 (STAA),[21] the Surface Transportation and Uniform Relocation Assistance Act of 1987 (STURAA),[22] the Intermodal Surface Transportation Efficiency Act of 1991 (ISTEA),[23] and the Transportation Equity Act for the 21st Century (TEA-2 1),[24] each of which contained a 10% minority or disadvantaged business participation goal on federally funded projects. Sometimes, Congress has coupled these goals with authority to meet them, as was the case with the goals for DOD, NASA, and the Coast Guard. Congress authorized these agencies to apply a price evaluation preference of up to 10% to bids submitted by businesses other than SDBs in order to meet their goals.[25] Recently, however, the Federal Circuit held that DOD's SDB program was unconstitutional.[26]

The *Adarand* Decision and Its Progeny

Background and History of *Adarand*

Litigation surrounding racial preferences in federal contracting has followed a convoluted course since 1995, when the Supreme Court settled the constitutional parameters of the issue but avoided a decision of the merits in *Adarand Constructors Inc. v. Pena (Adarand I).*[27] By the time it returned to the High Court six years later, as *Adarand Constructors Inc. v. Mineta*, the legal and factual framework of the case was considerably altered by multiple lower court decisions and appeals, and by changes in the plaintiff's legal standing, the details of the challenged federal program, and regulatory reforms to "amend, not end" federal affirmative action by the former Clinton Administration. To the chagrin of many legal observers, the Court in 2001 once again sidestepped the constitutional issues posed by the Adarand case and, after agreeing to reconsider the controversy, dismissed the appeal as "improvidently granted." The object of the Court's latest action—or inaction—was the Tenth Circuit's two-part ruling in *Adarand Constructors v. Slater (Adarand III).*[28] The federal appeals court there invalidated a federal highway program of financial incentives to promote minority and "disadvantaged" small business utilization in force at the time of *Adarand I.* But as revised and amended in 1997, the program was found to be narrowly tailored to a compelling governmental interest and passed constitutional muster.

Prior to *Adarand*, the U.S. Supreme Court had narrowly approved of congressionally mandated racial preferences to allocate the benefits of contracts on federally sponsored public works projects in *Fullilove v. Klutznick*,[29] while generally condemning similar actions taken by state and local entities to promote public contracting opportunities for minority entrepreneurs in *City of Richmond v. J.A. Croson Co.*[30] These disputes generated divergent views as to whether state affirmative action measures for the benefit of racial minorities were subject to the same "strict scrutiny" as applied to "invidious" racial discrimination under the Equal Protection Clause, an "intermediate" standard resembling the test for gender-based classifications, or simple rationality. In *Croson*, a 5 to 4 majority resolved that while "race-conscious" remedies could be legislated in response to proven past discrimination by the affected governmental entities, "racial balancing" untailored to "specific" and "identified" evidence of minority exclusion was impermissible.

Until *Adarand*, however, a different, more lenient standard was thought to apply to use of racial preferences in federally conducted activities. The majority there applied "strict scrutiny" to a federal transportation program of financial incentives for prime contractors who subcontracted to firms owned by socially and economically disadvantaged group members. Although the Court refrained from deciding the constitutional merits of the particular program before it, and remanded for further proceedings below, it determined that all "racial classifications" by government at any level must be justified by a "compelling governmental interest" and "narrowly tailored" to that end.

There have been three distinct phases to the *Adarand* litigation. The case originated with a now- discontinued "race-conscious subcontracting compensation clause (SCC)" program conducted by the Federal Highway Lands Program of the Federal Highway Administration. The SCC did not allocate or set-aside a specific percentage of subcontract awards for DBEs or require a commitment on the part of prime contractors to subcontract with minority firms. Rather, "incentive payments" varying from 1.5% to 2% of the contract amount were paid to prime contractors whose subcontracts with one or more qualified DBEs exceeded 10% of total contract value. The program incorporated the racial presumption from the Small Business Act and regulations, in effect relieving minority group subcontractors of the burden of demonstrating disadvantaged status imposed upon non-minorities.

Suit was brought by Adarand Constructors, Inc., a white-owned construction firm whose low bid on a subcontract for highway guard rails was rejected in favor of a higher bidding DBE. Both the federal trial court and the Tenth Circuit initially upheld the program by applying "lenient" judicial review—"resembling intermediate scrutiny"—rather than strict scrutiny, requiring far less remedial justification by the government. Because the program was not limited to racial minorities, and non-disadvantaged minority group members were ineligible to participate, the appeals court concluded, the program was "narrowly tailored." In *Adarand I*, the Supreme Court reversed this first round of decisions.

The majority in *Adarand I* rejected the equal protection approach that applied "intermediate scrutiny" or some other relaxed standard of review to racial line-drawing by the Congress. Because the "race-based rebuttable presumption" in the DOT program was an "explicit" racial classification, the Court determined, "it must be analyzed by a reviewing court under strict scrutiny," and to survive, must be "narrowly tailored" to serve a "compelling governmental interest." *Adarand I* undermined prior judicial holdings, which had afforded substantially greater latitude to Congress than to the states or localities when crafting affirmative action measures for racial or ethnic minorities. To "dispel the notion," however, that "strict scrutiny is 'strict in theory, but fatal in fact,'" the Court appeared to reserve a role for the national legislature as architect of remedies for past societal discrimination. "The unhappy persistence of both the practice and lingering effects of racial discrimination against minorities in this country is an unfortunate reality, and the government is not disqualified from acting in response to it."[31] Thus, a majority of the Court appeared to accept some forms of racial preference by Congress in at least some circumstances.[32] No further guidance was provided, however, as to the scope of remedial authority remaining in congressional hands or the conditions for its exercise. Indeed, the Court refrained even from deciding the merits of the constitutional claim before it in *Adarand I*, instead remanding the case to the lower courts to determine the outcome.

On remand, the district court in *Adarand II* decided that the "congruence" required by the Court did not mean that federal affirmative action must be supported by the same "particularized" showing of past discrimination as state and local programs.[33] Rather, as the national legislature, Congress was empowered to enact broad discrimination remedies based on nationwide findings derived from congressional hearings and statements of individual federal lawmakers. "Congress," in other words, "may recognize a nationwide evil and act accordingly, provided the chosen remedy is narrowly tailored so as to preclude the application of a race-conscious measure where it is not warranted." The DOT incentive program failed the "narrow tailoring" test, however, because it linked a race-based presumption to the award of financial "bonus[es]" to prime contractors whose choice of a subcontractor was based "only on race." The racial presumption was found to be both "overinclusive"—in that its benefits were available to all named minority group members—and "underinclusive"—because it excluded members of other minority groups or Caucasians who may share similar disadvantages. Although "more flexible" than a "rigid racial quota" or mandatory set-aside, the SCC program was tainted by the government-wide 5% goals and transportation set-asides which it implemented.[34]

The Tenth Circuit in 2000 issued its decision on the merits of the controversy.[35] The appellate panel in *Adarand III* reversed the district court injunction against future implementation of DOT's disadvantaged business enterprise (DBE) program in Colorado. In so doing, the court of appeals considered the constitutionality of the program, both as structured at the time of the district court decision and of later revisions to DBE regulations adopted in 1997. First, it generally agreed with the district court that the SCC system of financial incentives, in effect at the time of Adarand I, had not been narrowly enough tailored to satisfy the constitutional requirements of strict scrutiny. But after lengthy congressional hearings, the financial incentives were eliminated, and other reforms were adopted to DBE requirements imposed by DOT regulation on state and local highway aid recipients. As a result, the appeals court ultimately concluded that the DOT disadvantaged business enterprise program as currently structured—though not the former, discarded program of financial incentives—passed constitutional muster.

Initially, the appellate tribunal aligned itself with the district court's finding that the federal government had a "compelling interest" in preventing and remedying the effects of past discrimination in government contracting. And the scope of Congress's authority to act was not limited geographically or to specific instances of discrimination—as in the case of the states and localities under *Croson*—but extended "'society-wide' and therefore nationwide." The range of admissible evidence to support racial line-drawing by Congress was both direct and circumstantial, including post-enactment evidence and legislative history, demonstrating public and private discrimination in the construction industry. The court was largely dismissive of individual statements by members or from committee reports as "insufficient in themselves to support a finding of compelling interest." Congressional hearings over nearly a two-decade period, however, depicted the social and economic obstacles—e.g., "old boy networks," racism in construction trade unions, and denial of access to bonding, credit, and capital—faced by small and disadvantaged entrepreneurs, mainly minorities, in business formation and in competition for government contracts. Moreover, "disparity studies" conducted after *Croson* in most of the nation's major cities compared minority-owned business utilization with availability and "raise[d] an inference that the various discriminatory factors the government cites have created that disparity." This record satisfied the Tenth Circuit panel that Congress had a "strong basis in evidence" for concluding that passive federal complicity with private discrimination in the construction industry contributed to discriminatory barriers in federal contracting, a situation the government had a "compelling" interest in remedying.

The appellate tribunal adopted a two-stage review of the "narrowly tailored" requirement, focusing on the DBE program both as in effect prior to 1997 and later as revised to comply with *Adarand I*. Basically, it determined that many of the constitutional flaws that defeated the program in the district court's opinion—an outcome with which the appellate panel largely agreed—had been eliminated by the government's regulatory reforms. In effect, the latest decision lays the old program to rest while reversing the district court's order insofar as it would bar implementation of the revised version. The appeals court also clarified the scope of the DBE program under review. It disagreed with, and specifically reversed, elements of the district court judgment raising issues beyond the specific DBE program as applied by Colorado officials to federally funded highway procurements within that state. Because the 5% and 10% goals in the SBA and underlying transportation authorization measures "are merely aspirational and not mandatory," they were not the reason that "Adarand lost or will lose" contracts, and any challenge to those provisions were outside the scope of the remand in *Adarand I*. Thus, any broader potential implications of the district court ruling for § 8(a) set-asides or government-wide goals for DBE participation under the Small Business Act were largely blunted by the appellate panel.[36]

The constitutional virtues of the revised program over the pre-1996 SCC program at issue in *Adarand I* were several. First, race-neutral measures dating back to the 1958 enactment of the SBA had preceded Congressional adoption of "aspirational goals" and other affirmative action measures for minority groups in government-wide contracting. DOT had not considered such alternatives before adopting race-conscious subsidies for prime contractors who select minority subcontractors. However, this defect was cured by the revised regulations, which specifically directed recipients to exhaust race-neutral alternatives—bonding, financing, and technical assistance, etc.—before taking race into account.[37] Secondly, the revised regulations incorporated the time limits and graduation requirements for participation of disadvantaged businesses in the §§ 8(a) and 8(d) programs, thereby ensuring the later program's limited duration.[38] The court of appeals also found that the revised DOT program was more flexible than the mandatory set-asides in Fullilove and Croson because it was voluntary on the part of the prime contractors and because the post-1996 revisions adopted an express waiver.[39] Any use of "aspirational goals" by recipients of federal highway funds had to make "reference to the relative availability of DBEs in the market" and was restrained in other ways by the new regulations so that "there is little danger of arbitrariness in the setting of such goals.... "[40] The burden of the revised program on third parties was mitigated by placing monetary caps on subsidies to prime contractors—limiting the incentive to hire further DBEs—and by adopting "preponderance of the evidence" for proof of "social disadvantage" by members of "non-presumed" groups in lieu of the former "clear and convincing" standard. Finally, the revised program avoided the constitutional vice of over- and under-inclusiveness by "disaggregating the race-based presumption that encompassed both 'social' and 'economic' disadvantage" in the former regulation. Thus, an individualized showing of economic disadvantage is now required of all applicants to the program, minority and non- minority alike. This change, the appeal court believed, effectively satisfied the Croson requirement of an "inquiry into whether or not the particular MBE seeking a racial preference has suffered from the effects of past discrimination."[41]

The Supreme Court Declines to Decide the Case

The U.S. Supreme Court granted *certiorari* in an appeal from the Tenth Circuit's final decision, marking the third High Court appearance by the *Adarand* case. During oral arguments, the Justices appeared more concerned with procedural irregularities in the case, as outlined by the Justice Department, than with the substance of the constitutional claims. In essence, the government argued that Adarand's legal challenge was limited to the DOT program and regulations applicable to direct procurement of highway construction on federal lands, like the contract denied, not to the separate regulatory scheme governing federal highway assistance to states. Petitioner Adarand Constructors, Inc., made a parallel argument—but for a different reason—that the court of appeals misconceived the scope of the appeal. In particular, petitioner's brief contended, the Tenth Circuit's analysis considered revisions to DOT regulations applicable to federally assisted state and local highway projects, which are irrelevant to the separate set of rules governing direct federal procurement, thereby undermining the court's conclusion that the SDB program was narrowly tailored. Because the race conscious aspects of the original financial incentive program had been suspended in Colorado and several other states as the result of administration reforms to affirmative action rules after *Adarand I*, counsel for the company had difficulty arguing that its client "is still unable to compete on an equal footing" or had "lost a single contract under the provisions they are now challenging." Further complicating Adarand's position, the Tenth Circuit had rejected its earlier attack upon the entire statutory framework for federal small disadvantaged business programs, a ruling not appealed to the Supreme Court. The government, therefore, contended that Adarand's lawsuit had "outlived the program that provoked it," and in oral arguments to the Justices, the Solicitor General urged the Court to dismiss the petition for certiorari as improvidently granted.

It came as no great surprise, therefore, that the Justices complied with the government's request and dismissed the case.[42] In a per curiam opinion, the Court emphasized technical flaws with the present appeal, as framed during oral arguments. First, Adarand was challenging a by now defunct aspect of the program that the Tenth Circuit had not ruled upon, asking "whether the various race-based programs applicable to direct federal contracting could satisfy strict scrutiny." Nor had the company sought review of those aspects of the DOT statute and regulations respecting the state and local procurement program on whose constitutionality the appeals court had spoken. Consequently, the Supreme Court declined to reach the merits of a controversy regarding which neither the parties nor the courts below appeared to be reading from the same page.

Left unanswered, therefore, were two major questions presented by the petition for review. First was "whether the court of appeals misapplied the strict scrutiny standard in determining if Congress had a compelling interest to enact legislation designed to remedy the effects of past discrimination." The Tenth Circuit found that Congress had a "solid basis in evidence" for concluding race-conscious action necessary based on its dissection of hearing testimony, legislative reports, and state and local disparity studies. Generally, its approach conformed to earlier rulings, which have stressed deference to congressional fact-finding under section 5 of the Fourteenth Amendment. As the national legislature, Congress may not be constrained by the same requirements of specificity in regard to regional scope and classes of individuals benefitted by race conscious programs.

But later Court rulings parsing the scope of congressional § 5 power to override state sovereign immunity under a variety of federal civil rights laws have emphasized the need for "congruence and proportionality" of the remedy to any problem perceived by the Congress.[43] The ramifications of this principle for § 5 race discrimination legislation is undetermined, and questions remain. Conversely, some would argue, the affirmative grant of congressional authority to legislate remedies for equal protection violations by states conferred by § 5 is even broader than its power to place similar conditions on direct spending for federal procurements, which is limited by Fifth Amendment due process.

The second aspect of strict scrutiny analysis would have required the Court to determine whether the means chosen by DOT to promote minority group participation in the federal procurement process is "narrowly tailored." In this regard, the Tenth Circuit found that after eliminating financial bonus or subsidy, the adoption of "aspirational goals" for utilization of disadvantaged firms based on "good faith efforts," as required by current regulations, was a more flexible and narrowly tailored alternative. That conclusion, however, has been questioned by other courts, which have found that governmentally required goal-setting, coupled with enforcement sanctions—in Adarand's case, liquidated damages under § 8(d)—is inherently coercive and encourages racial quotas. The Ninth Circuit, for example, has invalidated a California affirmative action statute that required bidders on state contracts to subcontract a percentage of their work to female- and minority-owned firms or document a "good faith" effort to do so.[44] Similarly, in Lutheran *Church-Missouri Synod v. FCC*,[45] the D.C. Circuit blurred the distinction between so- called "inclusive" and exclusive "affirmative" action. FCC regulations required broadcast license holders (1) to engage in "critical self-analysis" of minority and female underrepresentation, and (2) to undertake affirmative outreach by using minority and female-specific recruiting sources. Strict scrutiny was held to be appropriate and the regulations were unlawful since beyond simple outreach, their effect was to influence ultimate hiring decisions; that is, the threat of government enforcement "coerced" stations to maintain a workforce that mirrors racial breakdown of the labor area.

The Court's disposition of the final *Adarand* appeal means that a definitive review of federally mandated affirmative action must be postponed to another day. That day, however, may not be too far distant. Percolating in the lower federal courts are cases that pose similar questions regarding the power of Congress to enact racial preferences in federal contracting as were bypassed by the Court's inconclusive determination in *Adarand*.

POST-*ADARAND* REGULATORY DEVELOPMENTS

Federal regulatory reforms put forward by the former Clinton Administration sought to "narrowly tailor" federal minority and disadvantaged small business programs in line with *Adarand*. The Justice Department in 1996 proposed a structure for reform of affirmative action in federal procurement, setting stricter certification and eligibility requirements for minority contractors claiming "socially and economically disadvantaged" status under § 8(a) and § 8(d) of the Small Business Act.[46] The plan suspended for two years set-aside programs in which only minority firms could bid on contracts. Statistical "benchmarks" developed by the Commerce Department and adjusted every five years were made the basis for estimating expected disadvantaged business participation as federal contractors, in the absence of discrimination, for nearly 80 different industries. Where minority participation in an industry falls below the benchmark, bid and evaluation credits or incentives are authorized for economically disadvantaged firms and prime contractors who commit to subcontract with such firms. Conversely, when such participation exceeds an industry benchmark, the credit would be lowered or suspended in that industry for the following year. The system is monitored by the Commerce Department, using data collected to evaluate the percentage of federal contracting dollars awarded to minority-owned businesses, and relies more heavily on "outreach and technical assistance" to avoid potential constitutional pitfalls.

The Justice Department's response to comments on its proposal, together with proposed amendments to the Federal Acquisition Regulation (FAR) to implement it, were published in 1997.[47] Several procurement mechanisms interact with benchmark limits pursuant to the FAR regulation jointly promulgated by DOD, the General Services Administration, and NASA. An "evaluation factor" applies to bids by non-minority prime contractors participating in joint ventures, teaming arrangements, or subcontracts with such firms, and contracting officers may employ "monetary incentives" to increase subcontracting opportunities for disadvantaged firms in negotiated procurements. "Benchmarking" by the Commerce Department is the key feature of the program, designed to narrowly tailor the government's use of race-conscious subcontracting in line with *Adarand*. The Commerce recommendation relies "primarily on census data to determine the capacity and availability of minority-owned firms." As explained by DOJ:

> [A] statistical calculation representing the effect discrimination has had on suppressing minority business development and capacity would be made, and that calculation would be factored into benchmarks.... The purpose of comparing utilization of minority-owned firms to the benchmark is to ascertain when the effects of discrimination have been overcome and minority-owned firms can compete equally without the use of race-conscious programs. Full utilization of minority-owned firms in [an] SIC code may well depend on continued use of race-conscious programs like price or evaluation credits. Where utilization exceeds the benchmark, the Office of Federal Procurement Policy may authorize the reduction or elimination of the level of price or evaluation credits, but only after analysis has projected the effect of such action.[48]

Final regulations implementing Justice Department recommendations with respect to the § 8(a) business development and small disadvantaged business program were issued by the SBA in 1998.[49] The reforms included a new process for certifying firms as small disadvantaged businesses[50] and, in place of set-asides, a price evaluation adjustment program administratively tied to the Commerce benchmarks. In the past, the government relied on self-certification for purposes of "disadvantaged" eligibility, which allowed firms to identify themselves as meeting certification requirements. Under the new procedure, SBA, or where SBA deems appropriate, SBA-approved state agencies, or private certifiers make a threshold determination as to whether a firm is actually owned or controlled by specified individuals claiming to be disadvantaged. After ownership or control is established, the application is reviewed by SBA for purposes of a determination of disadvantaged status.

The definition of social and economic disadvantage remains largely intact under the SBA regulation. Members of designated minority groups participating in disadvantaged small business programs continue to enjoy a statutory presumption of social disadvantage. They are required, however, to state their group identification and meet certification criteria for economic disadvantage and are subject to third-party challenge under current administrative mechanisms. Individuals who are not within the statutory presumption may qualify by proving that they are socially and economically disadvantaged under SBA standards. Under prior SBA § 8(a) certification standards, however, persons not members of presumed disadvantaged groups had to prove their status by "clear and convincing evidence." The revised SBA regulations ease this burden on non-minority applicants by adopting a "preponderance of evidence" rule.

U.S. Department of Transportation Revised Regulations

Similarly, USDOT responded to *Adarand Constructors* and its progeny by issuing revised regulations to implement minority set-aside provisions in current federal transportation authorization measures. The Transportation Equity Act for the 21st Century (TEA-21), as enacted by Congress in 1998, provided that

> [e]xcept to the extent that the Secretary [of Transportation] determines otherwise, not less than 10 percent of the amounts made available for any program under titles I, III, and V of this Act shall be expended with small business concerns owned and controlled by socially and economically disadvantaged individuals.[51]

One in a succession of laws dating back more than two decades, TEA-2 1 lapsed on May 31, 2005, but was extended by P.L. 109-59, signed into law during the 109th Congress.[52] The new law continued through FY2009 the longstanding DOT policy of setting aside 10% of federal highway and surface transportation funds for small disadvantaged firms "[e]xcept to the extent the Secretary of Transportation determines" otherwise.

The revised DOT regulations track the Small Business Act in defining disadvantaged business enterprises (DBEs), including the presumption regarding designated minority groups and women, except that any small business owner with more than $750,000 in assets—or who is otherwise shown not to be socially or economically disadvantaged—is disqualified. Members of non- designated groups (i.e., a white male) may qualify for DBE status if the individual demonstrates social and economic disadvantage in fact.[53]

Describing the 10% goal as merely "aspirational," the regulations de-centralize administration of the DBE program by delegating implementation to state agencies receiving federal transportation funds. A two-step process is established for states to determine "the level of DBE participation [that] would [be] expect[ed] absent the effects of discrimination."[54] First, the relative availability locally of "ready, willing, and able" DBEs must be calculated. This baseline figure is then adjusted upward or downward to reflect other capability factors and evidence of discrimination against DBEs drawn from statistical "disparity" studies. The final adjusted figure represents the portion of federal transportation funding that a state must allocate to DBEs for that year.

A state must meet the maximum feasible portion of this goal through race- (and sex-) neutral means. Race-conscious contract goals must be applied to achieve any portion of the utilization requirement not attainable by other means.[55] Even when race-conscious measures are necessary, however, the regulations do not require that DBE goals be included in every contract—or that they be set at the same level in every contract where used—as long as the overall effect is to obtain the required DBE participation level. Prime contractors to whom a state awards federally funded transportation contracts must undertake good faith efforts to satisfy any included goal by allocating the designated percentage of funds to DBEs.[56] States are prohibited from instituting rigid quotas that do not account for a prime contractor's good faith efforts to subcontract works to DBEs.[57]

Small Business Administration Rules for Women-Owned Businesses

During the Bush Administration, the SBA issued proposed regulations in 2007 that would have implemented Section 811 of the Small Business Reauthorization Act of 2000,[58] which added a new section 8(m) to the Small Business Act authorizing set asides for industries in which women- owned small businesses (WOSBs) are underrepresented or substantially underrepresented in federal procurement. Under the legislation, SBA was required to conduct a study to identify such industries, and the resulting study identified 28 different approaches for determining underrepresentation and substantial underrepresentation. In its proposed rule, the SBA announced the approach it had selected, identifying four industries in which WOSBs were underrepresented or substantially underrepresented in federal procurement.[59] However, the agency was criticized for adopting this approach by critics who claimed that the SBA unjustifiably selected the most restrictive methodology available under the study and instead should have chosen an approach that recognized a broader range of industries, including one methodology that would have classified 87% of industries as underrepresented. In response to this criticism, the SBA issued a final rule but delayed a final determination regarding industries that are underrepresented until it had solicited additional public comment and further examined the methodological issues at stake.[60] Subsequently, the agency announced that it was extending the comment period yet again in response to the Federal Circuit's decision in *Rothe Development Corporation v. Department of Defense*,[61] which is discussed in the next section of this report.

Although the SBA's final regulations did not identify industries in which WOSBs are underrepresented or substantially underrepresented in federal procurement, the new regulations do contain another controversial provision that requires a federal agency implementing the program with regard to a particular industry to determine whether the set-aside is substantially related to remedying sex discrimination in that industry and to conduct an analysis of its own procurement history to establish whether the agency itself had discriminated against WOSBs in the relevant industry. According to the SBA, this requirement is necessary in order to comply with constitutional equal protection standards that require the government to "establish probative evidence of discrimination in the relevant economic sphere in order to justify sex-based contracting preferences."[62]

In 2010, the Obama Administration issued new proposed regulations for the set-aside program for WOSBs.[63] These proposed regulations would do two things: (1) withdraw the never-finalized October 1, 2008 proposed rule that identified thirty-one industries in which women were underrepresented or substantially underrepresented; and (2) establish a new methodology for identifying eligible industries and eliminate the requirement for an agency-by-agency determination of discrimination.

The SBA does not explicitly address *Rothe* in its introductory comments to these proposed regulations. However, it notes that comments on earlier proposed rules indicated that the "disparity study analysis" conducted in identifying industries eligible for set-asides "is sufficient to satisfy the intermediate scrutiny standard that applies to the WOSB Program."[64] It also states that:

> The means chosen by Congress to implement the WOSB Program ensure that the Program is substantially related to its goals. Congress expressly limited application of the WOSB Program only to industries in which women are substantially underrepresented or underrepresented in contracting.[65]

The SBA may or may not be correct in stating that the set-asides for women-owned small businesses would survive intermediate scrutiny if challenged, although the disparity studies underlying the determinations of eligible industries would likely be the focus of any potential constitutional challenges.

POST-*ADARAND* JUDICIAL DECISIONS

Federal Affirmative Action Programs

Since *Adarand*, several lower federal courts have addressed the issue of congressional authority to fashion affirmative action remedies. Courts in these cases have, with one exception, generally concluded from the record of committee hearings and other documentary evidence before Congress that the government had a compelling interest for the program in question. However, in applying the constitutional demand for a "narrowly tailored" remedy, there is a divergence of judicial opinion as to whether states or localities must independently justify the use of racial preferences to implement federal mandates within their individual jurisdictions.

The Supreme Court in 2004 refused to revisit issues left unsettled by Adarand when it denied review of the Eighth Circuit's consolidated ruling in *Sherbrooke Turf, Inc. v. Minnesota Department of Transportation and Gross Seed Company v. Nebraska Department of Roads.*[66] The Sherbrooke court joined the Tenth Circuit in upholding the DBE program under current DOT regulations and, beyond that, approved specific state plans to implement that program. Pursuant to TEA-21 and the DOT revised regulations, state highway departments in Minnesota and Nebraska established specific goals for the award of federally-funded contracts to DBEs. In both states, white-owned contractors had submitted the low bid on DOT funded subcontracts, but were passed over in favor of a presumptively disadvantaged minority competitor. Petitioners challenged DBE contract awards, alleging unconstitutional race discrimination and that continued enforcement of the programs would deny them the right to compete on an equal basis for future contracts. Federal district courts in both states upheld the program.

The government conceded that the federal highway DBE program, on its face and as applied, is subject to strict scrutiny because it uses a race-based rebuttable presumption to define its beneficiaries and employs race conscious remedial measures. Such governmental consideration of race is constitutional only if narrowly-tailored to further a compelling governmental interest. Neither Sherbrooke nor Gross Seed disputed that the federal government has "a compelling interest in not perpetuating the effects of racial discrimination in its own distribution of federal funds and in remediating the effects of past discrimination in the government contracting markets created by its disbursements." Rather, petitioners argued that Congress and DOT have no "hard evidence" of widespread intentional discrimination in the contracting industry; they relied instead on a Justice Department summary of over 50 documents and 30 congressional hearings on minority-owned businesses prepared in response to the *Adarand* decision.[67] The Eighth Circuit nonetheless agreed with the Tenth Circuit conclusion in *Adarand* that "Congress has spent decades compiling evidence of race discrimination in federal highway contracting," and petitioners failed to meet the burden of showing that no remedial action was necessary.

Nor were the Minnesota DOT and Nebraska road department required to independently satisfy the compelling government interest aspect of strict scrutiny review. To be narrowly tailored, however, a national program must be limited to those parts of the country where its race-based measures are demonstrably needed. "To the extent the federal government delegates this tailoring function, a State's implementation becomes critically relevant to a reviewing court's strict scrutiny." Under the current DOT program, the opinion notes, race-conscious methods cannot be used unless race-neutral means are projected to fall short of achieving the overall goal, and racial preferences or set-asides are limited to those instances "when no other method could be reasonably expected to redress egregious instances of discrimination." In addition, because the goals for DBE participation are tied to the relevant labor markets, have built in durational limits, and are subject to "good faith" waiver and exemptions, the programs were deemed narrowly tailored on their face. Finally, the court reviewed Minnesota's and Nebraska's implementation, including each state's reliance on findings by independent consultants in setting goals for minority-owned business participation, and concluded that the DBE program was narrowly tailored as applied at the state level.

Similarly, the issue presented in *Western States Paving Co., Inc. v. Washington State Department of Transportation*[68] is whether TEA-21—which allocates 10% of certain federal transportation funds for small disadvantaged and minority contractors—is unconstitutional on its face, or as applied by the State of Washington. As discussed above, DOT regulations "presume" disadvantaged status for minority groups and women, provided the small business owner has a net worth of less than $750,000, but members of other groups are eligible if they can demonstrate, in fact, that they are "socially and economically disadvantaged." A three-judge panel of the Ninth Circuit agreed with the Eighth and Tenth Circuits that race and sex preferences for highway contractors under TEA-2 1 are facially valid. The compelling interest was in ensuring that federal funding is not distributed in a manner that reinforces the effects of either public or private discrimination within the transportation construction industry. The evidence relied on by Congress and reviewed by the court demonstrated a continuing pattern of race and sex discrimination in the industry.

The court further determined that the TEA-2 1 racial preferences were narrowly tailored to further compelling federal governmental interests. In this regard, the court pointed to several factors. First, the revised DOT regulations "explicitly prohibit the use of quotas" and require a state to "meet the maximum feasible portion of [its] overall goal by using race-neutral means."[69] Where racial goals are not met, the state may yet comply with federal standards by showing "good faith efforts" to achieve its goals. Moreover, "durational limitations" imposed by the legislative reauthorization process "ensure that Congress regularly evaluates" whether continuing need exists for the minority preference program. The regulation also makes clear that the statute's 10% DBE goal is "aspirational" only, with individual state goals determined by "the realities of [each state's] own labor market" and the availability locally of qualified minority contractors.

But these findings did not shield the Washington State program from Fourteenth Amendment challenge. Because the record was "devoid of any evidence suggesting that minorities currently suffer—or have ever suffered—discrimination" in the award of transportation infrastructure contracts within Washington State, the court found that the state's implementation program "is not narrowly tailored to further Congress' remedial objectives." A narrowly tailored remedy "depends on the absence or presence of discrimination," the court urged, and it was not enough "simply [that] the state complied with the federal program's requirements." Thus, each of the six principal minority groups identified in Washington's DBE program must be shown to have suffered contract award discrimination.

The ruling of another post-*Adarand* appellate tribunal imposes a heavier burden on the federal government for demonstrating a "strong basis in evidence" to establish a compelling governmental interest in support of minority contracting preferences. In *Rothe Development Corporation v. U.S. Department of Defense*,[70] a business owned by a non-minority woman, challenged the constitutionality of 10 U.S.C. § 2323, the statutory authority for DOD's SDB program, after losing a DOD contract to a business owned by Korean-Americans. Rothe argued that 10 U.S.C. § 2323 unconstitutionally deprived it of due process both as applied and on its face. Rothe's as-applied challenge focused upon 10 U.S.C. § 2323 in its 1992 reenactment, which governed the DOD's award of the contract to Rothe's competitor, while Rothe's facial challenge focused upon the 2006 reenactment of 10 U.S.C. § 2323, which was in effect at the time when the court heard the case.

The challenged SDB program in *Rothe* incorporates the SBA definition of small disadvantaged business, including the racial presumption, and establishes a 5% participation goal for such entities in DOD contracts.[71] The § 1207 program also authorizes DOD to apply a price evaluation adjustment of up to 10% in order to attain the 5% goal.[72] In effect, this means that DOD may raise the bids of non-DBEs by 10% in order to give disadvantaged entrepreneurs a preference. The statutory goal-setting provision in § 1207 was reauthorized in 1989, and again in 1992, 1999, 2002, and 2006.

After lengthy litigation and a complicated procedural history, which included repeated appearances before both the district court and the Federal Circuit, the trial court ultimately held that the DOD program was unconstitutional as applied because DOD failed to demonstrate that there was sufficient statistical evidence of discrimination before Congress when the statute was reenacted in 1992. In contrast, the district court held that the statute was facially constitutional because there was sufficient statistical evidence of discrimination before Congress when the statute was most recently reenacted in 2002.[73] However, the Federal Circuit reversed with respect to the facial challenge, holding that DOD's SBD program was unconstitutional on its face because Congress lacked a "strong basis in evidence" for concluding that race-conscious remedies were necessary when reenacting 10 U.S.C. § 2323 in 2006.[74] The district court had found that six state and local disparity studies, along with other statistical and anecdotal evidence, constituted a "strong basis in evidence,"[75] but the Federal Circuit disagreed.[76] It found that the six state and local disparity studies[77]—which had been the "primary focus of the district court's compelling interest analysis and of the parties' arguments on appeal"[78]—did not constitute a "strong basis in evidence" because they did not provide the "substantially probative and broad- based statistical foundation ... that must be the predicate for nationwide, race-conscious action."[79]

The Federal Circuit found significant methodological flaws with all of the disparity studies: two of the six studies failed to exclude unqualified businesses in calculating the number of minority businesses available for government contracts, and five of the six studies failed to account for the relative capacity of minority-owned small businesses in contracting with the government.[80] These flaws, coupled with the fact that the studies' findings addressed only six of the more than three thousand counties and equivalent regions making up the United States, prompted the Federal Circuit to find that the studies were insufficient to constitute a "strong basis in evidence" for the nation-wide SDB program.[81] The Federal Circuit also suggested, although reached no final holding on the issue, that the studies had not been "before Congress" at the time when 10 U.S.C. § 2323 was reenacted because they were (1) mentioned by name or discussed only in two floor speeches and (2) Congress did not make any findings concerning them. [82]

Other statistical data and anecdotes discussed by the parties and the district court proved similarly insufficient to constitute a "strong basis in evidence" for the SDB program, according to the Federal Circuit. The Federal Circuit discounted the remaining statistical evidence because it was mentioned only in floor speeches, without being the subject of congressional findings, or being "sufficiently described ... for [the Federal Circuit] to locate [it], let alone subject [it] to detailed, skeptical, non-deferential analysis."[83] It likewise discounted the anecdotal evidence, even though this evidence had been introduced at congressional hearings, because "anecdotal evidence is insufficient by itself to support [10 U.S.C. § 2323]."[84] The Federal Circuit further noted that the anecdotal evidence, including that compiled by the district court, did not address "a single instance of alleged discrimination by DOD in the course of awarding a prime contract, nor a single instance of alleged discrimination by a private contractor identified as the recipient of a prime defense contract."[85] The Federal Circuit found this lack of evidence of discrimination in DOD contracts significant because it suggested that the government might not be able to prove "passive participation" in discrimination, within the meaning of *Croson*, by the DOD as a justification for the Department's SDB program.[86]

Ultimately, the *Rothe* decision is of particular significance for several reasons. First, although the decision is binding precedent only within the Federal Circuit, *Rothe* now governs all future constitutional challenges to minority set-aside programs arising within the context of bid protests related to federal procurements because the Administrative Dispute Resolution Act gave the Court of Federal Claims—whose appellate court is the Federal Circuit—exclusive judicial jurisdiction over bid protests related to federal procurements arising after 2001. Moreover, *Rothe* appears to be the latest in a long line of cases that place an increasingly heavy evidentiary burden on Congress when it enacts race-conscious legislation. In the immediate aftermath of the Court's landmark decision in *Adarand*, the federal courts generally stressed deference to congressional authority to conduct fact-finding and to enact remedial legislation pursuant to section 5 of the Fourteenth Amendment. This deference to congressional authority has eroded over the years. As a result, Congress must now support any race-conscious measures it enacts by developing a strong record, as demonstrated in hearings and legislative findings, of methodologically sound, broad statistical evidence of discrimination capable of withstanding searching judicial inquiry.

Meanwhile, courts have also considered challenges to SBA's § 8(a) program for socially and economically disadvantaged businesses. While upholding the constitutionality of the § 8(a) program on its face, the district court in *Cortez III Service Corporation v. NASA* required federal officials "to decide whether there has been a history of discrimination in the particular industry at issue" before applying a race-based set-aside. [87] Other courts, however, have denied firms or individuals standing to challenge the racial presumption in the SBA statute and regulations on the rationale that they were disqualified from contract consideration because of inability to demonstrate "social and economic disadvantage," and not race.[88] Currently, a legal challenge to the § 8(a) program is pending in the U.S. District Court for the District of Columbia.[89]

Minority Contracting By State and Local Government

With increasing frequency, state and local affirmative action programs have met with constitutional objection from courts applying strict judicial scrutiny. Several federal circuit courts have addressed the legality of racial preferences in employment and public contracting programs since the Supreme Court's ruling in *Croson*.[90] *Croson* emphasized the obligation of state and local governments to anchor their affirmative action efforts by identifying with specificity the effects of past discrimination. This meant that the governmental entity has to have a "strong basis in evidence"—just short, perhaps, of that required to establish a "prima facie" case in a court of law—for its conclusion that minorities have been discriminatorily excluded from public contracts in the past.

In *Croson*, a 30% set-aside for minority subcontractors adopted by the City of Richmond failed this constitutional test. First, the program was premised on a comparison of minority contractor participation in city contracts with general minority population statistics rather than the percentage of qualified minority business enterprises (MBEs) in the relevant geographic market. There was, moreover, no evidence of discrimination in any aspect of city contracting as to certain groups—i.e., Orientals, Indians, Eskimos, and Aleuts—who nonetheless were granted a preference under the plan. With respect to "narrow tailoring," the 30% "quota" was deemed "too inflexible" and had been implemented by the city without any prior consideration of "race- neutral" alternatives. Finally, the "waiver" built into the Richmond plan was too "rigid" because it focused solely on minority contractor "availability" with "no inquiry into whether or not the particular MBE seeking a racial preference has suffered from the effects of past discrimination by the city or prime contractors."

The heightened standards of proof articulated by *Croson* and further developed by *Adarand* led many states, counties and municipalities to reevaluate existing minority business enterprise programs. Judicial challenges followed, and while several race-conscious programs survived,[91] many others were less successful, either because they lacked a compelling remedial justification or were not sufficiently "narrowly tailored" to withstand strict judicial scrutiny. As to the former, local jurisdictions primarily sought to establish a "strong basis in evidence" with "disparity" studies depicting the extent of minority exclusion from public contracting activity within the jurisdiction, coupled with any available "anecdotal" evidence. After the Court's 1995 *Adarand* decision, such studies were generally poorly received in the courts. Almost universally cited as the basis for judicial rejection of such statistical proof was over-reliance by the governmental unit on general or undifferentiated population data that failed to adequately reflect minority contractor availability or to account for contractor size and other factors relevant to contractor qualifications.[92] Other major faults have been failure to "narrowly tailor" the remedy—whether a minority participation goal, preference, set-aside, or other "sheltered" bidding arrangement—to any disparities revealed by statistics and anecdotal proof of discrimination;[93] the failure to properly limit the program in scope and duration;[94] the absence of a "waiver" provision;[95] or neglecting first to consider race-neutral alternatives, such as bonding and credit assistance programs, to ameliorate minority underutilization.[96]

The courts, however, have yet to resolve several important issues. As noted, the first relates to whether different fact-finding standards pertain to independent state or local minority contracting initiatives or to state plans explicitly adopted in aid of enforcing federal law. Notwithstanding *Croson*, decisions by three different circuit courts suggest that no independent findings may be required to establish a "compelling" governmental interest where the state agency acts not on its own authority, but pursuant to federal mandate requiring remedial state or local action to counteract the effects of past or present discrimination on federally funded projects.

> Compelling government interest looks at a statute or government program on its face. When the program is federal, the inquiry is (at least usually) national in scope. If Congress or the federal agency acted for a proper purpose and with a strong basis in the evidence, the program has the requisite compelling government interest nationwide, even if the evidence did not come from or apply to every state or locale in the Nation.[97]

The principle here seems to be that the evidentiary record compiled by Congress to find a compelling interest for the federal program provides the factual leverage necessary to sustain supporting action at the state and local level.

Likewise, in *Western State Paving Co. v. Washington DOT*, the Ninth Circuit reviewed "as applied" challenges to state programs mandated by federal law. [98] As discussed earlier, the court followed the Eighth Circuit in finding the 10% DBE set-aside of federal transportation funds under TEA-2 1 facially constitutional.[99] But even if Washington demonstrates compliance with TEA-2 1 and its implementing regulations, it must separately meet strict scrutiny to survive an as- applied challenge. Thus, the majority found that while the state does not have to re-establish a compelling state interest, it still has to show that its program is narrowly tailored. That, in turn, "depends upon the presence or absence or discrimination in the state's transportation contracting industry."

Washington admitted that no statistical studies were done to establish the existence of discrimination in the highway contracting industry. What arguments the state did make regarding discrimination—based on estimates of minority contractor participation in state transportation contracting—were rejected. The court concluded that those percentages proved little because they failed to account for factors affecting the capacity of minority contractors to undertake contracting work; for example, DBEs could be smaller, less experienced or concentrated in a particular part of the state. Moreover, the court observed that historical minority participation on contracts with affirmative action components "does not provide any evidence of discrimination against DBEs" in a race-neutral market. Washington also lacked anecdotal evidence of discrimination, which could not be inferred from statistics alone. Finally, "even when discrimination is present within a State, a remedial program is narrowly tailored if its application is limited to those minority groups that have actually suffered discrimination."[100]

In a more recent ruling, Northern Contracting *Inc. v. State of Illinois*,[101] the Seventh Circuit reached a result similar to the Ninth Circuit's ruling in *Western States Paving*. In affirming the district court, the Seventh Circuit "considered the question of whether the federal government's interest in remedying discrimination in highway contracting provided sufficient justification for the state to engage in a federally mandated DBE program, and ... concluded that it did." As a result, the only question that remained was whether the state highway contracting program was narrowly tailored to achieve this compelling interest. After reviewing the statistical evidence and evaluating the state's compliance with federal regulations, the court determined that the state's program was narrowly tailored and therefore passed constitutional muster.

By contrast, a more restrictive evidentiary approach is represented by a different Seventh Circuit ruling in *Builders Association of Greater Chicago v. County of Cook*,[102] a case that involved a locally adopted minority contracting program rather than a federal program. The district court there held that Cook County had failed to establish a compelling interest supporting its contract set-aside program. In defense of its program, the County presented anecdotal evidence that prime contractors failed to solicit minority- and women-owned subcontractors at the same rate as similarly situated firms owned by white males. In addition, the County put forward statistical data demonstrating that a number of firms rarely or never solicit minority- or women-owned firms for subcontract work. This evidence, however, failed to persuade the court of a systematic refusal to solicit such firms for subcontract work because it was based on the practice of a mere thirteen general contractors. In affirming the decision, the appeals court also noted that the program failed to link its set-aside levels (30% minorities, 10% women) to evidence of their availability on the relevant market.

Western States Paving and related cases may have important implications for future challenges against both state and federal affirmative action programs. Under the Ninth Circuit's rationale, while federal programs may be insulated by appropriate congressional fact-finding, state affirmative action in furtherance thereof must be supported by proof of discrimination on a stateby-state basis. Moreover, even federal programs could fall under question as the statistical foundation for their enactment becomes strained by the passage of time, perhaps necessitating renewed evidentiary justification. Meanwhile, DOT has issued guidance concerning the effects of the *Western States Paving* decision on recipients in the Ninth Circuit. [103]

Another issue that has divided the federal circuit courts since Croson is whether post-enactment evidence of discrimination is sufficient to justify minority set-asides and preferences. [104] In 1996, the Supreme Court in *Shaw v. Hunt* ruled that, in the context of racial gerrymandering, a legislature must have sufficient evidence to support a racial distinction "before it embarks on an affirmative action program."[105] *Shaw* demanded a "strong basis in evidence" for race-based governmental action, which has been interpreted by the Federal Circuit to mean that "the quantum of evidence that is ultimately necessary to uphold racial classifications must have actually been before the legislature at the time of enactment."[106] In this view, proof that the legislature had a constitutionally permissible intent requires strong pre-enactment evidence. But the Tenth Circuit decision in *Adarand III* allowed consideration of post-enactment evidence in addition to congressional findings because the defendants had gathered it in response to the Supreme Court's application of strict scrutiny to the statutes in question. [107] The Supreme Court chose not to address this and other issues when it declined an appeal from the Tenth Circuit ruling in *Concrete Works of Colorado, Inc. v. City and County of Denver.*[108]

In *Concrete Works*, the federal circuit court examined a city ordinance establishing goals for participation in the construction industry by minority- and female-owned businesses. In 1990, the Denver City Council passed Ordinance 513 to promote participation by minority-owned business enterprises (MBEs) and women-owned business enterprises (WBEs) in public work projects "to an extent approximating [their] availability and capacity." The city determined availability and capacity by conducting periodic studies of minority participation in each contract area. The Ordinance also directed the Office of Contract Compliance (OCC) to establish MBE and WBE participation goals on each individual city contract. The statutory goals for total annual expenditures were 16% for MBEs and 12% for WBEs. According to the ordinance, if the OCC established an individual project goal, all bidders had to either meet the goals or demonstrate their good faith efforts to do so. The city revised the program in 1996 and 1998, reducing the annual goals for MBEs and WBEs in construction contracts to 10% and prohibiting M/WBEs from counting self-performed work towards the goals.

Concrete Works of Colorado, a construction firm owned by a white male, sued the city in 1992, alleging that it had been denied three contracts for failure to meet the goals or to make good faith efforts, and sought injunctive relief and money damages. The city relied on three categories of evidence to demonstrate a compelling remedial purpose for the ordinance. First, major studies— in 1990, 1995, and 1997—revealed large disparities between M/WBE availability and utilization on city projects without goals. Census data revealed like patterns of minority and female underutilization as contractors and subcontractors in state-wide construction, public and private. At trial, M/WBEs also testified to discrimination they confronted in qualifying and bidding on private sector jobs, in obtaining capital and credit, in dealing with suppliers, and of harassment suffered at work sites, including physical assaults.

The principal issue presented by *Concrete Works* was whether the government's statistics and other evidence established a remedial justification for racial and gender preferences in public contracting. The circuit court adopted an expansive approach, finding that "irrefutable or definitive" proof of the city's own "guilty" actions was unnecessary where the city's "passive" participation in marketplace discrimination by its spending practices was shown.

> Denver's only burden was to introduce evidence which raised the inference of discriminatory exclusion in the local construction industry and link its spending to that discrimination.... Denver was under no burden to identify any specific practice or policy that resulted in discrimination. Neither was Denver required to demonstrate that the purpose of any such practice or policy was to disadvantage women or minorities. To impose such a burden on a municipality would be tantamount to requiring proof of discrimination and would eviscerate any reliance the municipality could place on statistical studies and anecdotal evidence.[109]

Croson's admonition against relying on "mere societal discrimination" did not apply, the opinion states, where evidence of discrimination in the industry targeted by the program is shown— whether motivated by an attitude "shared by society" or "unique to the industry" is constitutionally irrelevant. The trial court was wrong to require Denver to "show the existence of specific discriminatory policies and that those policies were more than a reflection of societal discrimination."

The trial court also faulted the city's disparity studies, in part, for failure to control for firm size, area of specialization, and whether the firm had actually bid on city contracts. Such factors were thought important because, due to their generally smaller size, M/WBEs might lack the requisite experience and qualifications, diminishing their availability and capacity to perform on city construction projects. The Tenth Circuit accepted the studies, nonetheless, reasoning that small firms can expand and contract to meet their bidding opportunities, and because size and experience are not race or gender-neutral variables: "M/WBE construction firms are generally smaller and less experienced because of discrimination." The disparities, moreover, were not shown to disappear when such variables were controlled for, or held constant, and taking the number of city bidders into account might distort the picture by including unqualified firms. Likewise, "lending discrimination" and "business formation" studies were properly relied on by the city for the "strong link" they demonstrated between disbursement of public funds and the "channeling" of those funds due to private discrimination. Private barriers precluded entry of M/WBEs into the market "at the outset" and made impossible "fair competition" for public contracts by minority firms that did submit bids.

An appeal from the Tenth Circuit ruling, filed by petitioner Concrete Works of Colorado, Inc., was denied by the Supreme Court.[110] In an unusual move, Justice Scalia was joined by Chief Justice Rehnquist in filing a written dissent from the Court's refusal to grant *certiorari*. The dissenters argued that Denver's policy violated the standards of proof required by the Court's 1989 decision in *Croson* and "invites speculation that case has effectively been overruled." According to their view, there must be some evidence that discrimination was so pervasive that any minority business would have suffered: "Absent such evidence of pervasive discrimination, Denver's seeming limitation of the set-asides to victims of racial discrimination is a sham, and the only function of the preferences is to channel a fixed percentage of city contracting dollars to firms identified by race." In declining review, Justice Scalia opined that his fellow Justices had "abandoned" their former insistence on a "strong basis in evidence," relying instead on the "good faith" of local governments to act responsibly when using racial preferences.

End Notes

[1] P.L. 85-536, § 8(a), 72 Stat. 384, 389-90 (July 18, 1958) (codified at 15 U.S.C. §637(a)).

[2] Minority Contracting: Joint Hearing Before the Senate Comm. on Small Business and the House Subcomm. on Minority Enterprise and General Oversight of the Comm. on Small Business, 95th Cong., 2d Sess. 37 (1978).

[3] E.O. 11625, 3 C.F.R. § 616 (1971), *reprinted in* 15 U.S.C. § 631, authorized the Office of Minority Business Enterprise created by preceding order, E.O. 11458, to provide financial assistance to public or private organizations that provided management or technical assistance to minority business enterprises. It also empowered the Secretary of Commerce to coordinate and review all federal activities to assist in minority business development.

[4] 15 U.S.C. § 637(a).

[5] Id. at § 637(a)(5).

[6] 13 C.F.R. § 124.103(b).

[7] Id. at § 124.103(c).

[8] The statute, 15 U.S.C. § 637(a)(6)(A), defines economic disadvantage to mean "socially disadvantaged individuals whose ability to compete in the free enterprise system has been impaired due to diminished capital and credit opportunities as compared to others who are not socially disadvantaged, and such diminished opportunities have precluded or are likely to preclude such individuals from successfully competing in the open market."

[9] 15 U.S.C. §§ 637(a)(5), (d). Criteria set forth in the regulations requires non-minority individuals to prove by "a preponderance of the evidence," that they have personally experienced "substantial and chronic social disadvantage in American society" as the result of "[a]t least one objective distinguishing feature," including "long-term residence in an environment isolated from the mainstream of American society," with a "negative impact" on his or her "entry into ... the business world." "In every case ... SBA will consider education, employment, and business history, where applicable, to see if the totality of circumstances shows disadvantage in entering into or advancing in the business world." 13 C.F.R. § 124. 103(c).

[10] See 49 C.F.R. Pt. 23, Subpt. D, App. C.

[11] 15 U.S.C. § 637(d). See also 13 C.F.R. § 124.104.

[12] 15 U.S.C. § 637(d)(4)(D) and (d)(5)(A).

[13] 15 U.S.C. § 637(d)(3)(C).

[14] 15 U.S.C. § 637(d)(4)(F).

[15] See 15 U.S.C. § 644(g)(2).

[16] P.L. 100-656, § 502, 102 Stat. 3887, codified at 15 U.S.C. § 644(g)(1).

[17] See, e.g., 49 C.F.R. § 26.15 (2007) (setting forth waiver criteria for the Department of Transportation).

[18] P.L. 103-355, 108 Stat. 3243, 3374, § 7106 (1994).

[19] See CRS Report R41038, *Survey of Federal Laws Containing Goals, Set-Asides, Priorities, or Other Preferences Based on Race, Gender, or Ethnicity* , by Jody Feder, Kate M. Manuel, and Julia Taylor.

[20] Department of Defense Authorization Act, 1987, P.L. 99-661 (codified at 10 U.S.C. § 2323).

[21] P.L. 97-424, § 105(f), 96 Stat. 2097 (1982).

[22] P.L. 100-17, § 106(c), 101 Stat. 132 (1987).

[23] P.L. 102-240, § 1003, 105 Stat. 1914 (1992).

[24] P.L. 105-178, § 1101, 112 Stat. 107 (1998). TEA-21 lapsed on May 31, 2005, but was extended through FY2009 by P.L. 109-59, signed into law during the 109th Congress. See § 1101(b) of P.L. 109-59, the Safe, Accountable, Flexible, Efficient Transportation Equity Act: A Legacy for Users (SAFETEA-LU), 119 Stat. 1144 (Aug. 10, 2005).

[25] Other agencies were briefly given similar authority to apply price evaluation adjustments to bids or offers from companies other than SDBs. This authority expired at the end of FY2000. See, Federal Acquisition Streamlining Act, P.L. 103-355, § 7102, 108 Stat. 3243, 3368-69 (Oct. 13, 1994).

[26] Rothe Development Corporation v. Department of Defense, 545 F.3d 1023 (Fed. Cir. 2008). For more on *Rothe*, see *infra* notes 68-84 and accompanying text.

[27] 515 U.S. 200 (1995).

[28] 228 F.3d 1147 (10th Cir. 2000).

[29] 448 U.S. 448 (1980).

[30] 488 U.S. 469 (1989).

[31] 515 U.S. at 217.

[32] In their separate concurrences, Justices Scalia and Thomas, espoused a far more restrictive view that would foreclose all governmental classifications by race or ethnicity. Justice Scalia declared that "government can never have a 'compelling interest' in discriminating on the basis of race in order to 'make up' for past racial discrimination in the opposite direction." Justice Thomas was of the view that the "racial paternalism" of affirmative action was more injurious than beneficial to minorities. "In my mind, government-sponsored racial discrimination based on benign prejudice is just as noxious as discrimination inspired by malicious prejudice. In each instance, it is racial discrimination, plain and simple."

[33] Adarand Constructors Inc. v. Pena, 965 F. Supp. 1556 (D.Colo. 1997).

[34] Two aspects of the district court's analysis of the "narrow tailoring" requirement were especially unsettling for federal small disadvantaged business programs. First, the "optional" or voluntary nature of the SCC program was not enough to save it, notwithstanding the fact that prime contractors were free to accept bid proposals from any subcontractor, regardless of race or ethnicity. The government's failure to prevail on this issue cast a long shadow over other federal minority contracting efforts—e.g., the § 8(a) set-aside, bid or evaluation preferences, and the like—which, under the district court's reasoning, may be viewed as imposing a "choice based only on race" at least as "mandatory" and "absolute" as the incentive payment to prime contractors in *Adarand*, if not more so. Similarly, the fact that the SCC program did not expressly incorporate any "goals, quotas, or set-asides" was not sufficient to divorce it, in the district court's view, from the percentage goal requirements imposed by statutes the program was designed to implement. Those statutory provisions—the 5% minimum disadvantaged small business goal in § 8(d) of the SBA and the parallel 10% requirement in STURAA and ISTEA—were deemed invalid for lack of narrow tailoring. In effect, the district court ruling questioned much of the federal government's statutory infrastructure for advancing minority small business participation in the procurement process by race-conscious means.

[35] Adarand Constructors Inc. v. Slater (Adarand III), 228 F.3d 1147 (10th Cir. 2000). This court of appeals decision was preceded by an intervening appellate ruling and Supreme Court review confined to procedural questions of standing and mootness occasioned by the plaintiff's change in circumstances. After the district decision in *Adarand II*, the State of Colorado did away with the racial presumption and certified the non-minority owner of Adarand Constructors Inc. as disadvantaged. As a result, the Tenth Circuit dismissed the case as moot and the vacated the judgment against the government. Adarand v. Slater, 169 F.3d 1292 (10th Cir. 1999). The district court decision was reinstated on January 20, 2000, however, when the Supreme Court rejected the mootness finding because there was nothing to prevent the government from reviving the abandoned policy, and returned the case to the circuit court for further proceedings. Adarand Constructors v. Slater, 528 U.S. 216 (2000).

[36] Specifically, the Tenth Circuit opinion states: "Subsection 8(a) does not involve the use of SCCs, nor has Adarand made any showing that it has been injured by non-inclusion in the § 8(a).... This case does not involve, nor has Adarand ever demonstrated standing to bring, a generalized challenge to the policy of maximizing contracting opportunities for small disadvantaged businesses set forth in 15 U.S.C. §§ 637 and 644(g), or to the various goals for fostering the participation of small minority-owned businesses promulgated pursuant to 15 U.S.C. § 644(g). Nor are we presented with any indication that Adarand has standing to challenge ... § 637d." 228 F.3d at 1152.

[37] 49 C.F.R. § 26.51(a),(b)(1999).

[38] Participation in the § 8(a) program is limited by statute and regulation to nine years, and each DBE is re-evaluated, and may be graduated from the program, based on the submission of financial and other information required annually.

[39] 49 C.F.R. § 2615 (1999)(allowing recipients to seek waivers and exemptions, despite the already non-mandatory nature of the program).

[40] The court of appeals found that the SCC had been based in part on an ill-defined 12-15% goal apparently adopted by the Federal Highway Administration, for which "it could find no explanation in the record." This alone would have warranted summary judgment for Adarand, it concluded.

[41] The current regulations impose additional requirements on applicants with regard to individualized showing: they must submit a narrative statement describing the circumstances of that purported economic disadvantage. 13 C.F.R. § 124.104(b)(1)(2008). See also, 49 C.F.R. § 26.67(b)(1)(2007)(providing a $750,000 net worth limit for DBEs under transportation programs); id. § 26.65(b)(stating that businesses exceeding a certain amount of gross receipts are ineligible for the DBE program).

[42] Adarand Constructors, Inc. v. Mineta, 534 U.S. 103 (2001).

[43] See, e.g., Bd. of Trs. of the Univ. of Alabama, 531 U.S. 356 (2001)(Congress could not abrogate state sovereign immunity to suit for compensatory damages under Title I of the Americans with Disability Act since historical record "fails to show that Congress did in fact identify a pattern of irrational state discrimination in employment against the disabled," and the rights and remedies provided against the state "raise the same sort of concerns as to congruence and proportionality" as found in previous cases.); Kimel v. Florida Bd. of Regents, 528 U.S. 62 (2000)(Applying "congruence and proportionality" standard, the Court determined that the Age Discrimination in Employment Act was not "appropriate legislation" under § 5); United States v. Morrison, 529 U.S. 598 (2000)(Court invalidated provision of Violence Against Women Act, providing victims of gender-motivated violence with a civil damages remedy, since even as a "prophylactic measure," it was "overbroad" and applied uniformly throughout the nation, rather than merely in states with congressionally documented records of this type of gender discrimination.).

[44] Monterey Mech. Co. v. Wilson, 125 F.3d 702 (9th Cir. 1997), reh'g en banc denied, 138 F.3d 1270 (9th Cir. 1998).

[45] 141 F.3d 344 (D.C.Cir. 1998).

[46] 61 F.R. 26042, Notice, Department of Justice, Proposed Reforms to Affirmative Action in Federal Procurement. (May 23, 1996).

[47] Response to Comments to Department of Justice Proposed Reforms to Affirmative Action in Federal Procurement, 62 F.R. 25648 (1997).

[48] Id. at 25650-52. An interim rule incorporating proposed DOJ revisions to the FAR regulation became effective in 1998. Federal Acquisition Regulation; Reform of Affirmative Action in Federal Procurement; Interim rule with request for comment, 63 F.R. 52426 (1998).

[49] 63 F.R. 35726, 35767 (1998).

[50] In 2008, the Small Business Administration moved to abandon its role in the certification process by issuing an interim final rule under which other agencies can certify firms as SDBs for prime contractors and firms can self-certify as SDBs for subcontracting purposes. SBA, Interim Final Rule: Small Disadvantaged Business Program, 73 F.R. 57490 (Oct. 3, 2008).

[51] § 1101(b)(1), 112 Stat. at 113.

[52] See § 1101(b) of P.L. 109-59, the "Safe, Accountable, Flexible, Efficient Transportation Equity Act: A Legacy for Users" (SAFETEA-LU), 119 Stat. 1144 (Aug. 10, 2005).

[53] 49 C.F.R. pt. 26 (2007).

[54] Id. at § 26.45.

[55] Id. at § 26.51.

[56] Id. at § 26.53 (a).

[57] Id at § 26.43(a).

[58] P.L. 106-554, codified at 15 U.S.C. § 637(m).

[59] Small Business Administration, Women-Owned Small Business Federal Contract Assistance Procedures, 72 F.R. 73285, December 27, 2007. The four industries identified were national security and international affairs; coating, engraving, heat treating, and allied activities; household and institutional furniture and kitchen cabinet manufacturing; and other motor vehicle dealers. After re-examining the data, the SBA subsequently revised its proposed rules and identified thirty-one industries in which women were underrepresented or substantially underrepresented. Small Business Administration, Women-Owned Small Business Federal Contract Assistance Procedures, 73 F.R. 57014, Oct. 1, 2008.

[60] Small Business Administration, The Women-Owned Small Business Federal Contract Assistance Procedures, 73 F.R. 56940, 56941-42, October 1, 2008.

[61] Small Business Administration. The Women-Owned Small Business Federal Contract Assistance Procedures: Eligible Industries, 74 F.R. 1153 (Jan. 12, 2009).

[62] Small Business Administration, The Women-Owned Small Business Federal Contract Assistance Procedures, 73 F.R. 56940, 56943, Oct. 1, 2008.

[63] Small Business Administration, Women-Owned Small Business Federal Contract Program: Proposed Rule, 75 F.R. 10029 (Mar. 4, 2010). Implementation of the set-asides for women-owned small businesses was also temporarily delayed by a provision of the Omnibus Appropriations Act, 2009, which precluded SBA from using funds appropriated under the act to implement a proposed rule on set-asides for women-owned small businesses issued by the SBA on October 1, 2008. *See* P.L. 111-8, Administrative Provisions—Small Business Administration, § 522. Similar provisions do not appear to have been included in the Consolidated Appropriations Act, 2010, P.L. 111-117.

[64] Id. at 10043.

[65] Id.

[66] 345 F.3d 964 (8th Cir. 2003), cert. denied 541 U.S. 1041 (2004).

[67] See Appendix—The Compelling Interest for Affirmative Action in Federal Procurement: A Preliminary Survey, 61 F.R. 26050 (May 23, 1996).

[68] 407 F.3d 983 (9th Cir. 2005), cert. denied, 546 U.S. 1170 (2006).

[69] 49 C.F.R. § 26.5 1(a).

[70] 545 F.3d 1023 (Fed. Cir. 2008).

[71] 10 U.S.C. § 2323. Although only some subsections of § 1207 were challenged, the district court's order implementing the Federal Circuit decision struck down § 1207 in its entirety, meaning that several other provisions were affected, including technical and infrastructure assistance programs for certain minority-serving institutions. Rothe Dev. Corp. v. Dep't of Defense, 606 F. Supp. 2d 648 (W.D. Tex. 2009). The 111th Congress responded to the district court's decision, in part, by establishing a new program to assist such institutions in performing "defense- related research, development, testing, and evaluation activities." P.L. 111-84, § 252 (codified at 10 U.S.C. § 2362).

[72] Later legislation, however, limited DOD's authority to apply the 10% price evaluation adjustment in pursuit of its 5% goal. Under the Strom Thurmond National Defense Authorization Act for Fiscal Year 1999, DOD was precluded from using the price evaluation adjustment in any fiscal year when the Secretary of Defense determines, at the start of that fiscal year, that DOD had achieved its 5% contracting goal in the most recent fiscal year for which data are available. P.L. 105-261, § 801, 112 Stat. 1921, 2080-81 (Oct. 17, 1998).

[73] Rothe Dev. Corp. v. U.S. Dep't of Defense, 324 F. Supp.2d 840 (W.D.Tex. 2004).

[74] Rothe Dev. Corp., 545 F.3d at 1050. In order to establish a compelling governmental interest in remedying a history of past discrimination, the governmental entity creating racial classifications must (1) identify public or

private discrimination with some specificity before resorting to race-conscious remedies and (2) establish a "strong basis in evidence" to conclude that race-conscious remedies are necessary before enacting or implementing those remedies. Shaw v. Hunt, 517 U.S. 899, 909-10 (1996); Concrete Works of Colorado, Inc. v. City & County of Denver, 321 F.3d 950, 958 (10th Cir. 2003). As regards the "strong basis in evidence" requirement, the government has the burden of producing statistical evidence sufficient to support an inference of discrimination. Concrete Works, 321 F.3d at 958. Once the government has done this, the plaintiffs challenging the governmental action have the burden of persuasion in refuting the government's evidence and establishing race-neutral explanations for the apparent disparity. Plaintiffs can do this by, among other things, (1) showing that the government's statistics are flawed; (2) demonstrating that the disparities shown by the government's statistics are not significant; or (3) presenting contrasting statistical data of their own. Coral Constr. Co. v. King County, 941 F.2d 910, 921 (9th Cir. 1991).

75 Rothe Dev. Corp., 545 F.3d at 1036.

76 *Id.* at 1045-46.

77 A disparity study is a "study attempting to measure the difference—or disparity—between the number of contracts or contract dollars *actually* awarded to minority-owned businesses in a particular contract market, on the one hand, and the number of contracts or contract dollars that one would *expect* to be awarded to minority-owned business given their presence in that particular contract market, on the other hand." *Id.* at 1037 (emphases in the original).

78 *Id.*

79 *Id.* at 1040. *See also id.* at 1045 ("To be clear, we do *not* hold that the defects in the availability and capacity analyses in these six disparity studies render the studies wholly unreliable for any purpose. ... But we hold that the defects we have noted detract dramatically from the probative value of these six studies, and, in conjunction with their limited geographic coverage, render the studies insufficient to form the statistical core of the 'strong basis in evidence' required to uphold the statute.") (emphasis in the original).

80 *Id.* at 1042-43.

81 *Id.* at 1046.

82 *Id.* at 1039-40 (noting that the studies had been mentioned by title, author, and date in two floor speeches—one by Senator Ted Kennedy and one by Representative Cynthia McKinney—but had been neither discussed in congressional hearings nor the subject of congressional findings). The Federal Circuit also suggested that the currency of the studies upon which Congress relies is relevant to the analysis of whether a "strong basis in evidence" exists. However, the Federal Circuit rejected Rothe's argument for a *per se* rule that studies more than five years old cannot constitute a "strong basis in evidence." *Id.* at 1038. The Federal Circuit suggested, instead, that Congress can rely upon the most recently available studies so long as these studies are reasonably up-to-date. *Id.* at 1039.

83 *Id.* at 1047.

84 *Id.* at 1048.

85 *Id.*

86 *Id.* Under *Croson*, when a government seeking to use a racial classification is not remedying its own prior discrimination, it can still use the classification if it can show that it has become a "passive participant" in a system of racial exclusion practiced by a local industry. *See* City of Richmond v. Croson, 488 U.S. 469, 492 (1989).

87 950 F. Supp. 357 (D.D.C. 1996). See also Klaver Constr. Co. v. Kansas Dep't of Transp., 211 F. Supp.2d 1296 (D.Kan. 2002).

88 See Interstate Traffic Control v. Beverage, 101 F. Supp. 2d 445 (S.D. W.Va. 2000); Ellsworth Associates v. United States, 926 F.Supp. 207 (D.D.C. 1996).

89 *See* Dynalantic Corp. v. U.S. Dep't of Defense, 503 F. Supp. 2d 262 (D.D.C. 2007) (denying parties' motions for summary judgment).

90 488 U.S. 469 (1989).

91 See, e.g., Indianapolis Minority Contractors Ass'n v. Wiley, 187 F.3d 743 (7th Cir. 1999); Associated Gen. Contractors of California v. Coalition, 950 F.2d 1401, 1416-18 (9th Cir. 1991), cert. denied, 503 U.S. 585 (1992); Coral Constr. Co. v. King County, 941 F.2d 910 (9th Cir. 1991), cert. denied, 502 U.S. 1033 (1992).

92 See, e.g., Builders' Ass'n of Greater Chicago v. Cook County, 256 F.3d 642 (7th Cir. 2001); Associated Gen. Contractors of Ohio, Inc. v. Drabik, 214 F.3d 730 (6th Cir. 2000), cert. denied, 531 U.S. 1148 (2001); W.H. Scott Constr. Co., Inc. v. City of Jackson, 199 F.3d 206 (5th Cir. 1999); Engineering Contractors Ass'n v. Metro. Dade County, 122 F.3d 895 (1 1th Cir. 1997), cert. denied, 523 U.S. 1004 (1998); Concrete Works of Colorado, Inc. v. City and County of Denver, 36 F.3d 196 (10th Cir. 1994), cert. denied 514 U.S. 1004 (1995); O'Donnell Constr. Co. v. District of Columbia, 963 F.2d 420 (D.C.Cir. 1992).

93 See, e.g., Contractors Ass'n of Eastern Pennsylvania, Inc. v. City of Philadelphia, 91 F.3d 586 (3rd Cir. 1996), cert. denied, 519 U.S. 1113 (1997); Associated Util. Contractors of Md., Inc. v. Mayor of Baltimore, 83 F. Supp. 2d 613 (D. Md. 2000); Main Line Paving Co. v. Bd. of Educ., 725 F. Supp. 1349 (E.D. Pa. 1989).

[94] See, e.g., Associated Gen. Contractors of Ohio v. Drabik, 214 F.3d 730 (6th Cir. 2000); Kornhass Constr., Inc. v. State of Oklahoma, 140 F. Supp. 2d 1232 (W.D. Okla, 2001); Webster v. Fulton County, Ga. 51 F. Supp.2d 1354 (N.D. Ga. 1999); Associated Gen. Contractors v. New Haven, 791 F. Supp. 941, 948 (D. Conn. 1992).

[95] Associated Gen. Contractors, 214 F.3d 730. Compare Builders Ass'n of Greater Chicago v. City of Chicago, 298 F. Supp. 2d., 725, 740 (finding DBE plan not to be narrowly tailored where waivers were "rarely or never granted") with N. Contr., Inc. v. Illinois, 2005 U.S. Dist. LEXIS 19868 (D. Ill. 2005), aff'd 2007 U.S. App. LEXIS 320 (7th Cir. 2007)(state transportation funding plan approved where flexibility assured by "the employment of individualized DBE goals on a contract-by-contract basis, and through the maintenance of a waiver provision to account for those situations in which achievement of the set DBE goals is not reasonably possible.").

[96] See, e.g., Contractors Ass'n of Eastern Pennsylvania, 91 F.3d 586; Associated Gen. Contractors of Ohio, 214 F.3d 730; Concrete Works of Colorado v. City and County of Denver, 86 F. Supp 2d 1042 (D.Colo. 2000).

[97] Sherbrooke Turf, 345 F.3d 964, 970 (8th Cir. 2003), cert. denied 541 U.S. 1041 (2004).; see also Milwaukee County Paver Ass'n v. Fiedler, 922 F.2d 419, 423 (7th Cir. 199 1)("If the state does exactly what the statute expects it to do, and the statute is conceded for the purposes of the litigation to be constitutional, we do not see how the state can be thought to have violated the Constitution.").

[98] 407 F.3d 983 (9th Cir. 2005), cert. denied, 546 U.S. 1170 (2006).

[99] Generally, the court determined that Congress had a compelling interest in creating a remedial scheme to overcome effects of past discrimination in the transportation contracting industry. Further, TEA-21 was narrowly tailored to this end because it created no quotas, it is limited in duration (Congress must periodically re-authorize it), and it contains income limits to lessen the burden on non-minority firms.

[100] Id. at 998.

[101] 473 F.3d 715 (7th Cir. 2007).

[102] 123 F.Supp.2d 1087 (N.D. Ill. 2000), aff'd 256 F.3d 642 (7th Cir. 2001).

[103] A notice describing DOT's implementation of the guidance was published in the *Federal Register* on Aug. 21, 2006. 71 F.R. 48579. Questions and answers regarding *Western States Paving* are available on the DOT website at http://www.fhwa.dot.gov/civilrights/dbe_memo_a5.htm.

[104] See, e.g., Rothe Dev. Corp. v. United States DOD, 262 F.3d 1306 (Fed. Cir. 2001); Associated Gen. Contrs. of Ohio, Inc. v. Drabik, 214 F.3d 730 (6th Cir. 2000); Eng'g Contractors Ass'n of S. Fla., Inc. v. Metro. Dade County, 122 F.3d 895, 911-13 (1 1th Cir. 1997); Contractors Ass'n of E. Pa., Inc. v. City of Philadelphia, 91 F.3d 586, 605 n.21 (3rd Cir. 1996); Concrete Works of Colo., Inc. v. City & County of Denver, 36 F.3d 1513, 1520-21 (10th Cir. 1994); Harrison & Burrowes Bridge Constructors, Inc. v. Cuomo, 981 F.2d 50, 60 (2nd Cir. 1992); Coral Constr. Co. v. King County, 941 F.2d 910, 919-20 (9th Cir. 1991).

[105] 517 U.S. 899 (1996).

[106] Rothe Dev. Corp. v. United States DOD, 262 F.3d 1306, 1327 (Fed. Cir. 2001).

[107] Adarand Constructors Inc. v. Slater, 228 F.3d 1147 (10th Cir. 2000).

[108] 321 F.3d 950 (10th Cir. 2003), cert. denied, 540 U.S. 1027 (2003).

[109] Id. at 973.

[110] Concrete Works of Colorado v. City and County of Denver, cert. denied 540 U.S. 1047 (2003).

In: Disadvantaged Small Businesses and the 8(a) Program ISBN: 978-1-61209-309-3
Editors: James P. Carlson and Andrea M. Bernard

Chapter 8

Rothe Development Corporation v. Department of Defense: The Constitutionality of Federal Contracting Programs for Minority-Owned and Other Small Businesses

Jody Feder and Kate M. Manuel

Summary

This report discusses *Rothe Development Corporation v. Department of Defense*, a case involving a constitutional challenge to a minority contracting program authorized under Section 1207 of the Department of Defense (DOD) Authorization Act of 1987. This program allowed DOD to take 10% off the price of offers submitted by "small disadvantaged businesses" in determining which offer had the lowest price or represented the best value for the government. Section 1207 also incorporated a presumption that minorities are socially and economically disadvantaged.

On November 4, 2008, the U.S. Court of Appeals for the Federal Circuit struck down the DOD preference program, holding that Section 1207 was facially unconstitutional because Congress did not have sufficient evidence to conclude that there was racial discrimination in defense contracting when it reauthorized the program in 2006. Later, on February 27, 2009, the U.S. District Court for the Western District of Texas, San Antonio Division, to which the case had been remanded for entry of judgment, enjoined defense agencies from implementing other programs authorized by Section 1207 because these programs were "contingent" on the subsections containing the price preference and must "also fall" when they do. These programs included technical and infrastructure assistance for certain minority-serving institutions (MSIs) of higher education, including historically black colleges and universities (HBCUs), Hispanic-serving institutions (HSIs), Alaska Native- and Native Hawaiian-serving institutions (ANNHIs), and majority-minority institutions (MMIs). However, the first session of the 111th Congress enacted legislation (P.L. 111-84) that authorizes defense agencies to provide assistance similar to that authorized under Section 1207 to MSIs.

The report examines the *Rothe* decision in detail; describes existing contracting programs for minority-owned and women-owned small businesses; and analyzes *Rothe's* potential effect on these programs, including the Business Development Program under Section 8(a) of the Small Business Act.

INTRODUCTION

On November 4, 2008, the U.S. Court of Appeals for the Federal Circuit issued its decision in *Rothe Development Corporation v. Department of Defense*, a case involving a challenge to the constitutionality of a "small disadvantaged business" (SDB) program of the Department of Defense (DOD). [1] As part of the SDB program, DOD could apply a 10% price evaluation adjustment to the offers of small businesses owned and controlled by socially and economically disadvantaged individuals in pursuit of its goal of awarding 5% of its contract dollars to such businesses, among others.[2] In determining which small businesses were socially and economically disadvantaged, the SDB program relied upon Section 8(d) of the Small Business Act, which presumes that minorities are socially and economically disadvantaged, while also allowing non-minorities to demonstrate disadvantage.[3] Rothe Development Corporation (RDC) challenged the constitutionality of the SDB program after losing a contract to a KoreanAmerican-owned firm. RDC's offer would have been lower had DOD not applied a 10% price evaluation preference to the Korean-American firm's offer.[4] RDC claimed that the SDB program was unconstitutional, both on its face and as applied, because the program denied it equal protection by treating minority and nonminority businesses differently.[5] Prior litigation had resolved the as-applied challenge in RDC's favor,[6] and, in its decision, the Federal Circuit resolved the facial challenge in RDC's favor as well. The Federal Circuit found that DOD's SDB program was unconstitutional because, when re-enacting the program in 2006, Congress lacked a "strong basis in evidence" for concluding that race-conscious contracting was necessary to remedy discrimination in the defense industry.[7]

The Federal Circuit's decision in *Rothe* prompted much debate. For example, Representative Edolphus Towns, chairman of the House Committee on Oversight and Government Reform, reportedly signaled his intention to hold hearings on discrimination in federal contracting in the hopes of ensuring a strong basis in evidence for future programs,[8] and the Bush Administration extended the comment period for a proposed rule on federal contracting programs for women- owned small businesses, in part because of *Rothe*.[9] Although not subject to strict scrutiny like race-conscious programs are, gender-based programs also receive heightened scrutiny from the courts, and the SBA "is reviewing" how the evidence underlying its determinations regarding the industries in which women are "substantially underrepresented" might fare under the standards set by *Rothe*.[10] Commentators also questioned the constitutionality of other federal contracting programs for "disadvantaged" small businesses in light of the *Rothe* decision.[11] Such commentators wonder whether the government could demonstrate a "strong basis in evidence" for these programs, which include the subcontracting programs under Sections 8(a) and (d) of the Small Business Act, if they were challenged.

The Federal Circuit's decision in *Rothe* was followed on February 27, 2009, by a decision of the U.S. District Court for the Western District of Texas, San Antonio Division, to which the case had been remanded for entry of judgment. [12] This decision enjoined defense agencies from implementing other programs authorized by Section 1207 because these programs were "contingent" on the subsections containing the price preference and must "also fall" when those subsections did.[13] These programs included technical and infrastructure assistance for certain minority-serving institutions (MSIs) of higher education, including historically black colleges and universities (HBCUs), Hispanic-serving institutions (HSIs), Alaska Native- and Native Hawaiian- serving institutions (ANNHIs), and majority-minority institutions (MMIs).[14] However, the first session of the 111th Congress responded to the District Court's decision by enacting legislation authorizing defense agencies to provide assistance similar to that authorized under Section 1207 to MSIs.[15]

The report examines the *Rothe* decision in detail; describes existing contracting programs for minority-owned and women-owned small businesses; and analyzes Rothe's potential effect on these programs, including the Business Development Program under Section 8(a) of the Small Business Act.

BACKGROUND

DOD's Small Disadvantaged Business Program

The *Rothe* case involved a constitutional challenge to one specific federal program for minority- owned small businesses: DOD's SDB program. This program was created by Section 1207 of the Department of Defense Authorization Act of 1987, which was captioned "Contract Goal for Minorities."[16] Section 1207 established, as a goal for DOD, that 5% of DOD's contract dollars for procurement, research and development, testing and evaluation, military construction, and operations and maintenance be awarded to "small business concerns ... owned and controlled by socially and economically disadvantaged individuals."[17] Section 1207 further required or allowed DOD to take certain steps in meeting this 5% goal. Among the steps DOD was required to take were (1) making advance payments[18] and (2) providing "technical assistance," such as advice regarding DOD procurement procedures and instruction in preparing proposals. DOD was also given discretion to "enter into contracts using less than full and open competitive procedures," which included applying price evaluation adjustments[19] of up to 10% to offers submitted by small disadvantaged businesses.[20] For purposes of the SDB program, "socially and economically disadvantaged" had the same meaning it has under Section 8(d) of the Small Business Act, which presumes that minorities are socially and economically disadvantaged but allows non-minorities to demonstrate disadvantage.[21]

Although Section 1207 originally applied only to DOD and only for FY1987 to FY1989, its reenactments encompassed the National Aeronautics and Space Administration (NASA) and the Coast Guard, as well as all fiscal years between 1989 and 2009.[22] These periodic re-enactments of Section 1207 to extend DOD's "contracting goal for minorities," illustrated by

Table 1, ultimately determined the outcome in *Rothe* because, according to the Federal Circuit, Congress did not have sufficient evidence of racial discrimination in defense contracting when it re-enacted Section 1207 in 2006. The Federal Acquisition Streamlining Act (FASA) temporarily granted other federal agencies the same authority that DOD, NASA, and the Coast Guard had under Section 1207.[23] However, these provisions of FASA were not reauthorized when they expired at the end of FY2000.[24]

The 5% goal for contracting with small disadvantaged businesses under Section 1207 is not the only government-wide or DOD goal for contracting with such businesses. Sections 644(g)(1) and (2) of the Small Business Act require (1) that the federal government award at least 5% of all contract dollars to small disadvantaged businesses and (2) that DOD establish, in conjunction with the SBA, similar goals that "realistically reflect the potential of ... small business concerns owned and controlled by socially and economically disadvantaged individuals ... to perform such contracts and to perform subcontracts under such contracts."[25] In FY2007, DOD's goal for contracting with small disadvantaged businesses under 15 U.S.C. § 644(g)(2) was 5.8%, and DOD met this goal.[26] However, while 15 U.S.C. § 644(g) establishes or requires goals for contracting with small disadvantaged businesses, such goals are purely aspirational. Section 644(g) does not authorize agencies to use price evaluation adjustments—or any other mechanism—to attain contracting goals. The constitutionality of § 644(g) was not challenged in *Rothe*, nor was that of any other federal contracting program benefiting minority-owned small businesses.

The Facts Underlying the *Rothe* Litigation

The constitutionality of Section 1207 was at issue in the *Rothe* case because DOD used its price evaluation adjustment authority under Section 1207 in awarding a contract to a competitor of the Rothe Development Corporation (RDC). Beginning in the late 1980s, RDC had a contract with the Department of the Air Force to maintain, operate, and repair computer systems at Columbus Air Force Base in Mississippi.[27] In the late 1 990s, the Air Force decided to consolidate the contract that RDC had with a contract for communications services.[28] When doing so, it also decided to let the contract pursuant to Section 1207 and issued a solicitation for competitive bids.[29] RDC bid $5.57 million.[30] However, RDC was not a small disadvantaged business, and International Computer and Telecommunications, Inc. (ICT), a minority-owned small business eligible for the price evaluation adjustment under Section 1207, bid $5.75 million.[31] When 10% (or $575,000) was subtracted from ICT's bid, its bid was lowest, and the Air Force awarded the contract to it.

Table 1. Chronology of Section 1207 Dates of Enactment and Re-enactment.

Year	Period of Extension
1986	3 years
1989	7 years
1999	3 years
2002	3 years
2006	3 years

Source: Congressional Research Service.

RDC filed suit in U.S. District Court for the Western District of Texas, San Antonio Division, alleging that Section 1207 deprived it of equal protection under the U.S. Constitution both as applied and on its face.[32] RDC's as-applied challenge focused upon Section 1207 in its 1992 reenactment, which governed DOD's award of the contract to ICT, while RDC's facial challenge ultimately focused upon the 2006 re-enactment of Section 1207, which was in effect at the time when the Federal Circuit heard the appeal. DOD countered that Section 1207 "satisfies the strict scrutiny standard established by the United States Supreme Court in *Adarand v. Peña*."[33] DOD did not contest whether Section 1207's presumption regarding race and disadvantage constituted a racial classification subjecting its SDB program to strict scrutiny.[34]

The Constitutional Principles at Issue in *Rothe*

The claims and defenses of the parties to the *Rothe* litigation rested on the U.S. Constitution and case law interpreting it. The Fifth Amendment to the Constitution guarantees due process of law to individuals in their dealings with the federal government.[35] Due process under the Fifth Amendment includes equal protection, or the constitutional assurance that the government will apply the law equally to all people and not improperly prefer one class of people over another.[36] For this reason, consideration of race by the federal government, even when intended to remedy past discrimination, is constitutional only if it meets the so-called strict scrutiny test, which requires that a race-conscious government program be narrowly tailored to further a compelling government interest.[37] An alleged government interest qualifies as a compelling one, for due process or equal protection purposes, only when the government entity creating the racial classification (1) identified public or private discrimination with some specificity before resorting to race-conscious remedies and (2) had a "strong basis in evidence" to conclude that race- conscious remedies were necessary before enacting or implementing these remedies.[38] As regards the "strong basis in evidence" requirement, the government has the burden of producing statistical evidence sufficient to support an inference of discrimination.[39] Once the government has done this, the plaintiffs challenging the government's action have the burden of persuasion in refuting the government's evidence and establishing race-neutral explanations for any apparent racial disparities alleged by the government.[40] Plaintiffs can do this by, among other things, showing that the government's statistics are flawed; demonstrating that the disparities shown by the government's statistics are not significant; or presenting contrasting statistical data of their own.[41]

Prior Litigation in the *Rothe* Case

In applying the legal tests for equal protection to the facts of the case, the federal courts issued several opinions prior to the Federal Circuit's November 2008 decision. On April 27, 1999, the district court granted summary judgment to DOD, upholding the constitutionality of Section 1207 and denying RDC relief, because it found "no illegitimate purpose, no racial preference, and no racial stereotyping" at work in Section 1207.[42] RDC appealed to the U.S.

Court of Appeals for the Fifth Circuit, which transferred the case to the Federal Circuit because RDC asserted claims under the Tucker Act as well as under the U.S. Constitution.[43] Tucker Act claims are within the exclusive appellate jurisdiction of the Federal Circuit.[44] It was because of this transfer of the case from the Fifth Circuit to the Federal Circuit that the Federal Circuit decided *Rothe* using Fifth Circuit law.[45] The Federal Circuit's reliance on Fifth Circuit precedent does not make Rothe precedent for the Fifth Circuit, however, because federal circuits are not bound by other circuits' interpretations of their law.[46] On November 8, 2000, the Federal Circuit vacated the district court's decision and remanded the case for further proceedings because the district court, in finding for DOD, had not applied strict scrutiny and impermissibly considered evidence of discrimination that arose after Section 1207 had been re-enacted.[47]

On July 2, 2004, the district court issued a second opinion, holding that Section 1207 was unconstitutional as applied in 1998, but constitutional on its face.[48] In reaching this holding, the court found that while DOD failed to demonstrate that Congress had sufficient evidence of discrimination when it re-enacted Section 1207 in 1992, DOD had shown that Congress had such evidence when it re-enacted Section 1207 in 2002. RDC appealed to the Federal Circuit, which affirmed the district court on the as-applied challenge and remanded the case for consideration of the merits of the facial challenge.[49] When the district court again granted summary judgment to DOD on RDC's facial challenge,[50] RDC filed the appeal that that gave rise to the Federal Circuit's decision on November 4, 2008. The primary question at issue in the decision that would become "*Rothe* VII" was whether Section 1207 was unconstitutional on its face as re-enacted in 2006.[51]

Federal Circuit's Decision Finding Section 1207 Unconstitutional

In its November 4, 2008, decision, the Federal Circuit found that Section 1207 was unconstitutional on its face because, when Congress re-enacted Section 1207 in 2006, it lacked a strong basis in evidence for concluding that race-conscious contracting was necessary to remedy discrimination in the defense industry.[52] The district court, which had upheld the constitutionality of the challenged SDB program in "*Rothe VI*," had found that six state and local disparity studies, along with other statistical and anecdotal evidence, constituted a strong basis in evidence for the re-enactment of Section 1207.[53] The Federal Circuit disagreed.[54] It found that the six state and local disparity studies—which had been the "primary focus of the district court's compelling interest analysis and of the parties' arguments on appeal"[55]—did not constitute a strong basis in evidence because they did not provide the "substantially probative and broad-based statistical foundation ... that must be the predicate for nationwide, race-conscious action."[56]

The Federal Circuit first found significant methodological flaws with all of the disparity studies. According to the Federal Circuit, two of the six studies failed to exclude unqualified businesses in calculating the number of minority businesses available for government contracts,[57] while five of the six studies failed to account for the relative capacity of minority-owned small businesses in contracting with the government.[58] These flaws, coupled with the fact that the studies' findings addressed only six of the more than 3,000 counties and equivalent regions making up the United States, prompted the Federal Circuit to find that the studies were insufficient to constitute a strong basis in evidence for the nationwide SDB program.[59] The Federal Circuit also suggested, although it reached no final holding on the issue, that the studies were not "before Congress" when Section 1207 was reenacted because they were mentioned by name or discussed only in two floor speeches and Congress did not make any findings concerning them. [60]

The Federal Circuit similarly found that other statistical data and anecdotes discussed by the parties and the district court were insufficient to constitute a strong basis in evidence for the SDB program.[61] The Federal Circuit discounted the remaining statistical evidence because it was mentioned only in floor speeches, without being the subject of congressional findings. In fact, the court noted that some of the purported evidence was not even "sufficiently described ... for [the Federal Circuit] to locate [it], let alone subject [it] to detailed, skeptical, non-deferential analysis."[62] It likewise discounted the anecdotal evidence, even though this evidence had been introduced at congressional hearings, because "anecdotal evidence is insufficient by itself to support *Section 1207*."[63] The Federal Circuit further noted that the anecdotal evidence, including that compiled by the district court, did not address "a single instance of alleged discrimination by DOD in the course of awarding a prime contract, nor a single instance of alleged discrimination by a private contractor identified as the recipient of a prime defense contract."[64] The Federal Circuit found this lack of evidence of discrimination in DOD contracts significant because it suggested that the government could not prove "passive participation" in discrimination, as required under *City of Richmond v. Croson*, as a justification for DOD's SDB program. [65] Under Croson, a government entity can resort to racial classifications in situations when it is not remedying its own prior discrimination if it can show it is a "passive participant" in a system of racial exclusion practiced by industry.[66]

District Court's Judgment Prohibiting Section 1207 Programs for Minority-Serving Institutions

At the end of its decision in *Rothe* VII, the Federal Circuit remanded the case to the U.S. District Court for the Western District of Texas, San Antonio Division, with instructions for the district court to enter a judgment declaring Section 1207, as re-enacted in 2006, facially unconstitutional and enjoining application of the current 10 U.S.C. § 2323.[67] The district court entered its judgment on February 27, 2009, prohibiting defense agencies not only from implementing price evaluation adjustments for offers from small disadvantaged businesses but also from implementing technical and infrastructure assistance programs for certain minority-serving institutions (MSIs) of higher education,[68] including historically black colleges and universities (HBCUs), Hispanic-serving institutions (HSIs), Alaska Native- and Native Hawaiian-serving institutions (ANNHIs), and majority-minority institutions (MMIs).[69]

Although the government argued on remand that the judgment should be limited to subsections (a)(1)(A) and (e)(3) of Section 1207, which incorporated the price evaluation adjustment authority applicable to the offers of small disadvantaged businesses that had been the focus of the parties' arguments and the Federal Circuit's decision,[70] the district court disagreed.[71] It struck down the totality of Section 1207 as presently codified in 10 U.S.C. § 2323, including

1. Provisions in subsection (a)(1)(A)-(D) allowing awards to qualified HUBZone small businesses, HBCUs, HSIs, ANNHIs, and MMIs to count toward DOD's 5% goal;
2. Provisions in subsections (c)(1)-(4) authorizing DOD to provide technical assistance to entities counting toward its 5% goal, as well as infrastructure assistance to minority institutions;[72]
3. Provisions in subsection (e)(2) allowing DOD to make advance payments to qualifying entities; and
4. Provisions in sections (f)-(k) containing definitions and addressing implementation of DOD's SDB program.[73]

In so deciding, the district court specifically rejected arguments that any preferences for HUBZone businesses are race neutral and that RDC lacks standing to challenge infrastructure assistance to colleges and universities.[74] The court's reasoning in doing so, and in issuing its judgment, was that the Federal Circuit struck down the totality of section (a) in its decision, and sections (b) through (k) are contingent upon section (a) and must "also fall" when section (a) does.[75]

On March 10, 2009, the Under Secretary of Defense (Acquisition, Technology & Logistics) responded to the District Court's decision by directing that

> ... any activity, which includes but is not limited to the award of contracts and orders under contracts, advance payments, and the award of grants or scholarships or the addition of funds to existing grants and scholarships, that rely exclusively on the authority of 10 U.S.C. § 2323 should cease.[76]

A subsequent memorandum from the Department of the Army clarified that, for purposes of Army programs, options under existing contracts "should be treated ... as separate contract action[s] and the contracting organization should not exercise the option if the funding authority for the underlying contract stemmed solely from Title 10 U.S.C. Section 2323."[77] The memorandum also stated that the Army's goals for assistance to HBCUs remain in effect as aspirational goals and that pre-existing agreements with HBCUs could be continued until they lapse because the district court's decision was prospective and governed only contracting and other actions initiated after February 26, 2009.[78]

The first session of the 111th Congress responded to the district court's decision, in part, by establishing a new program to assist HBCUs, HSIs, ANNHIs, MMIs, and other MSIs in performing "defense-related research, development, testing, and evaluation activities."[79] Among the forms of assistance that defense agencies may provide under this program are grants, scholarships, fellowships, and the acquisition of research equipment and instrumentation.[80] Because this legislation has already somewhat ameliorated the effects of the district court's decision on minority educational institutions, the following discussion focuses upon the potential effects of the Federal Circuit's decision upon federal contracting programs for small businesses.

IMPLICATIONS OF THE *ROTHE* DECISION FOR FEDERAL SMALL-BUSINESS CONTRACTING PROGRAMS

As numerous commentators and the SBA have recognized, the Federal Circuit's decision in *Rothe* could have significant implications for the percentage of federal contract dollars awarded to minority-owned small businesses and for other federal contracting programs for small businesses.[81] The demise of DOD's price evaluation adjustment authority under Section 1207 is not, in itself, necessarily all that significant, in part because other provisions of law have precluded DOD from exercising this authority for over a decade. Potentially more serious is the effect that the *Rothe* decision could have on other programs for small disadvantaged businesses, which minority-owned small businesses are presumed to be. The Rothe decision arguably suggests grounds upon which potential plaintiffs might be able to successfully challenge these programs. The *Rothe* decision could also potentially leave programs for women-owned small businesses vulnerable to constitutional challenges. While not subject to strict scrutiny like the program for minority contractors at issue in *Rothe*, these programs are subject to heightened scrutiny rather than rational basis review, which is the most deferential form of judicial scrutiny.[82] Other programs for small businesses should be unaffected by the *Rothe* decision.

Will *Rothe* Lead to a Decline in Federal Contracting with Minority- Owned Businesses?

Many commentators concerned about the potential effects of the *Rothe* decision have noted that the decision could cause the percentage of federal contract dollars awarded to minority-owned small businesses to decrease because it bars DOD from making price evaluation adjustments to the offers of minority-owned small businesses.[83] This concern has some basis, both because of DOD's prominent role in federal procurement activities and because Section 1207 was unique, among existing federal laws, in coupling contracting goals with authority to take specific steps in attempting to meet these goals. DOD accounts for a larger share of federal contract spending than all other federal agencies combined. In FY2008, DOD spent $392.1 billion on contract awards, or 74% of the $529.8 billion that the federal government spent on such awards.[84] DOD's prominent role in federal contracting would make it difficult for the federal government to meet its contracting goals for minority-owned small businesses if DOD failed to meet its goals, and DOD's authority under Section 1207 was the sole means of ensuring that DOD could meet its minority-contracting goal. Section 1207 was, in fact, the only provision under current federal law giving agencies authority to take specific steps in meeting their contracting goals.[85] At various times in the past, other provisions of federal law gave other agencies similar price evaluation adjustment authority, or gave DOD and other agencies other authority to take specific steps to increase the percentage of federal contract dollars awarded to minority-owned businesses.[86] However, these authorities were gradually removed by judicial decisions, agency rule-making or congressional action, leaving only Section 1207.[87] In short, by precluding DOD from using its authority under Section 1207, the *Rothe* decision effectively removes the only mechanism that the agency responsible for the vast majority of federal contracting could rely upon to ensure awards to minority-owned small businesses in certain circumstances (i.e., when the offers of such businesses were within 10% of what would otherwise be the lowest-priced offer).

Despite the existence of such grounds for concern, however, the *Rothe* decision, in itself, does not necessarily portend an immediate decline in federal contracting with minority-owned small businesses. There are two related reasons for this. First, because of other provisions of law, DOD has not exercised its price evaluation adjustment authority under Section 1207 for over a decade. Section 801 of the Strom Thurmond National Defense Authorization Act for Fiscal Year 1999 barred DOD from granting price evaluation adjustments in any fiscal year directly following a fiscal year in which DOD awarded at least 5% of its contract dollars to small disadvantaged businesses.[88] Because DOD met this goal in every fiscal year between 1997 and the present, Section 801 has operated to keep DOD from granting price evaluation adjustments in every fiscal year between 1998 and 2009.[89] Arguably, only if DOD failed to award at least 5% of its contract dollars to small disadvantaged businesses in a future fiscal year, or if Section 801 were repealed, would the full effects of *Rothe* on contracting with minority-owned small businesses be felt. Second, the 5% goal for contracting with small disadvantaged businesses established by Section 1207 is not DOD's only goal for contracting with such businesses. Similar goals are required under other provisions of law, most notably 15 U.S.C. § 644(g)(2), whose constitutionality was not at issue in *Rothe*.[90] Under 15 U.S.C. § 644(g)(2), DOD's goal for contracting with minority- owned small businesses was 5.8% in FY2007, and DOD met this goal.[91] In FY2007, many other agencies also had and met goals for contracting with minority-owned small businesses that exceed 5%.[92] The SBA's "Procurement Scorecards," which highlight agencies' achievements in contracting with various subcategories of small businesses, may help to keep agencies and the general public attuned to contracting goals and progress toward them.[93]

What Effect Could *Rothe* Have on Other Minority Contracting Programs?

Even if the demise of price evaluation adjustment authority under Section 1207 does not trigger an immediate decline in federal contracting with minority-owned small businesses, however, the *Rothe* decision could still have profound implications for such businesses by suggesting possible grounds for constitutional challenges to other programs.[94] The loss of some of these programs, particularly the Business Development Program under Section 8(a) of the Small Business Act, could potentially have a much more significant impact on minority-owned small businesses than the loss of DOD's SDB program, especially given the limits already placed on DOD's exercise of its price evaluation adjustment authority by other legislation. Small businesses participating in the 8(a) Business Development Program received $6.3 billion in revenue through the program in FY2008.[95] This amount is down somewhat from FY2006, when it reached $7.1 billion,[96] but still represents $6.3 billion that such businesses would not be assured of receiving in the absence of the 8(a) Program.

Overview of Existing Programs

There are currently several government-wide programs providing contracting assistance to small businesses at least 51% owned and unconditionally controlled by socially and economically disadvantaged individuals. These programs include

- aspirational goals for the percentage of prime contracts and subcontracts awarded to small disadvantaged businesses by the federal government, as a whole, and by individual federal agencies;[97]
- subcontracting agencies' prime contracts to small businesses owned and controlled by socially and economically disadvantaged individuals through the SBA under the 8(a) Business Development Program;[98]
- contract clauses and plans relating to subcontracting with small disadvantaged businesses that are incorporated into agencies' prime contracts and bind their prime contractors;[99]
- use of evaluation factors and monetary incentives in awarding agencies' prime contracts so as to encourage agencies' contractors to subcontract with small disadvantaged businesses;[100] and
- technical assistance and outreach programs for small disadvantaged businesses participating in the 8(a) Business Development Program.[101]

Because all of these programs include presumptions that minorities are socially and, sometimes, economically disadvantaged like the presumption underlying DOD's SDB program,[102] they also arguably entail the same sort of "explicit racial classification" that DOD's SDB program did.[103]

Potential Vulnerability of Existing Programs

Although all existing federal contracting assistance programs rely upon presumptions about disadvantage and race similar to that in Section 1207, not all of them may be equally vulnerable to constitutional challenges like that in *Rothe*. Some programs, such those involving aspirational goals and technical assistance and outreach, are probably immune from successful constitutional challenges because of the type of assistance provided, as well as difficulties that potential plaintiffs could have in establishing standing to challenge such programs. In comparison, other programs, such as the subcontracting programs under Sections 8(a) and (d) of the Small Business Act or the Federal Acquisition Regulation (FAR), may be more vulnerable because (1) standing often exists for bid protests and contract disputes and (2) *Rothe* could be precedent for the court hearing such cases. Even the comparatively more vulnerable programs could, however, potentially survive a constitutional challenge like that in *Rothe* depending upon the evidence of discrimination that was before Congress when it enacted or re-enacted the program.

Aspirational Goals

Aspirational goals encouraging the federal government or individual federal agencies to award certain percentages of their contract dollars to small disadvantaged businesses [104] are probably not vulnerable to constitutional challenges like that in *Rothe.*[105] Although aspirational goals reflect classifications among small businesses based on the race or ethnicity of their owners, among other factors, the mere existence of such classifications is generally not problematic because such goals are voluntary, not mandatory, and thus do not constitute disparate treatment of small business owners by the federal government.[106] Broadly speaking, the government can set goals for itself as it wishes. Problems arise only when the government takes actions to realize its goals that result in the disparate treatment of individuals who are similarly situated, and aspirational goals do not authorize or allow actions that would cause disparate treatment. The situation would be different if agencies also had authority to take specific steps to meet their contracting goals for small disadvantaged businesses, such as DOD had under Section 1207. However, no agencies other than DOD, NASA, and the Coast Guard had such authority immediately prior to *Rothe* ,[107] and *Rothe* precludes NASA and the Coast Guard, as well as DOD, from exercising this authority under Section 1207.[108]

Technical Assistance and Outreach

Technical assistance and outreach programs for minority-owned small businesses are also unlikely to be vulnerable to constitutional challenges like that in *Rothe*, at least when they are not "contingent" upon other programs that are found unconstitutional. [109] In considering such programs in 1996, in the aftermath of the Supreme Court's decision in *Adarand Constructors v. Peña*, the Department of Justice (DOJ) noted that, "[a]s a general proposition, these activities are not subject to strict scrutiny" even when they are targeted to minorities.[110] DOJ did not articulate the rationale for this statement, but was probably relying on judicial precedents holding that minority outreach and recruitment efforts are not subject to strict scrutiny because they do not subject individuals to unequal treatment.[111] Moreover, a court's opportunity to repudiate these precedents could be limited by the inability of potential plaintiffs to demonstrate standing to challenge technical assistance and outreach programs. The doctrine of standing requires that plaintiffs demonstrate (1) injury in fact, (2) causation, and (3) redressibility before a court hears the merits of their claims.[112] Standing to challenge technical assistance or outreach programs targeted to minorities could be difficult to show, in part because plaintiffs' injuries would lie in their allegedly decreased ability to compete with minority firms that are better managed and better informed about agencies' contracting opportunities. Even if such remote injuries were recognized, it would be hard to show that plaintiffs' decreased ability to compete with minority firms was primarily due to the federal programs, or would be remedied by the programs' cessation. Courts generally do not recognize "taxpayer standing," so potential plaintiffs could not claim to be harmed by the government's spending their tax dollars on technical assistance and outreach programs for minority-owned small businesses.[113]

Subcontracting Programs: 8(a), 8(d), Evaluation Factors, & Monetary Incentives

The various programs relating to subcontracting on agency prime contracts—the programs under the authority of Sections 8(a) and (d) of the Small Business Act and the Federal Acquisition Regulation (FAR)—are probably the most susceptible to *Rothe*-type challenges of all federal contracting programs for minority-owned small businesses. This heightened susceptibility arises, in part, because these programs allow agencies to take more concrete steps to assist small disadvantaged businesses than are involved in seeking to "expand [their] participation" in agency procurement contracts.[114] Furthermore, these programs could potentially be seen as subjecting individuals to different treatment by, for example, setting aside contracts for competitions limited to small businesses participating in the 8(a) Business Development Program. This heightened susceptibility is also due to the fact that these programs would likely be challenged in bid protests or contract disputes where potential plaintiffs often have standing and *Rothe* could be precedent. Various provisions of federal law provide that disappointed bidders or offerors, or would-be bidders or offerors, have standing to challenge agencies' procurement activities.[115] Challenges could thus potentially be made to agencies' decisions to subcontract certain prime contracts through the 8(a) program; require certain percentages of subcontracts under 8(d) subcontracting plans; award a contract based on evaluation factors that include subcontracting with small disadvantaged businesses; or use monetary incentives for subcontracting with small disadvantaged businesses that could prompt a prime contractor to favor a minority-contractor over a nonminority one.[116] Other provisions of federal law likewise provide incumbent contractors with standing to challenge agency actions in contract disputes,[117] such as could be triggered by terminating a contractor or imposing liquidated damages for failure to abide by an 8(d) subcontracting plan.[118]

In some of these cases, especially outside the 8(a) context, standing could potentially be hard to show because the injuries arguably become more remote—and less likely to be redressed by changes in government programs—when subcontractors allege that prime contractors did not select them due to aspects of federal programs that are arguably aspirational, not mandatory.

Subcontracting plans under 8(d), for example, merely require agencies to "encourage subcontracting opportunities" for small disadvantaged businesses and call for such businesses to "have the maximum practicable opportunity to participate in the performance of contracts."[119] The plans do not require or authorize agencies' prime contractors to take any specific steps to meet their goals under the plans. However, assuming standing were shown, *Rothe* could serve as precedent for the court deciding the challenge for several reasons. First, the U.S. Court of Federal Claims and the Federal Circuit are the only judicial forums with jurisdiction to hear federal bid protests and contract disputes,[120] and the Court of Federal Claims is subject to the precedents of the Federal Circuit.[121] Second, even assuming the constitutional challenge arose outside of a bid protest or contract dispute, plaintiffs can generally select their forum and would have little incentive to avoid courts where *Rothe* is precedent because *Rothe* arguably works in favor of those challenging the constitutionality of federal contracting programs for minority-owned small businesses.

Even when standing exists and *Rothe* is precedent, however, the programs under Sections 8(a) and (d) of the Small Business Act, as well as the evaluation factors and monetary incentives under the FAR, are arguably distinguishable from the price evaluation adjustment authority at issue in *Rothe* in ways that could potentially enable them to survive constitutional challenges. While not a rigid quota setting aside a fixed percentage of DOD contract dollars for minority-owned businesses, the 5% goal in Section 1207 can be seen as quota-like when coupled with the price evaluation adjustment authority. None of the other federal programs combine aspirational goals with mechanisms to meet them. Neither Section 8(a) of the Small Business Act nor the FAR seeks to have any fixed percentage of subcontracts awarded to minority-owned small businesses. Section 8(a) merely gives agencies discretion to subcontract through SBA when they "determine[] such action is necessary or appropriate,"[122] while the FAR says only that agencies "may consider" prime contractors' performance in subcontracting with small disadvantaged businesses as an evaluation factor and "may encourage increased subcontracting opportunities ... by providing monetary incentives."[123] Similarly, while the subcontracting plans required under Section 8(d) of the Small Business Act include percentage goals and potential sanctions (e.g., breach, liquidated damages) for failure to meet these goals,[124] Section 8(d) does not require or authorize contractors to take any specific or concrete steps in meeting their contracting goals. In fact, contractors' failure to meet goals in their 8(d) subcontracting plans is excused, by law, so long as the contractors acted in good faith in attempting to abide by the plan. [125]

Furthermore, evidence of discrimination sufficient to justify race-conscious programs might have been before Congress when it enacted, or re-enacted, one or all of these programs. The "strong basis in evidence" test focuses specifically upon the evidence that was before Congress when it decided to create a race-conscious remedy in response to purported discrimination. Each program is likely to have unique evidence underlying it, and the "failure" of the evidence underlying one program does not necessarily mean that the evidence underlying other programs would also prove inadequate. It is also possible that, even if Congress lacked a strong basis in evidence when enacting the statutes that authorize the evaluation factors and monetary incentives under the FAR, a sufficient basis for these programs was nonetheless created by the Secretary of Commerce's determinations about the industries in which these authorities may be exercised. By law, agencies can use evaluation factors and monetary incentives only when contracting in industries where the Secretary has found "substantial and pervasive evidence of ... persistent and significant underutilization of minority firms ... attributable to past discrimination and ... demonstrated incapacity to alleviate the problem by using [other] mechanisms."[126]

What Effect Could *Rothe* Have on Contracting Programs for Women-Owned Small Businesses?

Shortly after the Federal Circuit issued its decision in *Rothe*, the Small Business Administration (SBA) extended the comment period on its proposed rule for the contracting assistance program for women-owned small businesses under Section 8(m) of the Small Business Act. [127] The SBA did so, in part, because government programs that classify people on the basis of gender also involve a suspect classification for purposes of equal protection review under the Constitution. Gender classifications are subject to intermediate scrutiny, which is less rigid than strict scrutiny but nonetheless requires the government to show that gender classifications are substantially related to important government objectives.[128] In extending the comment period, the SBA indicated that it wanted to "review[]" the evidence underlying its determinations that women are underrepresented in certain industries.[129]

The SBA never finalized this proposed rule. However, on March 4, 2010, the SBA issued new proposed regulations for the set-aside program for women-owned small businesses. [130] The SBA does not explicitly address *Rothe* in its introductory comments on these regulations. However, it notes that comments on earlier proposed rules indicated that the "disparity study analysis" conducted in identifying industries eligible for set-asides "is sufficient to satisfy the intermediate scrutiny standard that applies to the WOSB [women-owned small business] Program."[131] It also states that:

> The means chosen by Congress to implement the WOSB Program ensure that the Program is substantially related to its goals. Congress expressly limited application of the WOSB Program only to industries in which women are substantially underrepresented or underrepresented in contracting.[132]

The SBA may or may not be correct in stating that the set-asides for women-owned small businesses would survive intermediate scrutiny if challenged. It is, however, probably correct in identifying the disparity studies underlying the determinations of eligible industries as a likely focus of any constitutional challenges.

What Effect Could *Rothe* Have on Other Contracting Programs for Small Businesses?

The Rothe decision should have no effect on other federal contracting programs for small businesses generally, or for small businesses owned by members of other demographic groups, including blind and handicapped individuals; Native Americans,[133] including Native Alaskans; veterans; service-disabled veterans; and individuals operating businesses in Historically Underutilized Business Zones (HUBZones).[134] Only programs that rely upon suspect classifications, such as race or gender, are subject to strict or intermediate scrutiny when their constitutionality is challenged. Programs based on non-suspect classifications—such as business size, military status, disability, geography, or poverty—are subject only to rational basis review, which is characterized by deference to legislative judgment. Under rational basis review, a challenged program will be found constitutional if it is rationally related to a legitimate government interest.[135] As a result, programs reviewed under this standard are generally upheld. [136]

CONGRESS'S ROLE IN ESTABLISHING FUTURE PROGRAMS

Currently, the extent to which the courts will apply the reasoning in *Rothe* to future legal challenges is unclear. As a result, it is difficult to provide clear guidance regarding the requirements that Congress must meet when enacting legislation that may be subject to equal protection review. However, a few points may be made.

First, if enacting race-conscious measures or other legislation that will be subject to strict scrutiny, Congress will be required to establish a "strong basis in evidence" to support the articulated compelling governmental interest. This requirement for a "strong basis in evidence" was originally introduced by the Supreme Court in *Wygant v. Jackson Board of Education*.[137] Over the years, subsequent court cases have provided some clarification of the meaning and nature of a "strong basis in evidence" by finding that such a basis existed,[138] or was lacking,[139] in particular circumstances. As these cases suggest, the *Rothe* court, which required the government to show the same types of evidence of racial discrimination as were required in other cases and subjected this evidence to the same scrutiny other courts had given it, arguably did not depart significantly from precedent in its approach to the "strong basis in evidence" requirement.

Nevertheless, *Rothe* appears to be the latest in a long line of cases that place an increasingly heavy evidentiary burden on Congress. In the immediate aftermath of the Court's landmark decision in *Adarand Constructors v. Peña,*[140] which, for the first time, applied strict scrutiny to racial preferences in federal contracting programs, the federal courts generally stressed deference to congressional authority to conduct fact-finding and to enact remedial legislation pursuant to Section 5 of the Fourteenth Amendment. This deference to congressional authority has eroded over the years. As a result, Congress must now support any race-conscious measures it enacts by developing a strong record, as demonstrated in hearings and legislative findings, of methodologically sound, broad statistical evidence of discrimination capable of withstanding searching judicial inquiry.

End Notes

[1] Rothe Dev. Corp. v. Dep't of Defense, 545 F.3d 1023 (Fed. Cir. 2008). The government did not seek certiorari from the Supreme Court.

[2] 10 U.S.C. § 2323(a)(1) (5% goal); 10 U.S.C. § 2323(e)(3)(A) (10% price evaluation adjustment).

[3] 15 U.S.C. § 637(d)(3)(C)(ii) ("The contractor shall presume that socially and economically disadvantaged individuals include Black Americans, Hispanic Americans, Native Americans, Asian Pacific Americans, and other minorities, or any other individual found to be disadvantaged by the [Small Business] Administration pursuant to section 8(a) of the Small Business Act."); 13 C.F.R. § 124.1002 (addressing requirements for proving social and economic disadvantage).

[4] Rothe Dev. Corp., 545 F.3d at 1029.

[5] *Id.* at 1026.

[6] *See* Rothe Dev. Corp. v. Dep't of Defense, 324 F. Supp. 2d 840, 850 (W.D. Tex. 2004).

[7] Rothe Dev. Corp., 545 F.3d at 1049.

[8] *See, e.g.*, Joe Davidson, Another Obstacle for Affirmative Action, and Congress Is Prepared to Fight, *Wash. Post*, Dec. 3, 2008, at D1.

[9] *See* U.S. Small Bus. Admin., The Women-Owned Small Business Federal Contract Assistance Procedures: Eligible Industries, 74 Fed. Reg. 1153 (Jan. 12, 2009). This proposed rule has since been withdrawn, and the Obama Administration has issued new proposed regulations for the set-aside program for women-owned small businesses. *See* U.S. Small Bus. Admin., Women-Owned Small Business Federal Contract Program: Proposed Rule, 75 Fed. Reg. 10029 (Mar. 4, 2010).

[10] *Id. See also* 15 U.S.C. § 637(m)(2)(C) (limiting any contracting set-asides for women-owned small businesses to industries in which the SBA has determined that such businesses are underrepresented).

[11] *See, e.g.*, Ruling Threatens 8(a) Program, Unless Congress Acts, *Set-Aside Alert*, Nov. 21, 2008; Elizabeth Newell, Decision in Defense Procurement Case Could Set Precedent, *GovExec.com*, Nov. 11, 2008, *available at* http://www.govexec.com/dailyfed/1108/111108e1.htm ("The 8(a) program is not dead yet but this decision, if allowed to stand, could really have an impact on the 8(a) program should another contractor try a similar challenge."). A legal challenge to the 8(a) Program like that in *Rothe* is pending in the U.S. District Court for the District of Columbia. *See* Dynalantic Corp. v. U.S. Dep't of Defense, 503 F. Supp. 2d 262 (D.D.C. 2007) (denying parties' motions for summary judgment).

[12] Rothe Dev. Corp. v. Dep't of Defense, 2009 U.S. Dist. LEXIS 22029, at *12 (W.D. Tex. 2009).

[13] *Id.* at *11-14.

[14] 10 U.S.C. § 2323(c)(1)-(3).

[15] National Defense Authorization Act for FY2010, P.L. 111-84, § 252, 123 Stat. 2242-43 (Oct. 28, 2009). Similar provisions have also been introduced as part of the Coast Guard Authorization Act of 2010, H.R. 3619, § 221.

[16] P.L. 99-661, § 1207, 100 Stat. 3816, 3973-75 (Nov. 14, 1986) (codified at 10 U.S.C. § 2323).

[17] *Id.* at § 1207 (a)-(b).

[18] *Id.* at § 1207 (c) (technical assistance) & § 1207 (e)(2) (advance payments). Advance payments are non-interest-bearing loans made by government agencies to eligible small businesses to assist them in meeting the financial requirements of performing agency contracts. The government is generally prohibited from making advance payments to contractors. *See* 31 U.S.C. § 3324.

[19] A price evaluation adjustment works as follows: when comparing a offer from a small disadvantaged business with one submitted by another business, the agency can subtract up to 10% of the price from the offer submitted by the small disadvantaged business in determining which offer has the lowest price or represents the best value. For example, if a business that is not a small disadvantaged business bids $100,000 and a small

disadvantaged business bids $110,000, the small disadvantaged business would win because it is the lower bidder after its price is reduced by 10% ($110,000- $11 ,000=$99,000).

[20] P.L. 99-661, § 1207 (e)(3).

[21] *Id.* at § 1207 (a)(1). *See* 15 U.S.C. § 637(d); 13 C.F.R. § 124.1002 (addressing requirements for proving social and economic disadvantage). Among other things, evidence of disadvantage must include (1) at least one objective distinguishing feature, such as race, gender, physical handicap, or geographic isolation, that has contributed to social disadvantage; (2) personal experiences of substantial and chronic social disadvantage in American society; and (3) negative impact on entry into or advancement in the business world because of the disadvantage.

[22] *See, e.g.*, 10 U.S.C. § 2323 (2006) (including NASA and the Coast Guard, as well as DOD); National Defense Authorization Act for Fiscal Year 2006, P.L. 109-163, § 842, 119 Stat. 3135, 3389 (Jan. 6, 2006) (extending the price evaluation adjustment authority under Section 1207 through September 2009).

[23] P.L. 103-355, § 7102, 108 Stat. 3243, 3368-69 (Oct. 13, 1994).

[24] *Id.*; DOD, General Services Administration, NASA, Expiration of the Price Evaluation Adjustment, 71 Fed. Reg. 20304 (Apr. 19, 2006).

[25] The goals presently in 15 U.S.C. § 644(g)(2) were created first. *See* P.L. 95-507, § 221, 92 Stat. 1757, 1771 (Oct. 24, 1978). Those presently in 15 U.S.C. § 644(g)(1) were added later by the Business Opportunity Development Reform Act of 1988. *See* P.L. 100-656, § 502, 102 Stat. 3853, 3881 (Nov. 15, 1988).

[26] FY2007 is apparently the last year in which SBA's "goaling" reports include agency-specific goals that are higher than the government-wide goals. Agency performance may, and often does, exceed the government-wide and agency- specific goals because these goals represent "floors," not "ceilings." *See* U.S. Small Bus. Admin., FY2006-FY2008 Goals and Achievements, *available at* http://www.sba.gov/aboutsba/sbaprograms/goals/index.html. Despite its title, this source also includes agency-specific goals for FY2009.

[27] Rothe Dev. Corp., 545 F.3d at 1030.

[28] *Id.*

[29] *Id.*

[30] *Id.*

[31] *Id.*

[32] Rothe Dev. Corp. v. Dep't of Defense, 49 F. Supp. 2d 937, 941 (W.D. Tex. 1999).

[33] *Id.*

[34] Some courts had previously denied firms or individuals standing to challenge programs with racial presumptions like that underlying Section 1207 on the grounds that the would-be plaintiffs were denied the contract because of inability to demonstrate social and economic disadvantage, not because of race. *See, e.g.*, Interstate Traffic Control v. Beverage, 101 F. Supp. 2d 445 (S.D. W.Va. 2000); Ellsworth Assocs. v. United States, 926 F. Supp. 207 (D.D.C. 1996).

[35] U.S. Const. amend. V.

[36] *See* Bolling v. Sharpe, 347 U.S. 497 (1954). Although the Fourteenth Amendment requires equal protection, it does not preclude the classification of individuals. The Supreme Court has noted that the Constitution does not require things which are "different in fact or opinion to be treated in law as though they were the same." Tigner v. Texas, 310 U.S. 141, 147 (1940).

[37] Adarand Constructors, Inc. v. Peña, 515 U.S. 200 (1995). *See generally* CRS Report RL33284, *Minority Contracting and Affirmative Action for Disadvantaged Small Businesses: Legal Issues*, by Jody Feder.

[38] Shaw v. Hunt, 517 U.S. 899, 909-10 (1996); Concrete Works of Colorado, Inc. v. City and County of Denver, 321 F.3d 950, 958 (10th Cir. 2003).

[39] Concrete Works, 321 F.3d at 958.

[40] *Id.*

[41] Coral Constr. Co. v. King County, 941 F.2d 910, 921 (9th Cir. 1991).

[42] Rothe Dev. Corp., 49 F. Supp. 2d at 954 ("*Rothe* I").

[43] Rothe Dev. Corp. v. Dep't of Defense, 194 F.3d 622 (5th Cir. 1999) ("*Rothe* II").

[44] 28 U.S.C. § 1295(a)(2).

[45] Rothe Dev. Corp., 545 F.3d at 1035 ("*Rothe* VII").

[46] The Federal Circuit is a court of subject-specific, not territorial, jurisdiction, so there is no geographic region in which its decisions are precedent. The Fifth Circuit, in contrast, is a territorial jurisdiction.

[47] Rothe Dev. Corp. v. Dep't of Defense, 262 F.3d 1306 (Fed. Cir. 2001) ("*Rothe* III").

[48] Rothe Dev. Corp. v. Dep't of Defense, 324 F. Supp. 2d 840 (W.D. Tex. 2000) ("*Rothe* IV").

[49] Rothe Dev. Corp. v. Dep't of Defense, 413 F.3d 1327 (Fed. Cir. 2005) ("*Rothe* V").

[50] Rothe Dev. Corp. v. Dep't of Defense, 499 F. Supp. 2d 775 (W.D. Tex. 2007) ("*Rothe* VI").

[51] The Federal Circuit focused upon the 2006 re-enactment of Section 1207 in deciding the facial challenge because this was the re-enactment in effect when the Federal Circuit heard the case. In its earlier proceeding, the district court had considered the 2002 re-enactment of Section 1207 for the same reason.

[52] Rothe Dev. Corp., 545 F.3d at 1049.

[53] *Id.* at 1036-37. A disparity study is a "study attempting to measure the difference—or disparity—between the number of contracts or contract dollars *actually* awarded to minority-owned businesses in a particular contract market, on the one hand, and the number of contracts or contract dollars that one would *expect* to be awarded to minority- owned business given presence in that particular contract market, on the other hand." *Id.* at 1037 (emphases in the original).

[54] *Id.* at 1046.

[55] *Id.* at 1037.

[56] *Id.* at 1040. *See also id.* at 1045 ("To be clear, we do *not* hold that the defects in the availability and capacity analyses in these six disparity studies render the studies wholly unreliable for any purpose.... But we hold that the defects we have noted detract dramatically from the probative value of these six studies, and, in conjunction with their limited geographic coverage, render the studies insufficient to form the statistical core of the 'strong basis in evidence' required to uphold the statute.") (emphasis in the original).

[57] *Id.* at 1042.

[58] *Id.* at 1043.

[59] *Id.* at 1045-46.

[60] *Id.* at 1039-40 (noting that the studies had been mentioned by title, author, and date in two floor speeches—one by Senator Ted Kennedy and one by Representative Cynthia McKinney—but had been neither discussed in congressional hearings nor the subject of congressional findings). The Federal Circuit also suggested that the currency of the studies upon which Congress relies is relevant to the analysis of whether a strong basis in evidence exists. However, the Federal Circuit rejected RDC's argument for a *per se* rule that studies more than five years old cannot constitute a strong basis in evidence. *Id.* at 1039. Instead, the Federal Circuit suggested that Congress can rely upon the most recently available studies so long as these studies are reasonably up-to-date. *Id.*

[61] *Id.* at 1046-49.

[62] *Id.* at 1047.

[63] *Id.* at 1048 (emphasis in original).

[64] *Id.*

[65] *Id.*

[66] *See City of Richmond v. Croson*, 488 U.S. 469, 492 (1989).

[67] Rothe Dev. Corp., 545 F.3d at 1050.

[68] Rothe Dev. Corp., 2009 U.S. Dist. LEXIS 22029, at *12. *See* 10 U.S.C. § 2323(c)(1)-(3) (listing the groups eligible for certain programs under the authority of 10 U.S.C. § 2323). The government did not appeal this decision.

[69] The definitions for these institutions may be found at 20 U.S.C. § 1061 (HBCUs), 20 U.S.C. § 1 101a (HSIs), 20 U.S.C. § 1059d (ANNHIs), and 20 U.S.C. § 1067k (MMIs). For more information on MSIs, see CRS Report RL32674, *Minority-Serving Higher Education Institutions: Analysis of Selected Institutional and Student Characteristics*, by Charmaine Mercer and James B. Stedman.

[70] *Id.* at *7.

[71] *Id.* at *10.

[72] Under Section 1207, "technical assistance" means information about the program, advice about agency procurement procedures, instruction in the preparation of proposals, and other similar assistance considered appropriate by the head of the contracting agency. *See* 10 U.S.C. § 2323(c)(2). Infrastructure assistance includes (1) establishing or enhancing undergraduate, graduate, or doctoral programs in scientific disciplines; (2) making DOD personnel available to advise and assist faculty; (3) establishing partnerships between defense laboratories and minority institutions; (4) awarding scholarships and fellowships, or establishing cooperative work-education programs, in scientific disciplines; (5) attracting and retaining faculty involved in scientific disciplines; (6) equipping and renovating laboratories; (7) expanding and equipping Reserve Officer Training Corps activities; and (8) providing other similar assistance. *See* 10 U.S.C. § 2323(c)(3)(A)-(H).

[73] Rothe Dev. Corp., 2009 U.S. Dist. LEXIS 22029, at *11-14.

[74] *Id.* at *7.

[75] *Id.* at *11-14. The District Court subsequently denied Rothe Development Corporation's request for attorney's fees under the Equal Access to Justice Act because the Department of Defense's legal position was reasonable given that DOD had previously prevailed in similar cases. Rothe Dev. Corp. v. U.S. Dep't of Defense, W.D. Tex., No. SA-98- CV-1011-XR, 8/11/09.

[76] Dep't of Defense, Under Secretary of Defense (Acquisition, Technology & Logistics), Immediate Cessation of Activities Relying on 10 U.S.C. § 2323, Mar. 10, 2009, *available at* http://www.acq.osd.mil/osbp/policy 09%20Signed.pdf.

[77] Dep't of the Army, Under Secretary of Defense (Acquisition, Technology & Logistics (AT&L)) Rothe Memo—Immediate Cessation of Activities Relying on Title 10 United States Code (U.S.C.) Section 2323, May 22, 2009. Agencies were, however, instructed to exercise options that could be funded under other authority.

[78] *Id.*

[79] P.L. 111-84, § 252 (codified at 10 U.S.C. § 2362).

[80] *Id.* at § 252(c).

[81] *See, e.g.*, Davidson, *supra* note 8 (noting the possible effects of the *Rothe* decision on other programs for small businesses); DOD Confused by Recent Court Decision on Affirmative-Action Rule, *The Front Runner*, Dec. 3, 2008 (worrying that *Rothe* could lead to a decline in federal contracting with minority-owned small businesses); U.S. Small Bus. Admin., *supra* note 9 (extending the comment period on a proposed rule relating to the contracting assistance program for women-owned small businesses).

[82] *See* Craig v. Boren, 429 U.S. 190, 197 (1976). In *United States v. Virginia*, the Court required the State of Virginia to provide an "exceedingly persuasive justification" for its policy of maintaining an all-male military academy. 518 U.S. 515 (1996). It is unclear whether this standard is in fact more strict than the intermediate scrutiny standard of review that has long applied to gender classifications.

[83] *See, e.g.*, DOD Confused, *supra* note 81.

[84] Federal Contract Awards by Major Contracting Agency, *usaspending.gov*, last updated Dec. 14, 2009, *available at* http://www.usaspending.gov/fpds/tables.php?tabtype=t1&subtype=at&rowtype=f.

[85] The primary federal statute pertaining to contracting goals is 15 U.S.C. § 644(g), which created purely "aspirational goals," or goals unaccompanied by authority to take specific steps in meeting them.

[86] *See generally Minority Contracting and Affirmative Action for Disadvantaged Small Businesses*, *supra* note 37, for a description of prior authorities and their removal.

[87] *See id.*

[88] P.L. 105-261, § 801, 112 Stat. 1921, 2080-81 (Oct. 17, 1998).

[89] Rothe Dev. Corp., 545 F.3d at 1028 (addressing DOD's authority in fiscal years 1998 to 2007); 48 C.F.R. § 19.11 (2008) (suspending DOD's price evaluation adjustment authority for FY2008); Dep't of Defense, Suspension of the Price Evaluation Adjustment for Small Disadvantaged Businesses, 74 Fed. Reg. 7671 (Feb. 19, 2009) (suspending DOD's price evaluation adjustment authority for FY2009).

[90] *See also* 22 U.S.C. § 2864(e) ("Not less than 10 percent of the amount of funds obligated for local guard contracts for Foreign Service buildings subject to subsection (c) of this section shall be allocated to the extent practicable for contracts with United States minority small business contractors."); 49 U.S.C. § 47113(b) ("Except to the extent that the Secretary decides otherwise, at least 10 percent of amounts available in a fiscal year under section 48103 of this title shall be expended with small business concerns owned and controlled by socially and economically disadvantaged individuals or qualified HUBZone small business concerns."). Similarly, the 5% government-wide goal for contracting with small disadvantaged businesses under 15 U.S.C. § 644(g)(1) is a floor, not a ceiling. That is, the government-wide goal must be at least 5%, but could be higher.

[91] *See supra* note 26.

[92] *See* U.S. Small Bus. Admin., FY2008 Goals and Achievements, *available at* http://www.sba.gov /idc/groups/public/ documents/sba_homepage/fy2008goals_and_achievements.html. The government-wide goal for contracting with small disadvantaged businesses also tends to be met. *See* U.S. Small Bus. Admin., FY2008 Goals and Achievements, *available at* http://www.sba.gov/idc/groups/public/documents/sba_homepage/fy2008goals_and_achievements.html.

[93] *See, e.g.*, U.S. Small Bus. Admin., FY2008 Government-wide Scorecard, *available at* http://www.sba.gov/idc/groups/public/documents/sba_homepage/goals_08_gov_wide.pdf.

[94] *Cf.* Ruling Threatens 8(a), *supra* note 11; Newell, *supra* note 11.

[95] U.S. Small Bus. Admin., Office of Business Development, FY2008 Annual Report to Congress, *available at* http://www.sba.gov/idc/groups/public/documents/sba_program_office/8abd_408_fy2008report.pdf.

[96] U.S. Small Bus. Admin., Office of Business Development, FY2006 Annual Report to Congress, *available at* http://www.sba.gov/idc/groups/public/documents/sba_program_office/8abd_408_2006_finalreport.pdf.

[97] 15 U.S.C. § 644(g)(1)-(2).

[98] 15 U.S.C. § 637(a).

[99] 15 U.S.C. § 637(d).

[100] 48 C.F.R. § 19.1202-3 (evaluation factors); 48 C.F.R. § 19.1203 (monetary incentives). Use of these authorities is limited to contracts involving industries where the Secretary of Commerce has found "substantial and pervasive evidence of persistent and significant underutilization of minority firms ... attributable to past discrimination and a demonstrated incapacity to alleviate the problem by using [other] mechanisms." 48 C.F.R. § 19.20 1(b)(1)-(2). The Department of Commerce has apparently not updated its list of such industries since 1999-2000, and it is unclear to what extent agencies exercise these authorities. *See* Industries Eligible for the 10% Price Evaluation Adjustment, *available at* http://www.acquisition.gov/references/sbdadjustments.htm.

[101] *See, e.g.*, 15 U.S.C. § 636(j) (financial assistance to public or private organizations that provide various sorts of programs for 8(a) small businesses); 15 U.S.C. § 637(a)(10) (outreach to potential 8(a) businesses); 15 U.S.C. § 638(j)(2)(F) (outreach to increase the participation of 8(a) businesses in technological innovation); 13 C.F.R. § 124.520(b) (SBA's Mentor-Protégé program).

[102] *See* 15 U.S.C. § 637(a)(4) (presumption regarding social disadvantage underlying the 8(a) subcontracting program); U.S.C. § 637(d)(3)(C) (presumptions regarding social and economic disadvantage underlying the 8(d) subcontracting program); 48 C.F.R. § 19.20 1(b) (focusing on underrepresentation of minority firms in

determining which industries are eligible for evaluation factors and monetary incentives under the Federal Acquisition Regulation (FAR)).

[103] *See* Rothe Dev. Corp., 545 F.3d at 1035 ("Because Section 1207 incorporates an explicit racial classification—the presumption that members of certain minority groups are 'socially disadvantaged' for purposes of obtaining SDB status and the benefits that flow from that status under Section 1207 itself—the statute is subject to strict scrutiny.").

[104] *See, e.g.*, 15 U.S.C. § 644(g)(1)-(2).

[105] A challenge to the constitutionality of the federal government's aspirational goals under 15 U.S.C. § 644(g) is pending, however. *See* Dynalantic Corp. v. U.S. Dep't of Defense, 503 F. Supp. 2d 262.

[106] *See, e.g.*, Adarand Constructors, Inc. v. Slater, 228 F.3d 1147, 1181 (10th Cir. 2000) (permitting the constitutionality of aspirational goals in statutes, because such goals are not mandatory).

[107] The price evaluation adjustment authority that other agencies had under FASA expired at the end of FY2000. *See supra* note 24.

[108] *See* Rothe Dev. Corp., 2009 U.S. Dist. LEXIS 22029 (enjoining application of the entirety of 10 U.S.C. § 2323).

[109] *See id.* at *9. Technical and infrastructure assistance programs were among those struck down by the district court's judgment in *Rothe*. The court included these programs not because they were unconstitutional in their own right, but because they were "contingent" upon other programs that had been found unconstitutional.

[110] Dep't of Justice, Proposed Reforms to Affirmative Action in Federal Procurement, 61 Fed. Reg. 26041, 26048 (May 23, 1996).

[111] Courts have reasoned that "inclusive" activities, such as outreach, do not impose burdens or benefits, and do not subject individuals to unequal treatment, unlike "exclusive" activities such as quotas, set-asides, and layoff preferences. For this reason, they have concluded that "inclusive" activities are not subject to strict scrutiny, whereas "exclusive" activities are. *See, e.g.*, Duffy v. Wolle, 123 F.3d 1026, 1038-39 (8th Cir. 1997) ("An employer's affirmative efforts to recruit female and minority applicants does not constitute discrimination."); Allen v. Ala. State Bd. of Educ., 164 F.3d 1347, 1352 (11th Cir. 1999) (refusing to subject racially conscious outreach efforts to strict scrutiny); Billish v. City of Chicago, 962 F.2d 1269, 1290 (7th Cir. 1992) (characterizing aggressive recruiting as a "race-neutral procedure[]"), *rev 'd on other grounds*, 989 F.2d 890 (7th Cir.) (en banc).

[112] *See, e.g.*, Valley Forge Christian College v. Americans United for Separation of Church and State, Inc., 454 U.S. 464, 472 (1982); Allen v. Wright, 468 U.S. 737, 751 (1984); Lujan v. Defenders of Wildlife, 504 U.S. 555, 560-6 1 (1992).

[113] *See, e.g.*, Massachusetts v. Mellon, 262 U.S. 447 (1923) (finding that the plaintiff lacked standing to challenge alleged "taxation for illegal purposes" because the administration of federal statutes "likely to produce addition taxation to be imposed upon a vast number of taxpayers" is essentially a matter of public, and not individual, concern).

[114] *See* 15 U.S.C. § 644(g)(2).

[115] *See* 31 U.S.C. § 3556 (allowing "interested parties" to bring bid protests before the U.S. Court of Federal Claims; the Government Accountability Office; or procuring agencies); 31 U.S.C. § 355 1(2)(A) (defining an "interested party" as "an actual or prospective bidder or offeror whose direct economic interest would be affected by the award of a contract or by failure to award the contract.").

[116] Although a prime contractor might have difficulty demonstrating standing to challenge a monetary incentive for subcontracting with small disadvantaged businesses, a subcontractor might be able to do so. *Adarand Constructors, Inc. v. Peña*, 515 U.S. 200 (1995), for example, involved such a constitutional challenge by a subcontractor objecting to a monetary incentive for subcontracting with minority businesses.

[117] *See* 41 U.S.C. § 605 (allowing incumbent contractors to make claims arising during the course of contract performance against the government); 41 U.S.C. § 609 (providing for judicial review of contractor's claims).

[118] 15 U.S.C. § 637(d)(8) (breach); 48 C.F.R. § 19.705-7 (liquidated damages).

[119] 15 U.S.C. § 637(d)(3) & (4)(E).

[120] The Administrative Dispute Resolution Act of 1996 provided that the jurisdiction of federal district courts over bid protests would terminate on January 1, 2001, leaving the Court of Federal Claims as the exclusive trial-level federal judicial forum for bid protests. P.L. 104-320, § 12(d), 110 Stat. 3869, 3870 (Oct. 19, 1996). Disputes between contractors and agencies under existing contracts are subject to the Contract Disputes Act (CDA) of 1978. The CDA provides that the Court of Federal Claims is the sole federal trial-level court that can hear post-award disputes involving government contracts. 41 U.S.C. §§ 606 & 609(a). Federal district courts have no such jurisdiction. 28 U.S.C. § 1346(a)(2).

[121] Although the Federal Circuit applied Fifth Circuit law, not its own law, in deciding *Rothe*, *Rothe* can probably be viewed as precedent for both the Court of Federal Claims and the Fifth Circuit because the Federal Circuit relied upon its interpretations of Supreme Court decisions in reaching its holdings. *See* Rothe Dev. Corp., 545 F.3d at 1035 n.5 ("We note that while we stand in the shoes of the Fifth Circuit, the bulk of relevant, controlling authority comes directly from the Supreme Court, and we have interpreted much of that authority in our prior opinions in this case.").

[122] 15 U.S.C. § 637(a)(1). *See also* 15 U.S.C. § 637(a)(1)(A) ("In any case in which the [SBA] certifies to any officer of the Government having procurement powers that the [SBA] is competent and responsible to perform any specific Government procurement contract to be let by any such officer, such officer shall be *authorized in his discretion* to let such procurement contract to the [SBA] upon such terms and conditions as may be agreed upon between the [SBA] and the procurement officer.") (emphasis added).

[123] 48 C.F.R. § 19.1202-3 (evaluation factors); 48 C.F.R. § 19.1203 (monetary incentives).

[124] *See* 15 U.S.C. § 637(d)(8)(breach); 48 C.F.R. § 19.705-7 (liquidated damages).

[125] 15 U.S.C. § 637(d)(4)(F)(ii).

[126] 48 C.F.R. § 19.20 1(b)(1)-(2).

[127] Women-Owned Small Business Federal Contract Assistance Procedures, *supra* note 9.

[128] *See supra* note 82.

[129] Women-Owned Small Business Federal Contract Assistance Procedures, *supra* note 9, at 1153.

[130] Women-Owned Small Business Federal Contract Program, *supra* note 9. Implementation of the set-asides for women-owned small businesses was also temporarily delayed by a provision of the Omnibus Appropriations Act, 2009, which precluded SBA from using funds appropriated under the act to implement a proposed rule on set-asides for women-owned small businesses issued by the SBA on October 1, 2008. *See* P.L. 111-8, Administrative Provisions— Small Business Administration, § 522. Similar provisions do not appear to have been included in the Consolidated Appropriations Act, 2010, P.L. 111-117.

[131] *Id.* at 10043.

[132] *Id.*

[133] Although the classification of individuals as "Native Americans" might seem to be a racial one, courts have found that federal programs focused solely upon Native Americans living on or near a reservation do not constitute such a classification. *See, e.g.*, Morton v. Mancari, 417 U.S. 535, 548 (1973). Rather, such programs have been upheld by the Supreme Court under the Constitution based on the Government's historical trust relationship with the Tribes and the "unique legal status [of] Indians" in matters relating to tribal affairs "on or near" the reservation. According to the accepted legal view, such "special treatment" constitutes neither "racial discrimination" nor "even a 'racial' preference." It is based instead on a "criterion reasonably designed to further the cause of Indian self-government" which "as applied, is granted to Indians not as a discrete racial group, but, rather, as members of quasi-sovereign tribal entities...." *Id.* at 554.

[134] *See, e.g.*, 15 U.S.C. § 63 7(d) (contracting plans and clauses relating to contracting with small businesses owned and controlled by veterans or service-disabled veterans); 15 U.S.C. § 637(m) (set-asides for small businesses owned and controlled by women); 15 U.S.C. § 644 (set-asides for small businesses generally); 15 U.S.C. § 644(c) (programs for the blind and "handicapped individuals"); 15 U.S.C. § 657a (set-asides and sole-source awards for Historically Underutilized Business Zone (HUBZone) small businesses); 15 U.S.C. § 657f (set-asides and sole-source awards for service-disabled veteran-owned small businesses).

[135] *See, e.g.*, United States v. Carolene Products Co., 304 U.S. 144 (1938).

[136] *See, e.g.*, Pers. Adm'r of Mass. v. Feeney, 442 U.S. 256 (1979) (holding that a Massachusetts law that gave veterans lifetime preference for state employment did not violate the equal protection clause); San Antonio Indep. School Dist. v. Rodriguez, 411 U.S. 1, 29 (1973) ("[W]ealth discrimination alone [does not provide] an adequate basis for invoking strict scrutiny."); McGowan v. Md., 366 U.S. 420, 427 (1961) (holding that "the Equal Protection Clause relates to equality between persons as such, rather than between areas and that territorial uniformity is not a constitutional prerequisite."); *but see* City of Cleburne v. Cleburne Living Center, 473 U.S. 432, 442 (1985) (applying rational basis review in striking down a city ordinance that targeted mentally disabled individuals).

[137] 476 U.S. 267 (1986).

[138] W. States Paving Co. v. Wash. State DOT, 407 F.3d 983 (9th Cir. 2005); Concrete Works of Colo. v. City & County of Denver, 321 F.3d 950 (10th Cir. 2003); Sherbrooke Turf, Inc. v. Minn. DOT, 345 F.3d 964 (8th Cir. 2003).

[139] City of Richmond v. Croson, 488 U.S. 469 (1989); Eng'g Contrs. Ass'n v. Metropolitan Dade County, 122 F.3d 895 (11th Cir. 1997); Contractors Ass'n v. City of Philadelphia, 91 F.3d 586 (3d Cir. 1996).

[140] 515 U.S. 200, 237 (1995).

CHAPTER SOURCES

The following chapters have been previously published:

Chapter 1 – This is an edited, excerpted and augmented edition of a United States Congressional Research Service publication, Report Order Code R40987, dated March 18, 2010.

Chapter 2 – This is an edited, excerpted and augmented edition of a United States Congressional Research Service publication, Report Order Code R40744, dated June 1, 2010.

Chapter 3 – This is an edited, excerpted and augmented edition of a United States Government Accountability Office publication, Report Order Code GAO-10-353, dated March 2010.

Chapter 4 – This is an edited, excerpted and augmented edition of a United States Government Accountability Office publication, Report Order Code GAO-10-425, dated March 2010.

Chapter 5 – This is an edited, excerpted and augmented edition of a United States Government Accountability Office publication, Report Order Code GAO-07-125T, dated September 19, 2007.

Chapter 6 – This is an edited, excerpted and augmented edition of a United States Congressional Research Service publication, Report Order Code R40855, dated March 17, 2010.

Chapter 7 – This is an edited, excerpted and augmented edition of a United States Congressional Research Service publication, Report Order Code RL33284, dated April 1, 2010.

Chapter 8 – This is an edited, excerpted and augmented edition of a United States Congressional Research Service publication, Report Order Code R40440, dated March 12, 2010.

INDEX

#

A

B

C

D

E

F

J

K

L

M

N

O

P

Q

R

S

T

U

V

W